Ao Haru Ride

The scent of air after rain...
In the light around us, I felt your heartbeat.

9

IO SAKISAKA

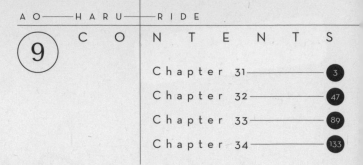

C O N T E N T S

S T O R Y
T H U S
F A R

Futaba Yoshioka was quiet and awkward around boys in junior high, but she's taken on a tomboy persona in high school. It's there that she once again meets her first love, Tanaka (now Kou Mabuchi), and falls for him again.

Just as Kou is starting to smile again, Yui appears, bringing up memories of their shared past.

In hopes of moving on, Futaba tells Kou she likes him, and as she expects, she is rejected. Although he turns her down, Kou feels conflicted because he cares about her. Meanwhile, Toma tells Futaba that he likes her.

Futaba and Kou run into each other at the shrine where they shared an important moment years ago, and Kou embraces her. Futaba pushes him away and immediately calls Toma. Kou picks up his phone and calls Yui...

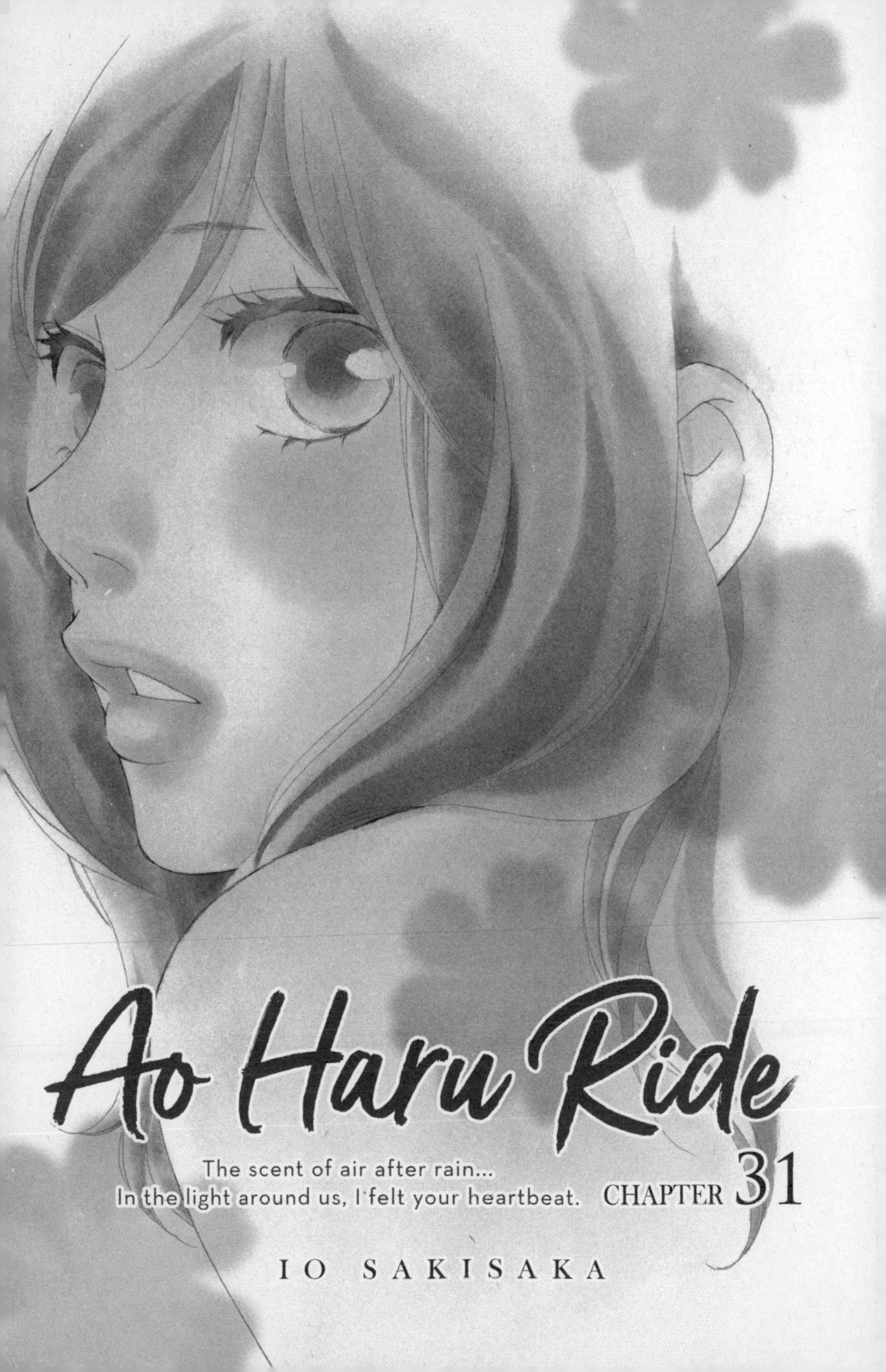
Ao Haru Ride
The scent of air after rain...
In the light around us, I felt your heartbeat.
CHAPTER 31
IO SAKISAKA

GREETINGS

Hi! I'm Io Sakisaka. Thank you for picking up a copy of *Ao Haru Ride* volume 9!

Human emotions are wondrous and complicated, but at times utterly concealed from the people experiencing them. It's challenging for me to write the exact dialogue to express each emotion... With a complicated emotion, words can define its meaning too quickly, making it so the reader does not get the opportunity to fully understand that emotion. This is because words have the power to be understood, and words also have the power to be misunderstood. I often get stuck trying to illustrate the detailed nuances of a certain emotion in my manga. Sometimes, after going back and forth over a specific line, I just use "...". Figuring out how to express a specific emotion through a combination of words, body language and facial expressions is constant trial and error. It's extremely challenging but also extremely fun. I suspect the fact that I find joy in this is partly the reason I've been able to come so far in this line of work. I don't think I did a very good job explaining all this, but I do hope you enjoy *Ao Haru Ride* volume 9 through to the end!

☆☆☆ Io Sakisaka ☆☆☆

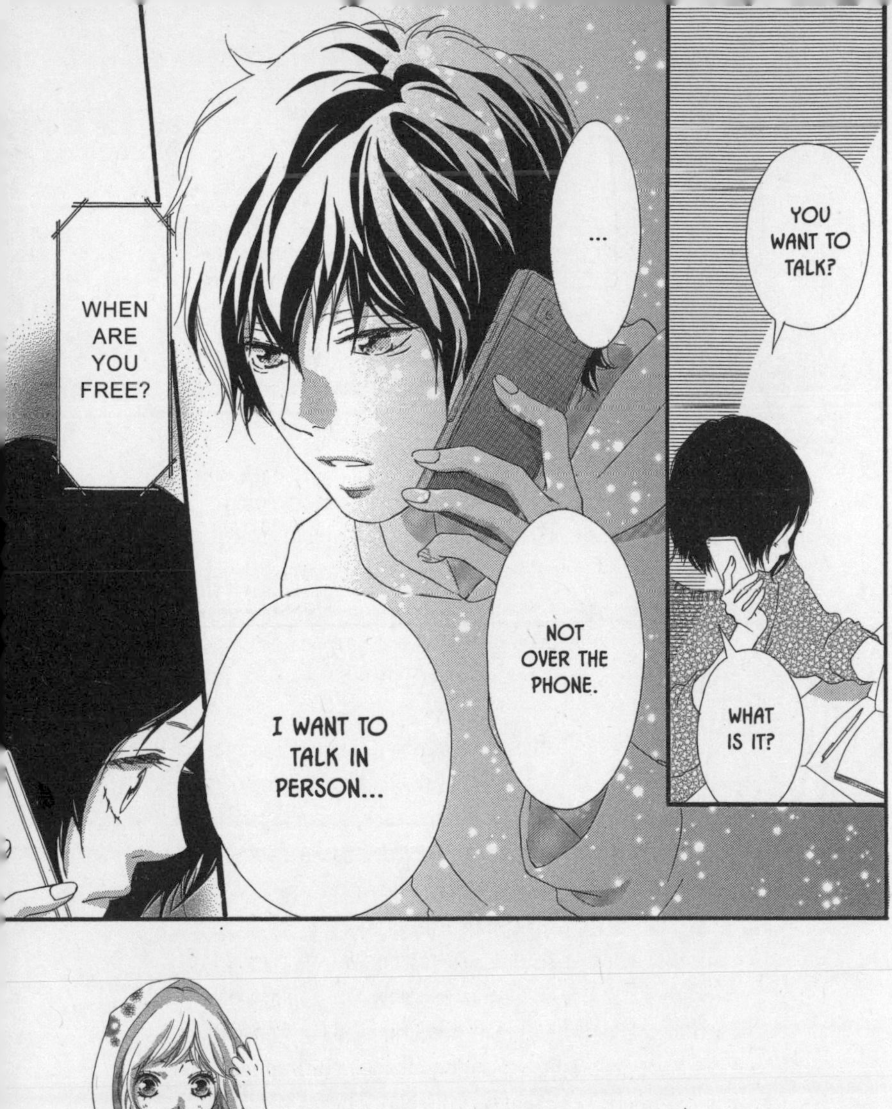
YOU WANT TO TALK?
WHAT IS IT?
...
NOT OVER THE PHONE.
I WANT TO TALK IN PERSON...
WHEN ARE YOU FREE?

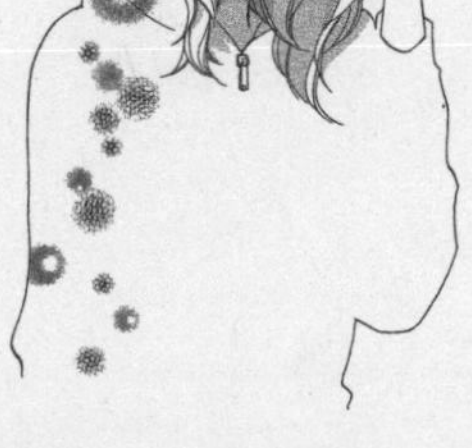

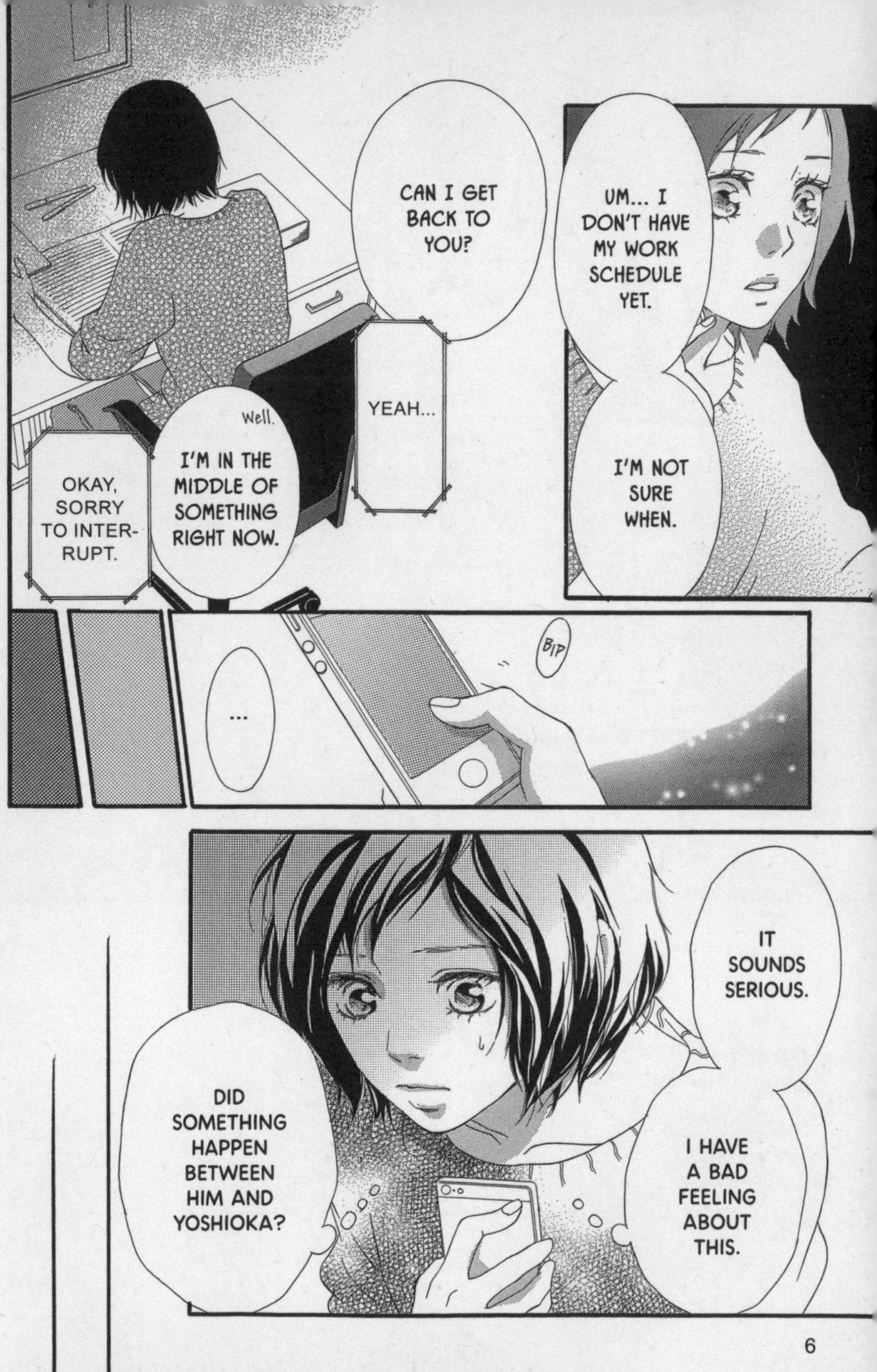
UM... I DON'T HAVE MY WORK SCHEDULE YET.
I'M NOT SURE WHEN.
CAN I GET BACK TO YOU?
YEAH...
Well.
I'M IN THE MIDDLE OF SOMETHING RIGHT NOW.
OKAY, SORRY TO INTER-RUPT.
BIP
...
IT SOUNDS SERIOUS.
I HAVE A BAD FEELING ABOUT THIS.
DID SOMETHING HAPPEN BETWEEN HIM AND YOSHIOKA?

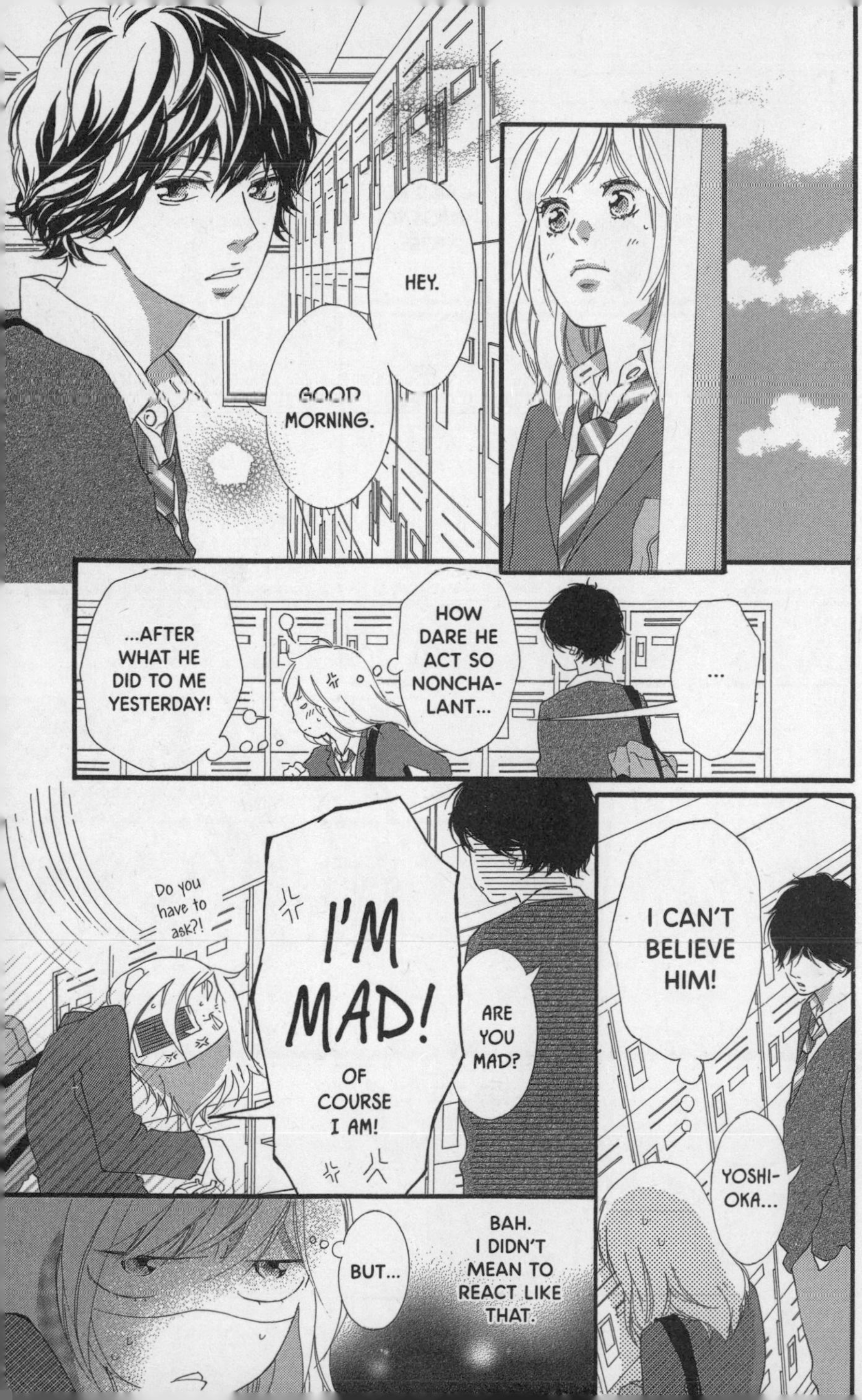
HEY.
GOOD MORNING.
...
HOW DARE HE ACT SO NONCHA-LANT...
...AFTER WHAT HE DID TO ME YESTERDAY!
I CAN'T BELIEVE HIM!
YOSHI-OKA...
ARE YOU MAD?
I'M MAD!
OF COURSE I AM!
Do you have to ask?!
BAH. I DIDN'T MEAN TO REACT LIKE THAT.
BUT...

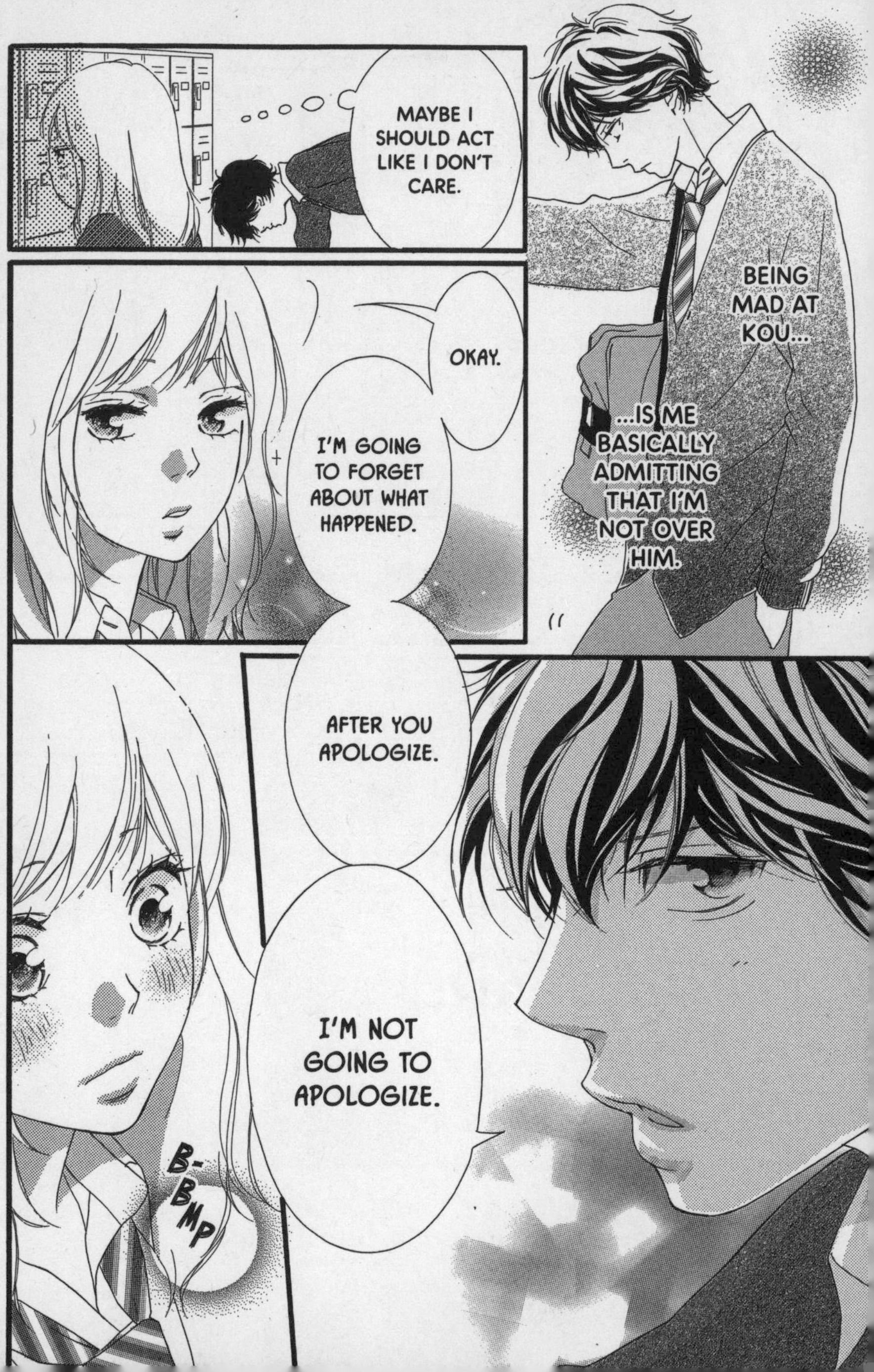
BEING MAD AT KOU...
...IS ME BASICALLY ADMITTING THAT I'M NOT OVER HIM.
MAYBE I SHOULD ACT LIKE I DON'T CARE.
OKAY.
I'M GOING TO FORGET ABOUT WHAT HAPPENED.
AFTER YOU APOLOGIZE.
I'M NOT GOING TO APOLOGIZE.
B-BMP

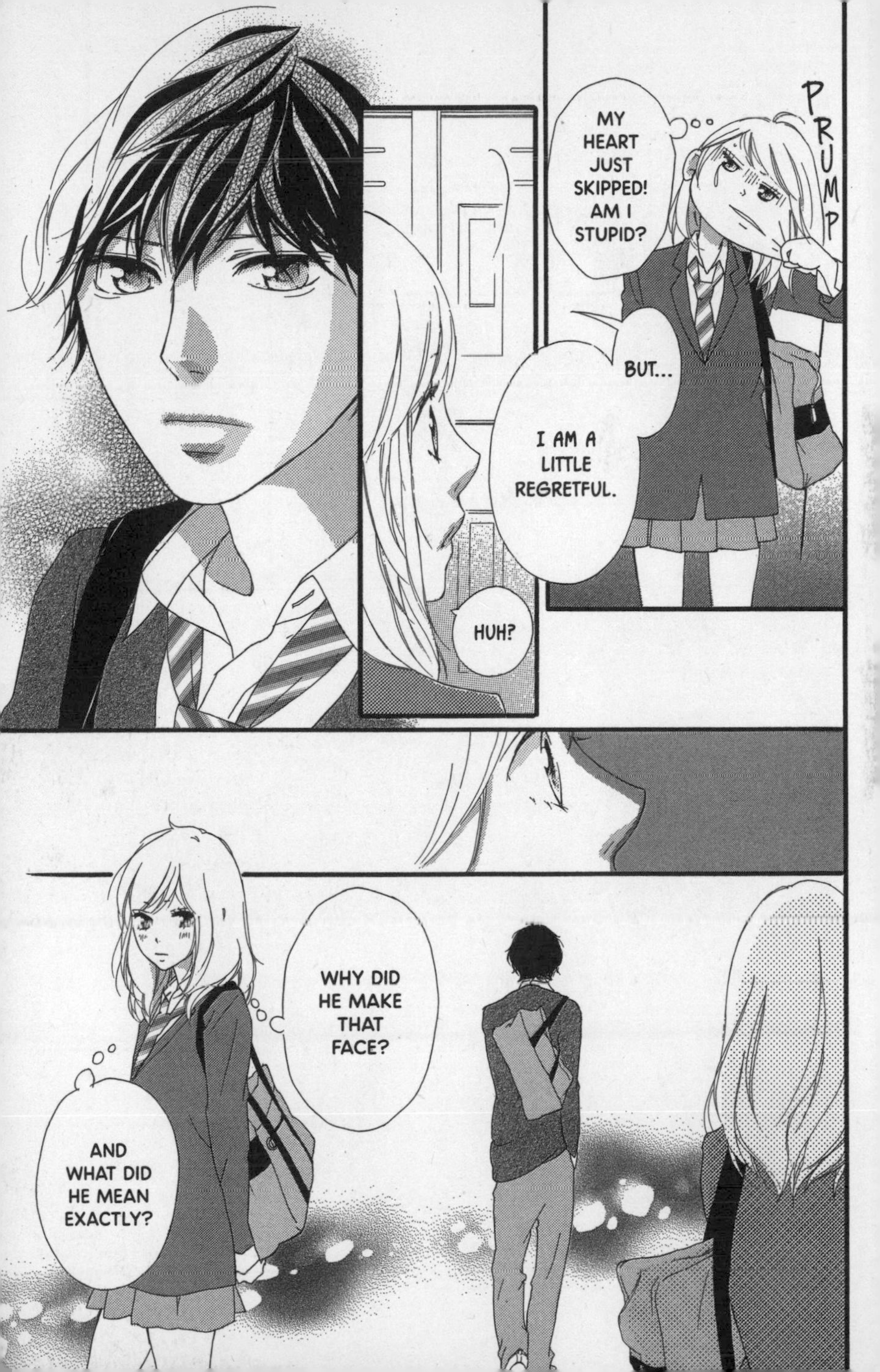
PRUMP
MY HEART JUST SKIPPED! AM I STUPID?
BUT...
I AM A LITTLE REGRETFUL.
HUH?
WHY DID HE MAKE THAT FACE?
AND WHAT DID HE MEAN EXACTLY?

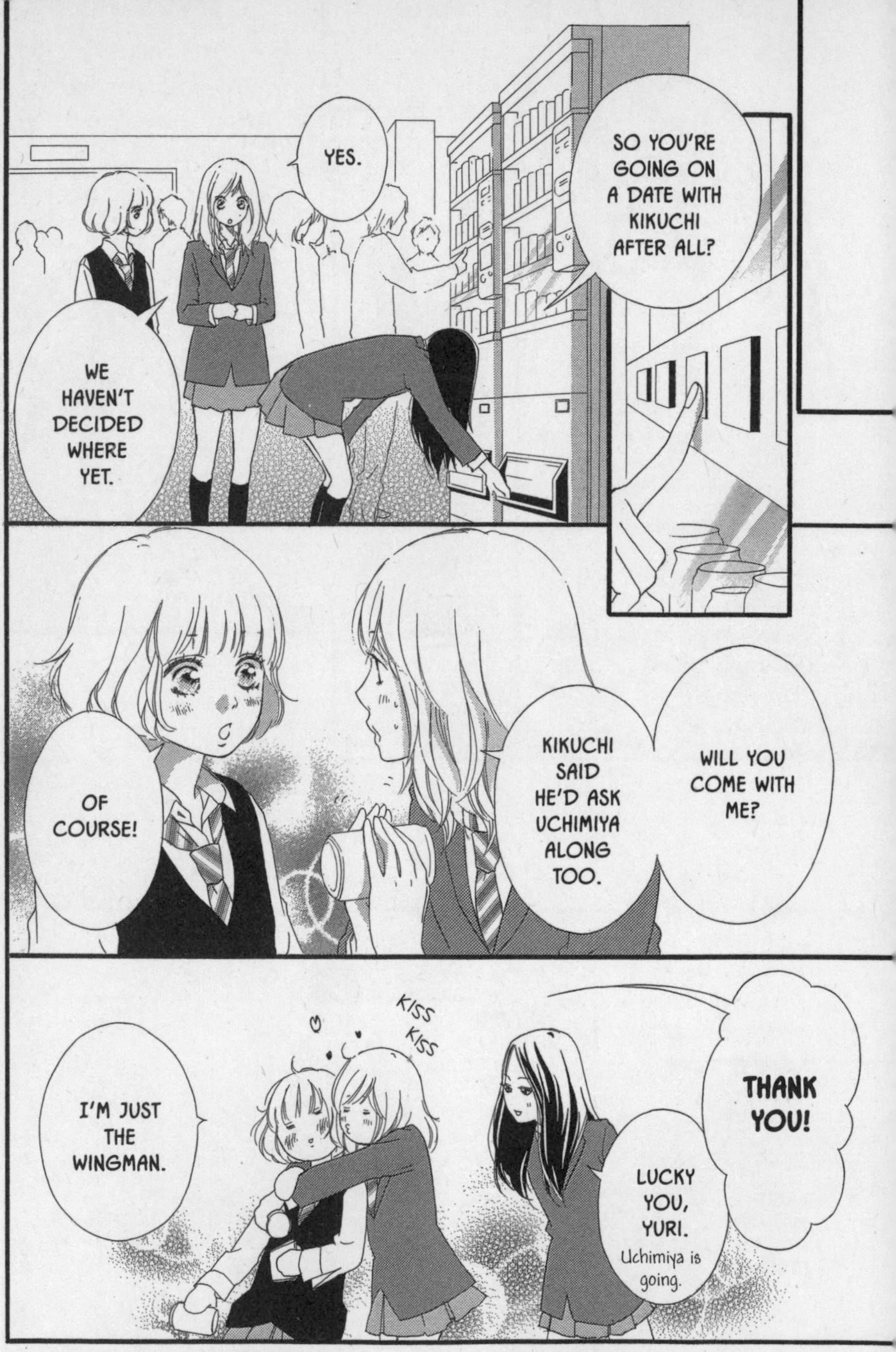
SO YOU'RE GOING ON A DATE WITH KIKUCHI AFTER ALL?
YES.
WE HAVEN'T DECIDED WHERE YET.
WILL YOU COME WITH ME?
KIKUCHI SAID HE'D ASK UCHIMIYA ALONG TOO.
OF COURSE!
THANK YOU!
KISS KISS
LUCKY YOU, YURI.
Uchimiya is going.
I'M JUST THE WINGMAN.

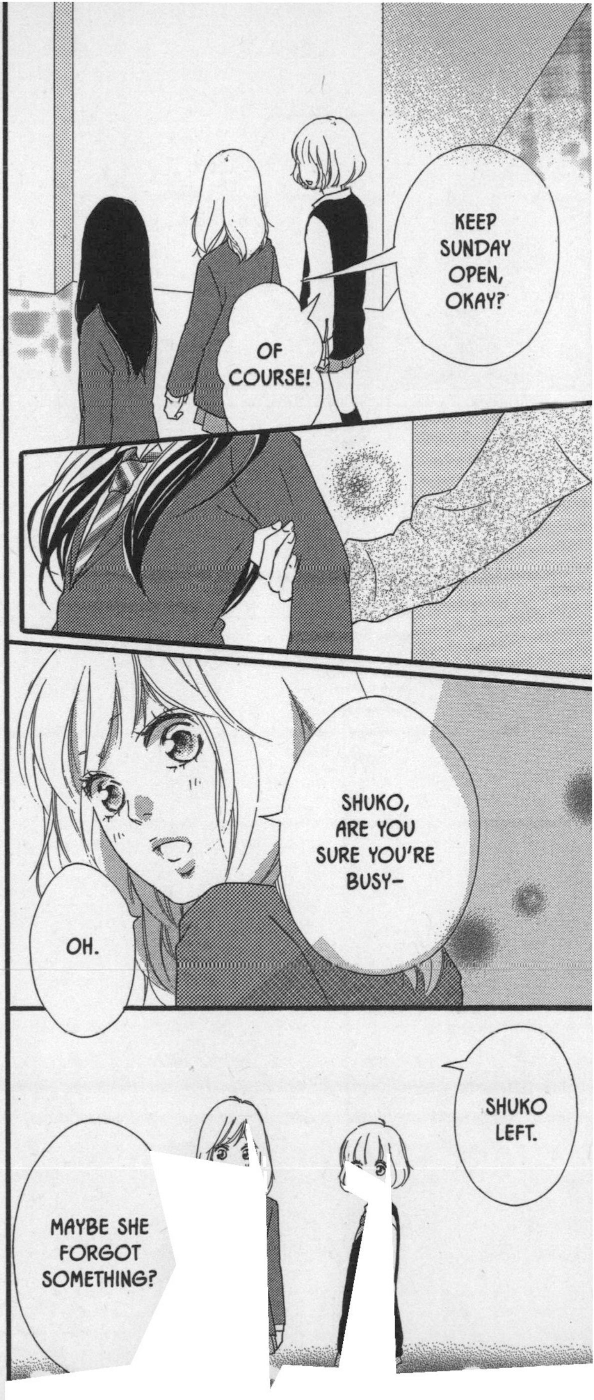
KEEP SUNDAY OPEN, OKAY?
OF COURSE!
SHUKO, ARE YOU SURE YOU'RE BUSY—
OH.
SHUKO LEFT.
MAYBE SHE FORGOT SOMETHING?

I think I was in third or fourth grade when I saw a circular rainbow. We had just gotten out of P.E. and were walking across the campus back to the classroom. One of my classmates noticed it and said "Hey, what's that?" When we looked up, there was a rainbow in a circle, just floating in the air. I was about 10 at the time. I hadn't seen many rainbows in my life yet, so all I thought was, "Huh, rainbows come in circles too." Now that I'm an adult, I know circular rainbows are extremely rare. If I had known it back then, I probably would have just sat and stared at it forever. I regret my ignorance.

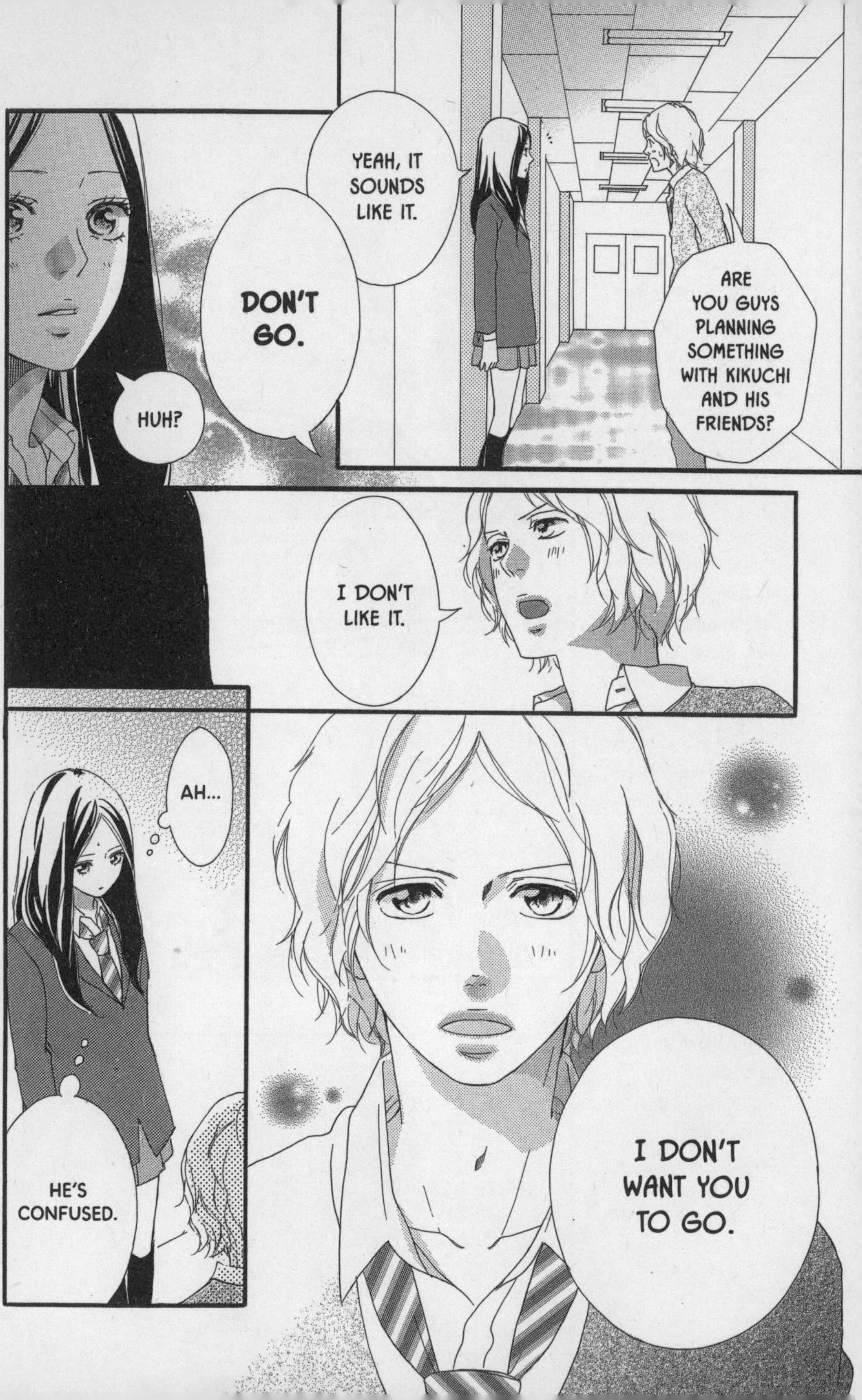
ARE YOU GUYS PLANNING SOMETHING WITH KIKUCHI AND HIS FRIENDS?
YEAH, IT SOUNDS LIKE IT.
DON'T GO.
HUH?
I DON'T LIKE IT.
I DON'T WANT YOU TO GO.
AH...
HE'S CONFUSED.

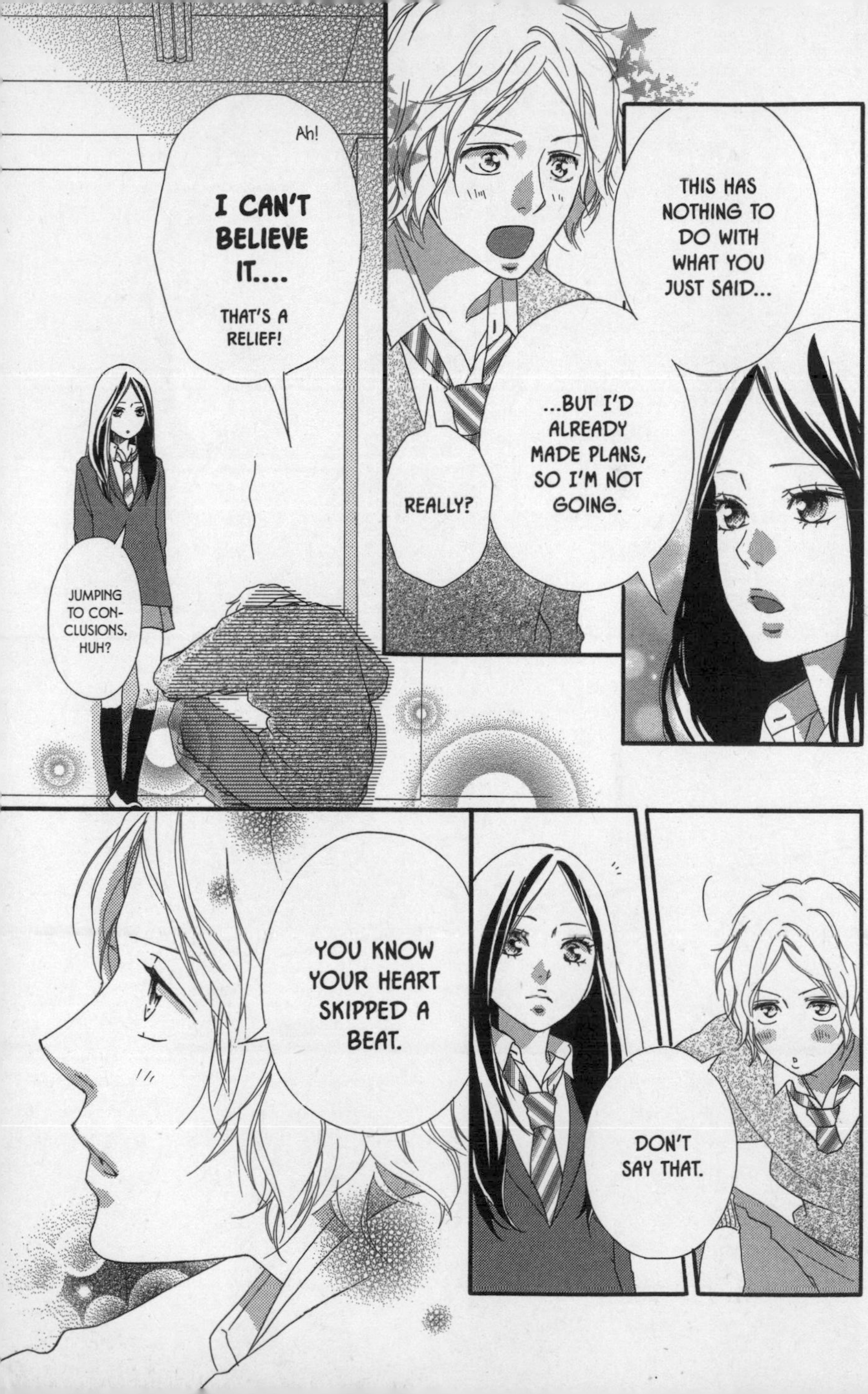
THIS HAS NOTHING TO DO WITH WHAT YOU JUST SAID...
...BUT I'D ALREADY MADE PLANS, SO I'M NOT GOING.
REALLY?
Ah!
I CAN'T BELIEVE IT....
THAT'S A RELIEF!
JUMPING TO CONCLUSIONS, HUH?
DON'T SAY THAT.
YOU KNOW YOUR HEART SKIPPED A BEAT.

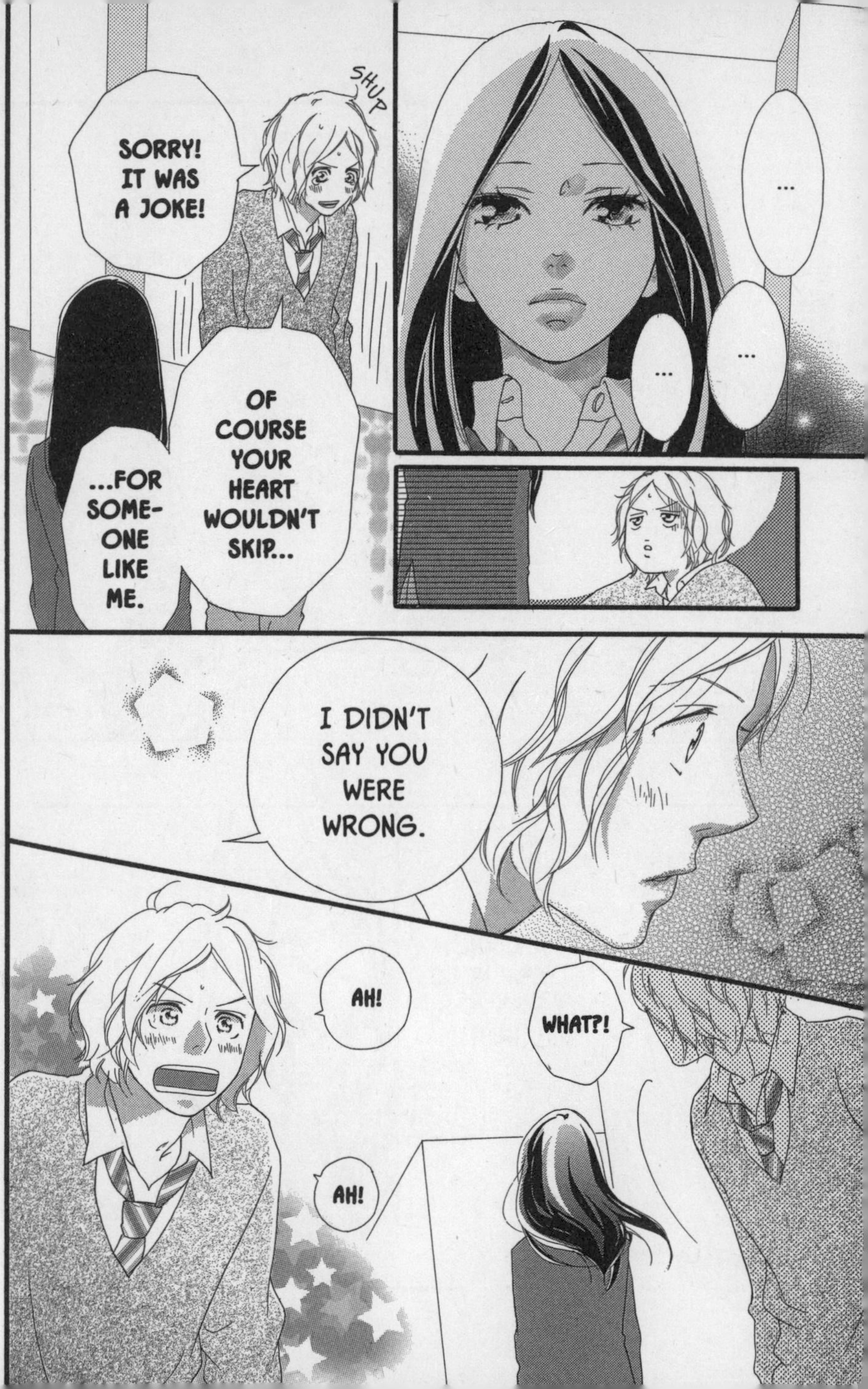
...
...
...
SHUP
SORRY! IT WAS A JOKE!
OF COURSE YOUR HEART WOULDN'T SKIP...
...FOR SOME-ONE LIKE ME.
I DIDN'T SAY YOU WERE WRONG.
WHAT?!
AH!
AH!

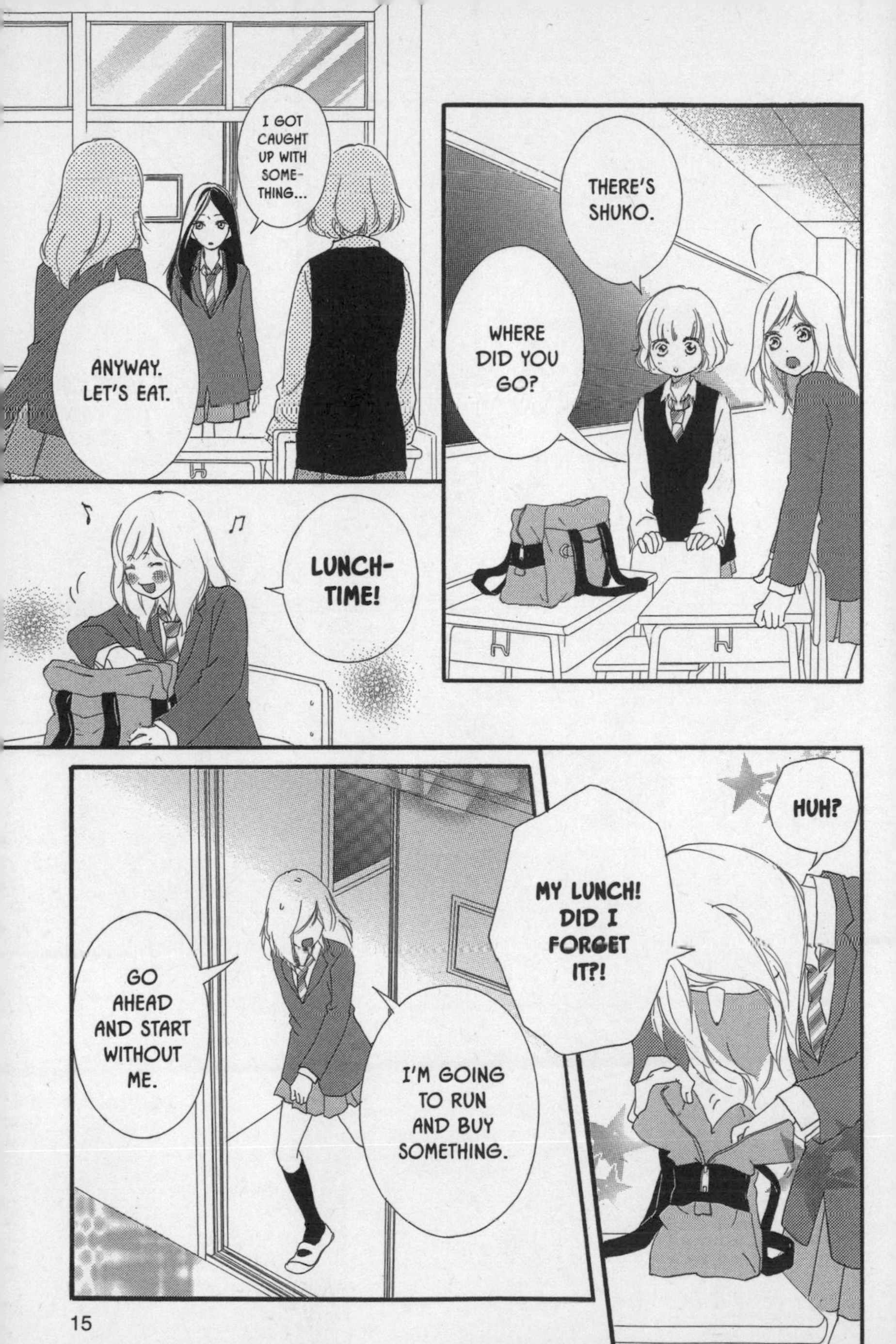
THERE'S SHUKO.
WHERE DID YOU GO?
I GOT CAUGHT UP WITH SOME-THING...
ANYWAY. LET'S EAT.
LUNCH-TIME!
HUH?
MY LUNCH! DID I FORGET IT?!
I'M GOING TO RUN AND BUY SOMETHING.
GO AHEAD AND START WITHOUT ME.

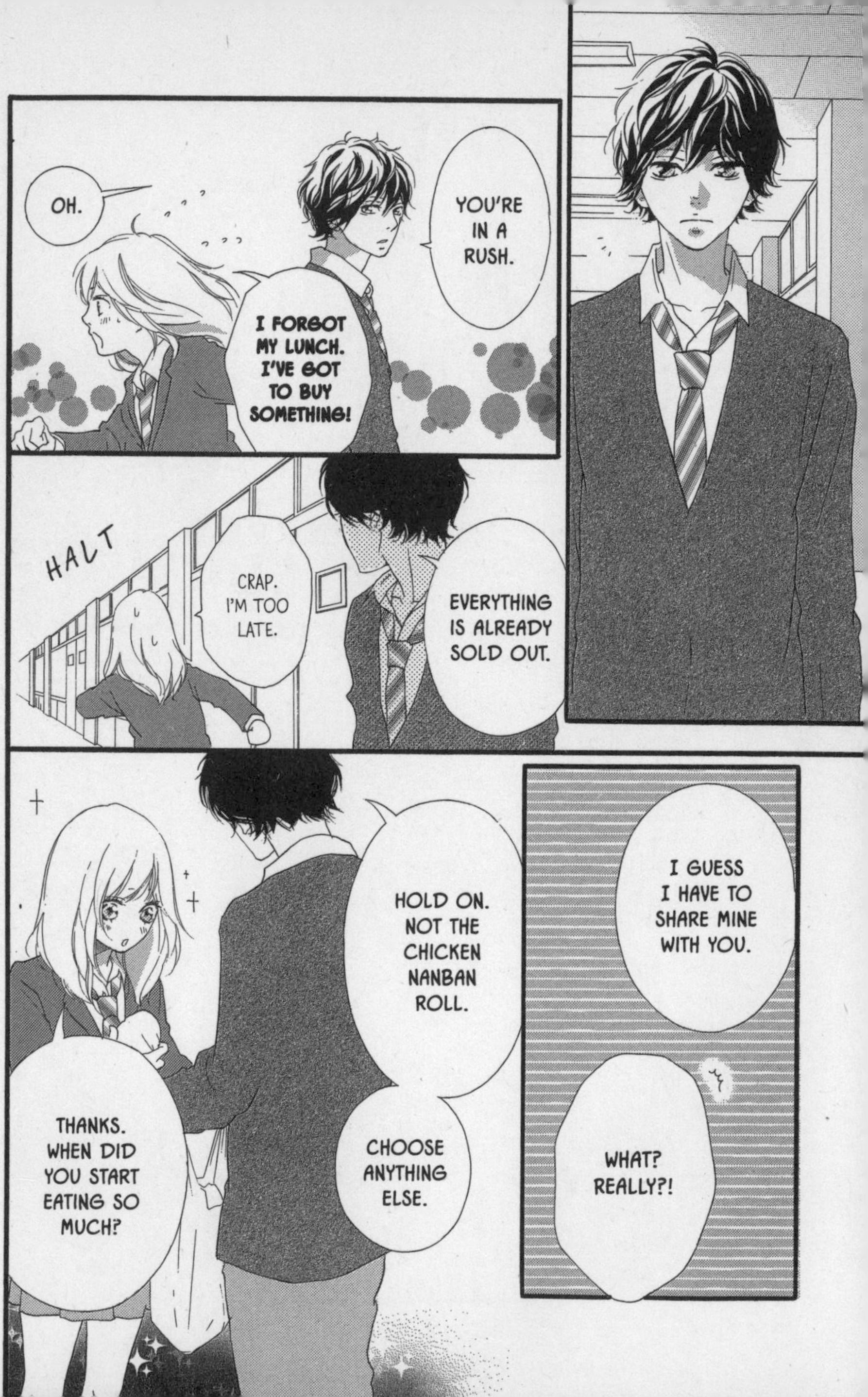
YOU'RE IN A RUSH.
OH.
I FORGOT MY LUNCH. I'VE GOT TO BUY SOMETHING!
EVERYTHING IS ALREADY SOLD OUT.
CRAP. I'M TOO LATE.
HALT
I GUESS I HAVE TO SHARE MINE WITH YOU.
WHAT? REALLY?!
HOLD ON. NOT THE CHICKEN NANBAN ROLL.
CHOOSE ANYTHING ELSE.
THANKS. WHEN DID YOU START EATING SO MUCH?

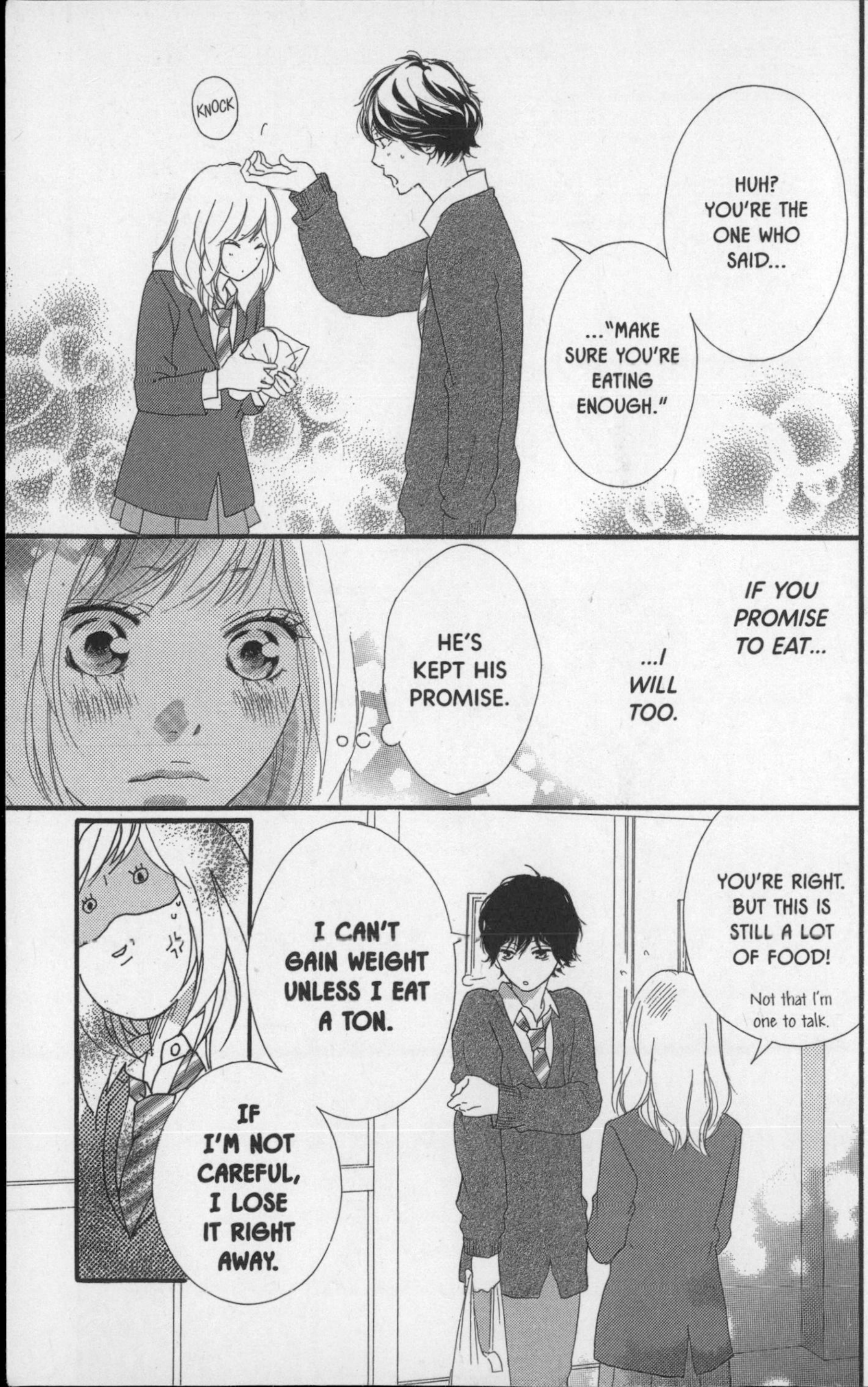
HUH? YOU'RE THE ONE WHO SAID...
..."MAKE SURE YOU'RE EATING ENOUGH."
KNOCK
IF YOU PROMISE TO EAT...
...I WILL TOO.
HE'S KEPT HIS PROMISE.
YOU'RE RIGHT. BUT THIS IS STILL A LOT OF FOOD!
Not that I'm one to talk.
I CAN'T GAIN WEIGHT UNLESS I EAT A TON.
IF I'M NOT CAREFUL, I LOSE IT RIGHT AWAY.

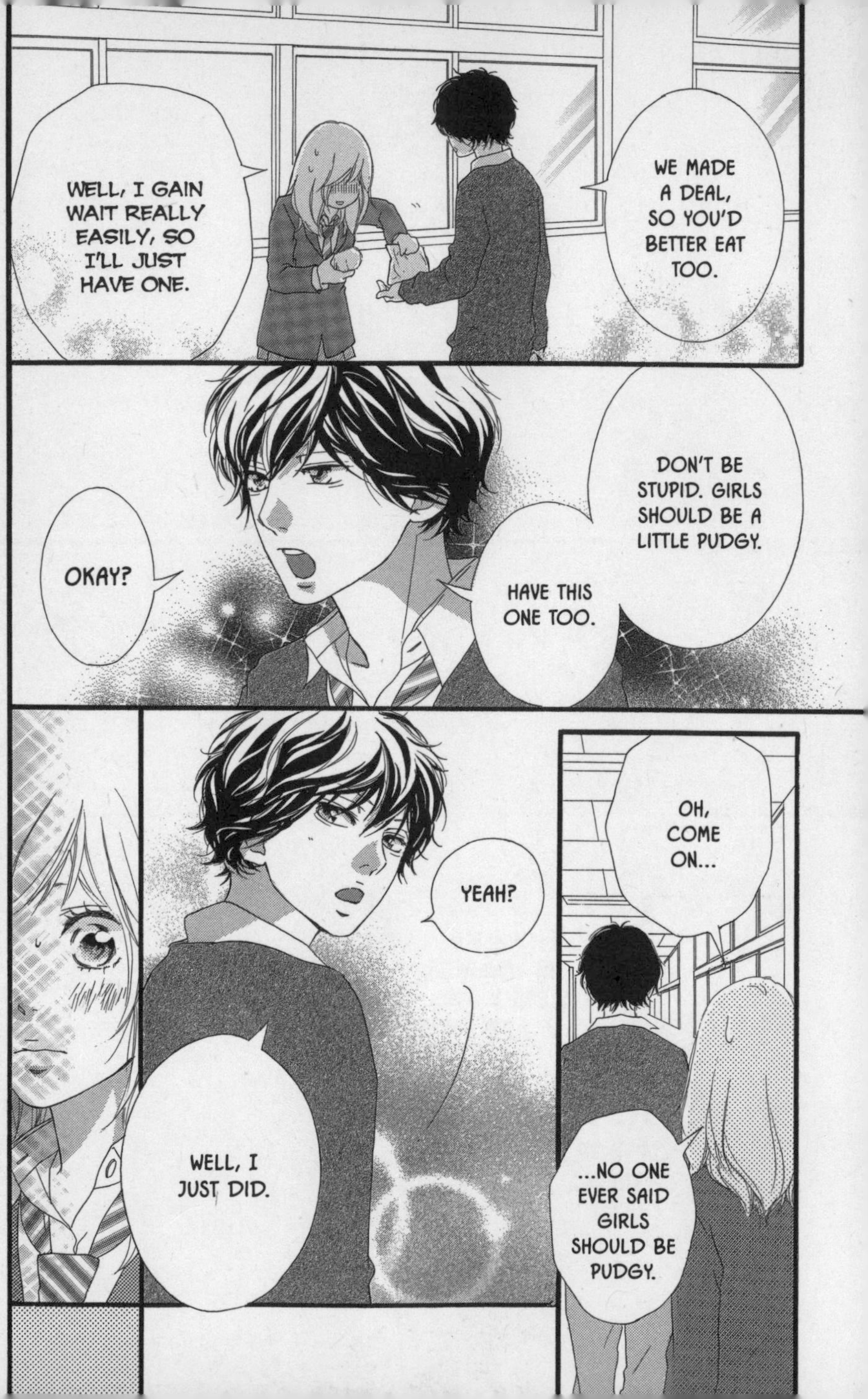
WE MADE A DEAL, SO YOU'D BETTER EAT TOO.
WELL, I GAIN WAIT REALLY EASILY, SO I'LL JUST HAVE ONE.
DON'T BE STUPID. GIRLS SHOULD BE A LITTLE PUDGY.
HAVE THIS ONE TOO.
OKAY?
OH, COME ON...
...NO ONE EVER SAID GIRLS SHOULD BE PUDGY.
YEAH?
WELL, I JUST DID.

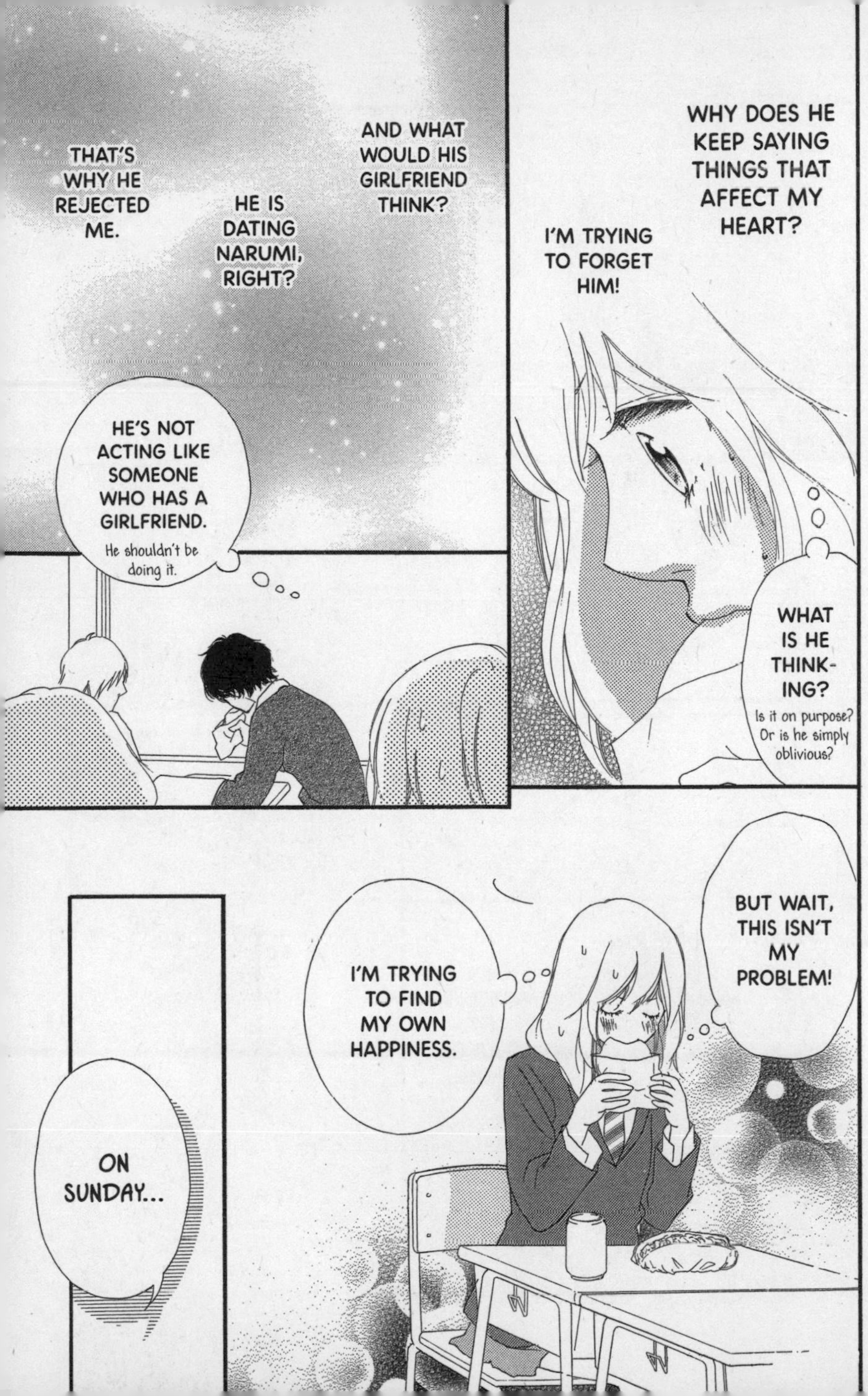
WHY DOES HE KEEP SAYING THINGS THAT AFFECT MY HEART?
I'M TRYING TO FORGET HIM!
WHAT IS HE THINKING?
Is it on purpose? Or is he simply oblivious?
AND WHAT WOULD HIS GIRLFRIEND THINK?
HE IS DATING NARUMI, RIGHT?
THAT'S WHY HE REJECTED ME.
HE'S NOT ACTING LIKE SOMEONE WHO HAS A GIRLFRIEND.
He shouldn't be doing it.
BUT WAIT, THIS ISN'T MY PROBLEM!
I'M TRYING TO FIND MY OWN HAPPINESS.
ON SUNDAY...

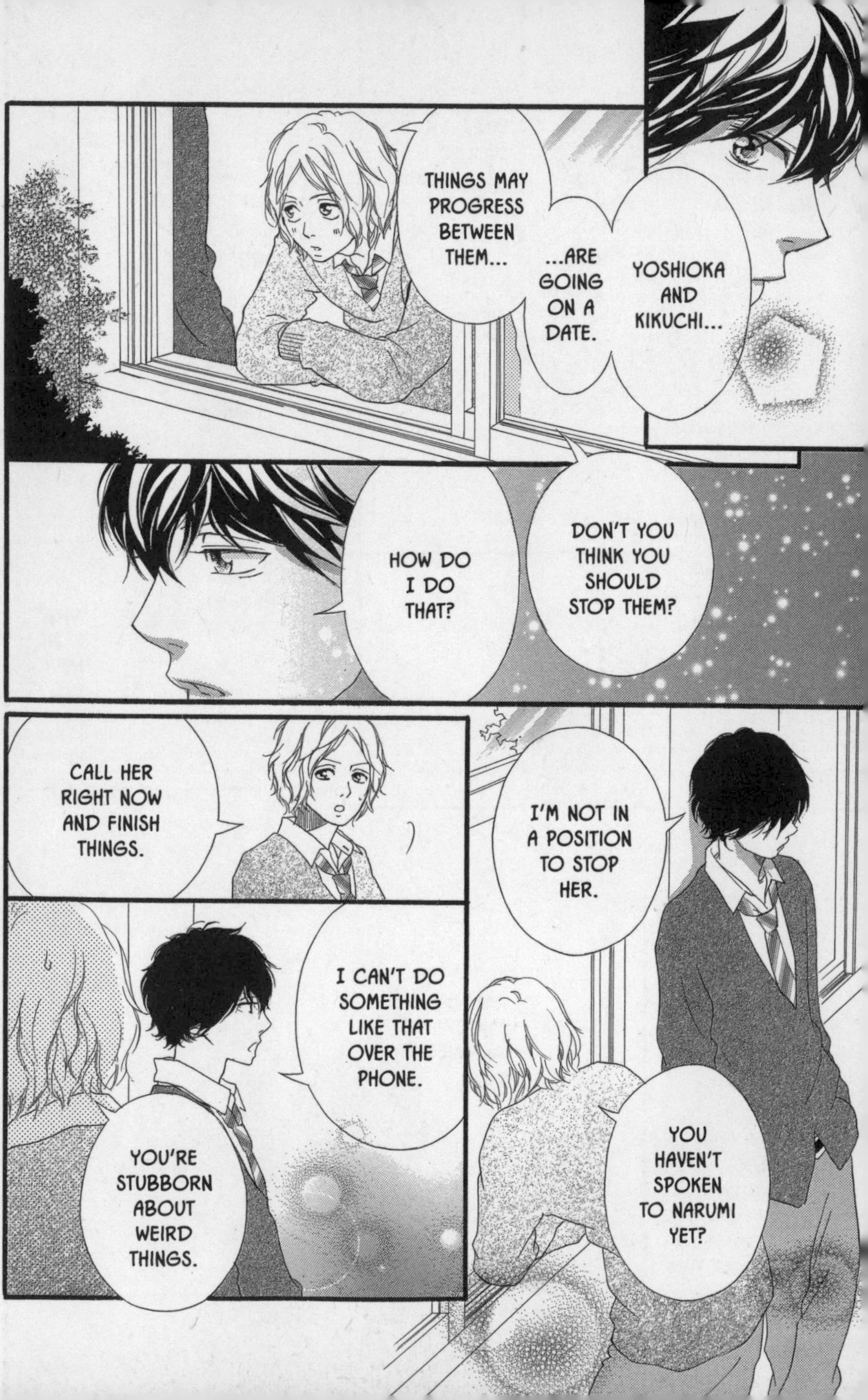
YOSHIOKA AND KIKUCHI...
...ARE GOING ON A DATE.
THINGS MAY PROGRESS BETWEEN THEM...
DON'T YOU THINK YOU SHOULD STOP THEM?
HOW DO I DO THAT?
I'M NOT IN A POSITION TO STOP HER.
YOU HAVEN'T SPOKEN TO NARUMI YET?
CALL HER RIGHT NOW AND FINISH THINGS.
I CAN'T DO SOMETHING LIKE THAT OVER THE PHONE.
YOU'RE STUBBORN ABOUT WEIRD THINGS.

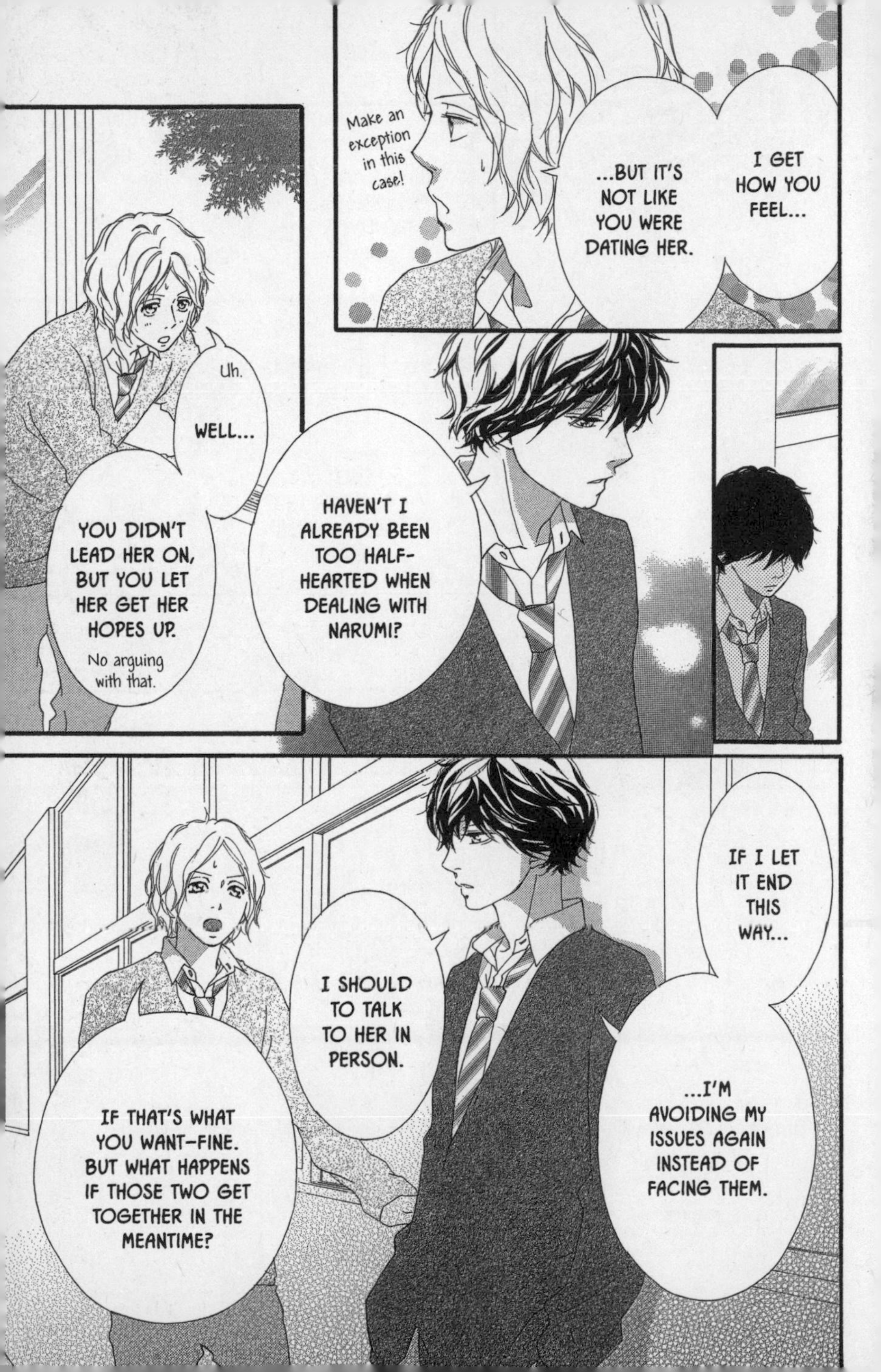
I GET HOW YOU FEEL...
...BUT IT'S NOT LIKE YOU WERE DATING HER.
Make an exception in this case!
Uh.
WELL...
YOU DIDN'T LEAD HER ON, BUT YOU LET HER GET HER HOPES UP.
No arguing with that.
HAVEN'T I ALREADY BEEN TOO HALF-HEARTED WHEN DEALING WITH NARUMI?
IF I LET IT END THIS WAY...
...I'M AVOIDING MY ISSUES AGAIN INSTEAD OF FACING THEM.
I SHOULD TO TALK TO HER IN PERSON.
IF THAT'S WHAT YOU WANT—FINE. BUT WHAT HAPPENS IF THOSE TWO GET TOGETHER IN THE MEANTIME?

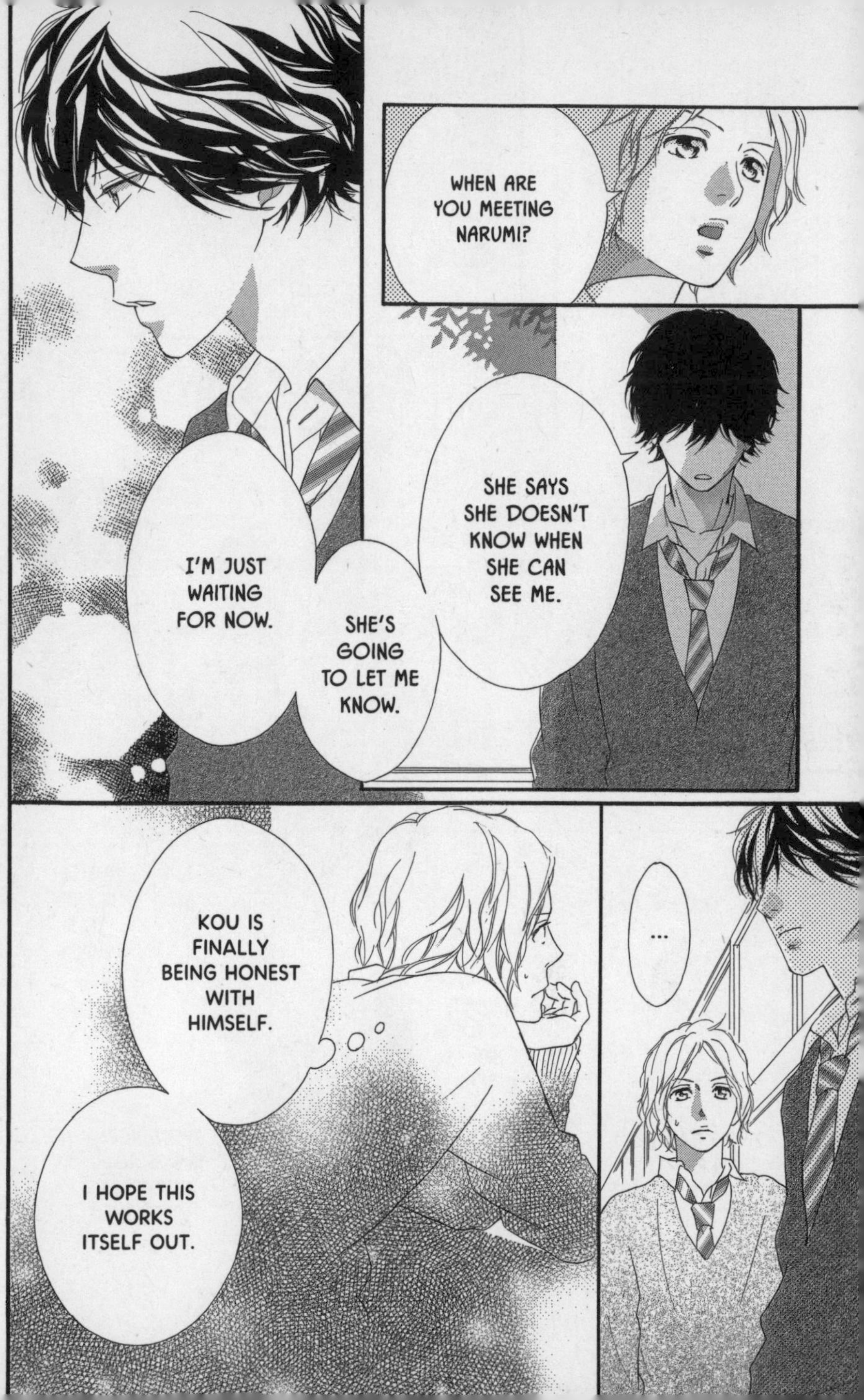
WHEN ARE YOU MEETING NARUMI?
SHE SAYS SHE DOESN'T KNOW WHEN SHE CAN SEE ME.
SHE'S GOING TO LET ME KNOW.
I'M JUST WAITING FOR NOW.
...
KOU IS FINALLY BEING HONEST WITH HIMSELF.
I HOPE THIS WORKS ITSELF OUT.

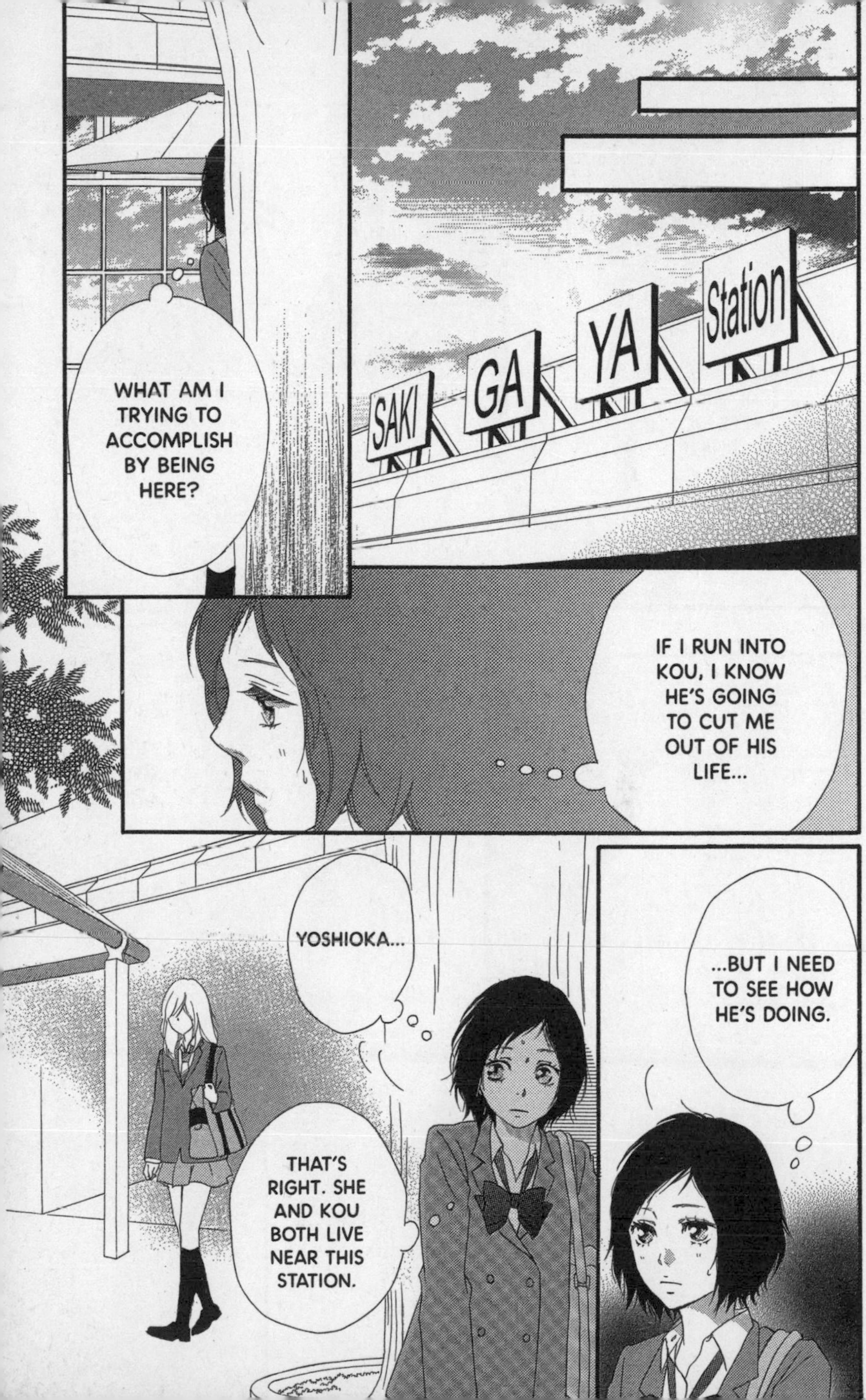
SAKI GA YA Station
WHAT AM I TRYING TO ACCOMPLISH BY BEING HERE?
IF I RUN INTO KOU, I KNOW HE'S GOING TO CUT ME OUT OF HIS LIFE...
...BUT I NEED TO SEE HOW HE'S DOING.
YOSHIOKA...
THAT'S RIGHT. SHE AND KOU BOTH LIVE NEAR THIS STATION.

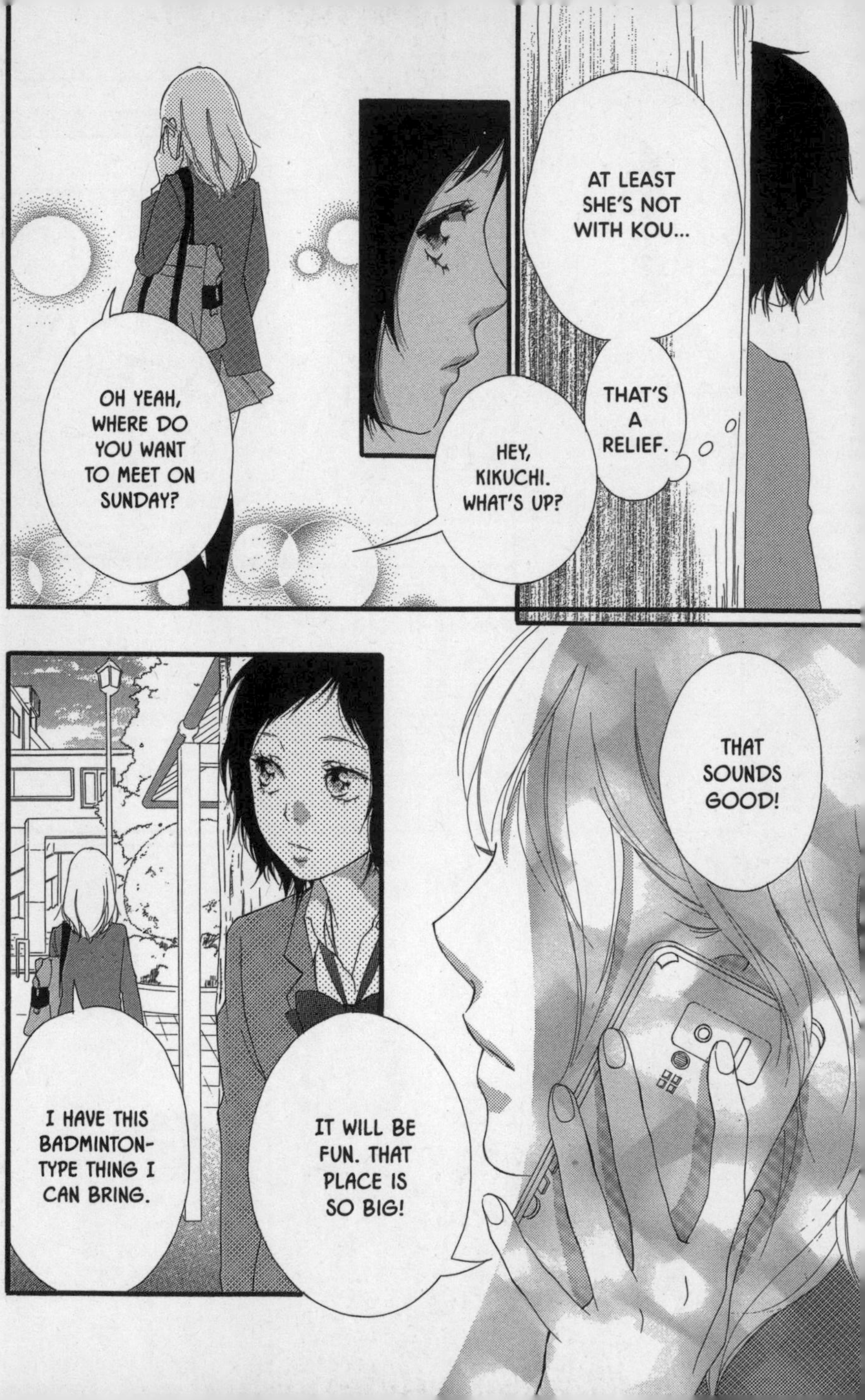
AT LEAST SHE'S NOT WITH KOU...
THAT'S A RELIEF.
HEY, KIKUCHI. WHAT'S UP?
OH YEAH, WHERE DO YOU WANT TO MEET ON SUNDAY?
THAT SOUNDS GOOD!
IT WILL BE FUN. THAT PLACE IS SO BIG!
I HAVE THIS BADMINTON-TYPE THING I CAN BRING.

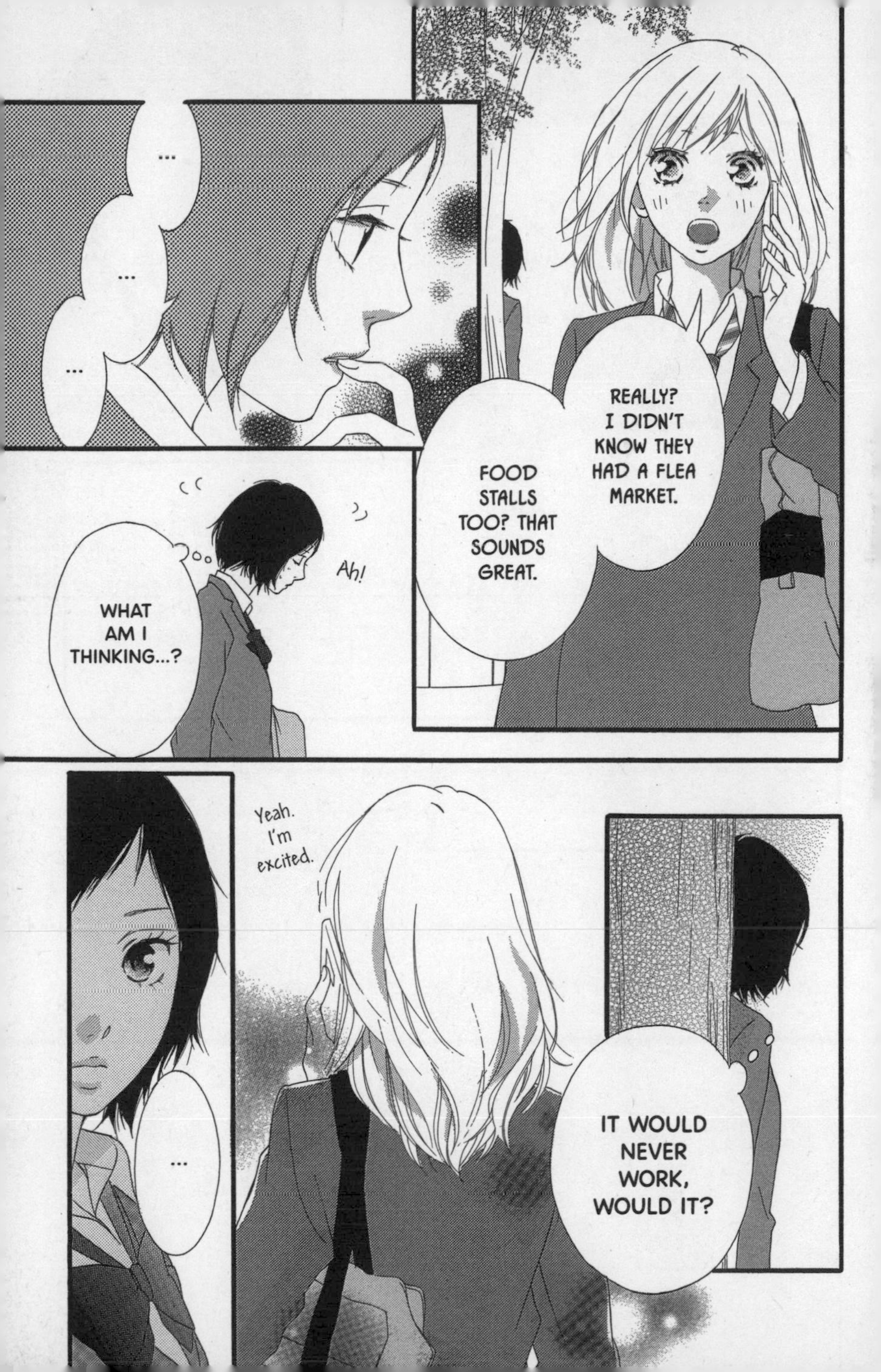
REALLY? I DIDN'T KNOW THEY HAD A FLEA MARKET.
FOOD STALLS TOO? THAT SOUNDS GREAT.
...
...
...
Ah!
WHAT AM I THINKING...?
IT WOULD NEVER WORK, WOULD IT?
Yeah. I'm excited.
...

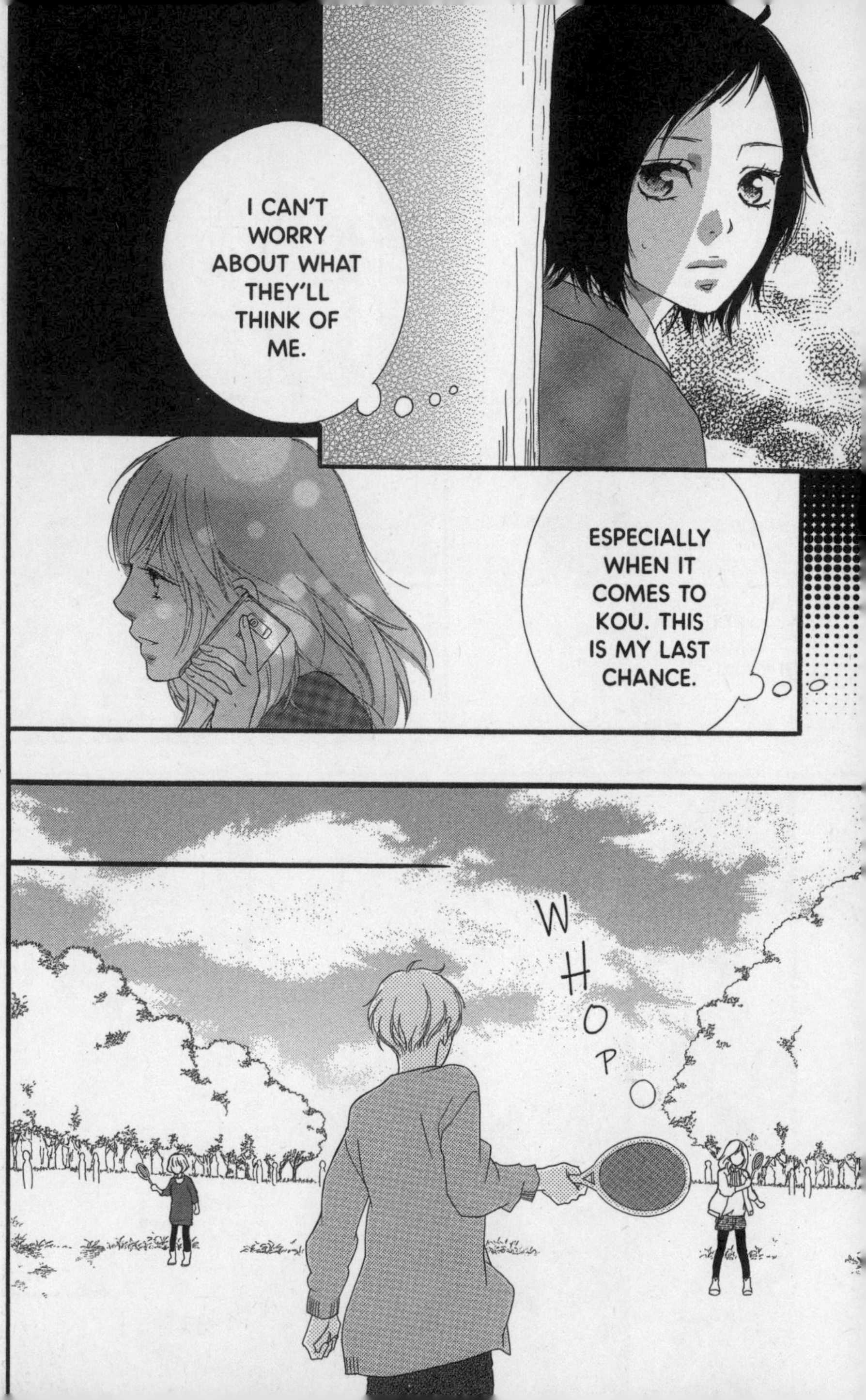
I CAN'T WORRY ABOUT WHAT THEY'LL THINK OF ME.
ESPECIALLY WHEN IT COMES TO KOU. THIS IS MY LAST CHANCE.
WHOP

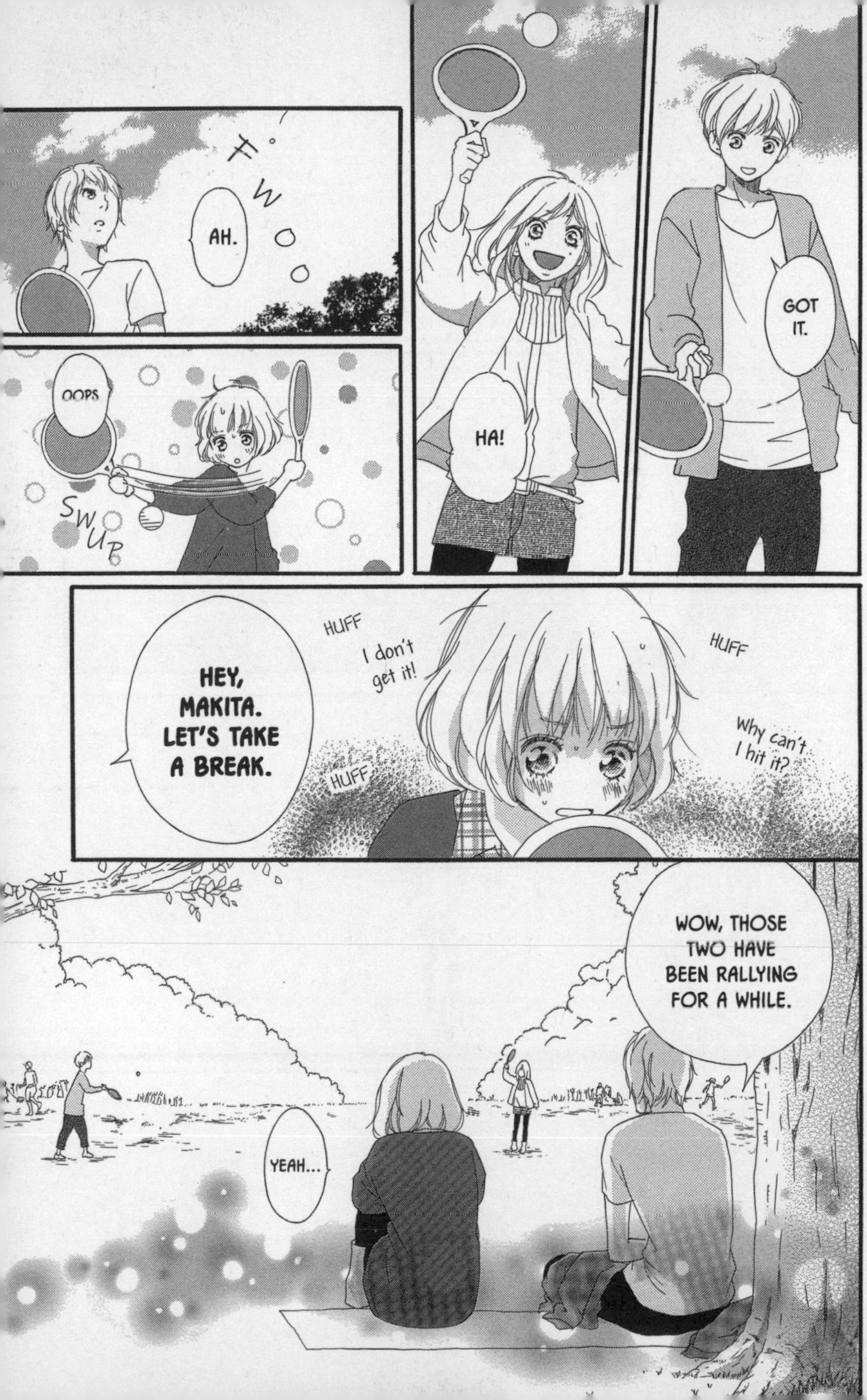
GOT IT.
HA!
AH.
FWOOO
OOPS
SWUP
HUFF
Why can't I hit it?
I don't get it!
HUFF
HUFF
HEY, MAKITA. LET'S TAKE A BREAK.
WOW, THOSE TWO HAVE BEEN RALLYING FOR A WHILE.
YEAH...

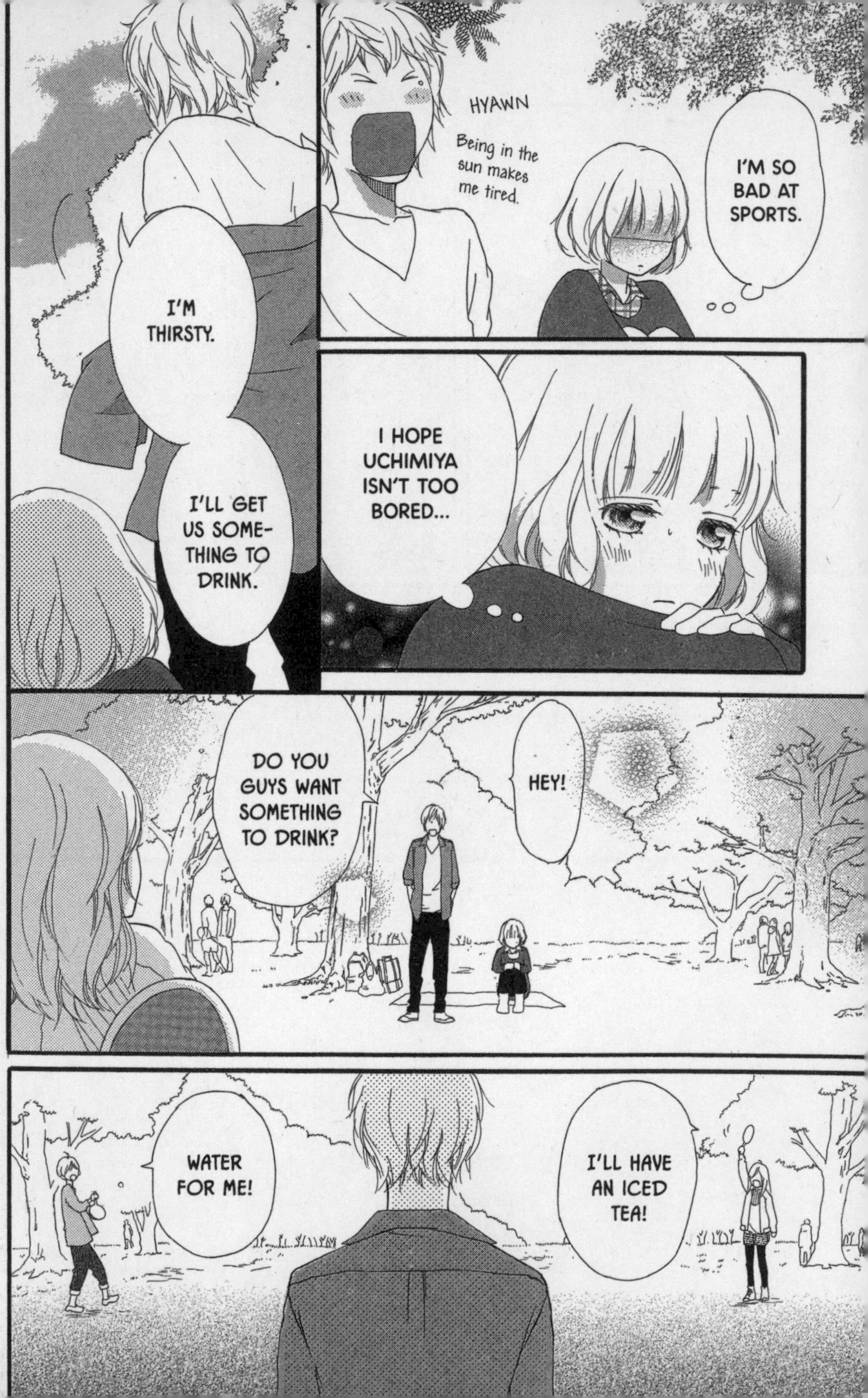
I'M SO BAD AT SPORTS.
HYAWN
Being in the sun makes me tired.
I HOPE UCHIMIYA ISN'T TOO BORED...
I'M THIRSTY.
I'LL GET US SOME-THING TO DRINK.
HEY!
DO YOU GUYS WANT SOMETHING TO DRINK?
I'LL HAVE AN ICED TEA!
WATER FOR ME!

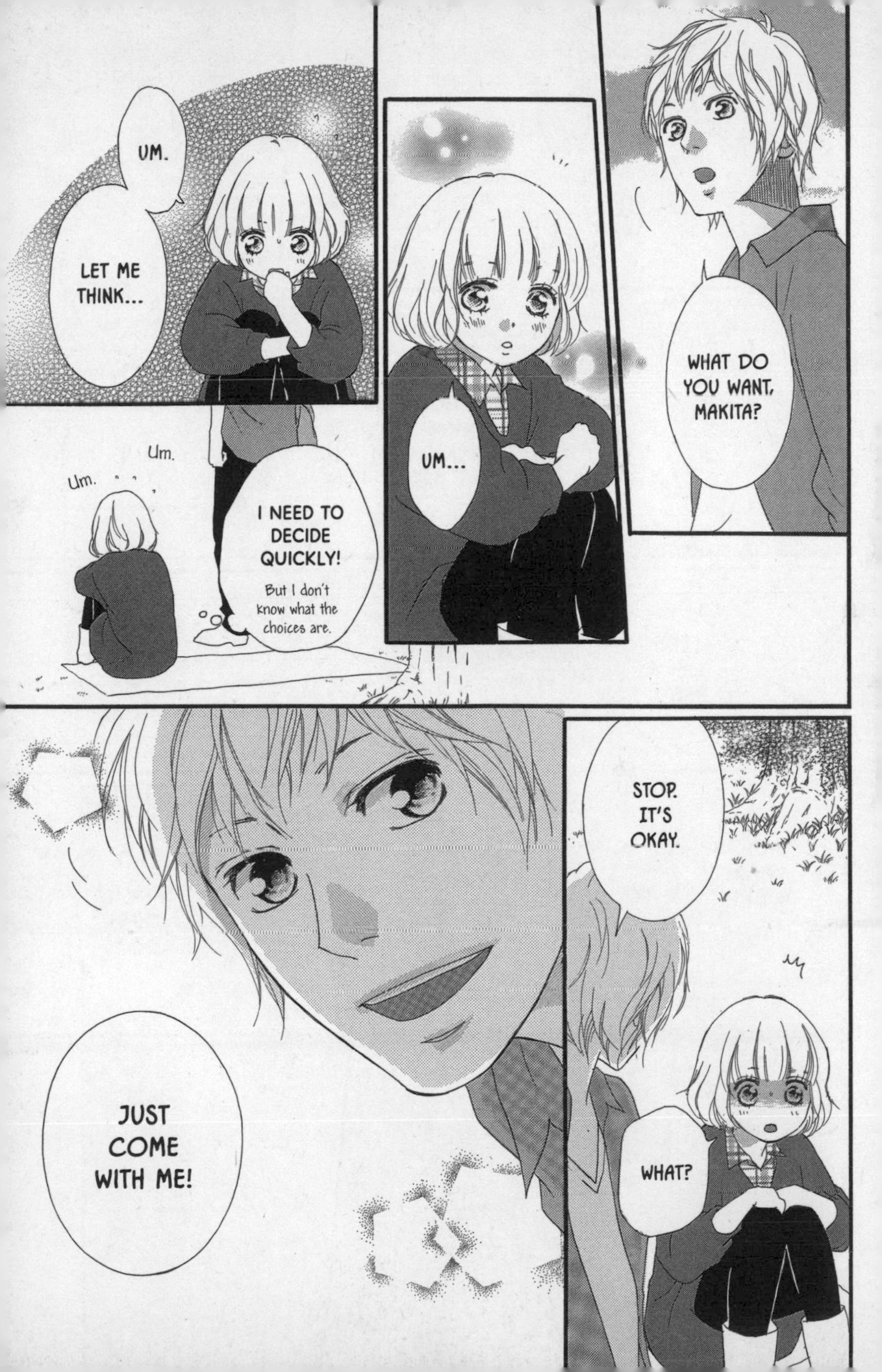
WHAT DO YOU WANT, MAKITA?
UM...
UM.
LET ME THINK...
I NEED TO DECIDE QUICKLY!
But I don't know what the choices are.
Um.
Um.
STOP. IT'S OKAY.
WHAT?
JUST COME WITH ME!

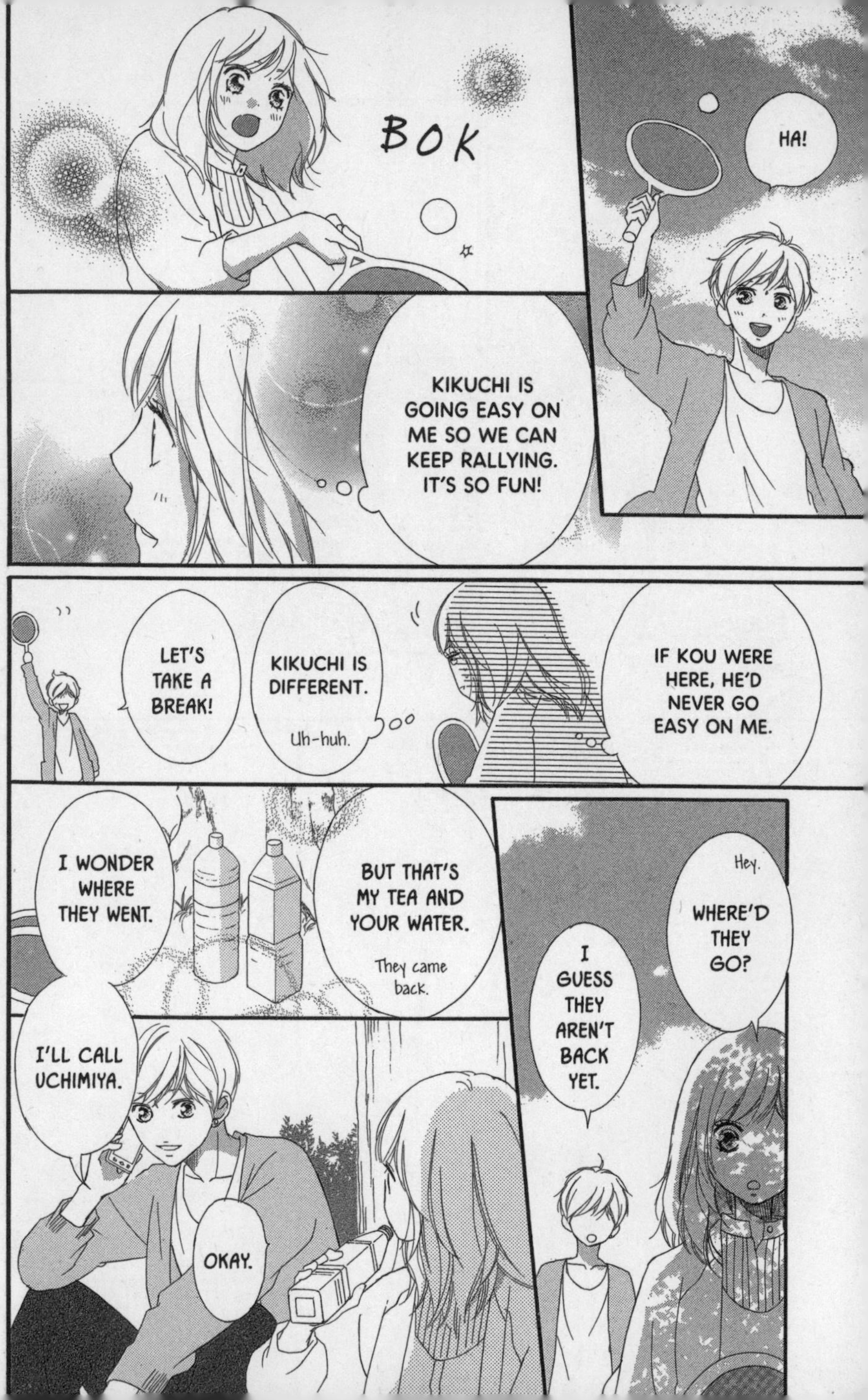
HA!
BOK
KIKUCHI IS GOING EASY ON ME SO WE CAN KEEP RALLYING. IT'S SO FUN!
IF KOU WERE HERE, HE'D NEVER GO EASY ON ME.
KIKUCHI IS DIFFERENT.
Uh-huh.
LET'S TAKE A BREAK!
Hey.
WHERE'D THEY GO?
I GUESS THEY AREN'T BACK YET.
BUT THAT'S MY TEA AND YOUR WATER.
They came back.
I WONDER WHERE THEY WENT.
I'LL CALL UCHIMIYA.
OKAY.

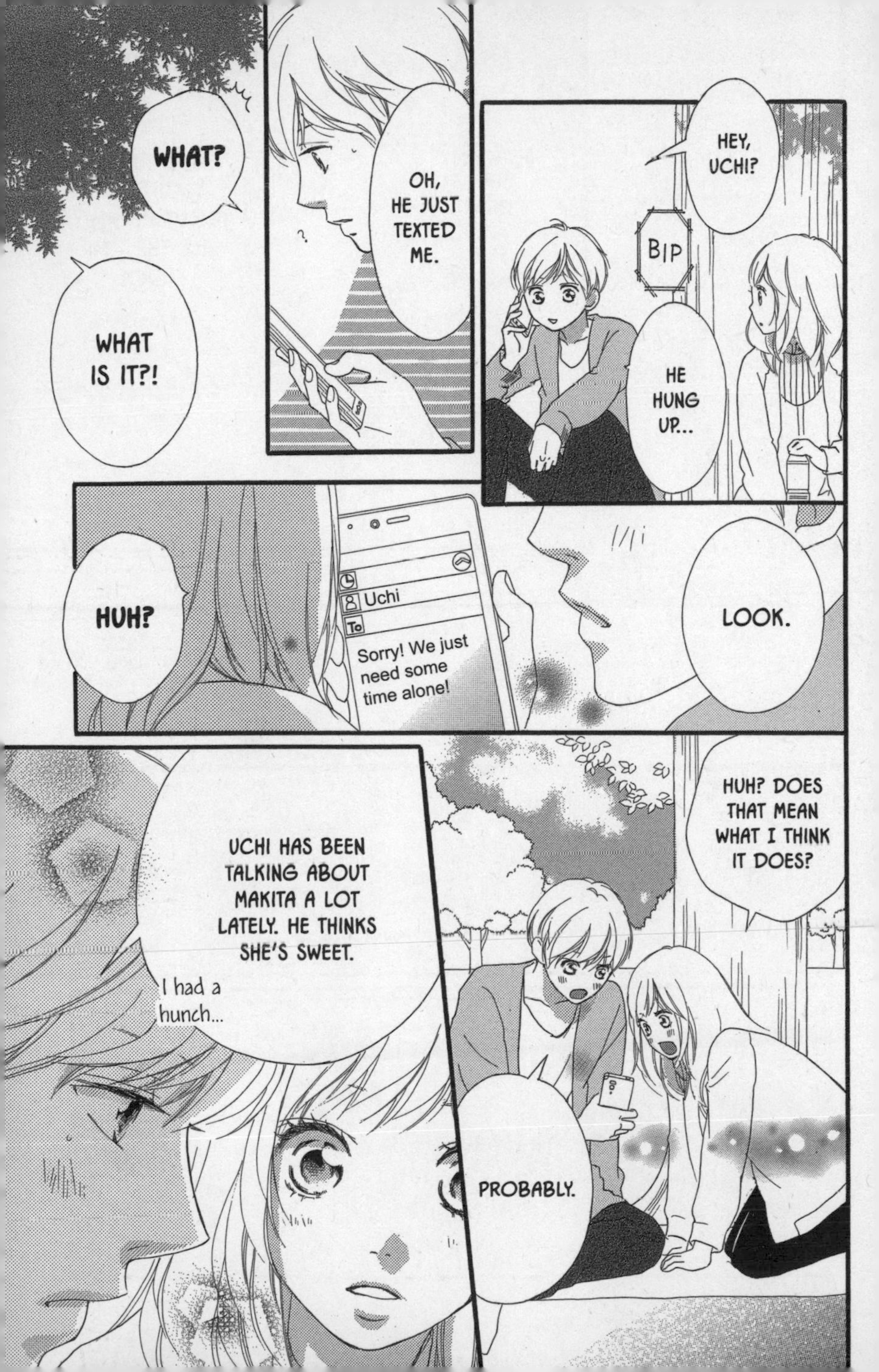
HEY, UCHI?
BIP
HE HUNG UP...
OH, HE JUST TEXTED ME.
WHAT?
WHAT IS IT?!
LOOK.
Uchi
To
Sorry! We just need some time alone!
HUH?
HUH? DOES THAT MEAN WHAT I THINK IT DOES?
PROBABLY.
UCHI HAS BEEN TALKING ABOUT MAKITA A LOT LATELY. HE THINKS SHE'S SWEET.
I had a hunch...

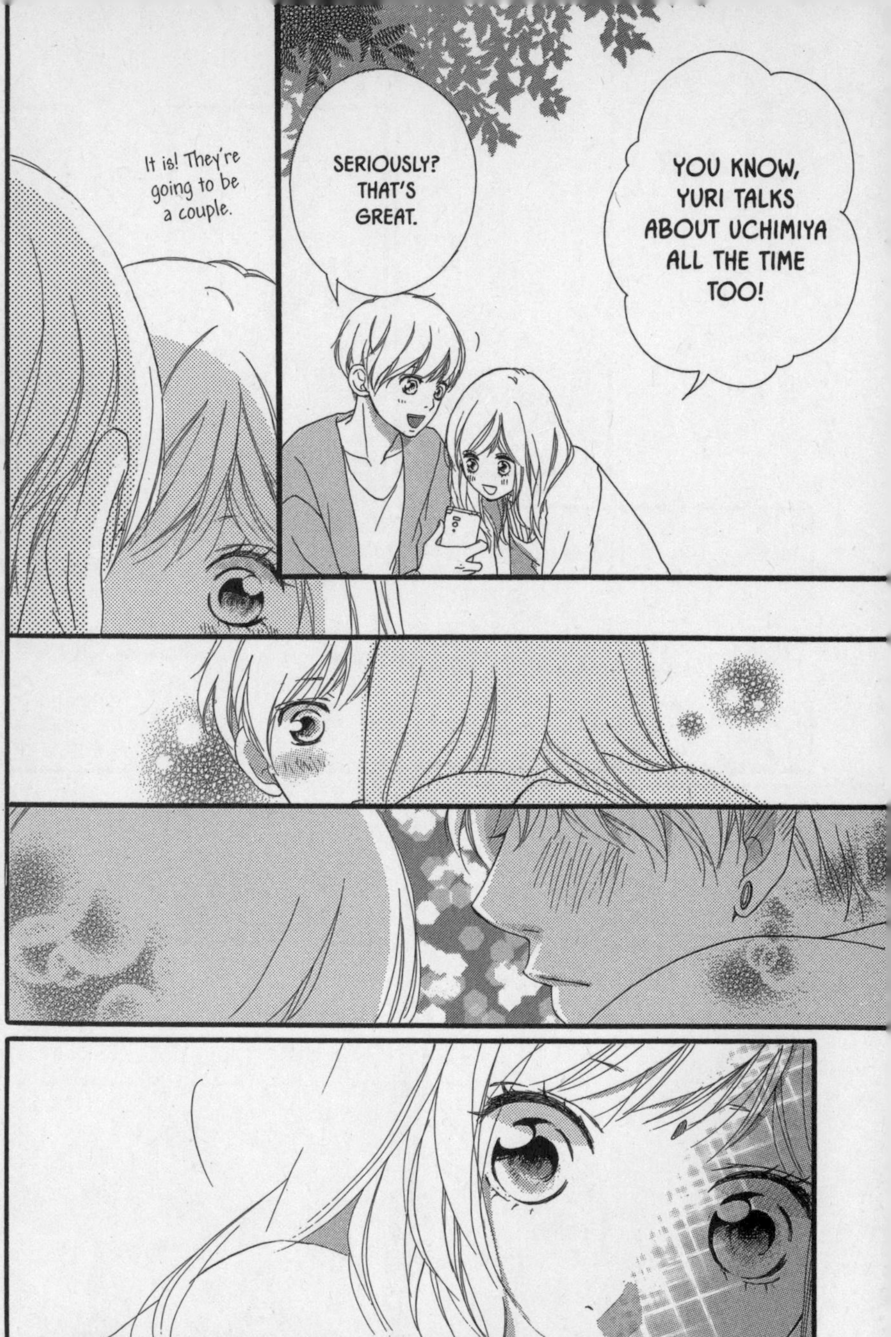
YOU KNOW, YURI TALKS ABOUT UCHIMIYA ALL THE TIME TOO!
SERIOUSLY? THAT'S GREAT.
It is! They're going to be a couple.

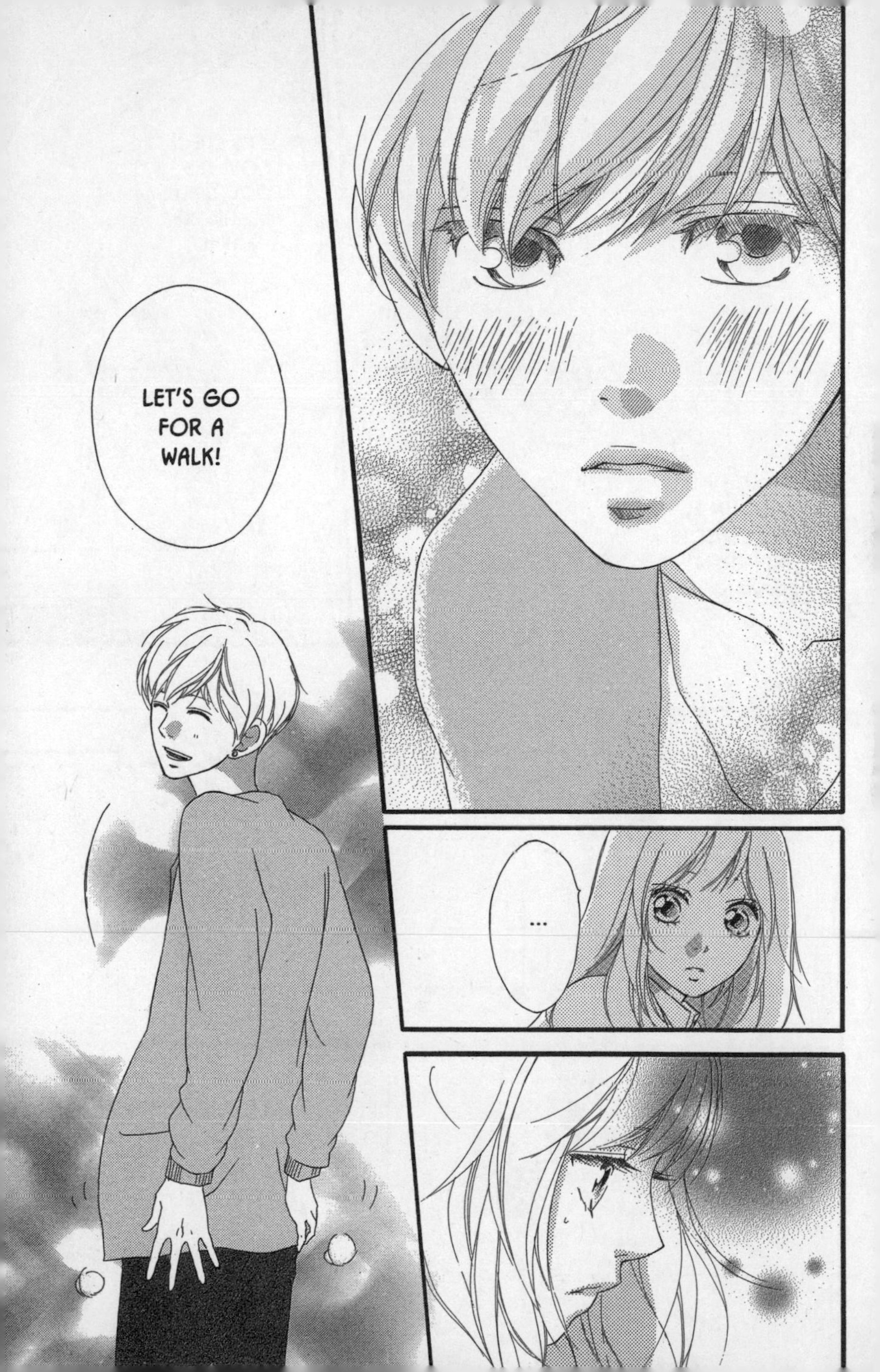
...
LET'S GO FOR A WALK!

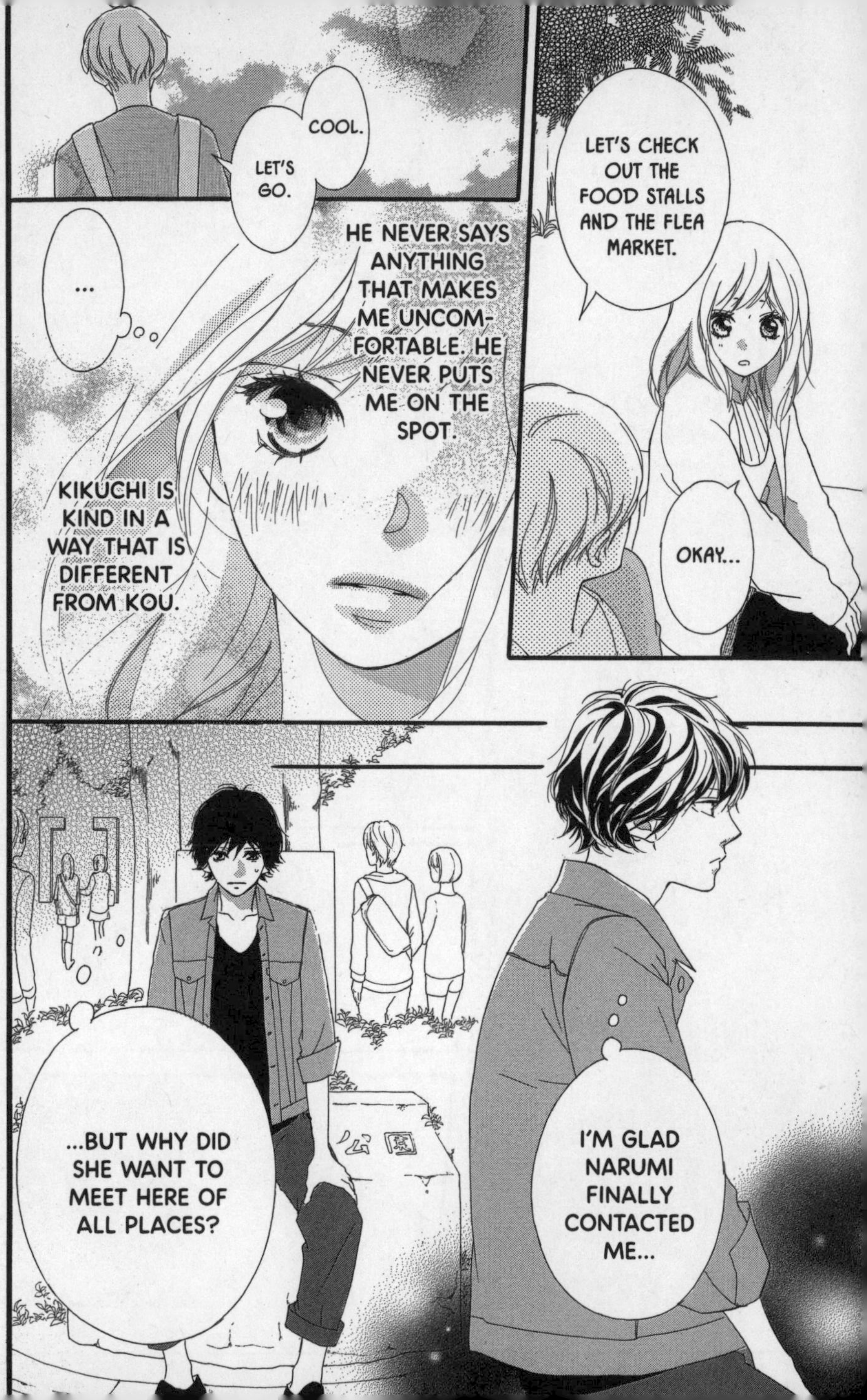
LET'S CHECK OUT THE FOOD STALLS AND THE FLEA MARKET.
OKAY...
COOL.
LET'S GO.
HE NEVER SAYS ANYTHING THAT MAKES ME UNCOMFORTABLE. HE NEVER PUTS ME ON THE SPOT.
...
KIKUCHI IS KIND IN A WAY THAT IS DIFFERENT FROM KOU.
I'M GLAD NARUMI FINALLY CONTACTED ME...
...BUT WHY DID SHE WANT TO MEET HERE OF ALL PLACES?

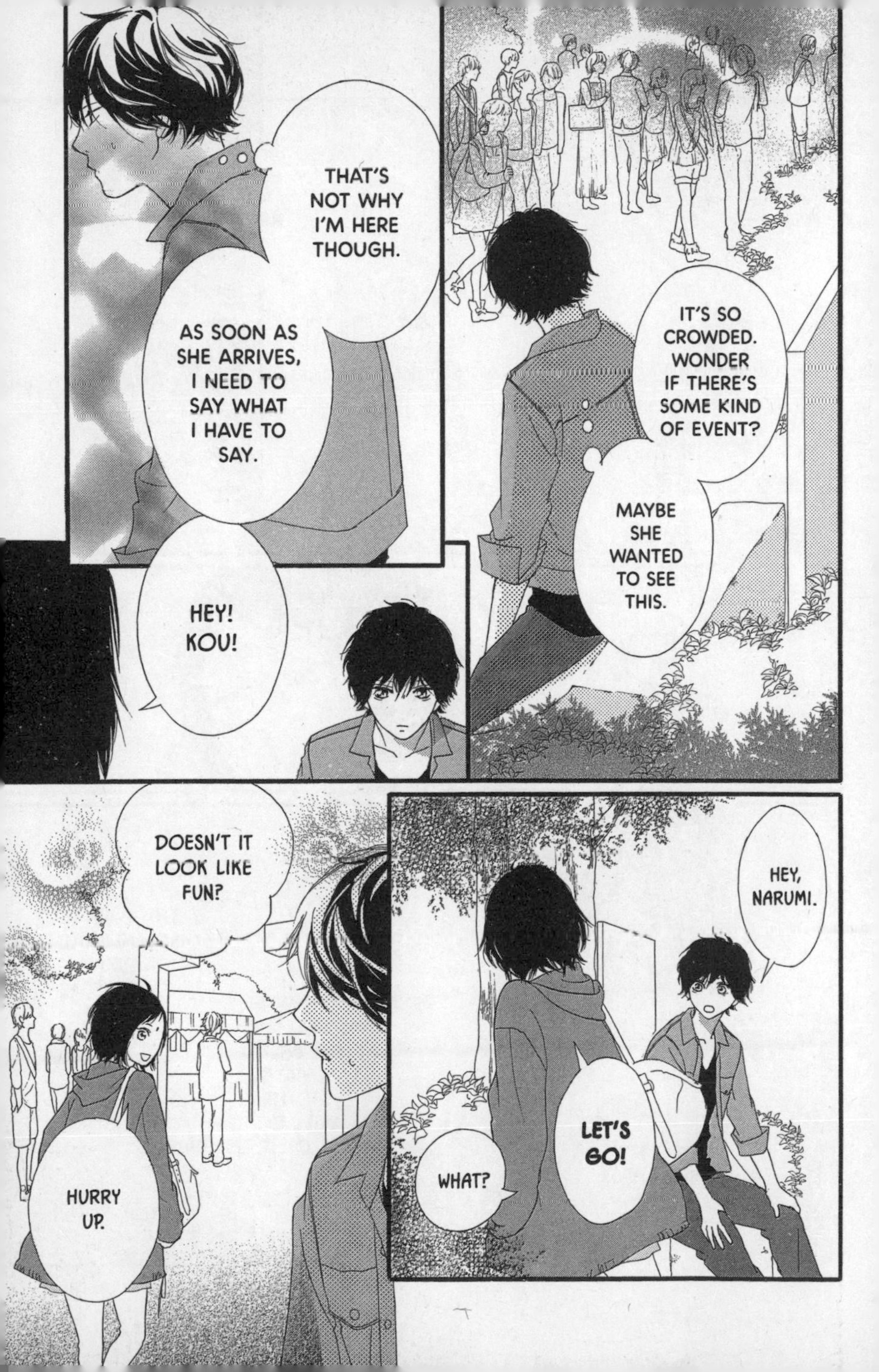
IT'S SO CROWDED. WONDER IF THERE'S SOME KIND OF EVENT?
MAYBE SHE WANTED TO SEE THIS.
THAT'S NOT WHY I'M HERE THOUGH.
AS SOON AS SHE ARRIVES, I NEED TO SAY WHAT I HAVE TO SAY.
HEY! KOU!
HEY, NARUMI.
LET'S GO!
WHAT?
DOESN'T IT LOOK LIKE FUN?
HURRY UP.

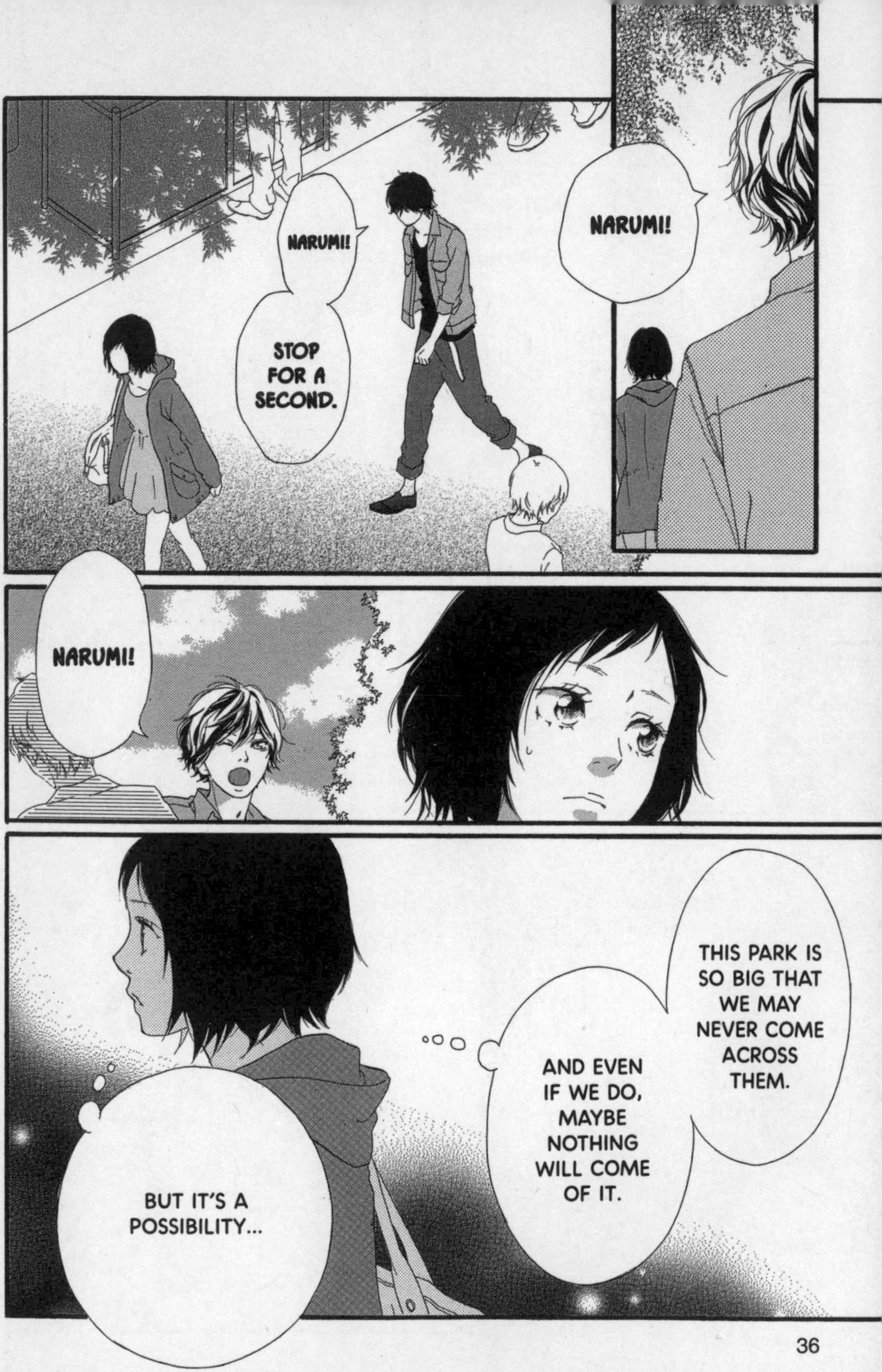
NARUMI!
NARUMI!
STOP FOR A SECOND.
NARUMI!
THIS PARK IS SO BIG THAT WE MAY NEVER COME ACROSS THEM.
AND EVEN IF WE DO, MAYBE NOTHING WILL COME OF IT.
BUT IT'S A POSSIBILITY...

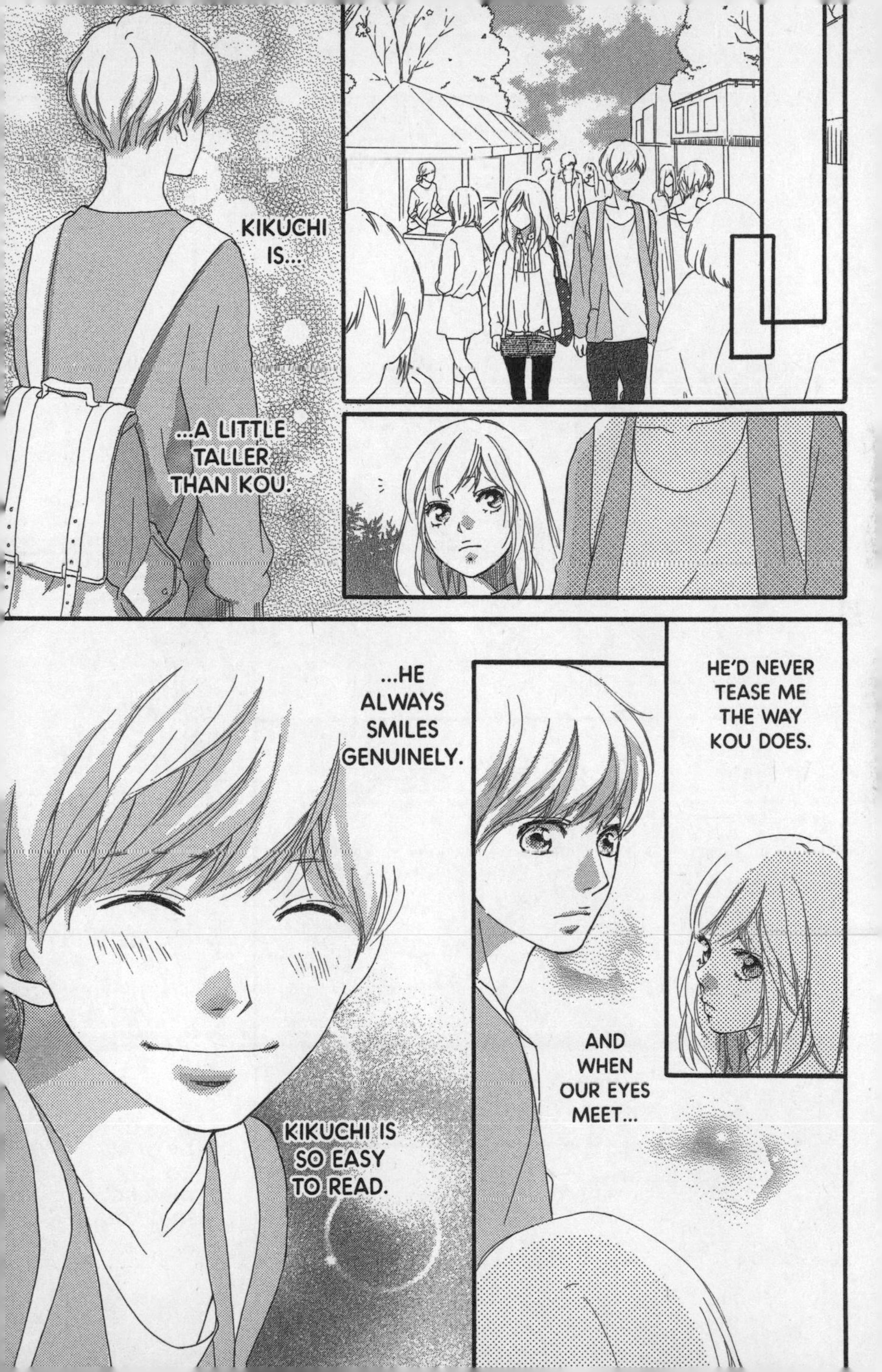
KIKUCHI IS...
...A LITTLE TALLER THAN KOU.
HE'D NEVER TEASE ME THE WAY KOU DOES.
AND WHEN OUR EYES MEET...
...HE ALWAYS SMILES GENUINELY.
KIKUCHI IS SO EASY TO READ.

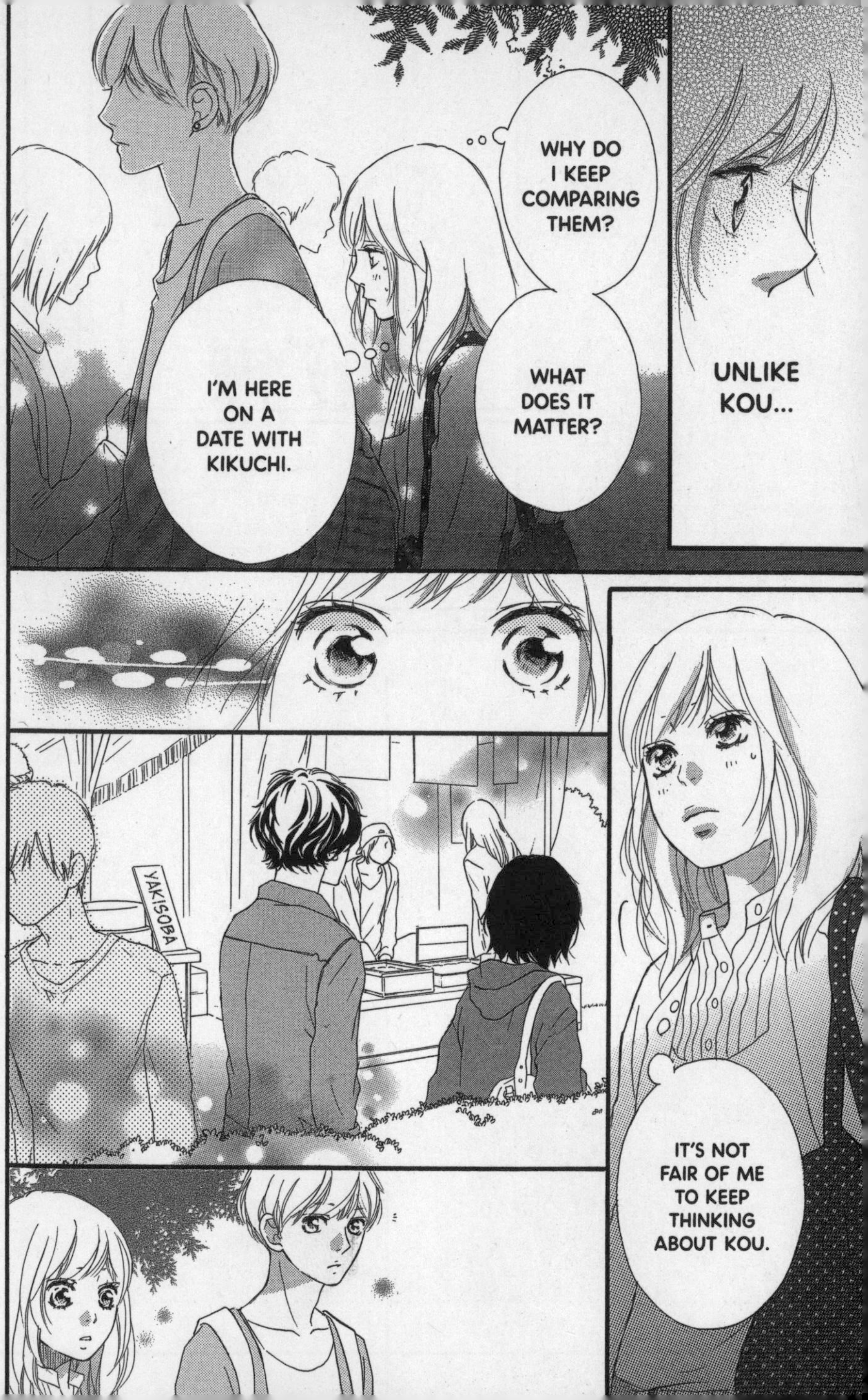
UNLIKE KOU...
WHY DO I KEEP COMPARING THEM?
WHAT DOES IT MATTER?
I'M HERE ON A DATE WITH KIKUCHI.
IT'S NOT FAIR OF ME TO KEEP THINKING ABOUT KOU.
YAKISOBA

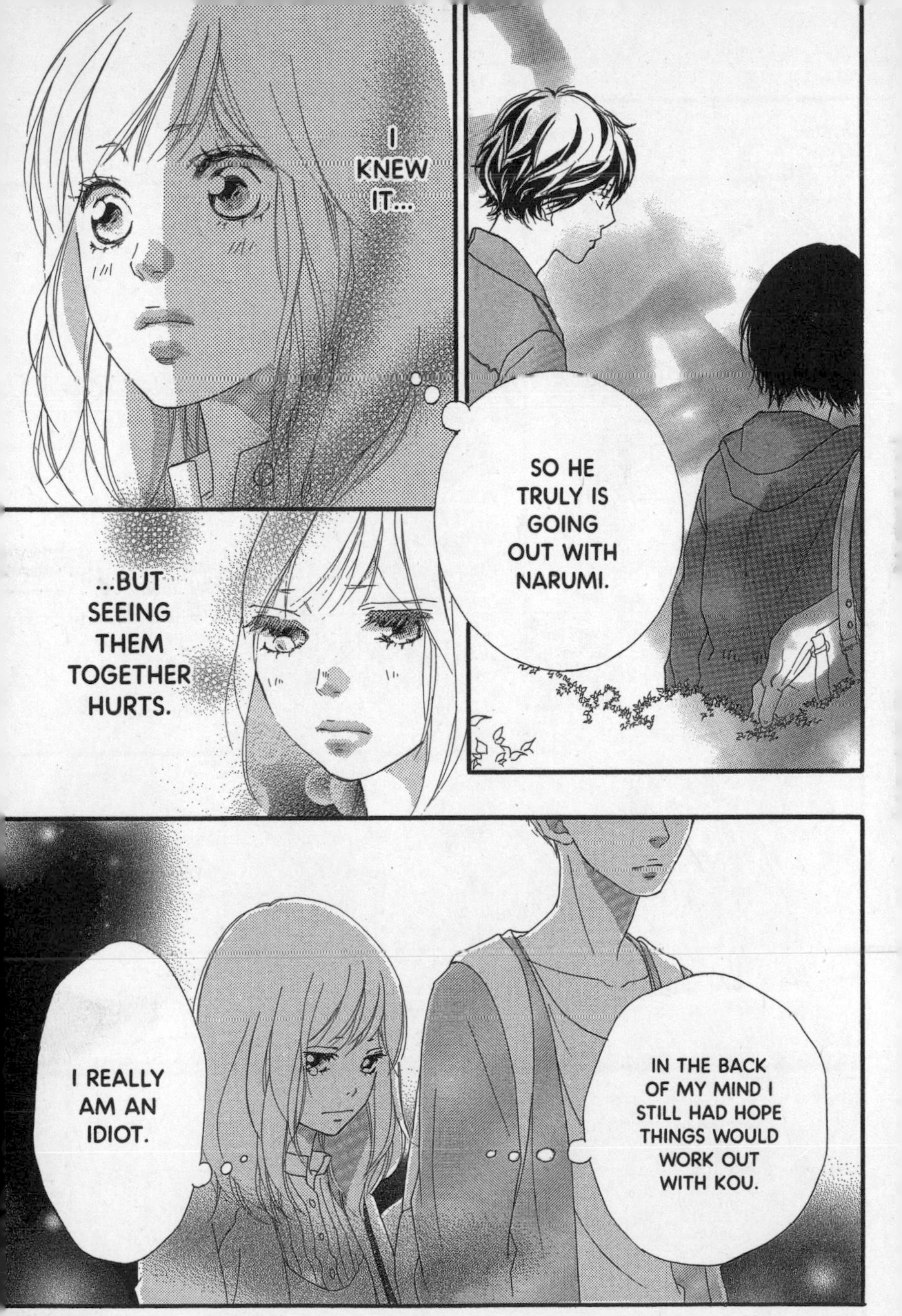
SO HE TRULY IS GOING OUT WITH NARUMI.
I KNEW IT...
...BUT SEEING THEM TOGETHER HURTS.
IN THE BACK OF MY MIND I STILL HAD HOPE THINGS WOULD WORK OUT WITH KOU.
I REALLY AM AN IDIOT.

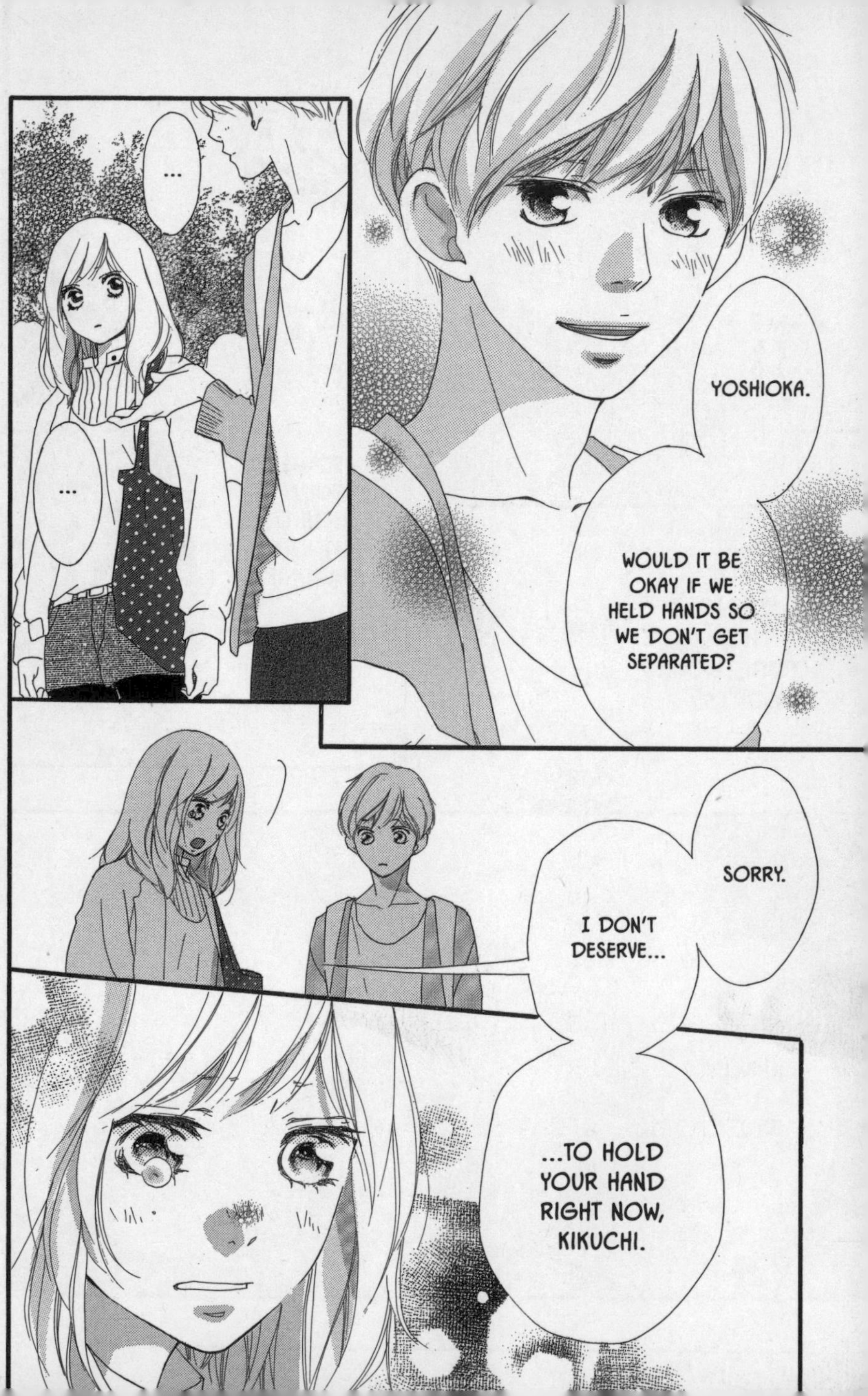
YOSHIOKA.
WOULD IT BE OKAY IF WE HELD HANDS SO WE DON'T GET SEPARATED?
...
...
SORRY.
I DON'T DESERVE...
...TO HOLD YOUR HAND RIGHT NOW, KIKUCHI.

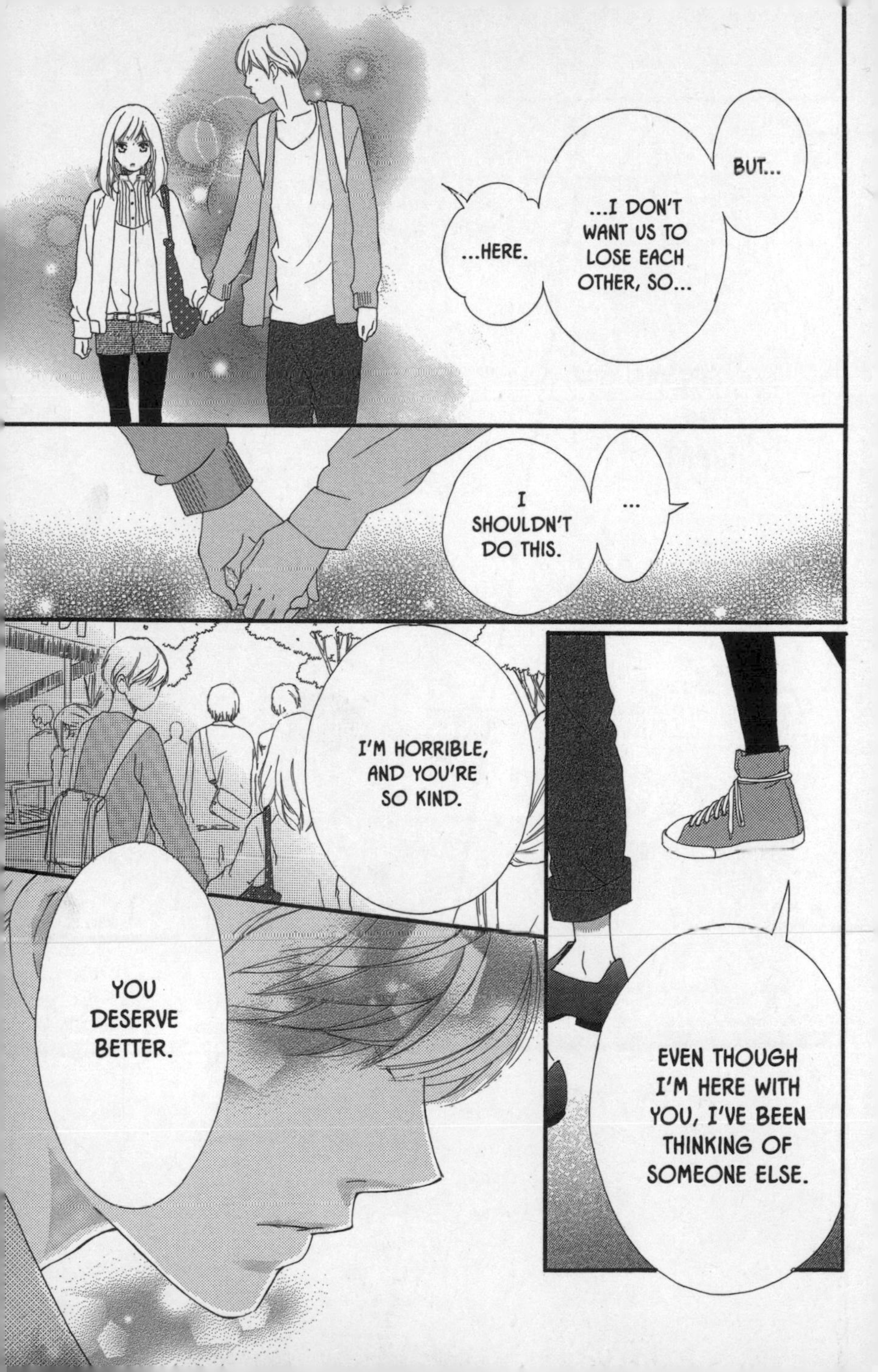
BUT...
...I DON'T WANT US TO LOSE EACH OTHER, SO...
...HERE.
...
I SHOULDN'T DO THIS.
EVEN THOUGH I'M HERE WITH YOU, I'VE BEEN THINKING OF SOMEONE ELSE.
I'M HORRIBLE, AND YOU'RE SO KIND.
YOU DESERVE BETTER.

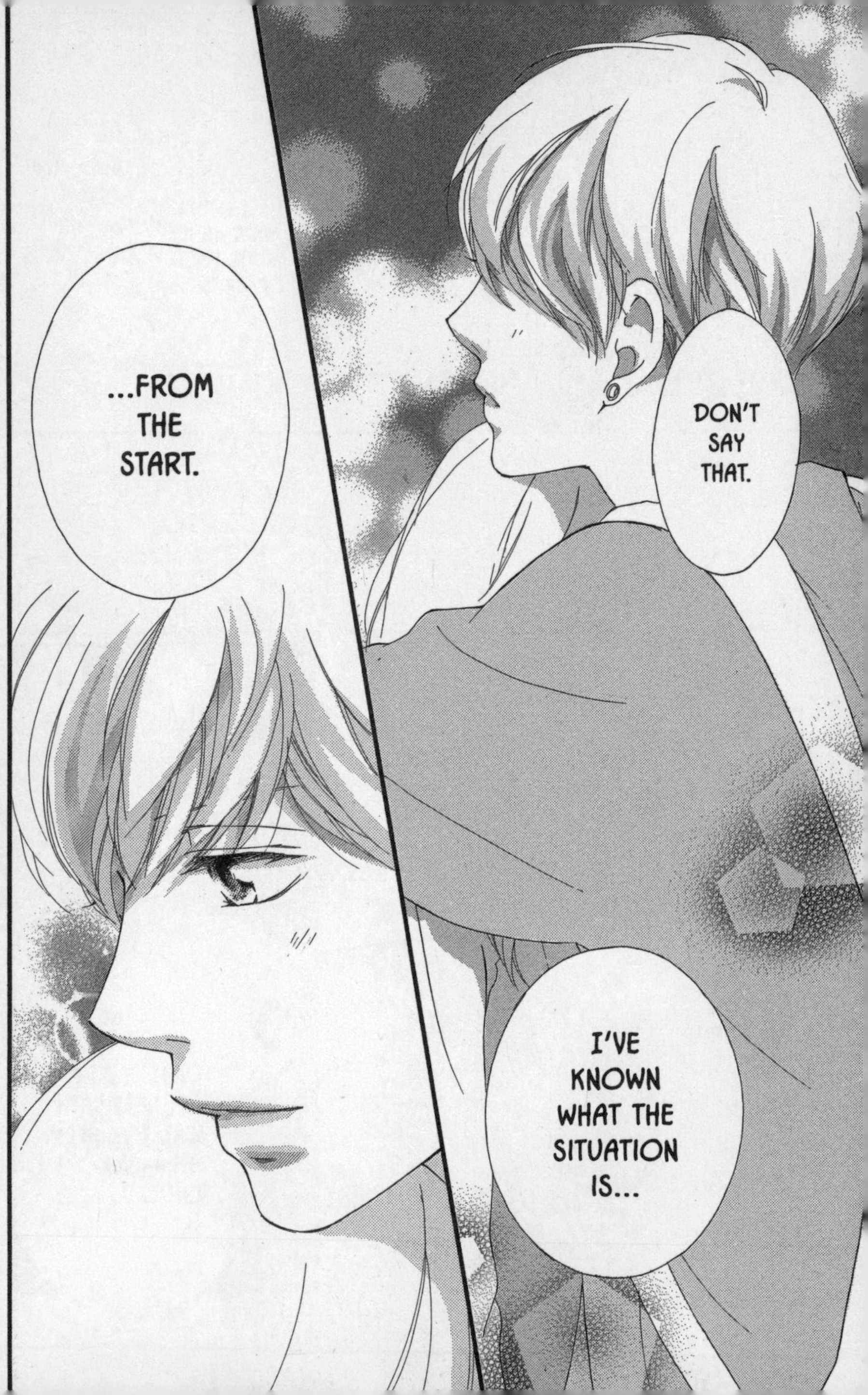
DON'T SAY THAT.
I'VE KNOWN WHAT THE SITUATION IS...
...FROM THE START.

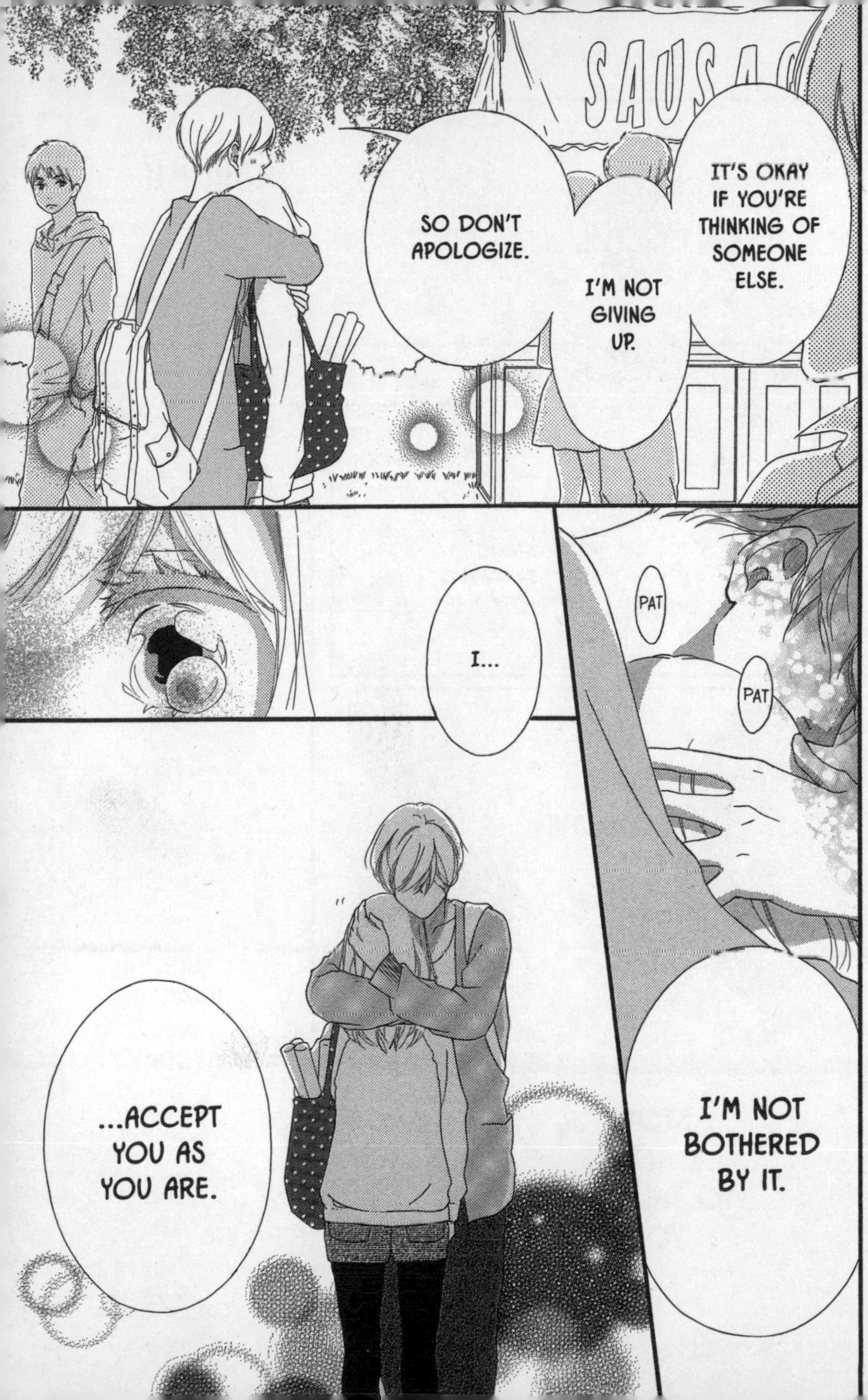
IT'S OKAY IF YOU'RE THINKING OF SOMEONE ELSE.
I'M NOT GIVING UP.
SO DON'T APOLOGIZE.
PAT
PAT
I'M NOT BOTHERED BY IT.
I...
...ACCEPT YOU AS YOU ARE.

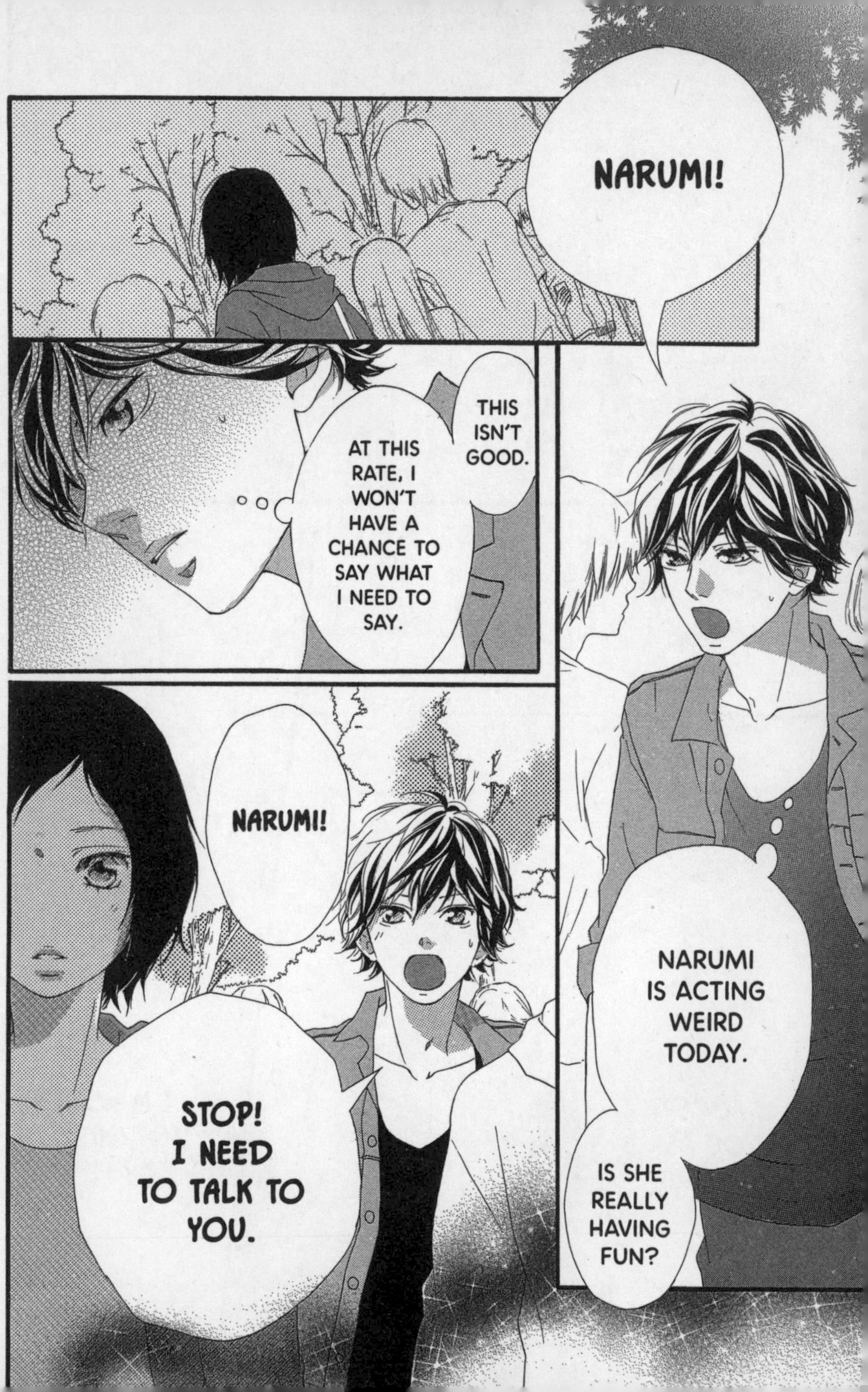
NARUMI!
NARUMI IS ACTING WEIRD TODAY.
IS SHE REALLY HAVING FUN?
THIS ISN'T GOOD.
AT THIS RATE, I WON'T HAVE A CHANCE TO SAY WHAT I NEED TO SAY.
NARUMI!
STOP! I NEED TO TALK TO YOU.

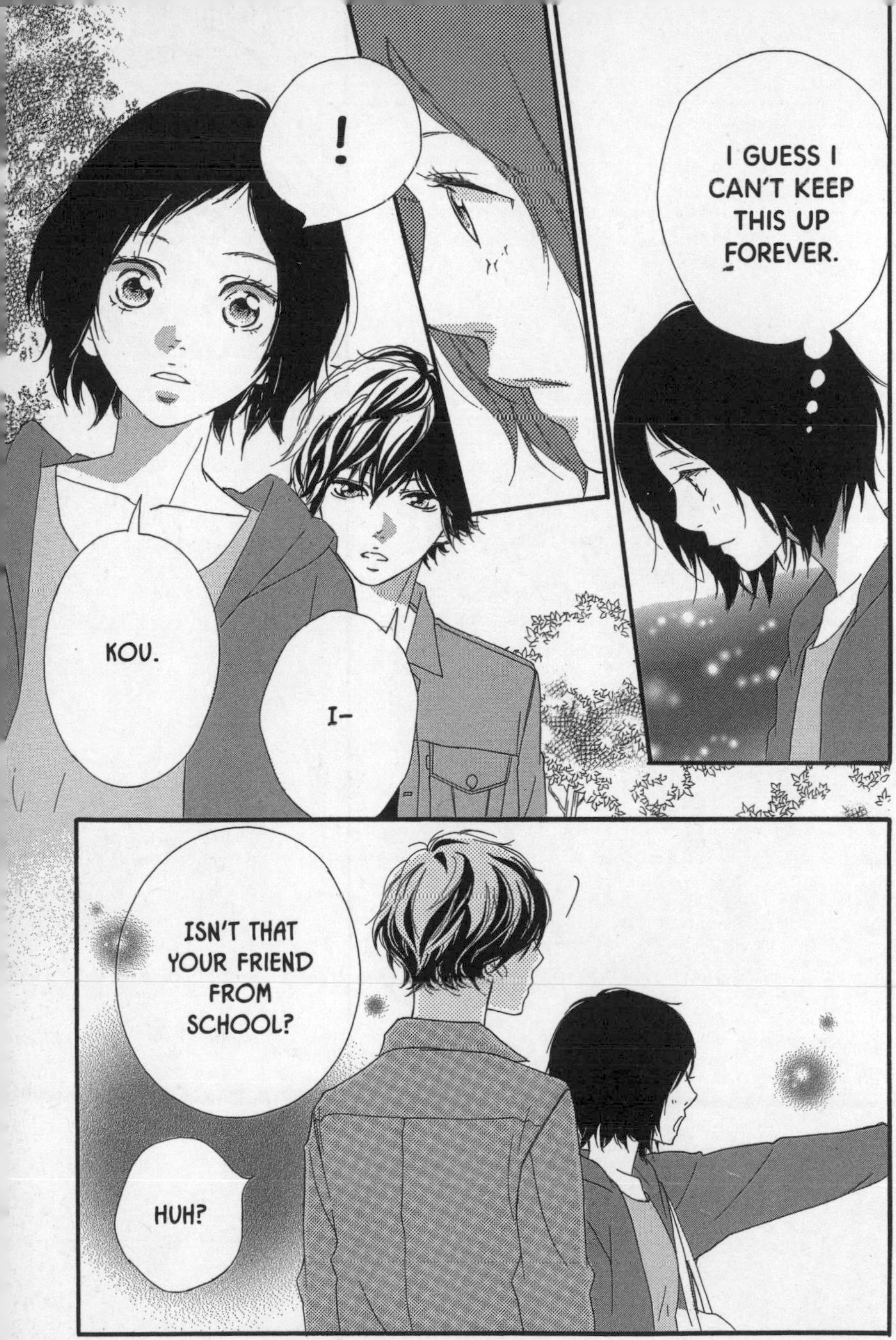
I GUESS I CAN'T KEEP THIS UP FOREVER.
!
KOU.
I-
ISN'T THAT YOUR FRIEND FROM SCHOOL?
HUH?

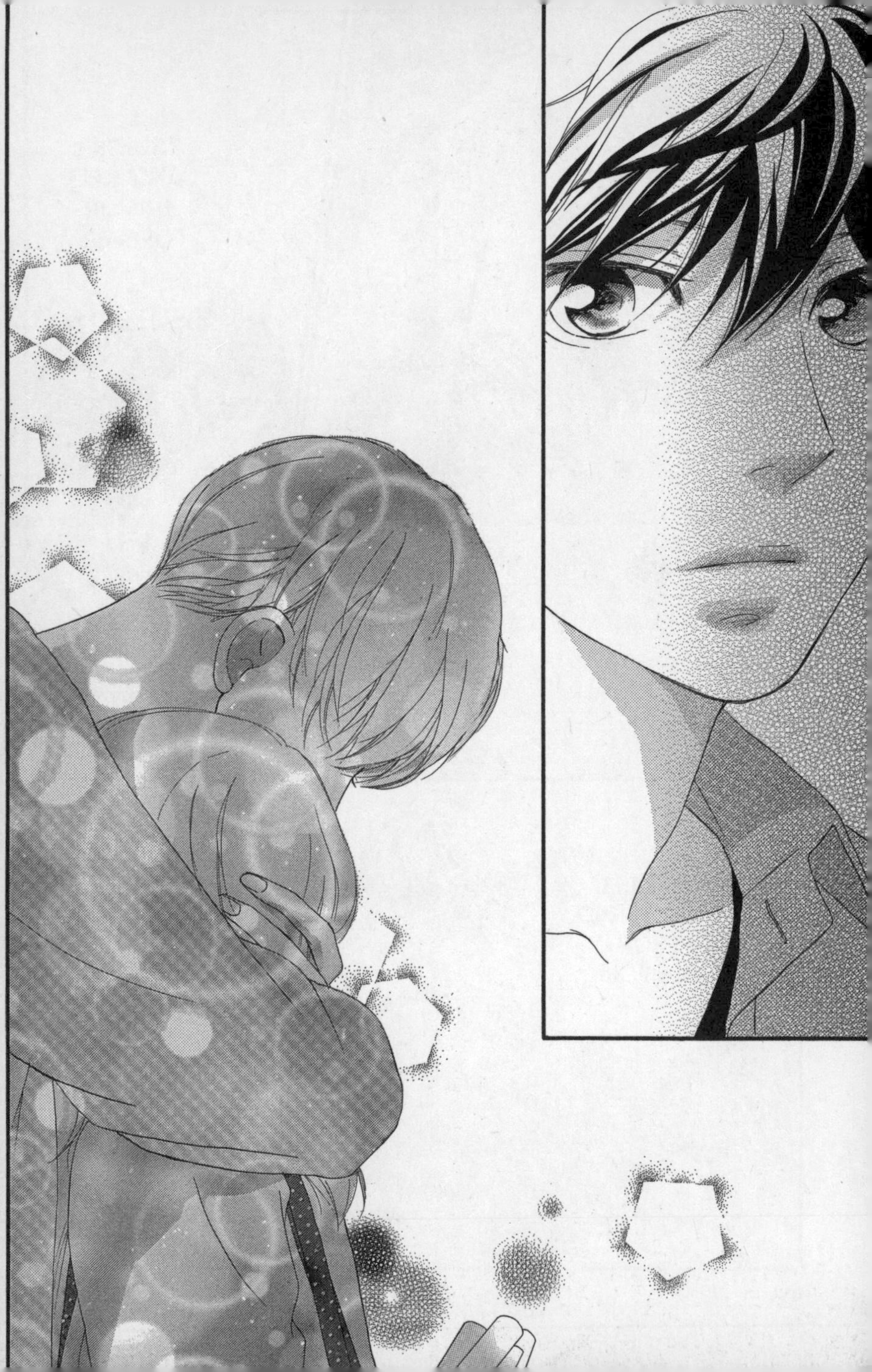

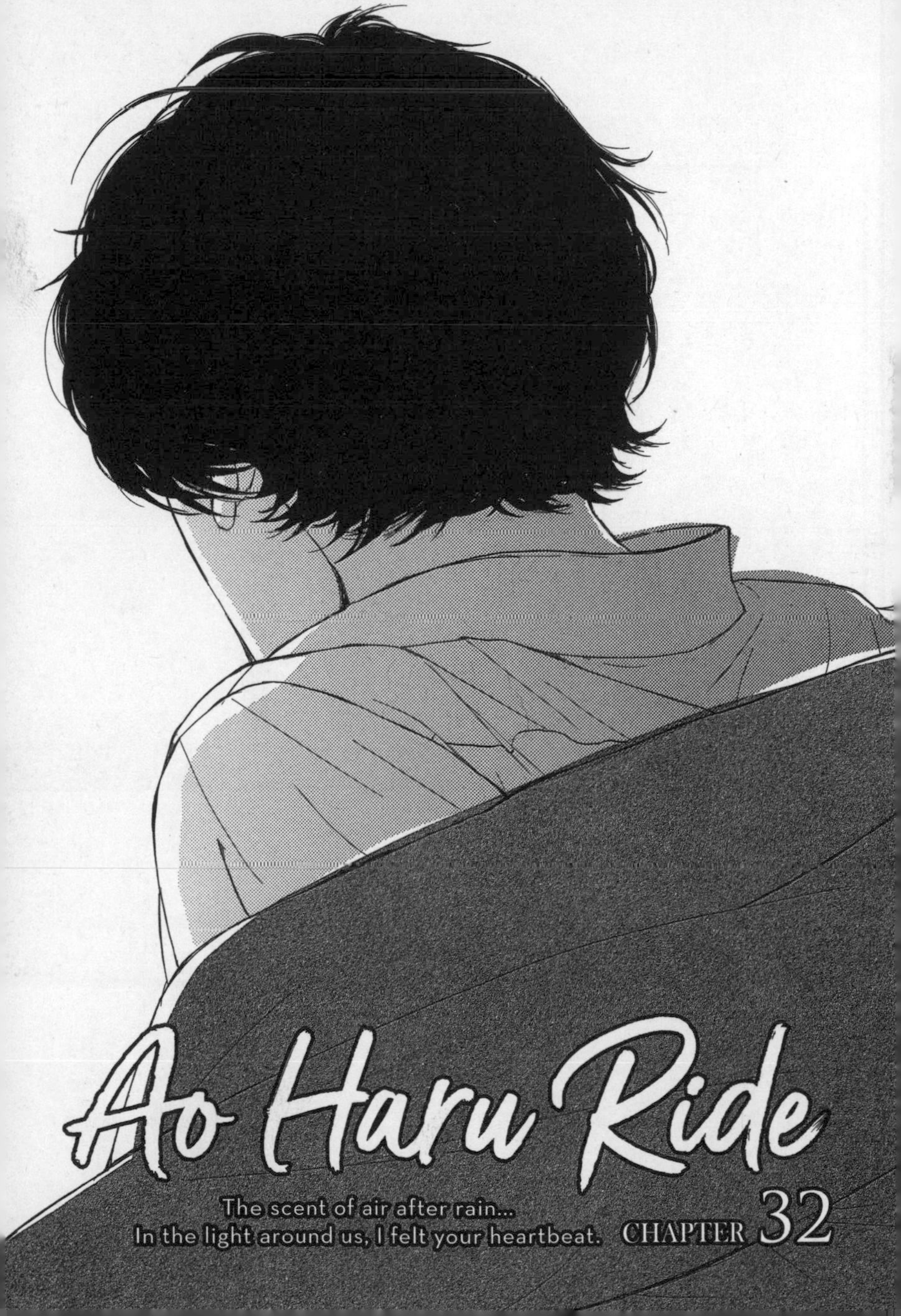
Ao Haru Ride
The scent of air after rain...
In the light around us, I felt your heartbeat.
CHAPTER 32

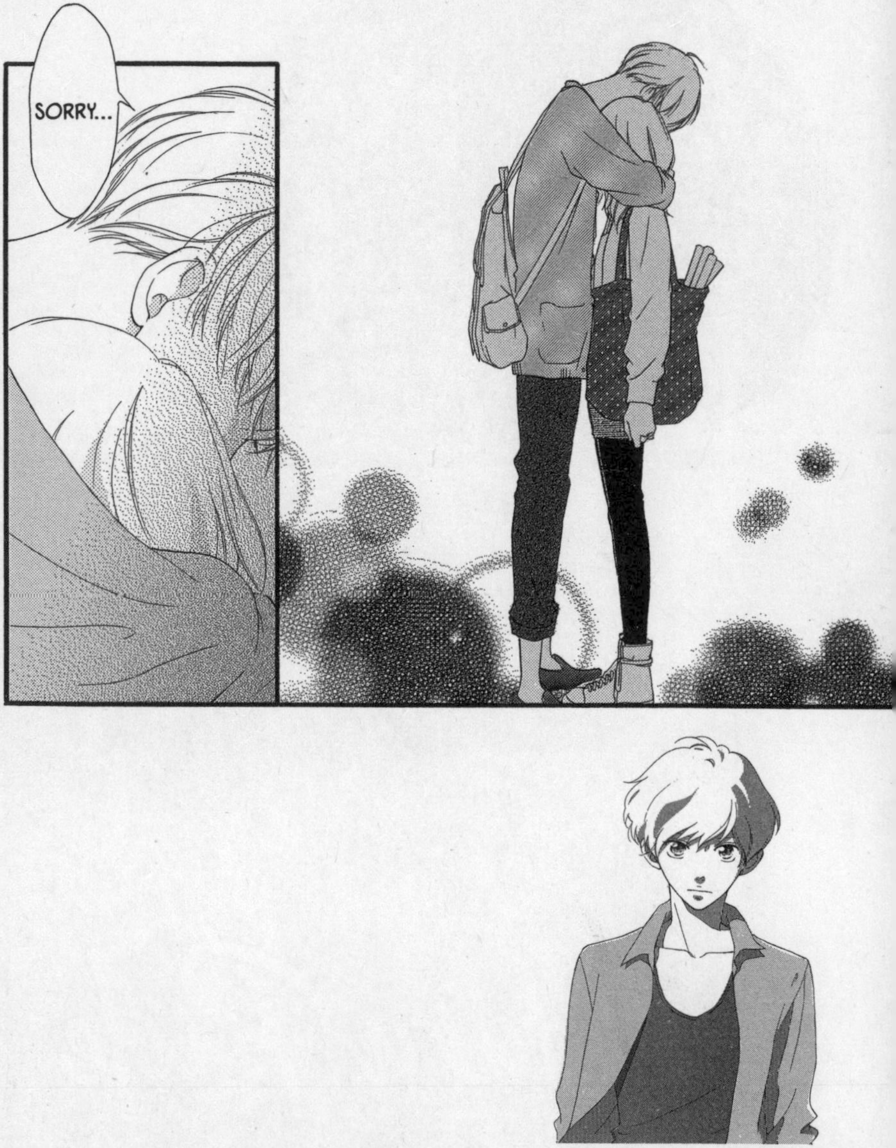
SORRY...

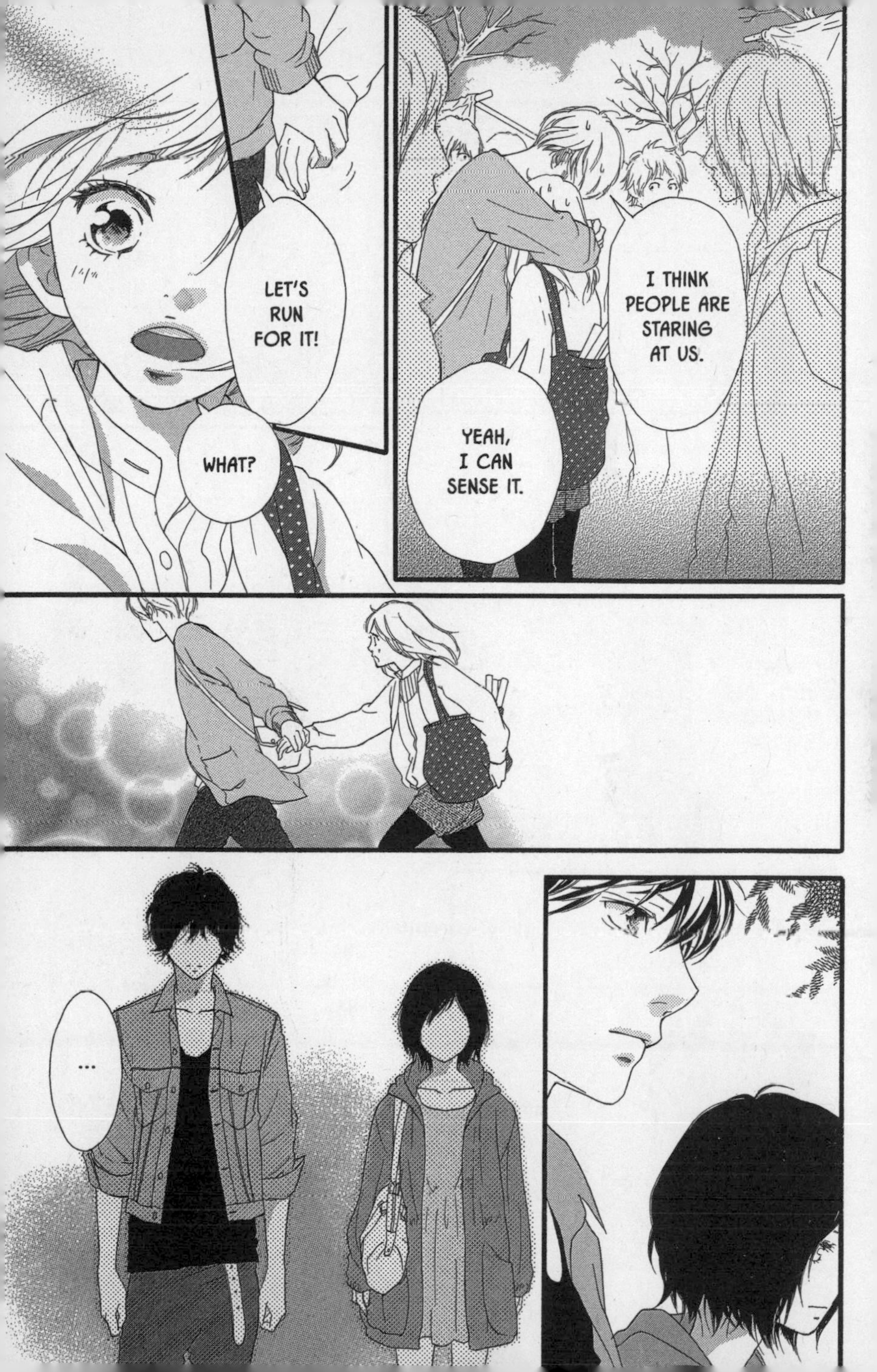
I THINK PEOPLE ARE STARING AT US.
YEAH, I CAN SENSE IT.
LET'S RUN FOR IT!
WHAT?
...

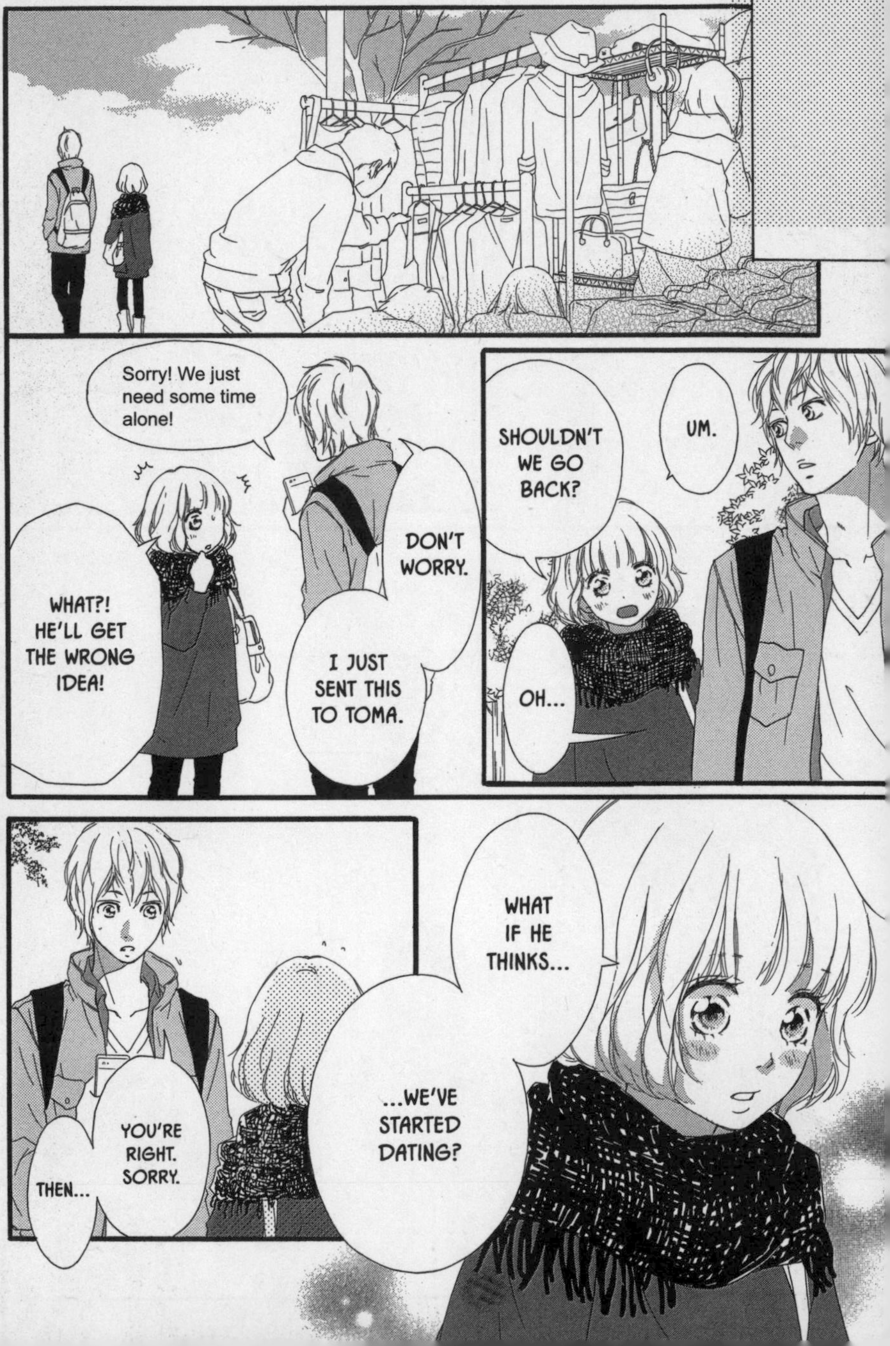
UM.
SHOULDN'T WE GO BACK?
OH...
DON'T WORRY.
I JUST SENT THIS TO TOMA.
Sorry! We just need some time alone!
WHAT?! HE'LL GET THE WRONG IDEA!
WHAT IF HE THINKS...
...WE'VE STARTED DATING?
YOU'RE RIGHT. SORRY.
THEN...

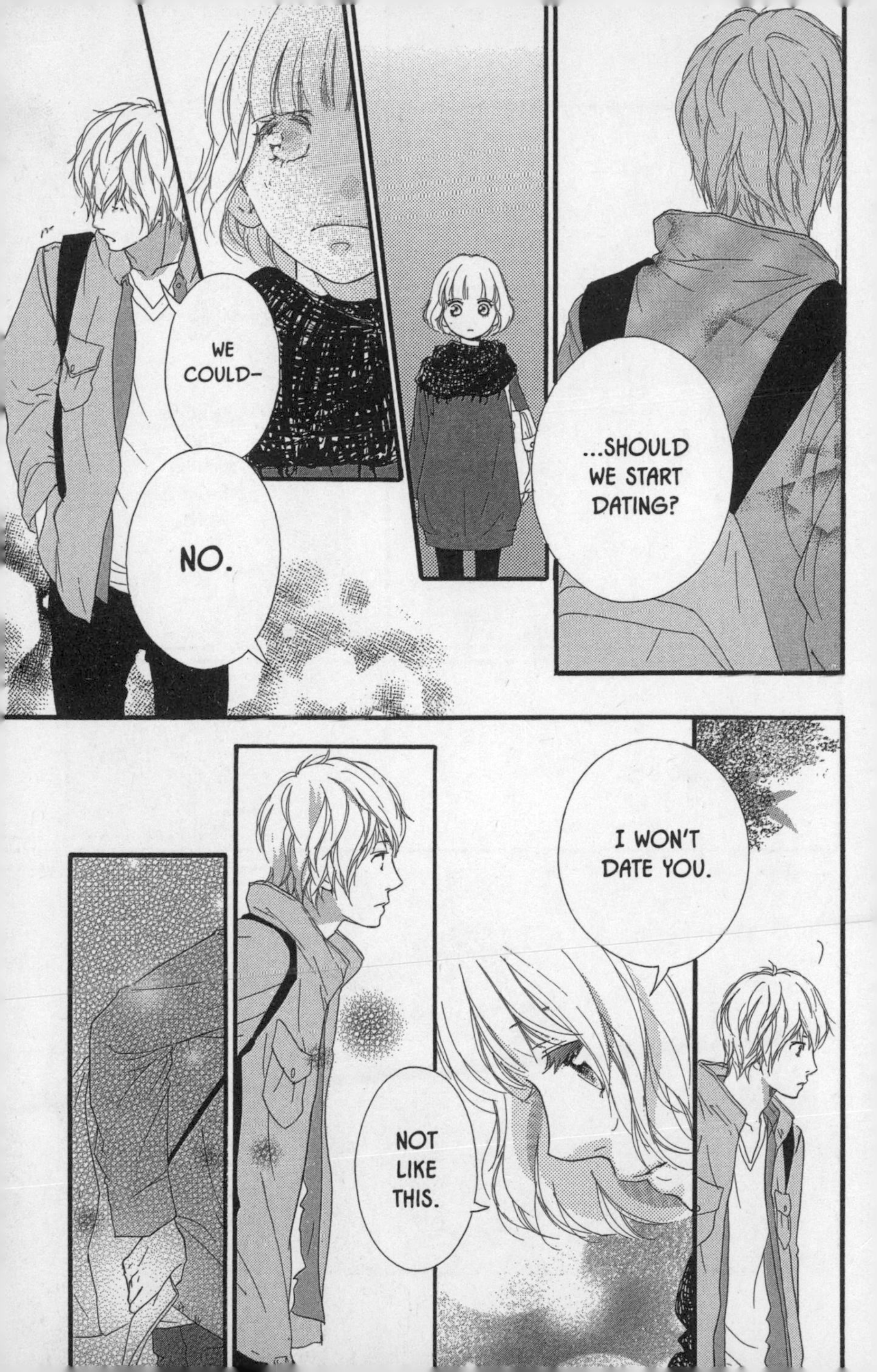
...SHOULD WE START DATING?
WE COULD-
NO.
I WON'T DATE YOU.
NOT LIKE THIS.

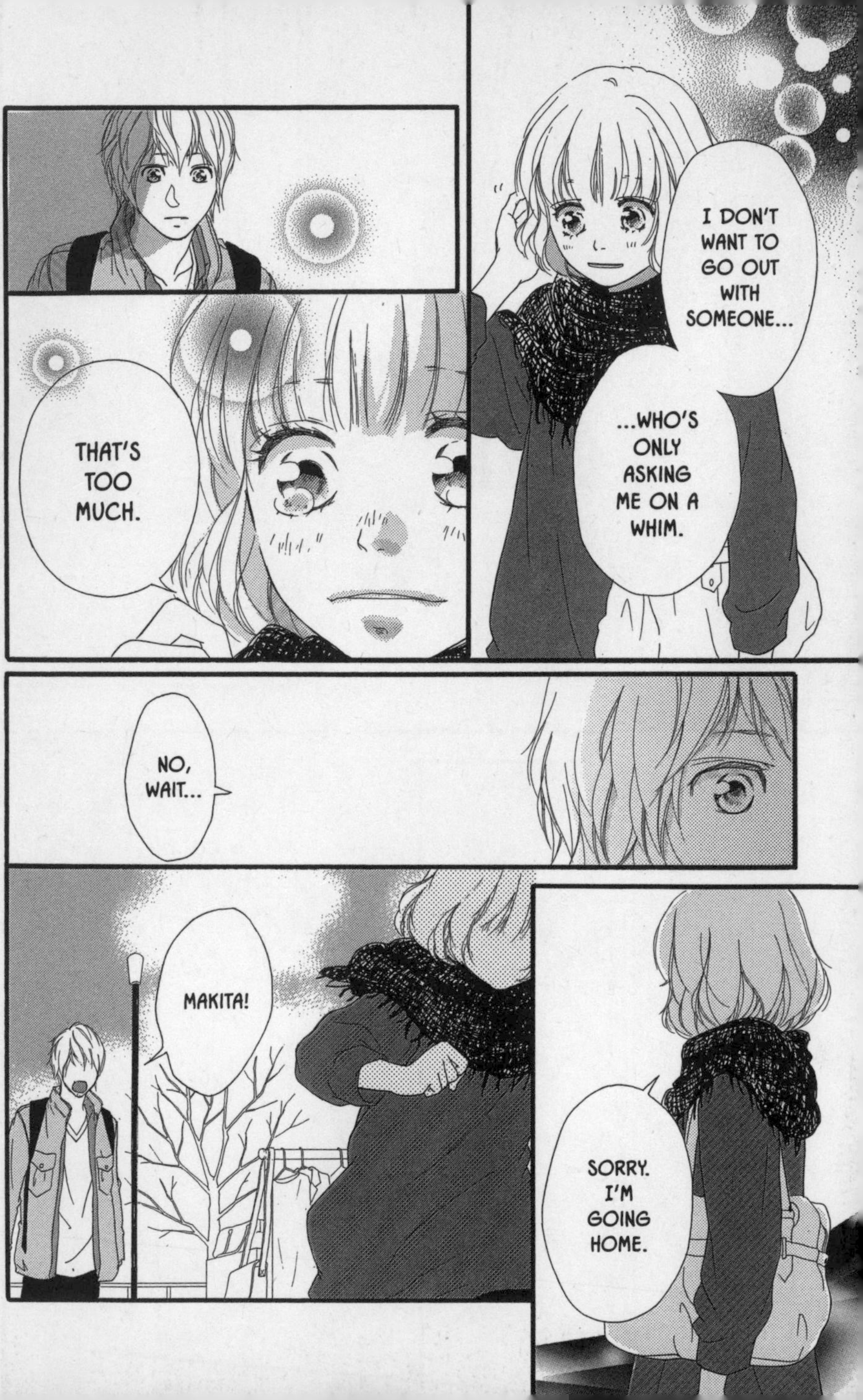
I DON'T WANT TO GO OUT WITH SOMEONE...
...WHO'S ONLY ASKING ME ON A WHIM.
THAT'S TOO MUCH.
NO, WAIT...
SORRY. I'M GOING HOME.
MAKITA!

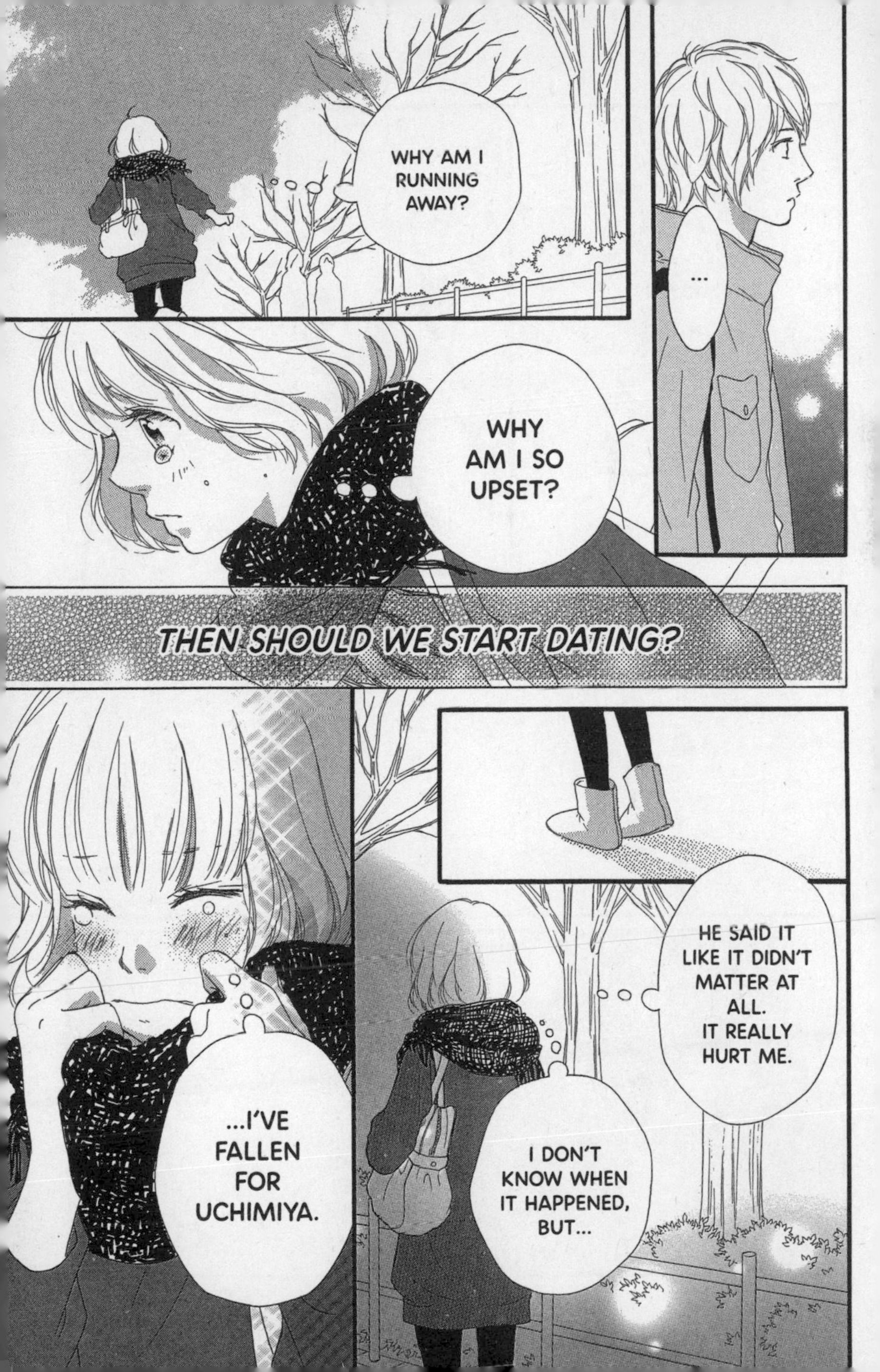
...
WHY AM I RUNNING AWAY?
WHY AM I SO UPSET?
THEN SHOULD WE START DATING?
HE SAID IT LIKE IT DIDN'T MATTER AT ALL. IT REALLY HURT ME.
I DON'T KNOW WHEN IT HAPPENED, BUT...
...I'VE FALLEN FOR UCHIMIYA.

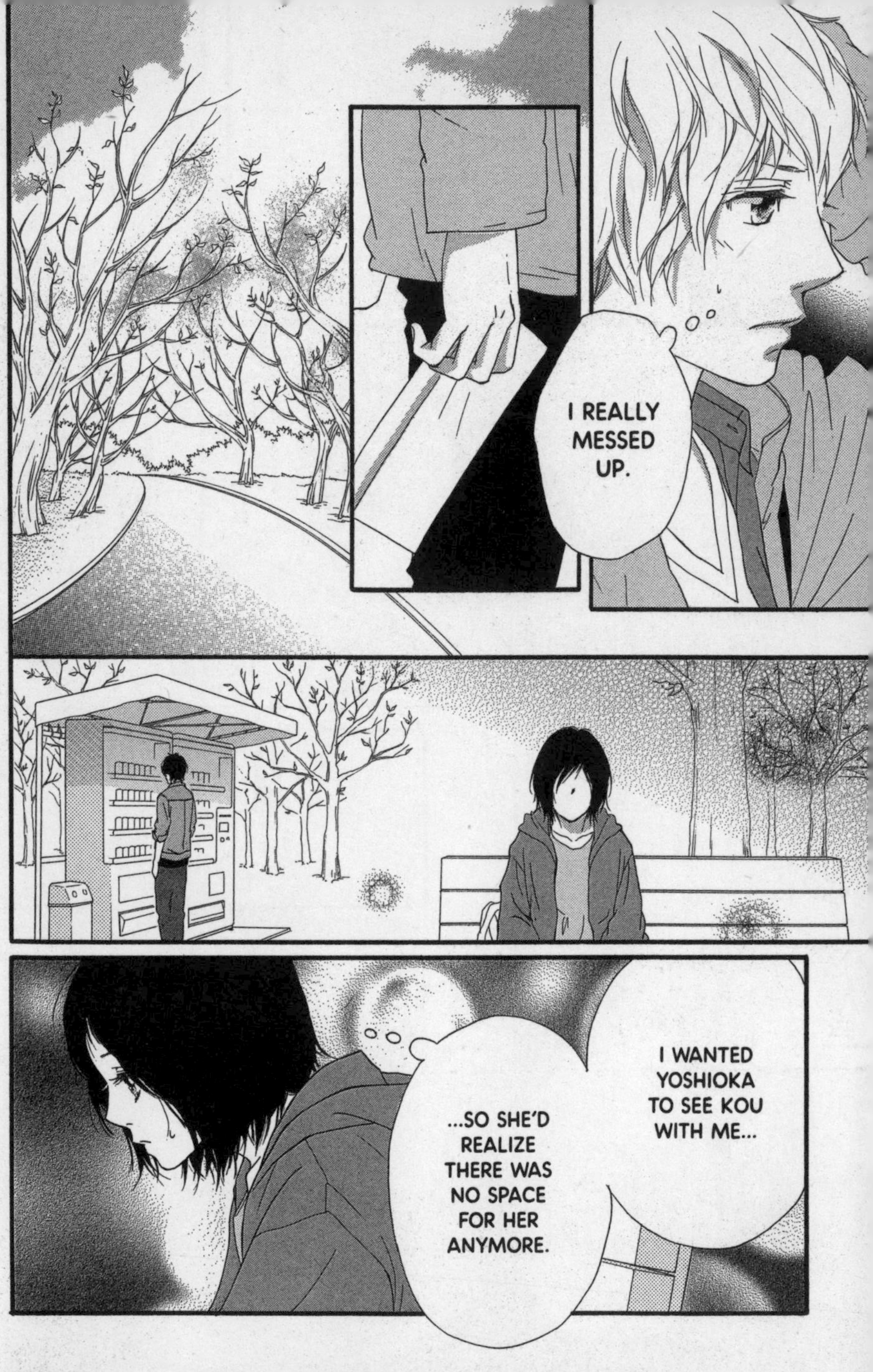
I REALLY MESSED UP.
I WANTED YOSHIOKA TO SEE KOU WITH ME...
...SO SHE'D REALIZE THERE WAS NO SPACE FOR HER ANYMORE.

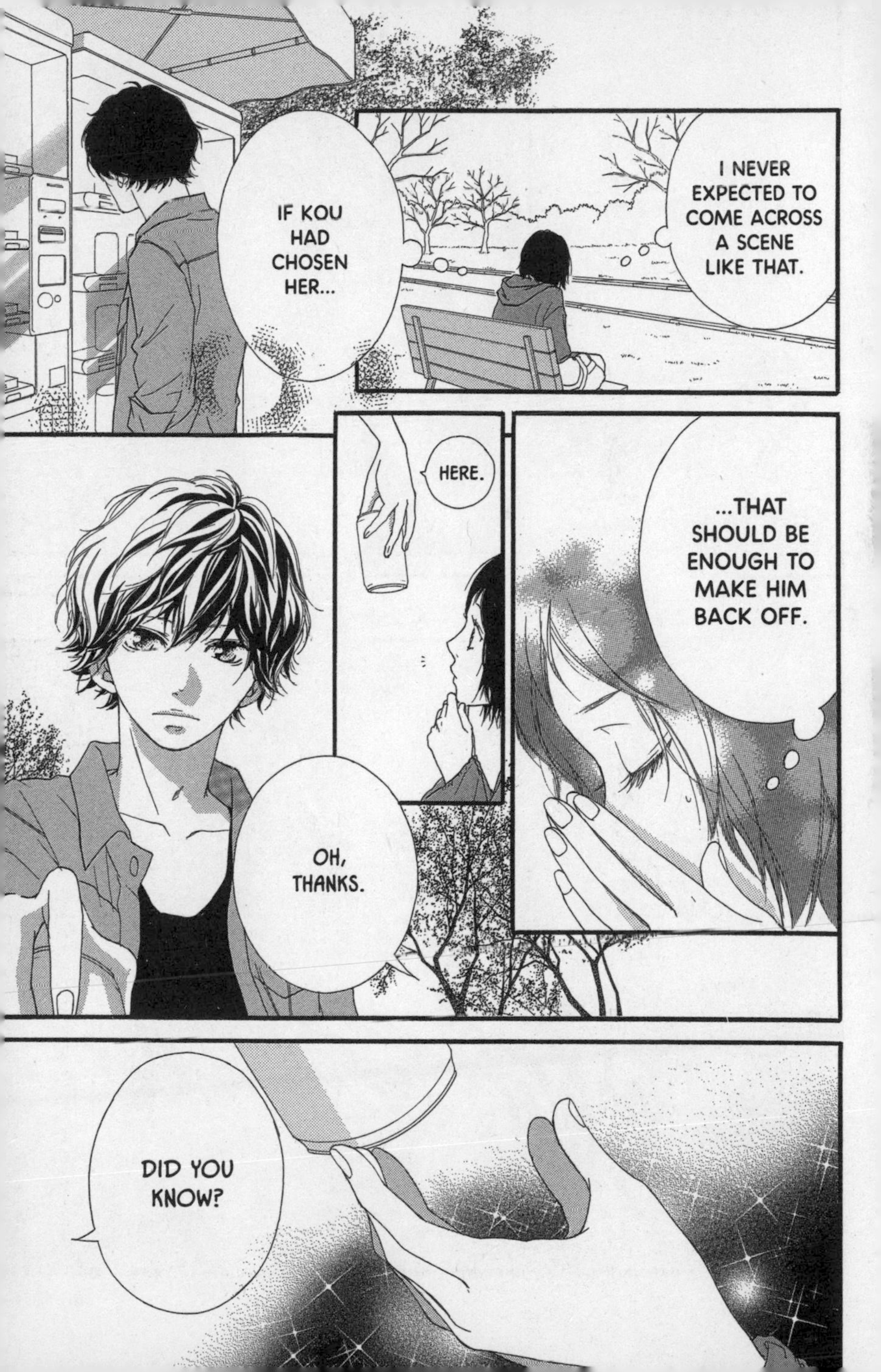
I NEVER EXPECTED TO COME ACROSS A SCENE LIKE THAT.
IF KOU HAD CHOSEN HER...
...THAT SHOULD BE ENOUGH TO MAKE HIM BACK OFF.
HERE.
OH, THANKS.
DID YOU KNOW?

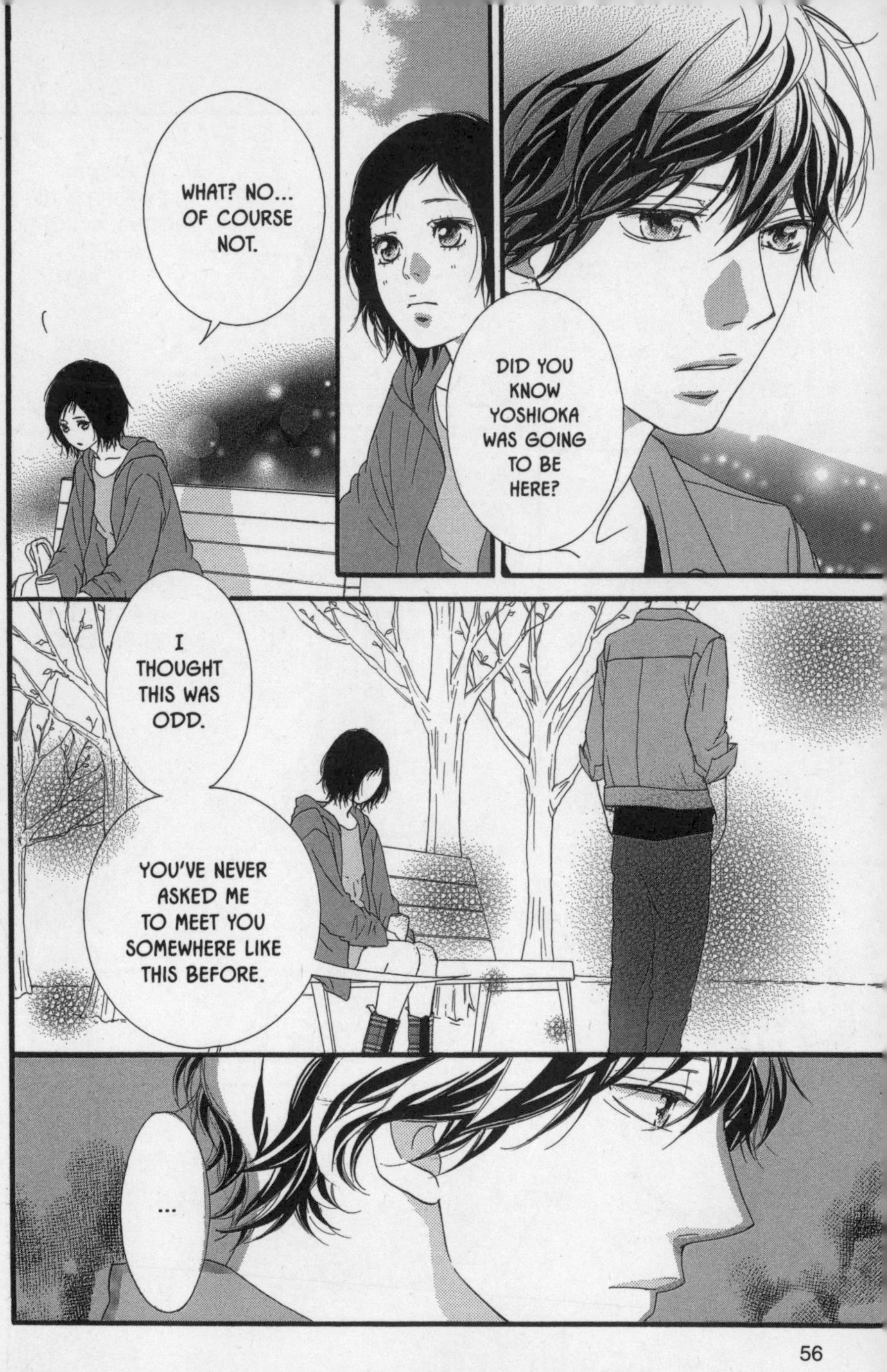
DID YOU KNOW YOSHIOKA WAS GOING TO BE HERE?
WHAT? NO... OF COURSE NOT.
I THOUGHT THIS WAS ODD.
YOU'VE NEVER ASKED ME TO MEET YOU SOMEWHERE LIKE THIS BEFORE.
...

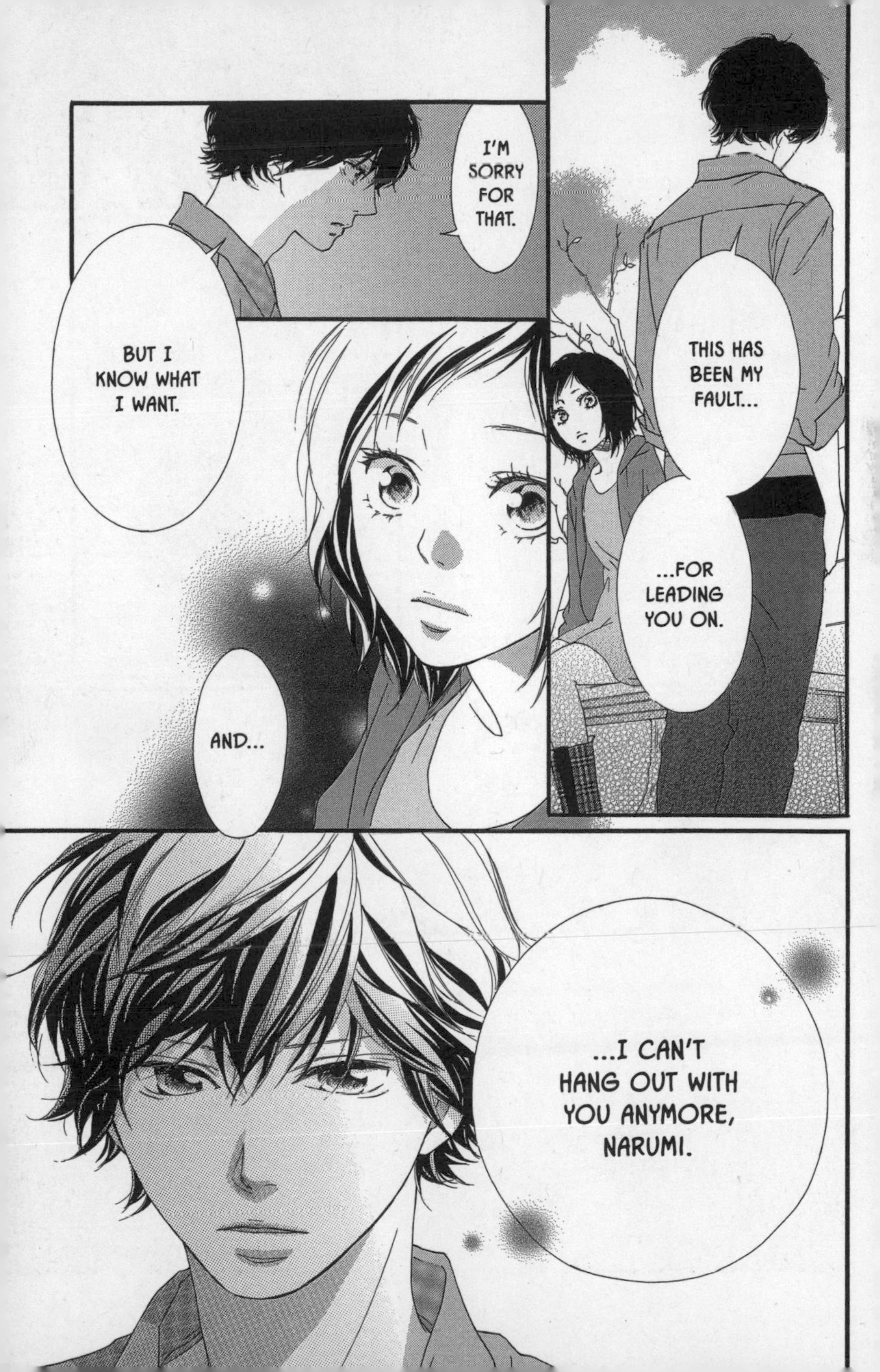
THIS HAS BEEN MY FAULT...
...FOR LEADING YOU ON.
I'M SORRY FOR THAT.
BUT I KNOW WHAT I WANT.
AND...
...I CAN'T HANG OUT WITH YOU ANYMORE, NARUMI.

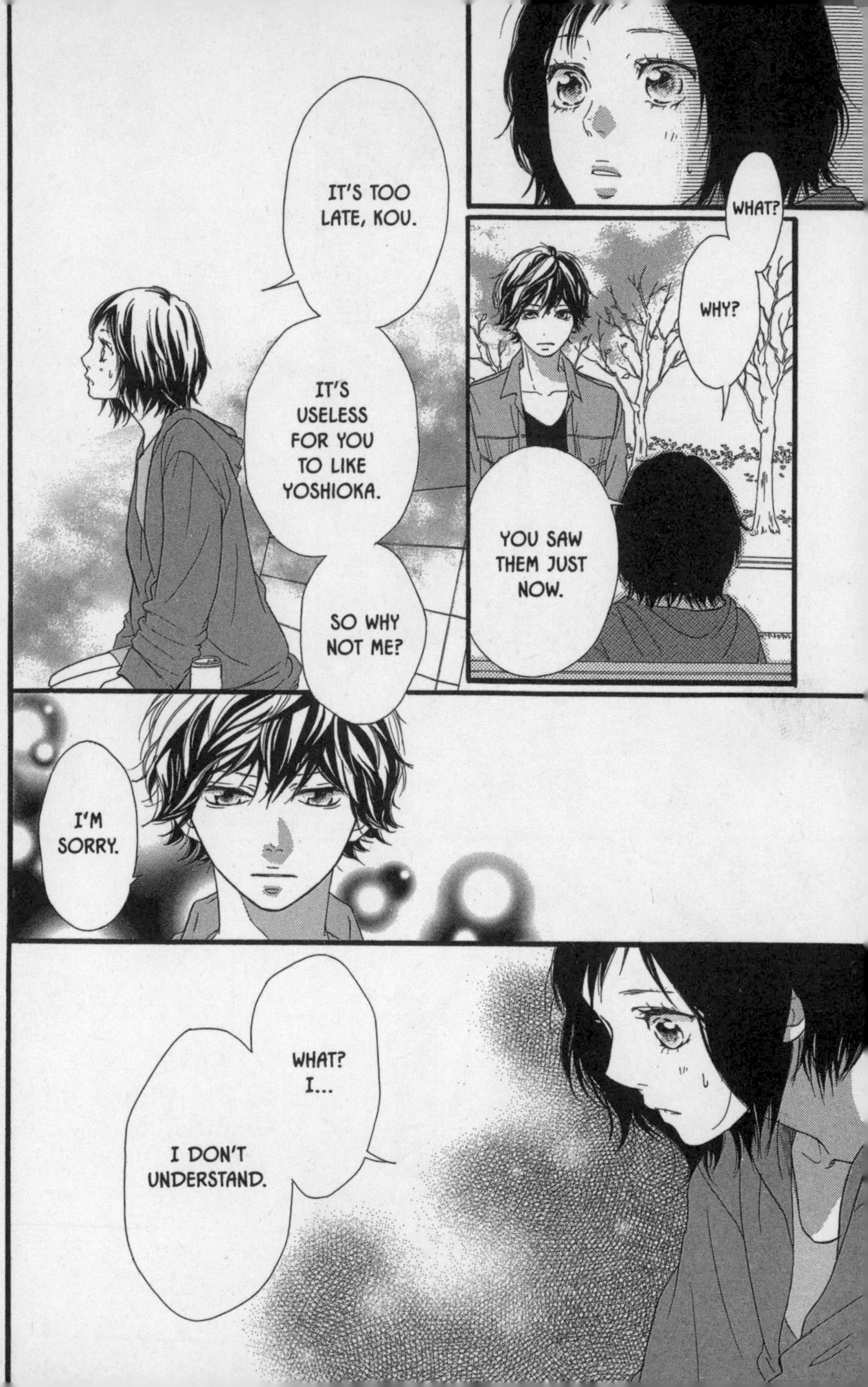
WHAT?
WHY?
YOU SAW THEM JUST NOW.
IT'S TOO LATE, KOU.
IT'S USELESS FOR YOU TO LIKE YOSHIOKA.
SO WHY NOT ME?
I'M SORRY.
WHAT? I...
I DON'T UNDERSTAND.

As a followup to my story about the circular rainbow, I'd like to share a story about my circular bald spot. It happened all of a sudden one day. I was brushing my hair as I usually do when a huge chunk fell out. I gasped. It didn't hurt, but I suddenly felt like I could relate to a boulder! Fearfully, I reached towards the back of my head, and discovered one spot was completely smooth! I propped up two mirrors to check it out and was shocked to discover a bald spot the size of a 500-yen coin. I was stunned! I burst into tears. I'll admit that I was dealing with some stress at the time...but was it really necessary for me to lose all that hair? While I was still reeling from that knowledge, I wound up needing to get my hair done, and when my hair stylist saw the spot she gasped. She offered words of encouragement, saying that many people experience regrowth in half a year, and that's exactly how long it took. This happened about 10 years ago.

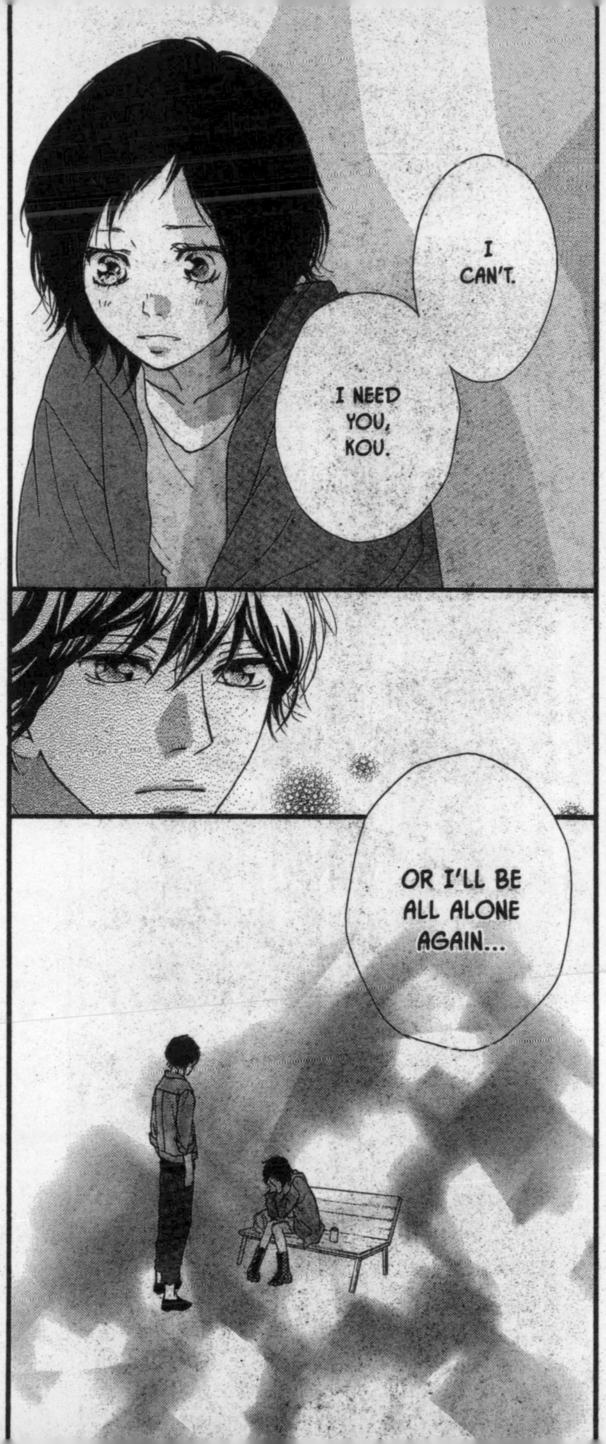

I CAN'T.
I NEED YOU, KOU.
OR I'LL BE ALL ALONE AGAIN...

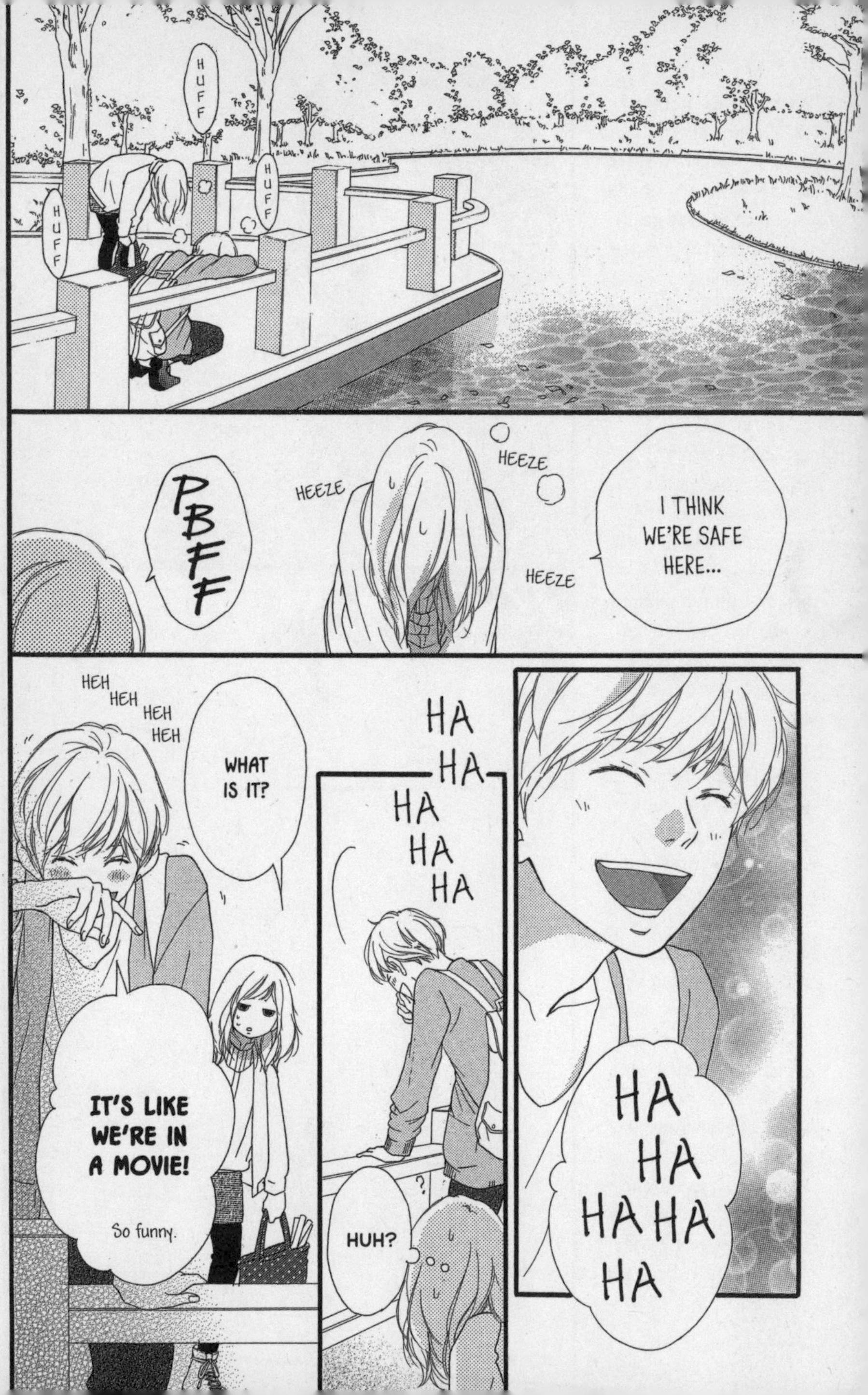
HUFF
HUFF
HUFF
I THINK WE'RE SAFE HERE...
HEEZE
HEEZE
HEEZE
PBFF
HA HA HA HA HA HA
HA HA
HA HA HA
HUH?
HEH HEH HEH HEH
WHAT IS IT?
IT'S LIKE WE'RE IN A MOVIE!
So funny.

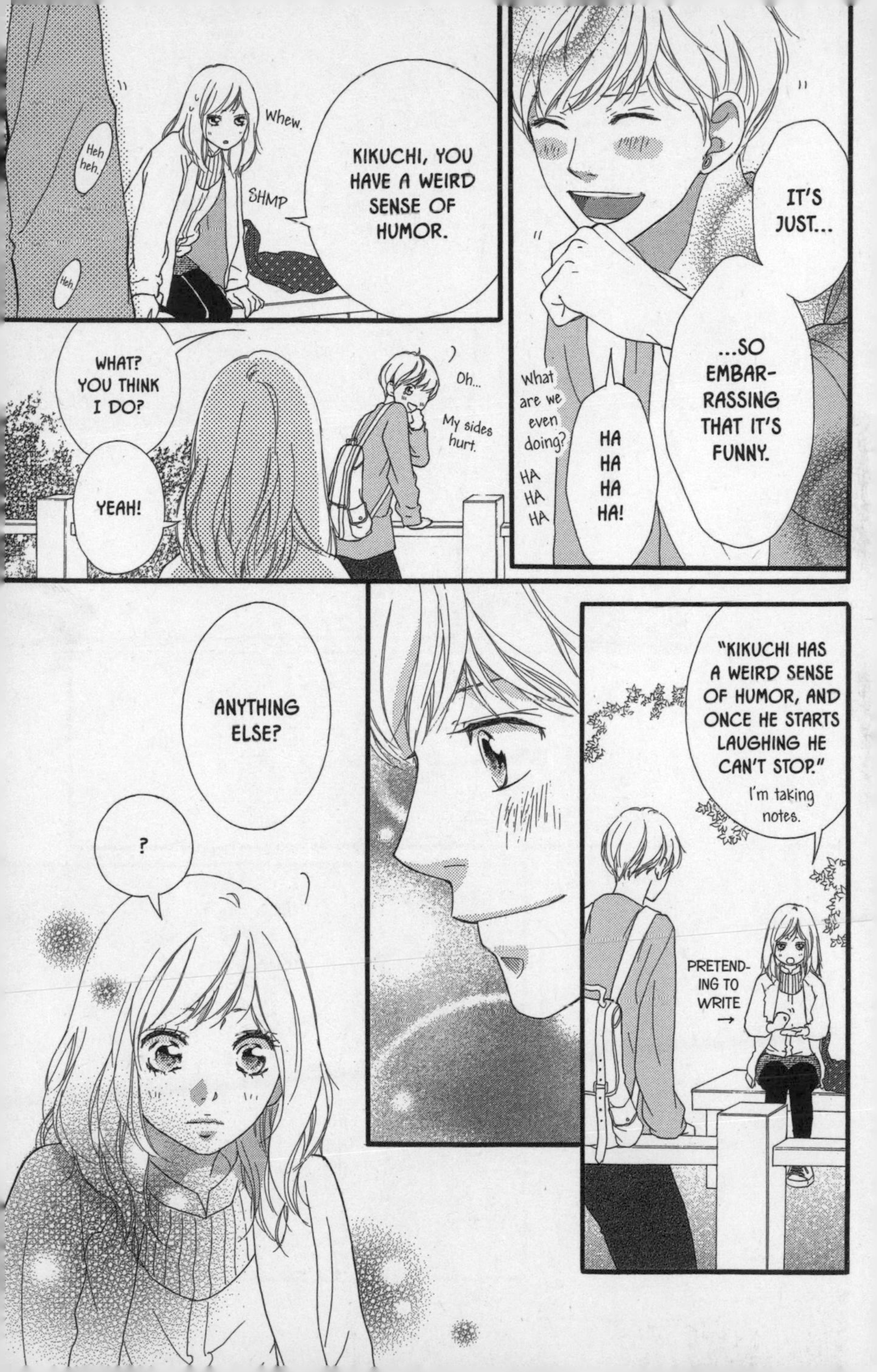
IT'S JUST...
...SO EMBARRASSING THAT IT'S FUNNY.
HA HA HA HA!
HA HA HA
What are we even doing?
Whew.
KIKUCHI, YOU HAVE A WEIRD SENSE OF HUMOR.
Heh heh.
Heh
SHMP
Oh...
My sides hurt.
WHAT? YOU THINK I DO?
YEAH!
"KIKUCHI HAS A WEIRD SENSE OF HUMOR, AND ONCE HE STARTS LAUGHING HE CAN'T STOP."
I'm taking notes.
PRETENDING TO WRITE →
ANYTHING ELSE?
?

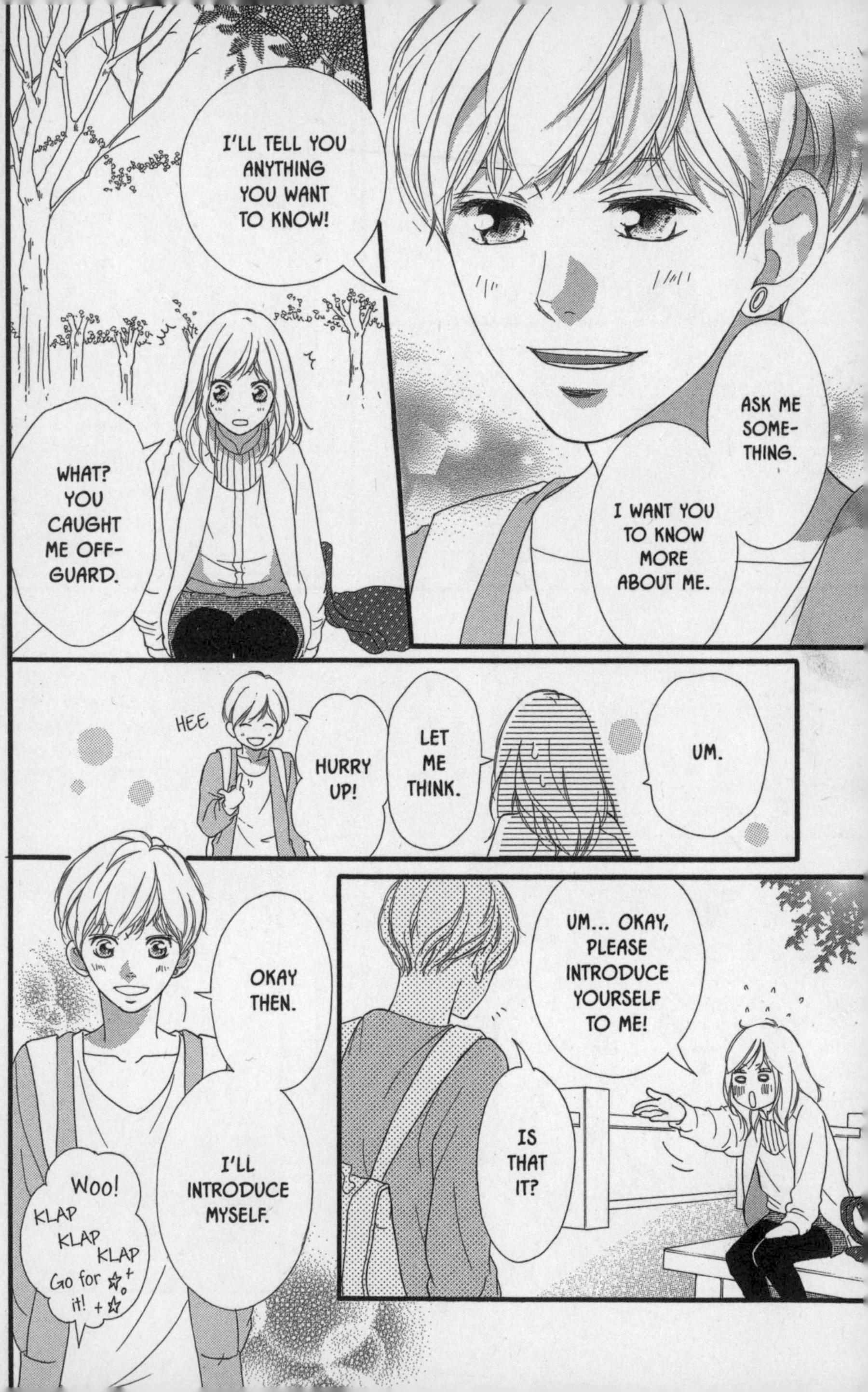
ASK ME SOME-THING.
I WANT YOU TO KNOW MORE ABOUT ME.
I'LL TELL YOU ANYTHING YOU WANT TO KNOW!
WHAT? YOU CAUGHT ME OFF-GUARD.
UM.
LET ME THINK.
HURRY UP!
HEE
UM... OKAY, PLEASE INTRODUCE YOURSELF TO ME!
IS THAT IT?
OKAY THEN.
I'LL INTRODUCE MYSELF.
Woo! KLAP KLAP KLAP Go for it!

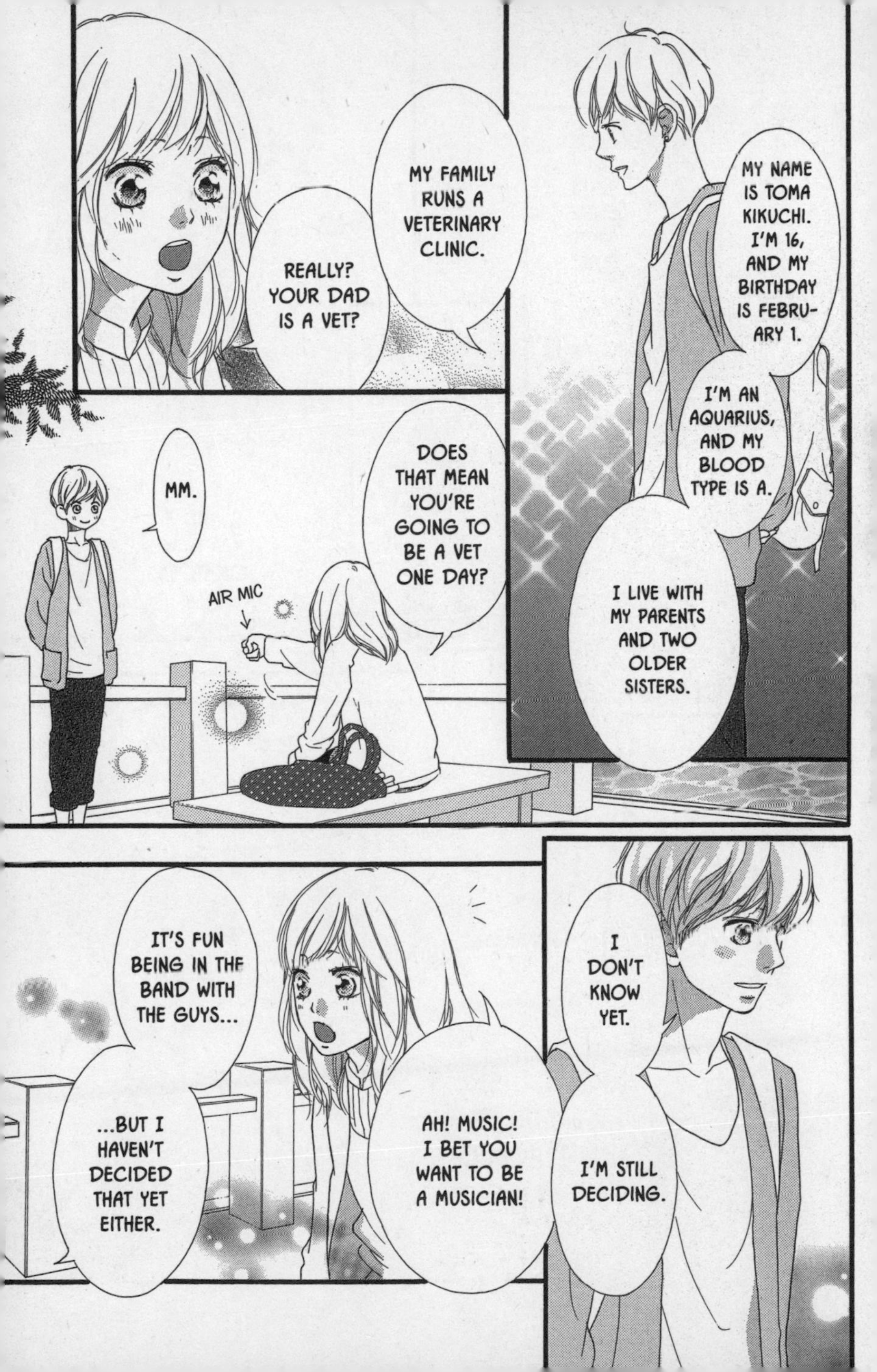
MY NAME IS TOMA KIKUCHI. I'M 16, AND MY BIRTHDAY IS FEBRU- ARY 1.
I'M AN AQUARIUS, AND MY BLOOD TYPE IS A.
I LIVE WITH MY PARENTS AND TWO OLDER SISTERS.
MY FAMILY RUNS A VETERINARY CLINIC.
REALLY? YOUR DAD IS A VET?
DOES THAT MEAN YOU'RE GOING TO BE A VET ONE DAY?
AIR MIC
MM.
I DON'T KNOW YET.
I'M STILL DECIDING.
AH! MUSIC! I BET YOU WANT TO BE A MUSICIAN!
IT'S FUN BEING IN THE BAND WITH THE GUYS...
...BUT I HAVEN'T DECIDED THAT YET EITHER.

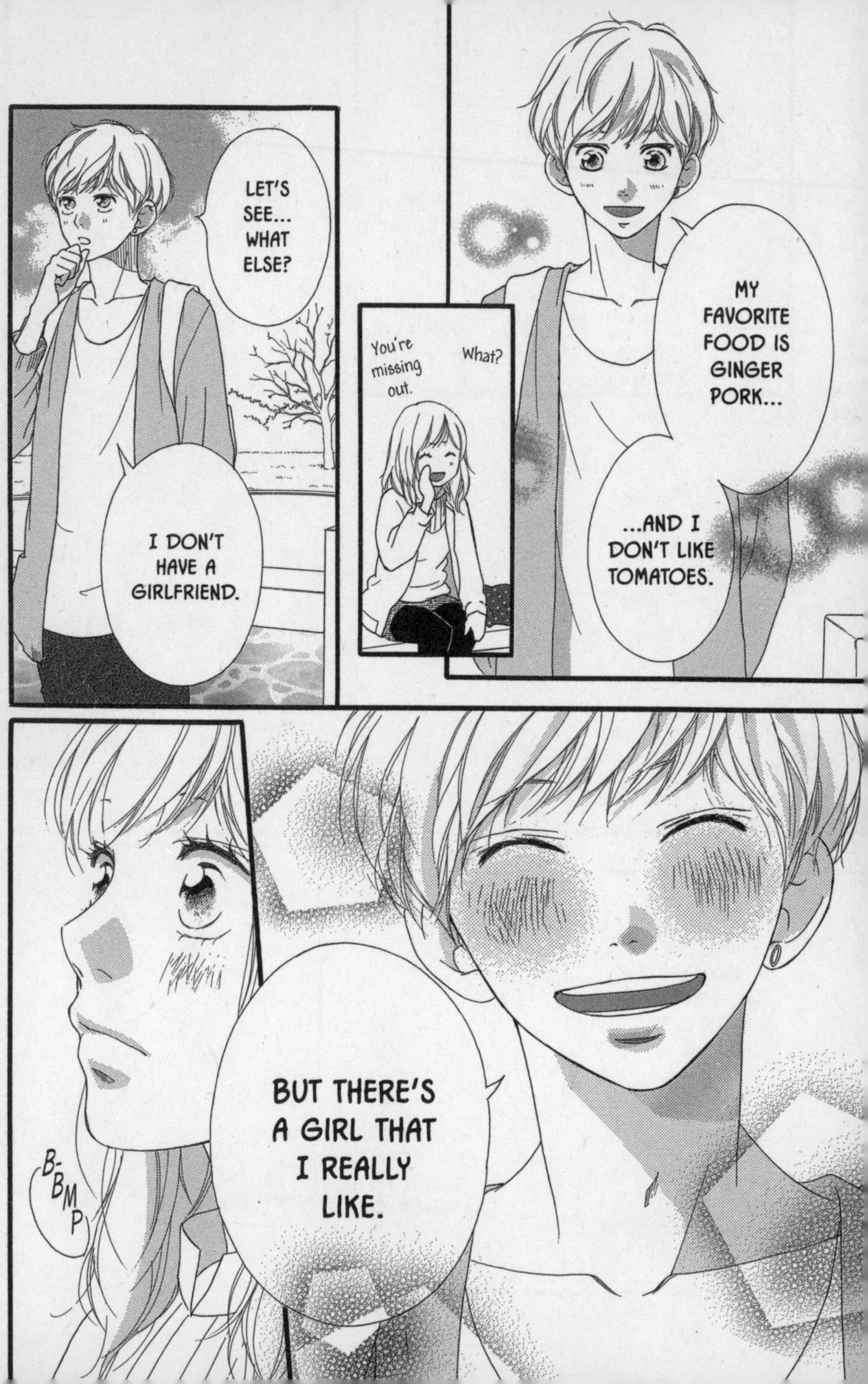
MY FAVORITE FOOD IS GINGER PORK...
...AND I DON'T LIKE TOMATOES.
What?
You're missing out.
LET'S SEE... WHAT ELSE?
I DON'T HAVE A GIRLFRIEND.
BUT THERE'S A GIRL THAT I REALLY LIKE.
B-BMP

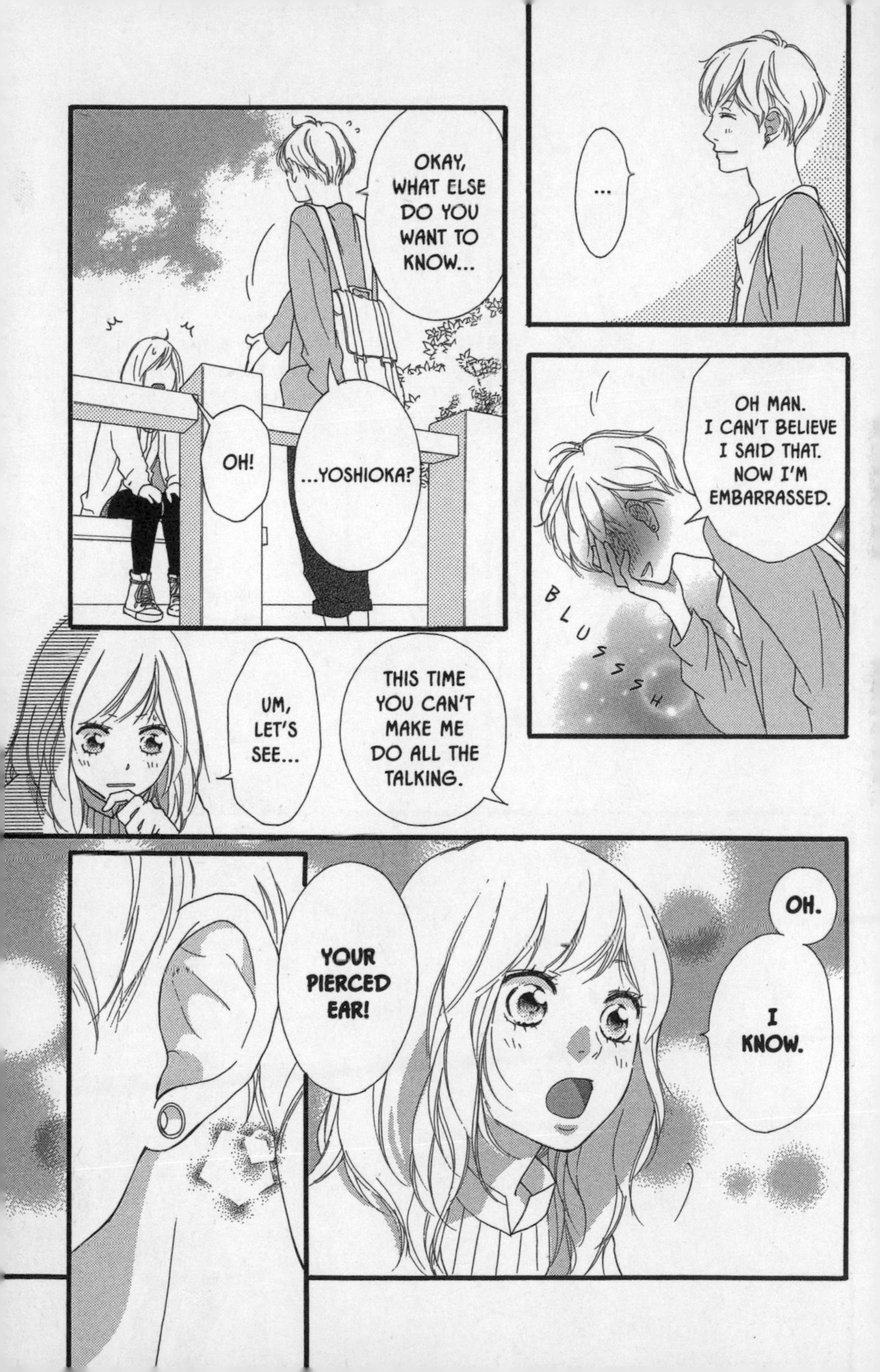
...
OH MAN. I CAN'T BELIEVE I SAID THAT. NOW I'M EMBARRASSED.
BLUSSSH
OKAY, WHAT ELSE DO YOU WANT TO KNOW...
...YOSHIOKA?
OH!
THIS TIME YOU CAN'T MAKE ME DO ALL THE TALKING.
UM, LET'S SEE...
OH.
I KNOW.
YOUR PIERCED EAR!

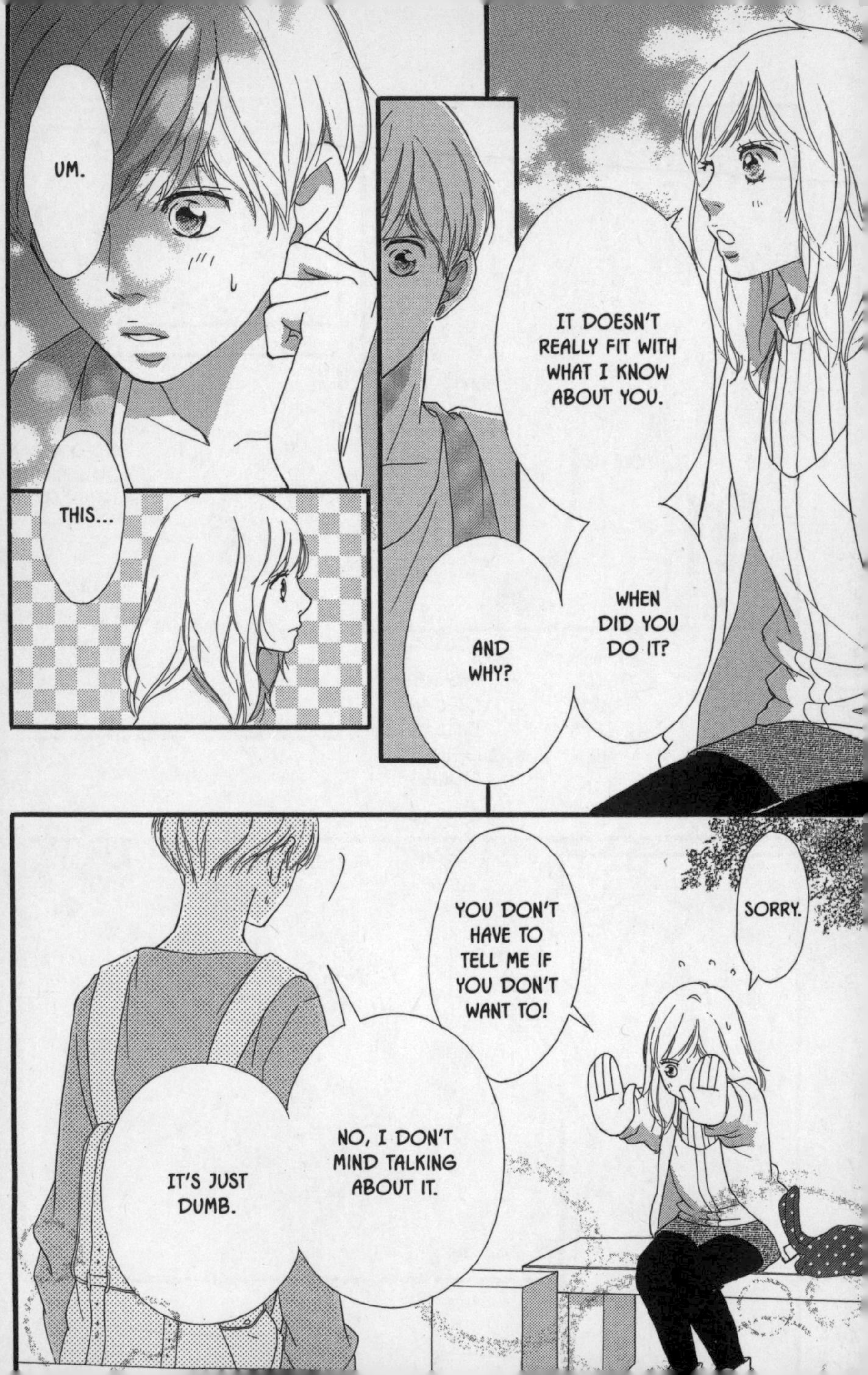
IT DOESN'T REALLY FIT WITH WHAT I KNOW ABOUT YOU.
WHEN DID YOU DO IT?
AND WHY?
UM.
THIS...
SORRY.
YOU DON'T HAVE TO TELL ME IF YOU DON'T WANT TO!
NO, I DON'T MIND TALKING ABOUT IT.
IT'S JUST DUMB.

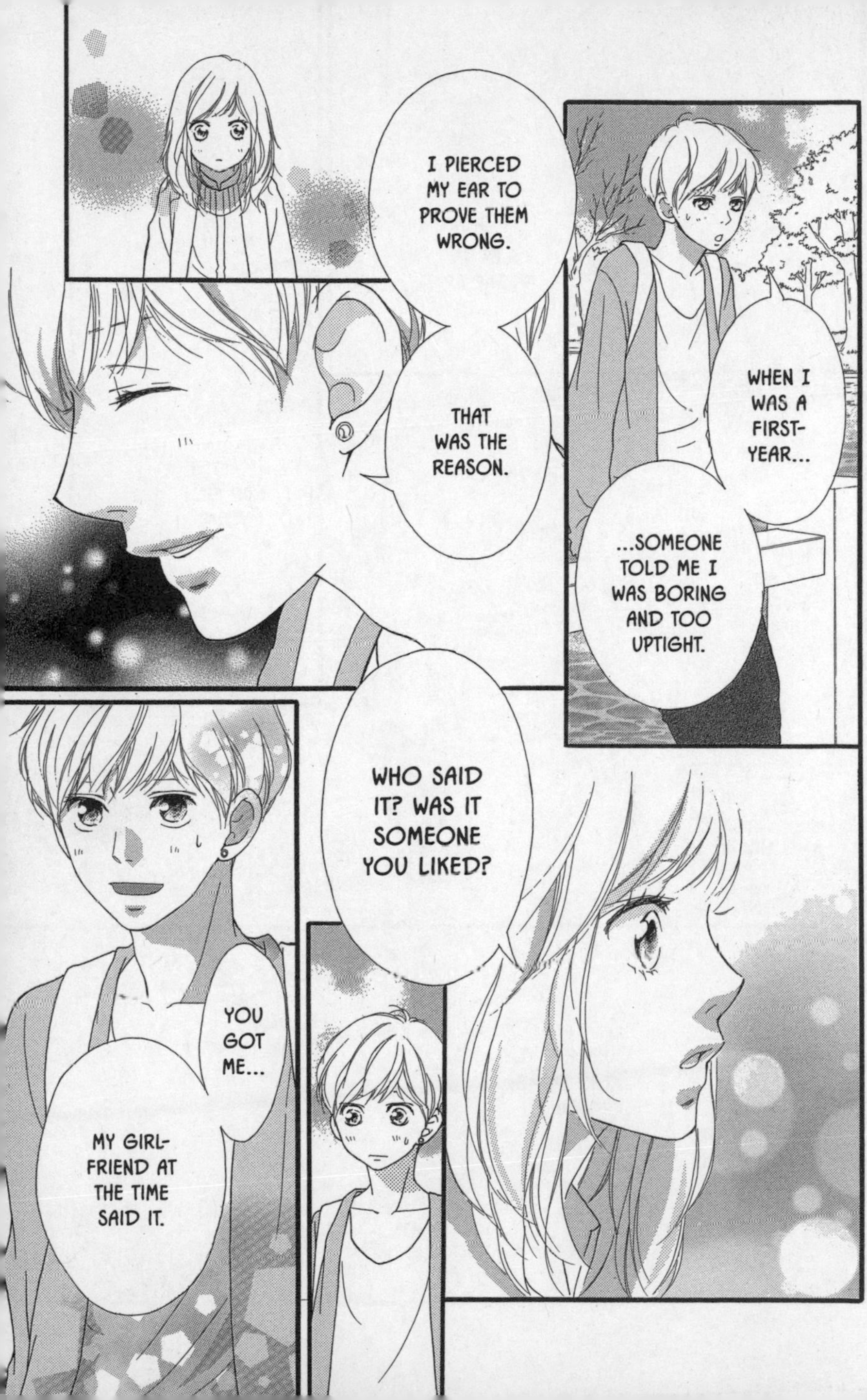
WHEN I WAS A FIRST-YEAR...
...SOMEONE TOLD ME I WAS BORING AND TOO UPTIGHT.
I PIERCED MY EAR TO PROVE THEM WRONG.
THAT WAS THE REASON.
WHO SAID IT? WAS IT SOMEONE YOU LIKED?
YOU GOT ME...
MY GIRL-FRIEND AT THE TIME SAID IT.

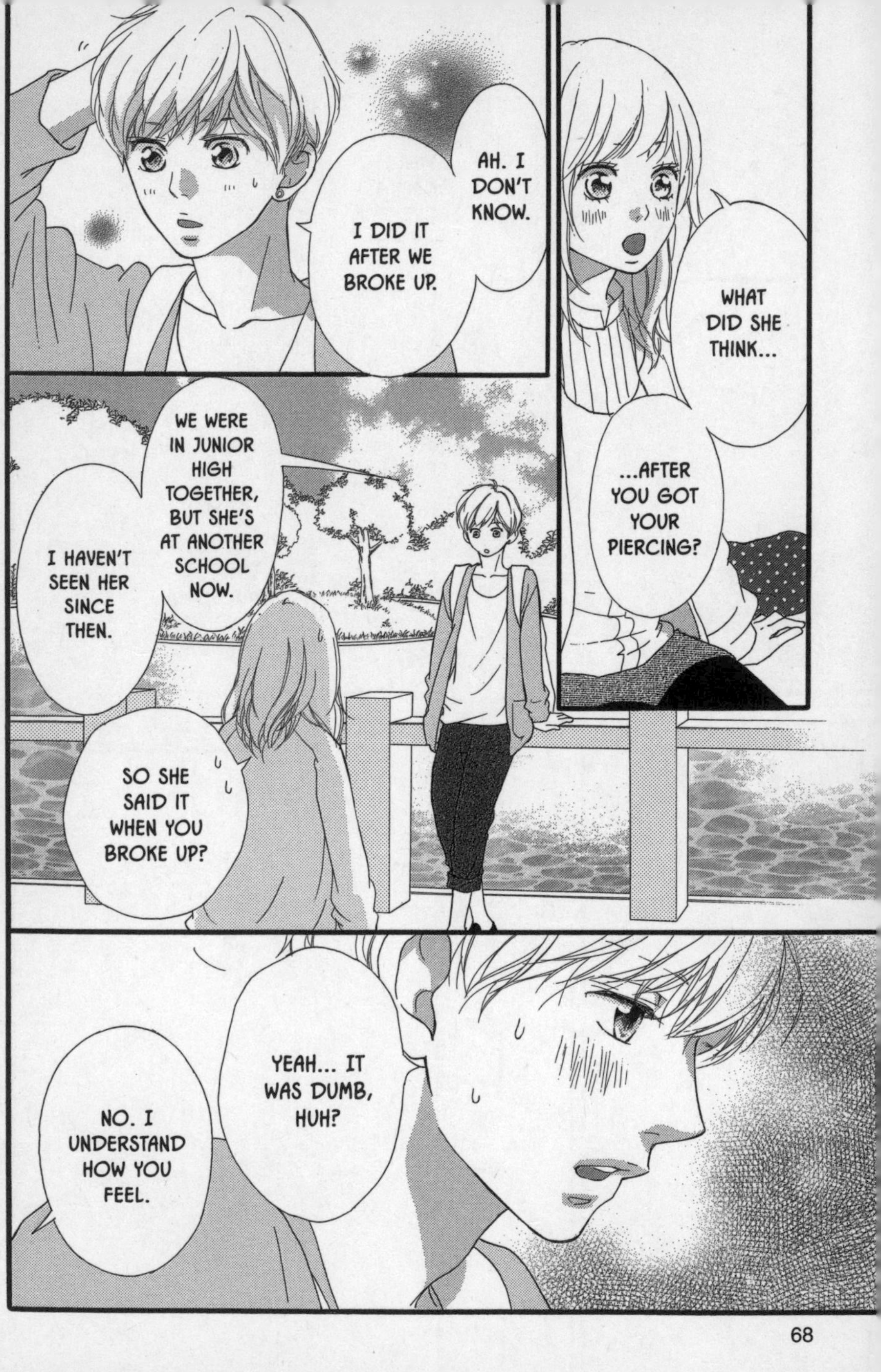
WHAT DID SHE THINK...
...AFTER YOU GOT YOUR PIERCING?
AH. I DON'T KNOW.
I DID IT AFTER WE BROKE UP.
WE WERE IN JUNIOR HIGH TOGETHER, BUT SHE'S AT ANOTHER SCHOOL NOW.
I HAVEN'T SEEN HER SINCE THEN.
SO SHE SAID IT WHEN YOU BROKE UP?
YEAH... IT WAS DUMB, HUH?
NO. I UNDERSTAND HOW YOU FEEL.

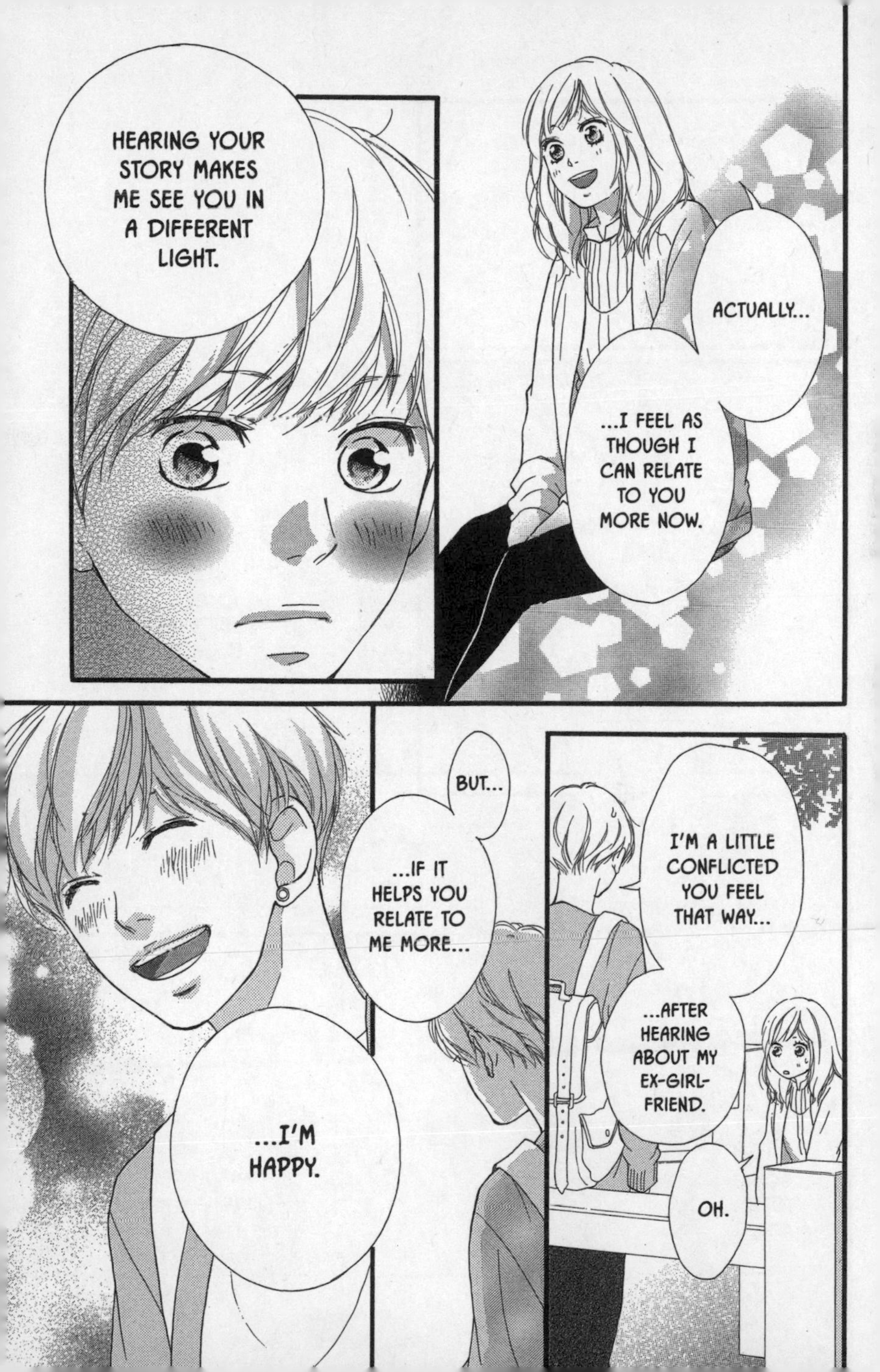
ACTUALLY...
...I FEEL AS THOUGH I CAN RELATE TO YOU MORE NOW.
HEARING YOUR STORY MAKES ME SEE YOU IN A DIFFERENT LIGHT.
I'M A LITTLE CONFLICTED YOU FEEL THAT WAY...
...AFTER HEARING ABOUT MY EX-GIRL-FRIEND.
OH.
BUT...
...IF IT HELPS YOU RELATE TO ME MORE...
...I'M HAPPY.

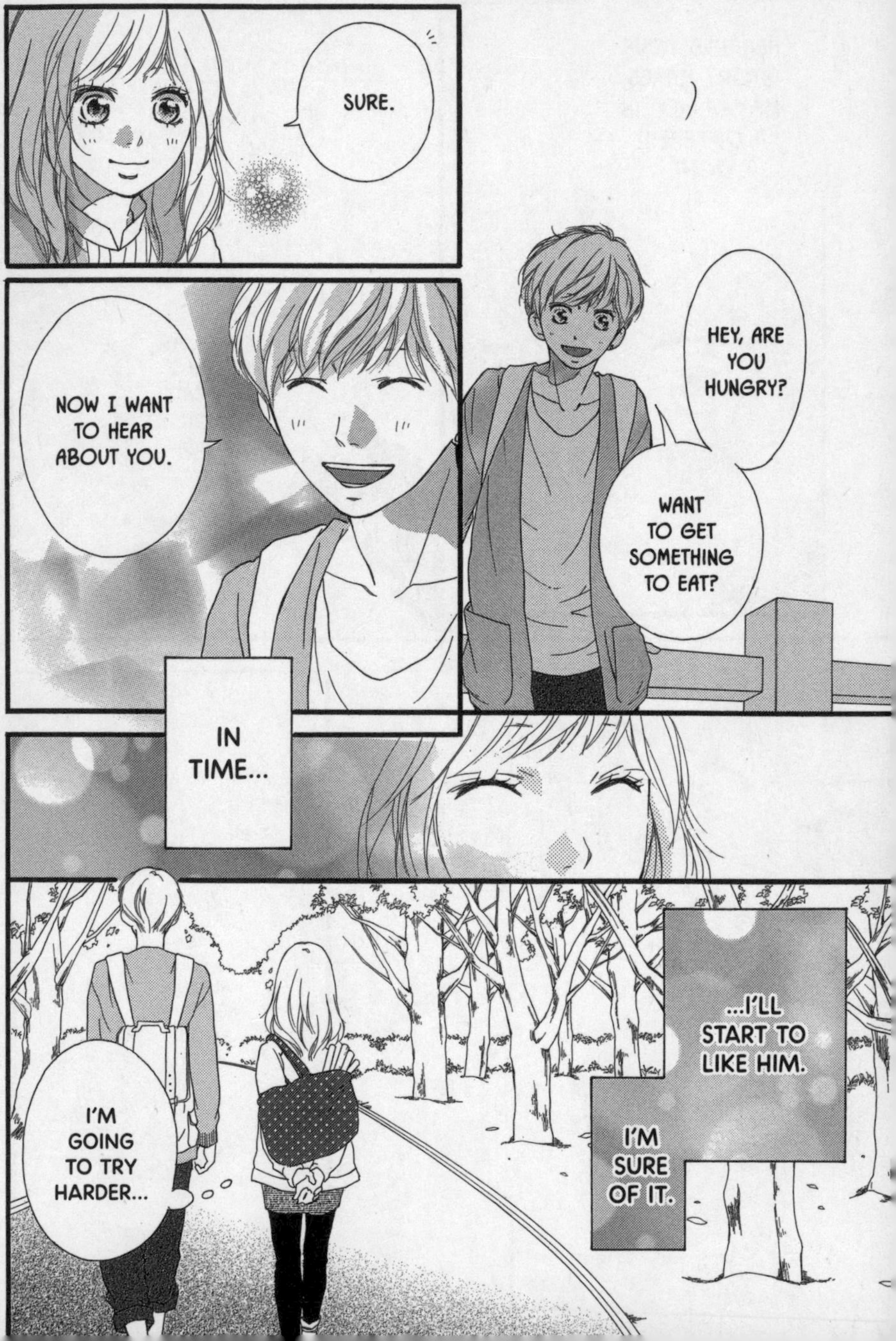
HEY, ARE YOU HUNGRY?
WANT TO GET SOMETHING TO EAT?
SURE.
NOW I WANT TO HEAR ABOUT YOU.
IN TIME...
...I'LL START TO LIKE HIM.
I'M SURE OF IT.
I'M GOING TO TRY HARDER...

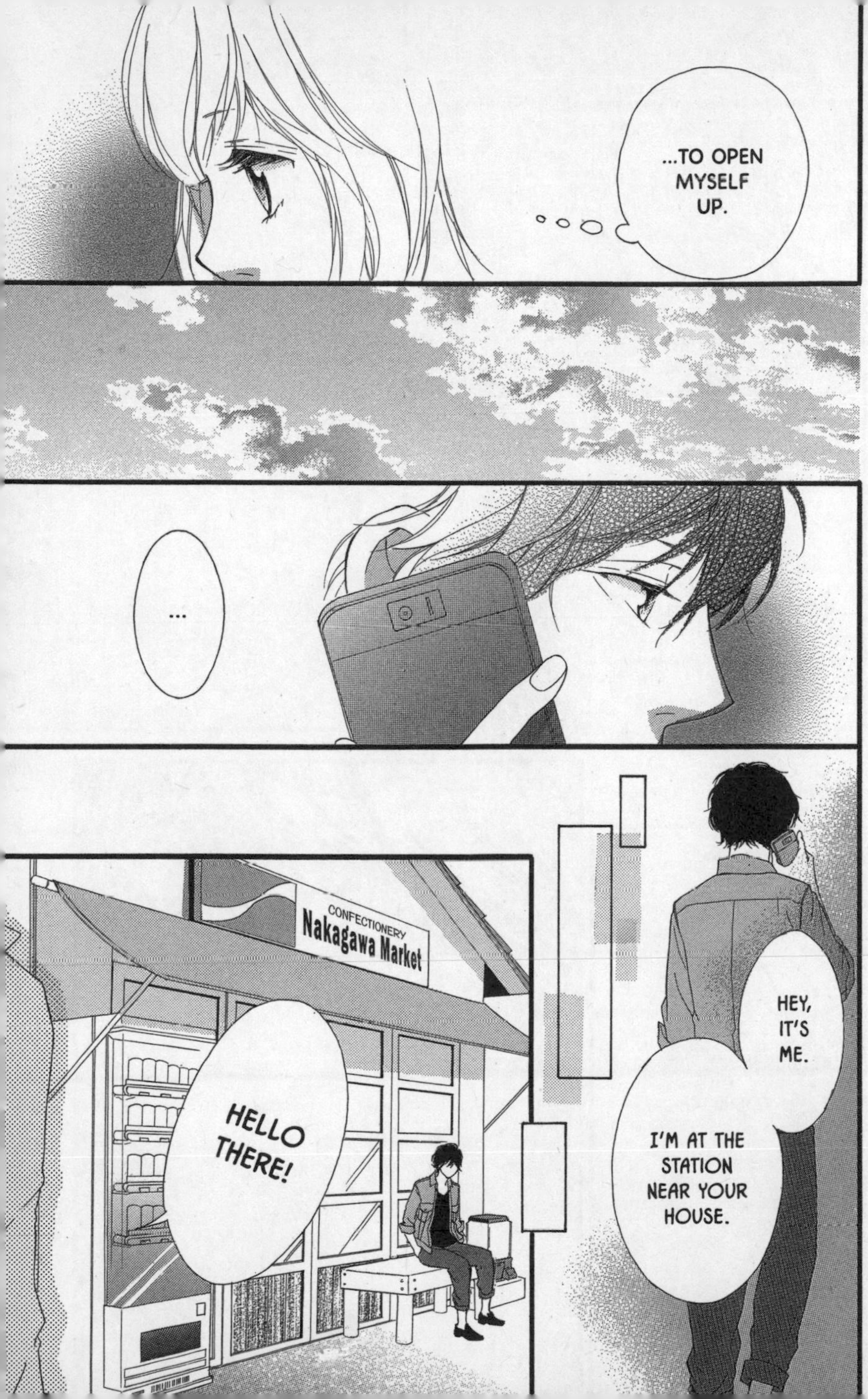
...TO OPEN MYSELF UP.
...
HEY, IT'S ME.
I'M AT THE STATION NEAR YOUR HOUSE.
CONFECTIONERY
Nakagawa Market
HELLO THERE!

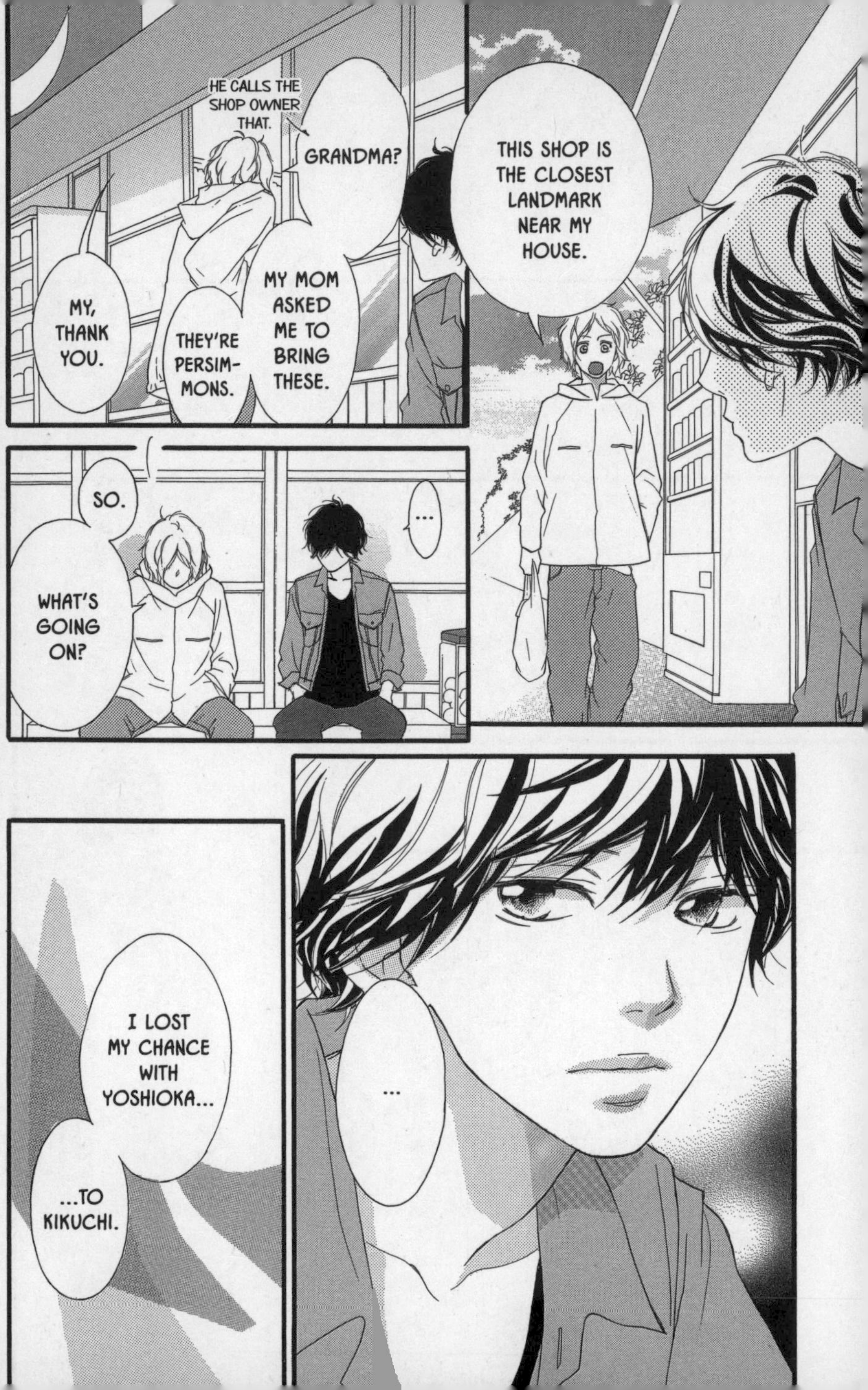
THIS SHOP IS THE CLOSEST LANDMARK NEAR MY HOUSE.
GRANDMA?
HE CALLS THE SHOP OWNER THAT.
MY MOM ASKED ME TO BRING THESE.
THEY'RE PERSIM-MONS.
MY, THANK YOU.
...
SO.
WHAT'S GOING ON?
...
I LOST MY CHANCE WITH YOSHIOKA...
...TO KIKUCHI.

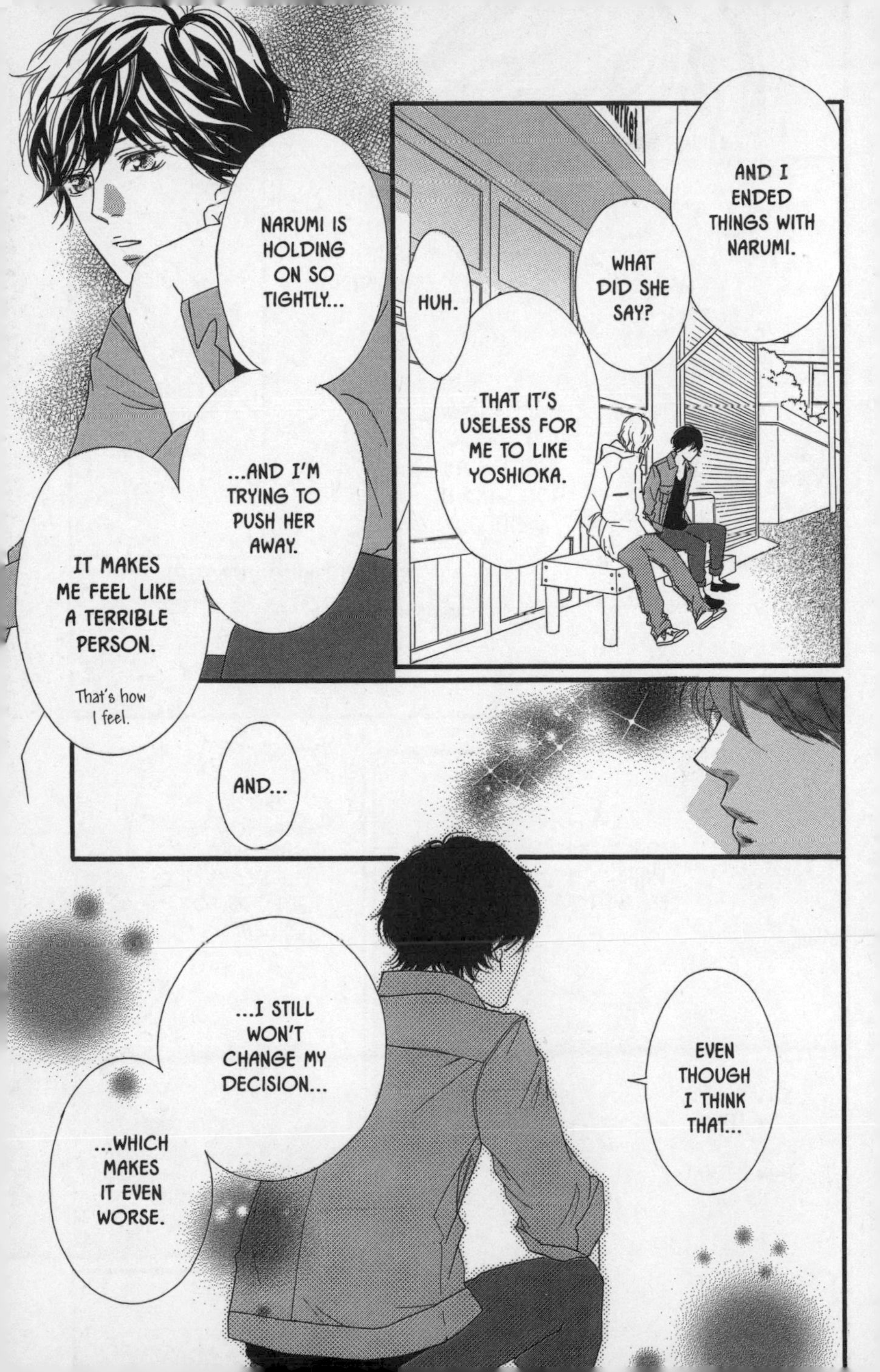
AND I ENDED THINGS WITH NARUMI.
WHAT DID SHE SAY?
HUH.
THAT IT'S USELESS FOR ME TO LIKE YOSHIOKA.
NARUMI IS HOLDING ON SO TIGHTLY...
...AND I'M TRYING TO PUSH HER AWAY.
IT MAKES ME FEEL LIKE A TERRIBLE PERSON.
That's how I feel.
AND...
EVEN THOUGH I THINK THAT...
...I STILL WON'T CHANGE MY DECISION...
...WHICH MAKES IT EVEN WORSE.

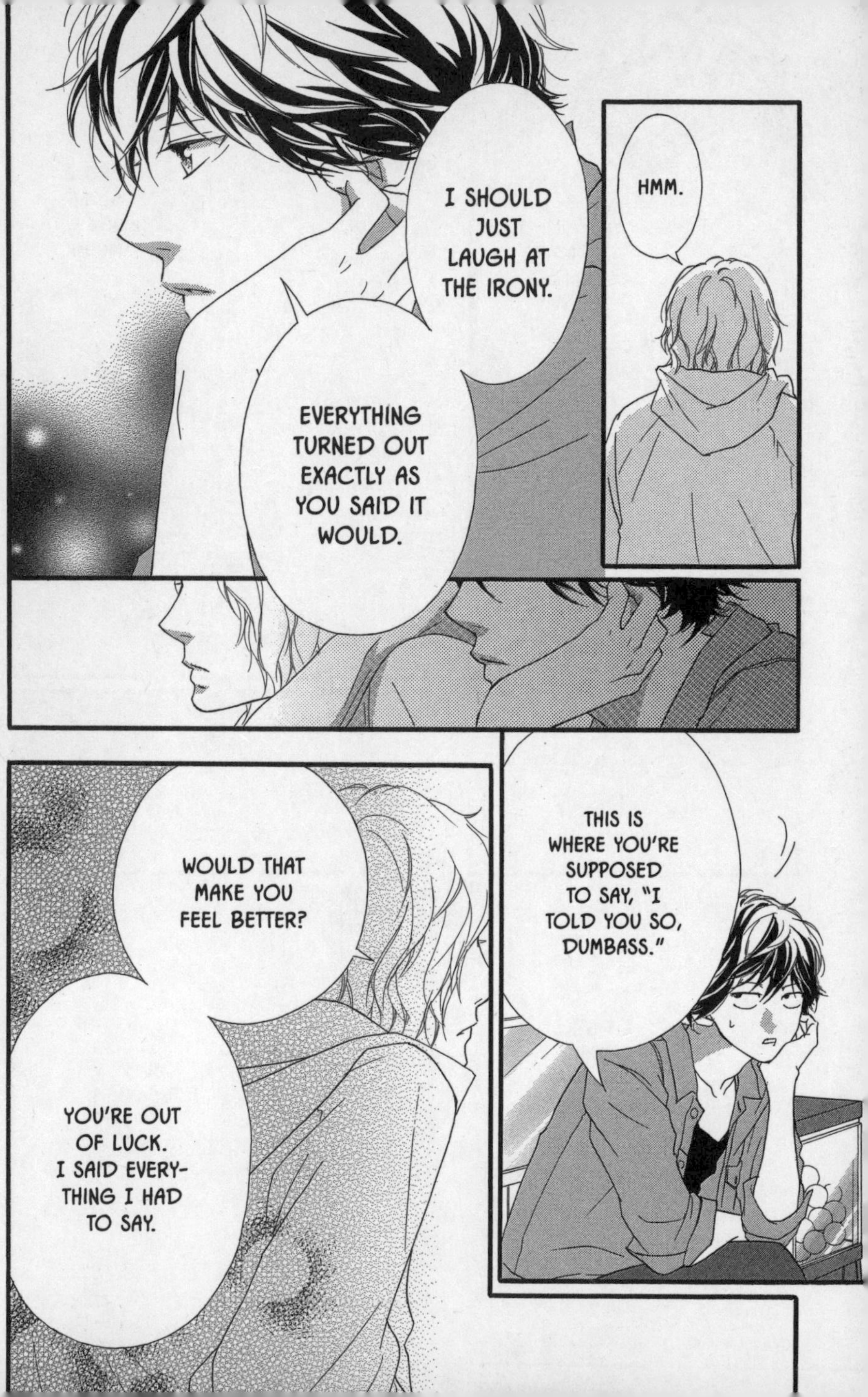
HMM.
I SHOULD JUST LAUGH AT THE IRONY.
EVERYTHING TURNED OUT EXACTLY AS YOU SAID IT WOULD.
THIS IS WHERE YOU'RE SUPPOSED TO SAY, "I TOLD YOU SO, DUMBASS."
WOULD THAT MAKE YOU FEEL BETTER?
YOU'RE OUT OF LUCK. I SAID EVERY-THING I HAD TO SAY.

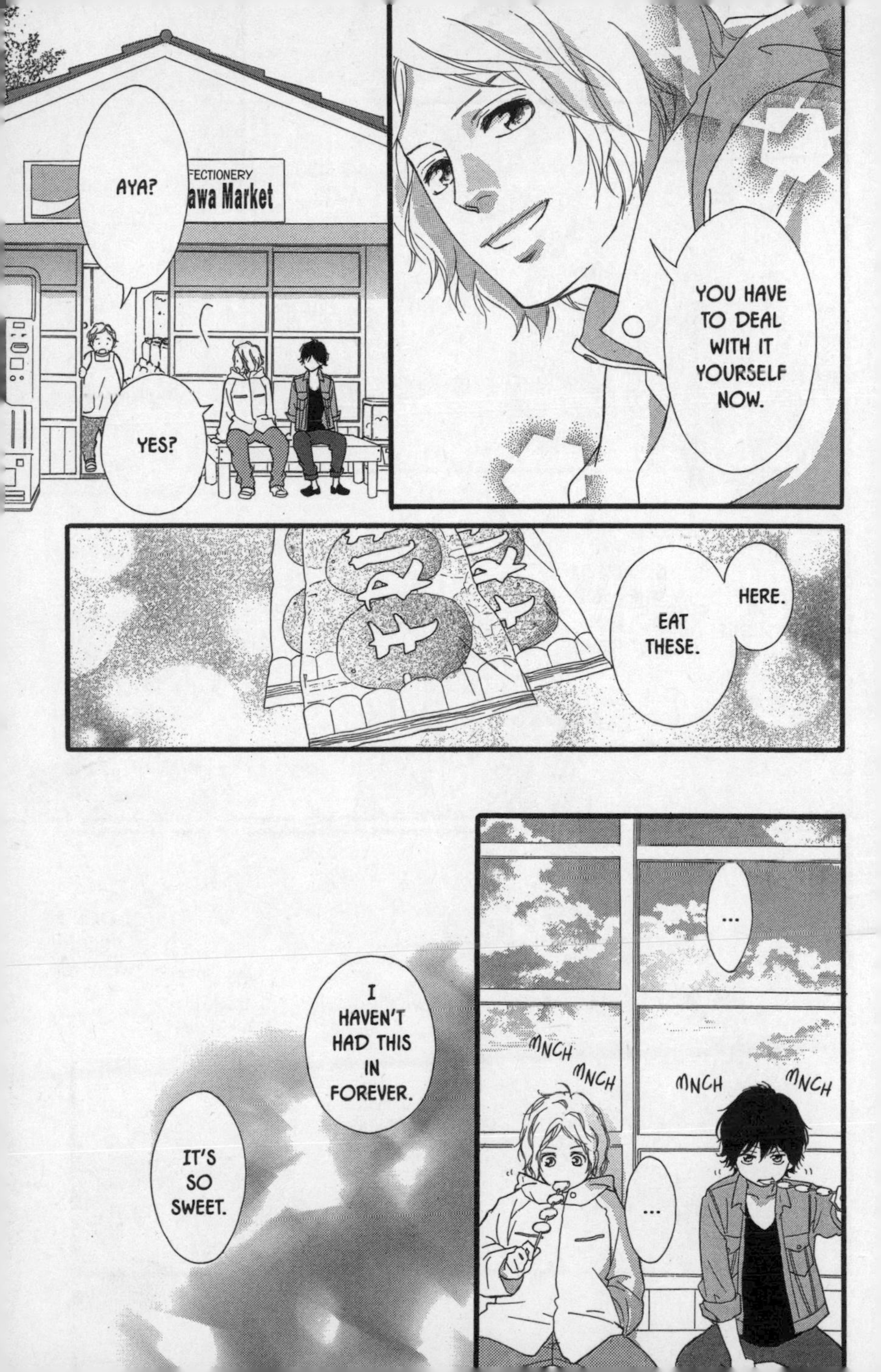
YOU HAVE TO DEAL WITH IT YOURSELF NOW.
FECTIONERY
awa Market
AYA?
YES?
HERE.
EAT THESE.
...
MNCH MNCH
MNCH MNCH
...
I HAVEN'T HAD THIS IN FOREVER.
IT'S SO SWEET.

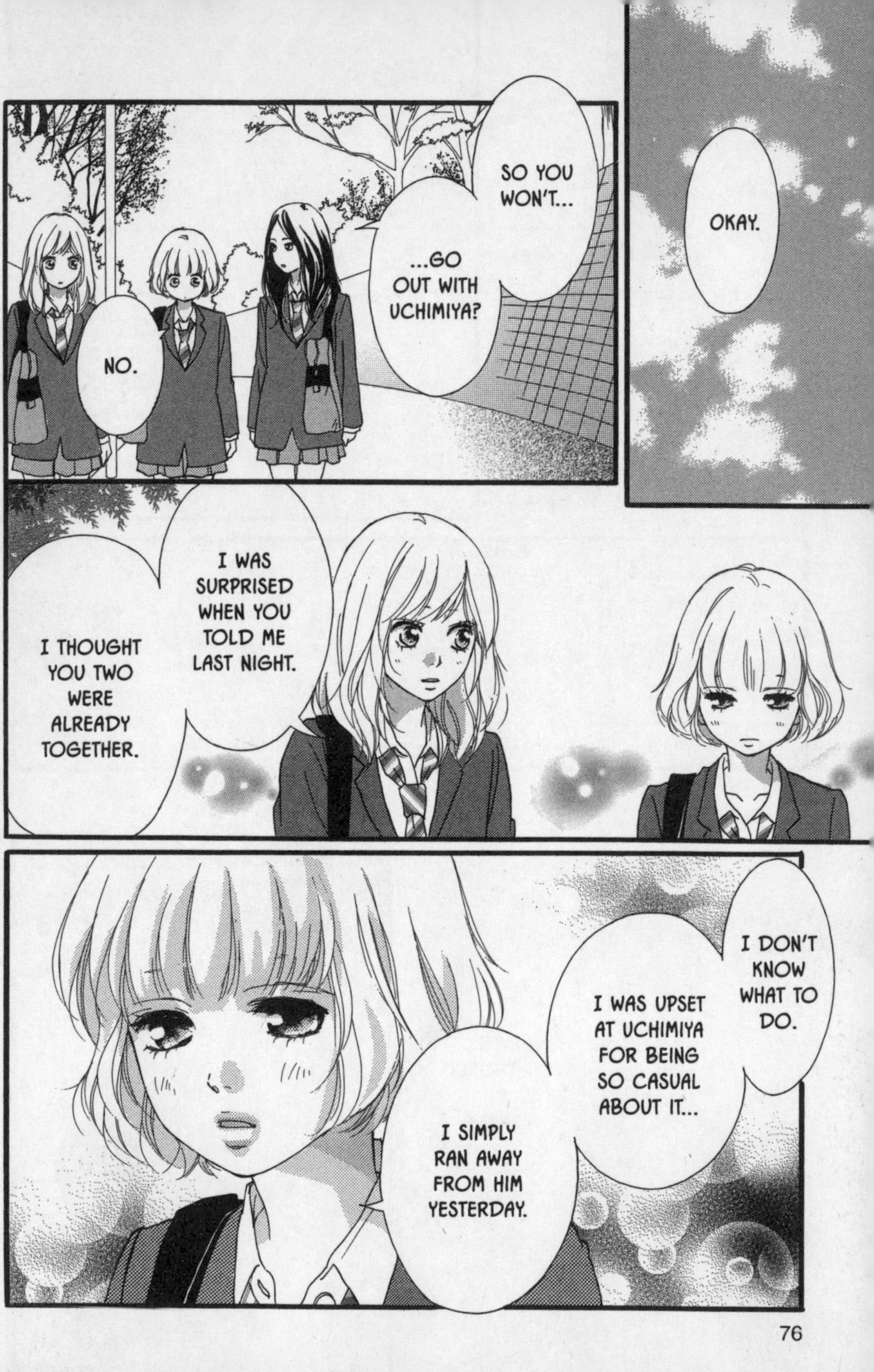
OKAY.
SO YOU WON'T...
...GO OUT WITH UCHIMIYA?
NO.
I WAS SURPRISED WHEN YOU TOLD ME LAST NIGHT.
I THOUGHT YOU TWO WERE ALREADY TOGETHER.
I DON'T KNOW WHAT TO DO.
I WAS UPSET AT UCHIMIYA FOR BEING SO CASUAL ABOUT IT...
I SIMPLY RAN AWAY FROM HIM YESTERDAY.

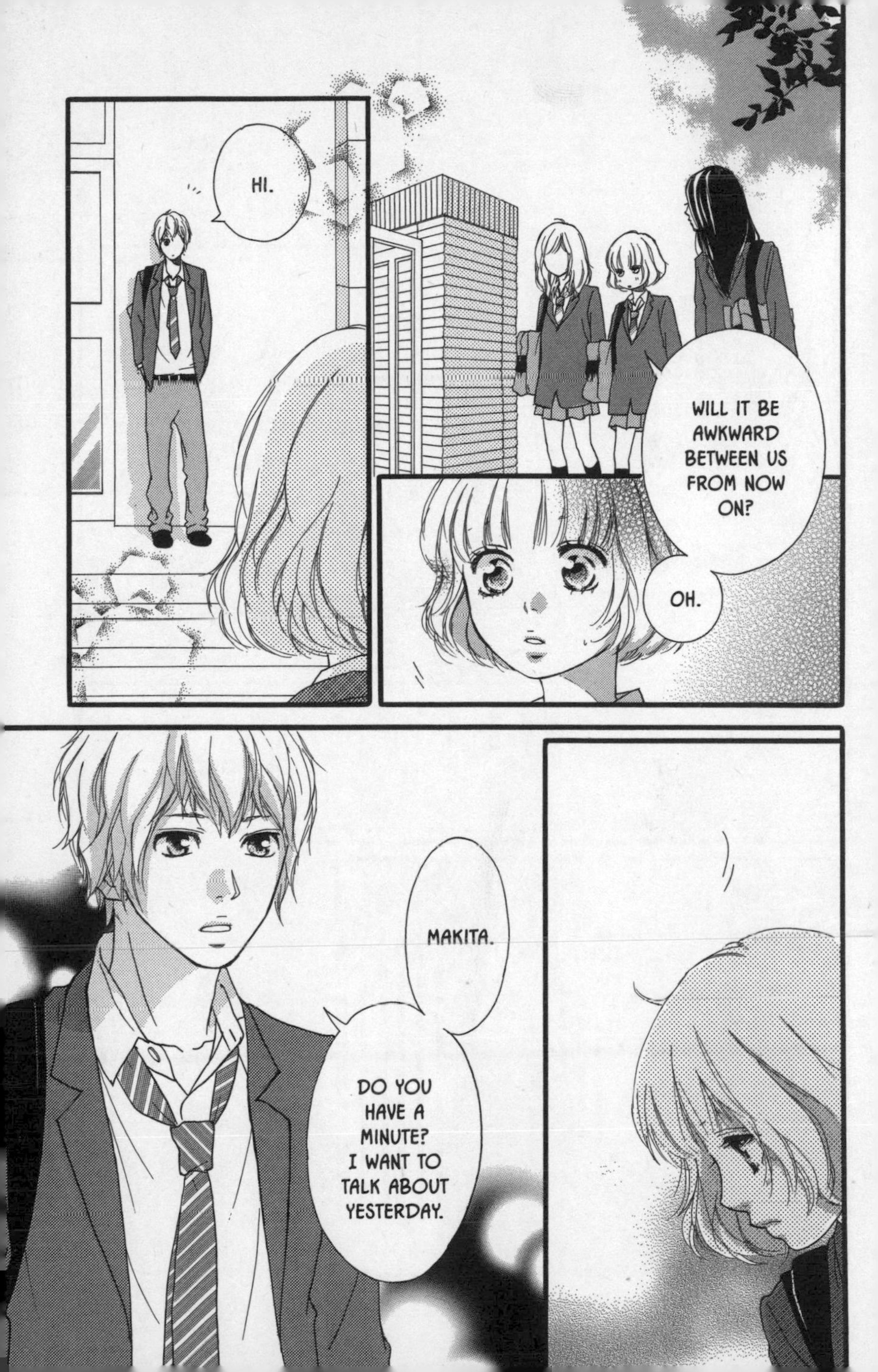
WILL IT BE AWKWARD BETWEEN US FROM NOW ON?
OH.
HI.
MAKITA.
DO YOU HAVE A MINUTE? I WANT TO TALK ABOUT YESTERDAY.

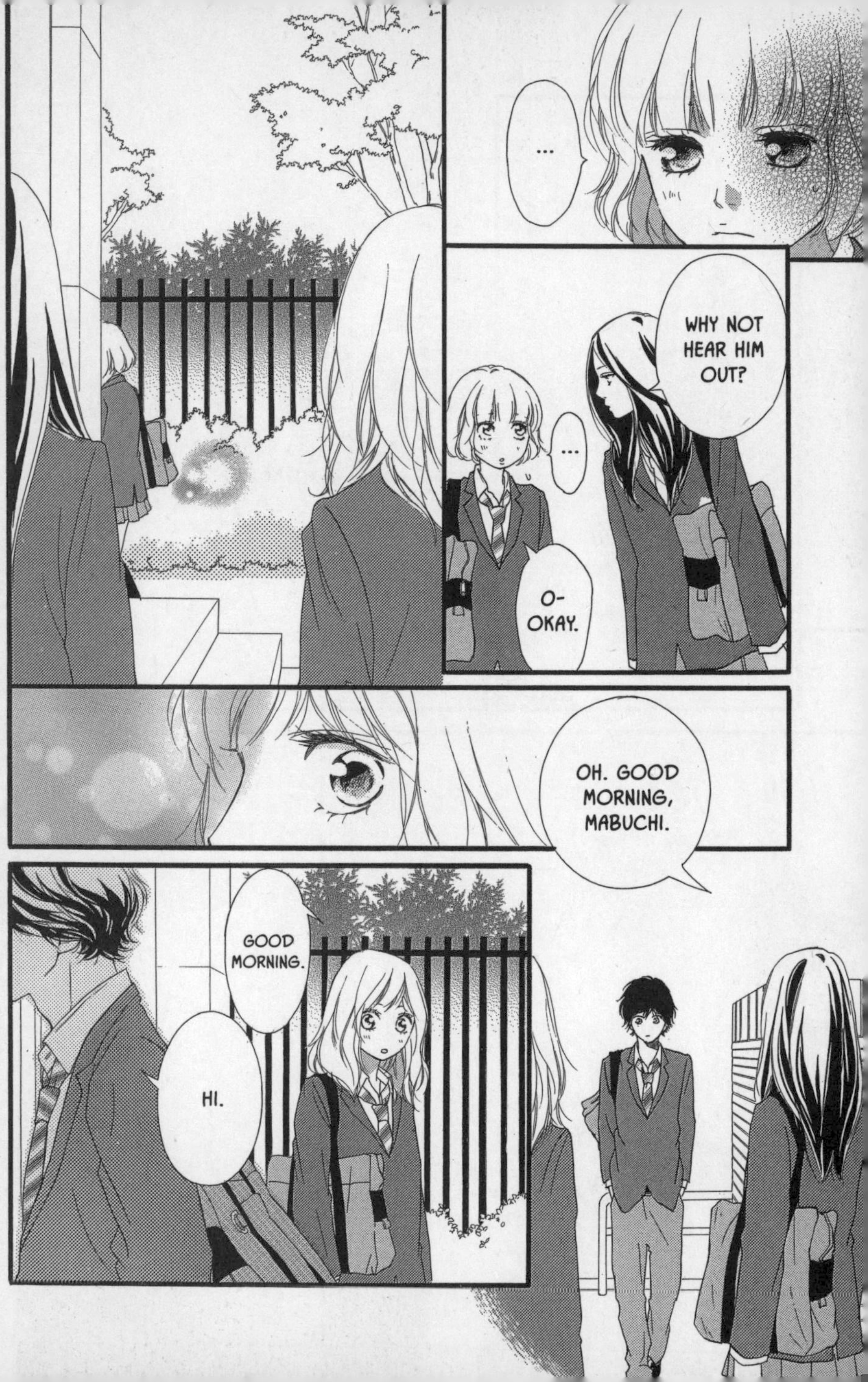
...
WHY NOT HEAR HIM OUT?
...
O-OKAY.
OH. GOOD MORNING, MABUCHI.
GOOD MORNING.
HI.

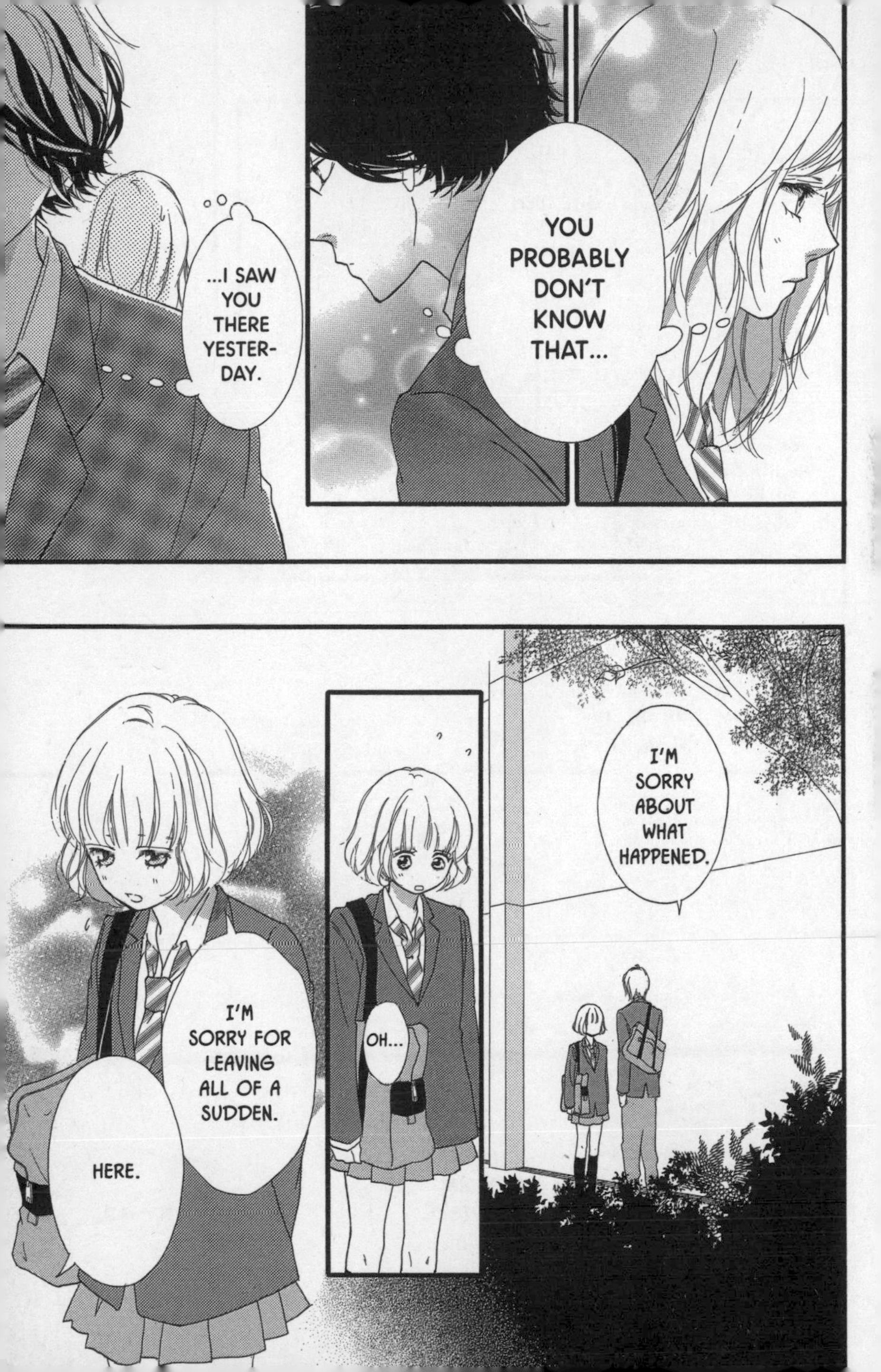
YOU PROBABLY DON'T KNOW THAT...
...I SAW YOU THERE YESTER-DAY.
I'M SORRY ABOUT WHAT HAPPENED.
OH...
I'M SORRY FOR LEAVING ALL OF A SUDDEN.
HERE.

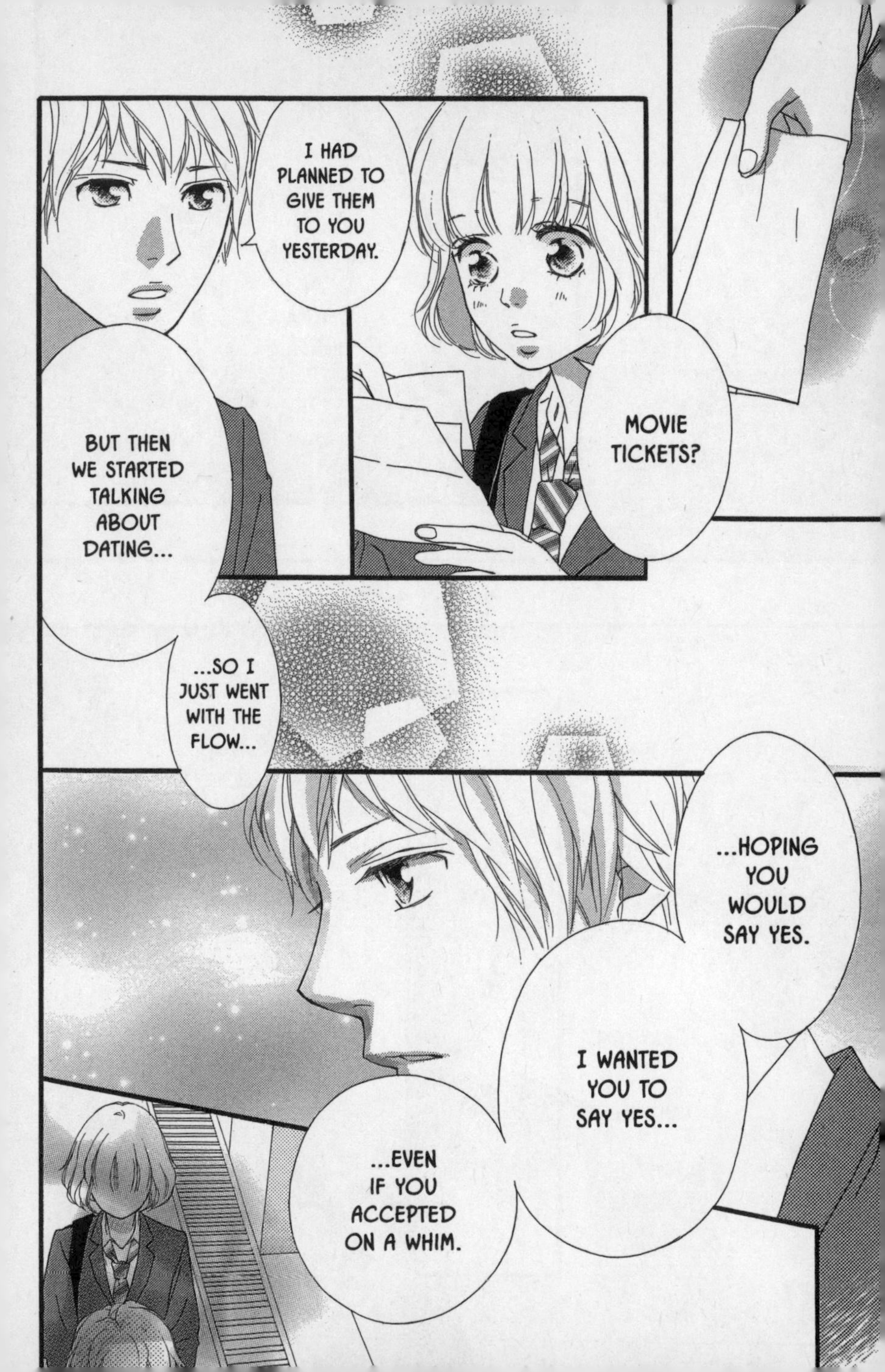
MOVIE TICKETS?
I HAD PLANNED TO GIVE THEM TO YOU YESTERDAY.
BUT THEN WE STARTED TALKING ABOUT DATING...
...SO I JUST WENT WITH THE FLOW...
...HOPING YOU WOULD SAY YES.
I WANTED YOU TO SAY YES...
...EVEN IF YOU ACCEPTED ON A WHIM.

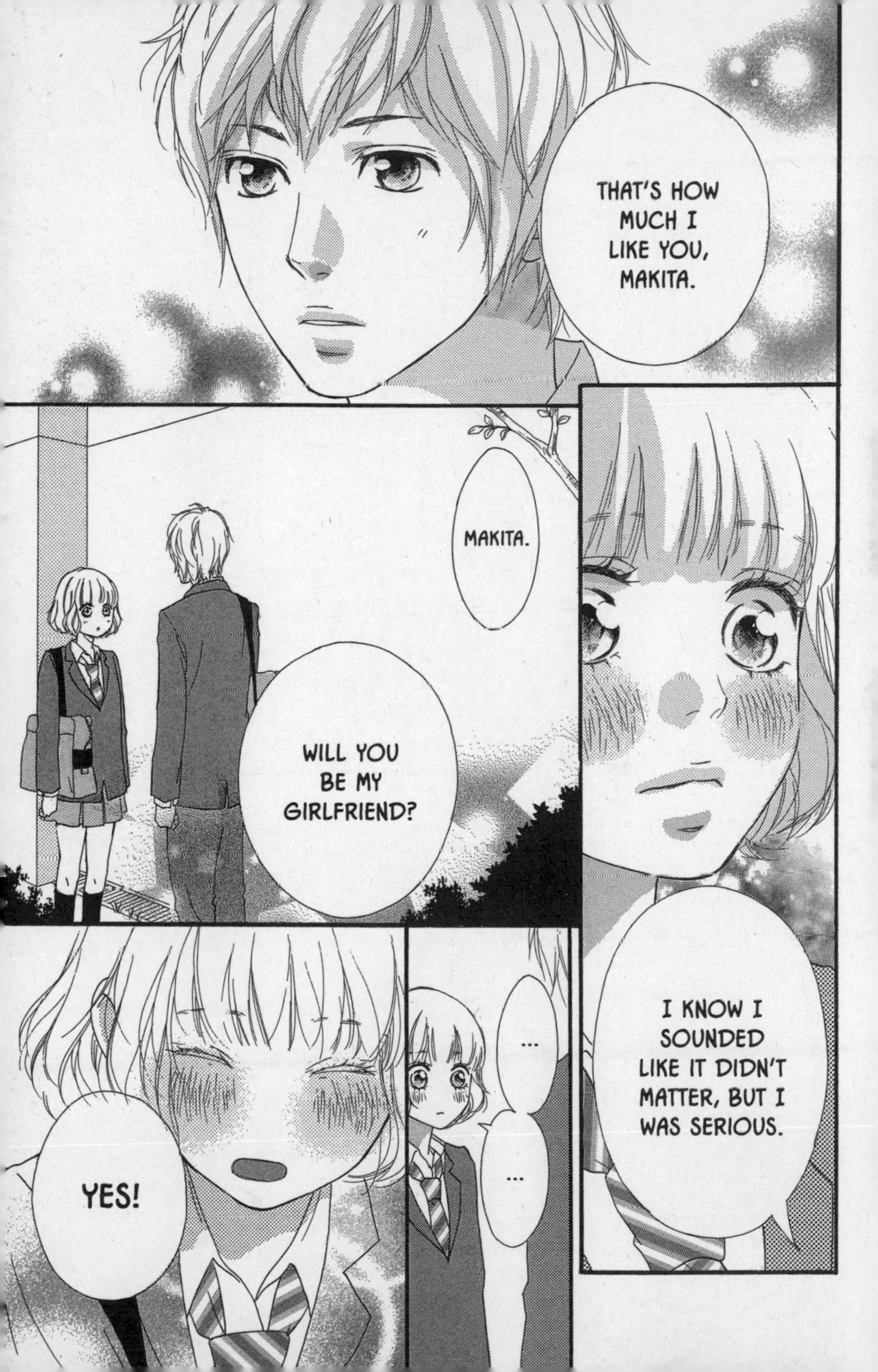
THAT'S HOW MUCH I LIKE YOU, MAKITA.
I KNOW I SOUNDED LIKE IT DIDN'T MATTER, BUT I WAS SERIOUS.
MAKITA.
WILL YOU BE MY GIRLFRIEND?
...
...
YES!

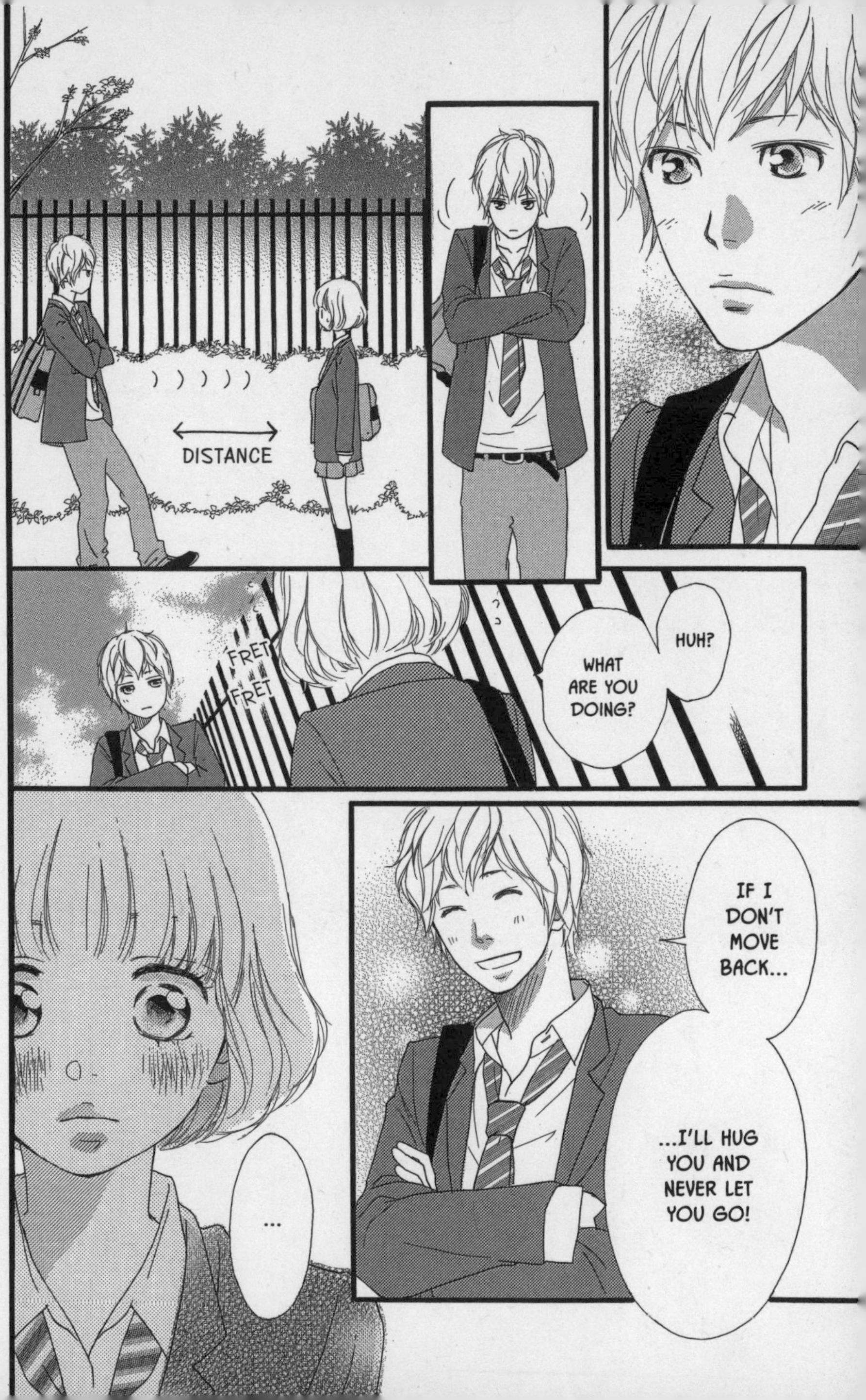
DISTANCE
HUH?
WHAT ARE YOU DOING?
FRET FRET
IF I DON'T MOVE BACK...
...I'LL HUG YOU AND NEVER LET YOU GO!
...

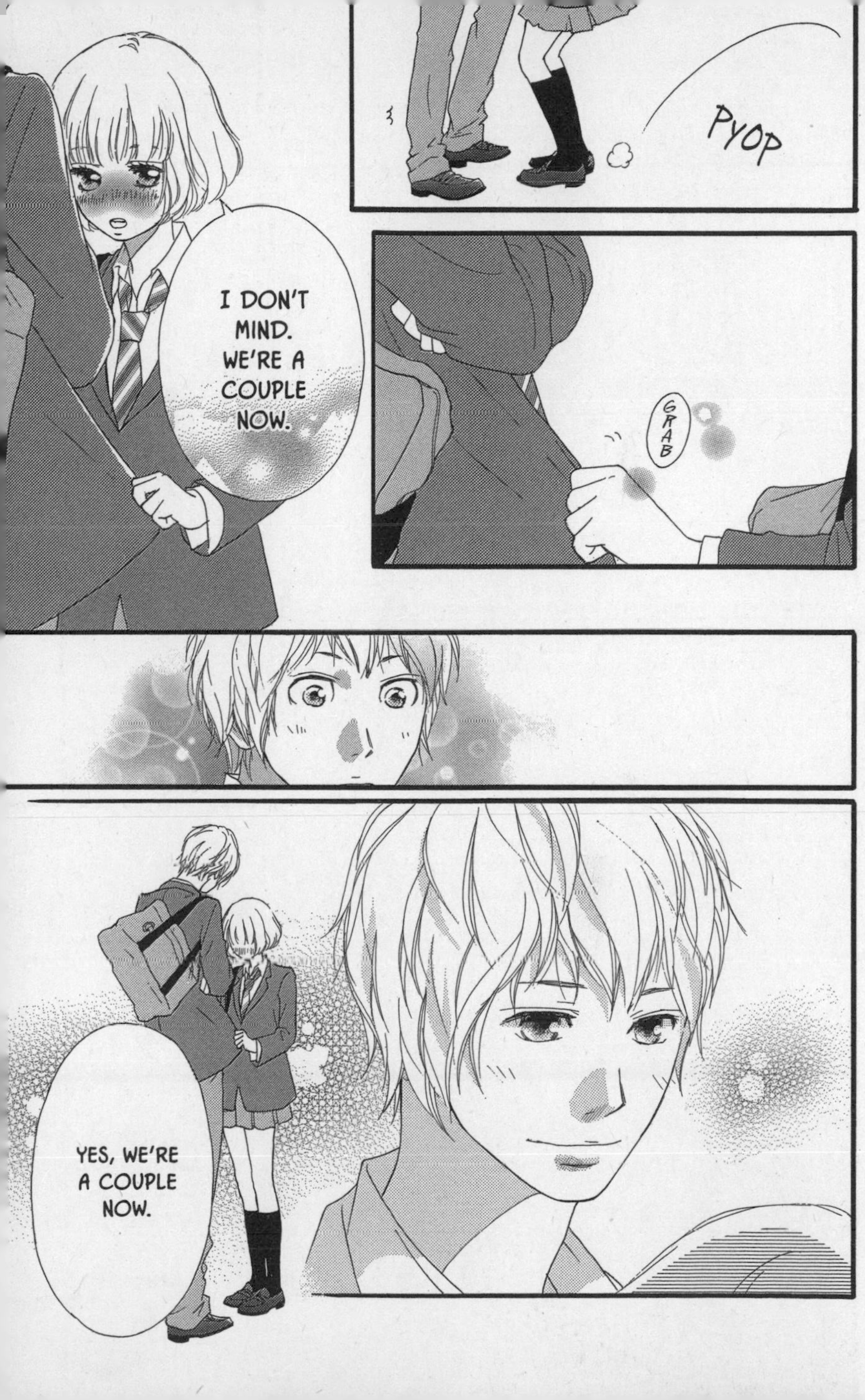
PYOP
GRAB
I DON'T MIND. WE'RE A COUPLE NOW.
YES, WE'RE A COUPLE NOW.

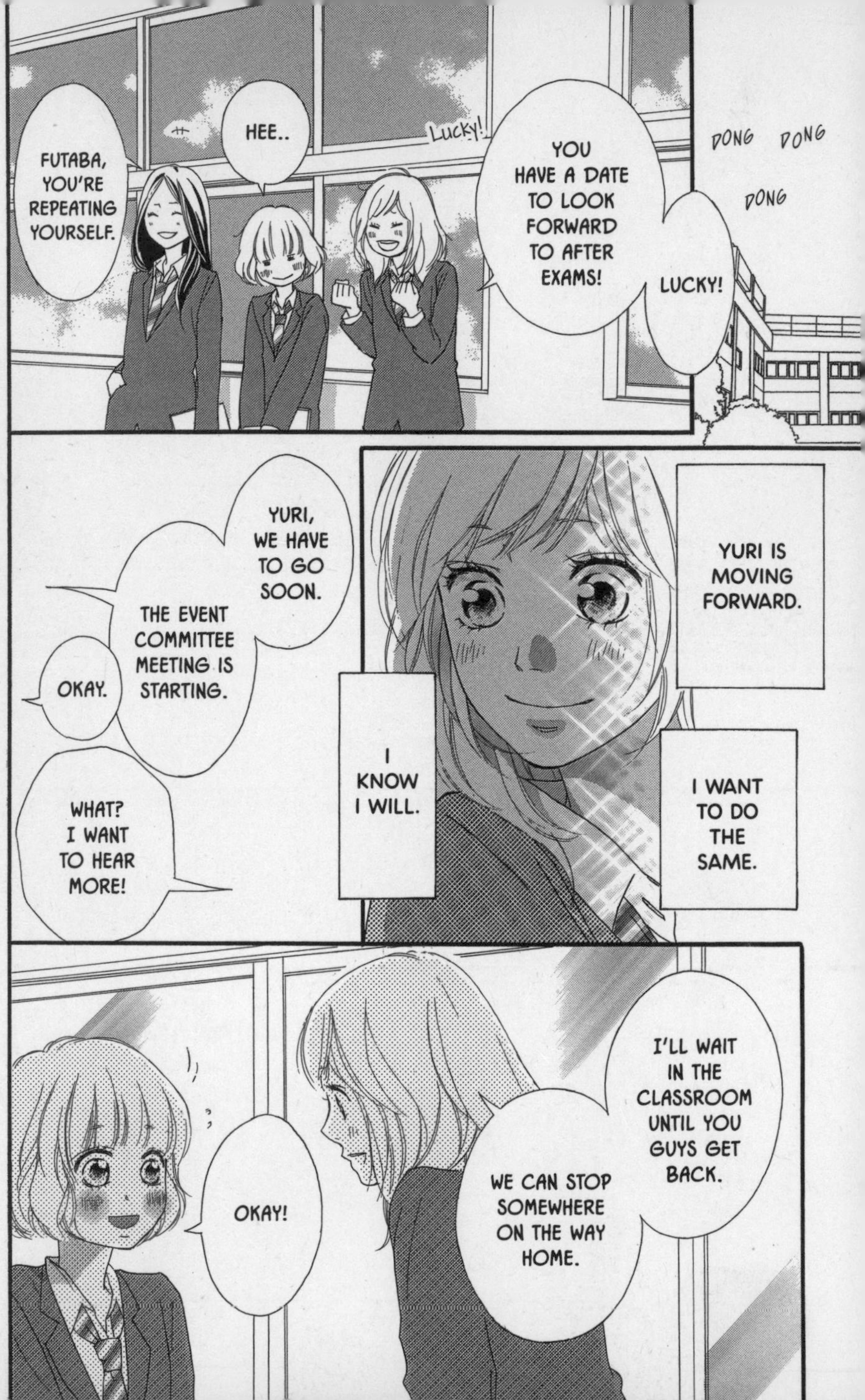
DONG DONG
DONG
LUCKY!
YOU HAVE A DATE TO LOOK FORWARD TO AFTER EXAMS!
Lucky!
HEE..
FUTABA, YOU'RE REPEATING YOURSELF.
YURI IS MOVING FORWARD.
I WANT TO DO THE SAME.
I KNOW I WILL.
YURI, WE HAVE TO GO SOON.
THE EVENT COMMITTEE MEETING IS STARTING.
OKAY.
WHAT? I WANT TO HEAR MORE!
I'LL WAIT IN THE CLASSROOM UNTIL YOU GUYS GET BACK.
WE CAN STOP SOMEWHERE ON THE WAY HOME.
OKAY!

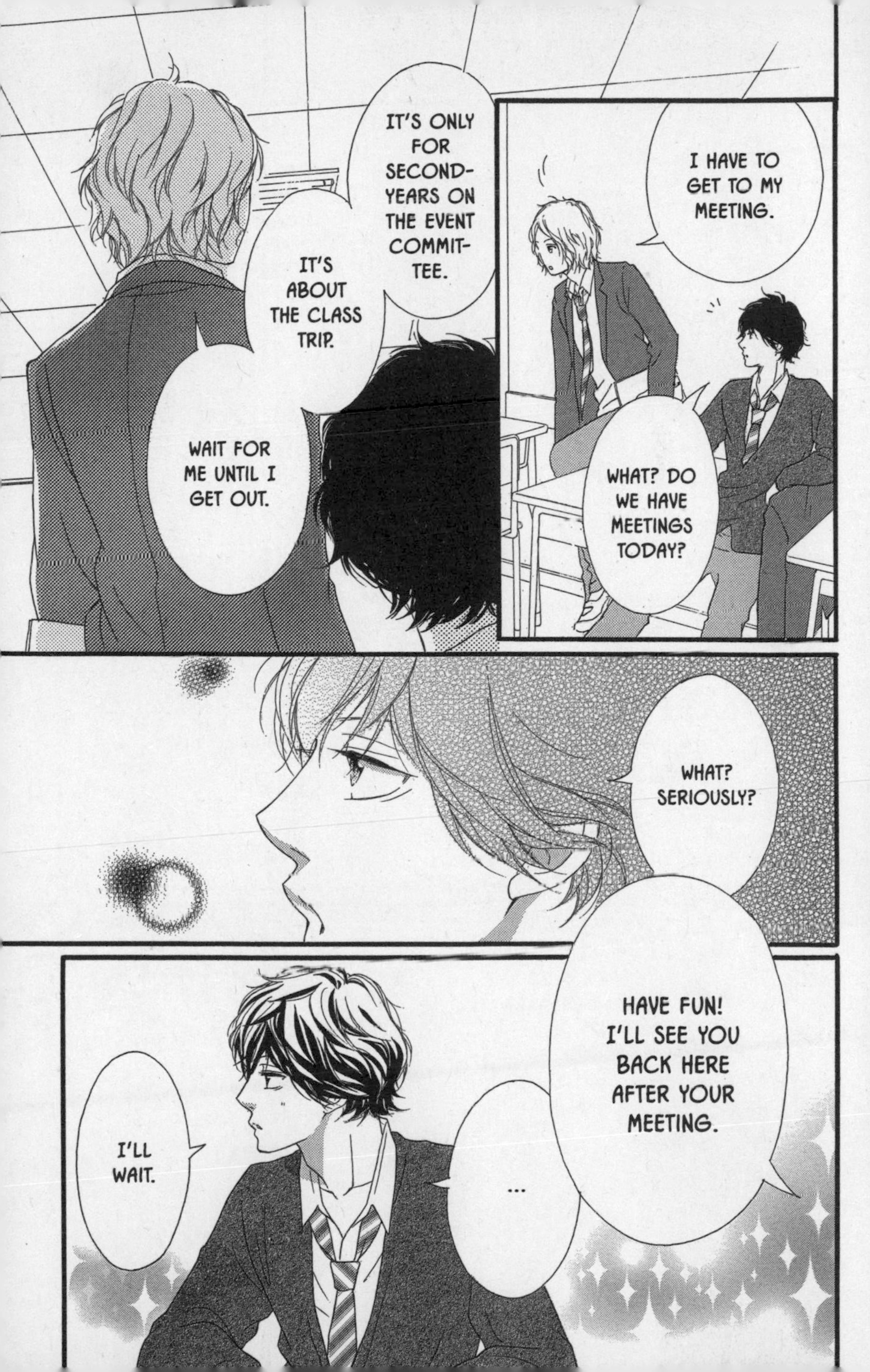
I HAVE TO GET TO MY MEETING.
WHAT? DO WE HAVE MEETINGS TODAY?
IT'S ONLY FOR SECOND-YEARS ON THE EVENT COMMIT-TEE.
IT'S ABOUT THE CLASS TRIP.
WAIT FOR ME UNTIL I GET OUT.
WHAT? SERIOUSLY?
HAVE FUN! I'LL SEE YOU BACK HERE AFTER YOUR MEETING.
...
I'LL WAIT.

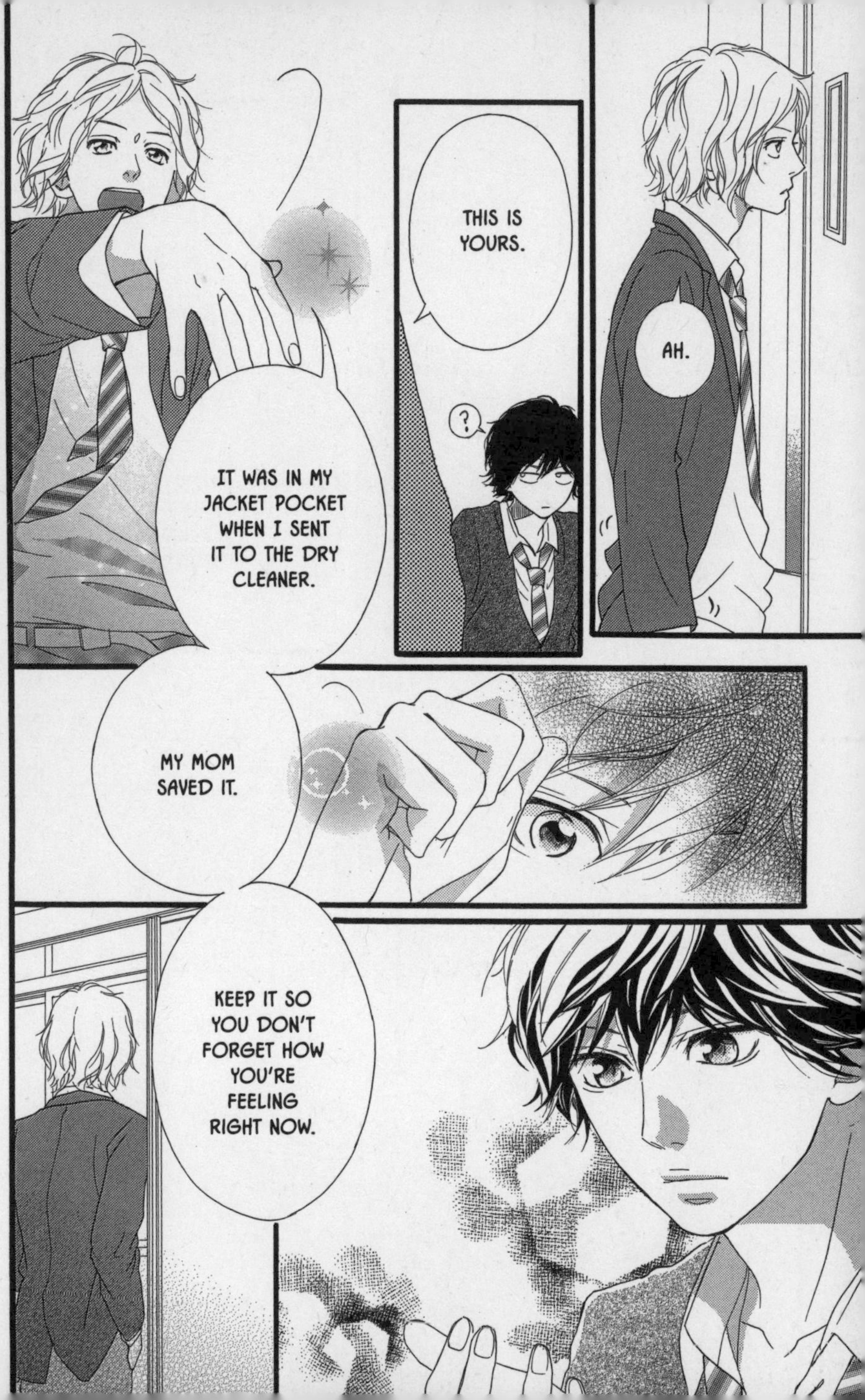
AH.
THIS IS YOURS.
?
IT WAS IN MY JACKET POCKET WHEN I SENT IT TO THE DRY CLEANER.
MY MOM SAVED IT.
KEEP IT SO YOU DON'T FORGET HOW YOU'RE FEELING RIGHT NOW.

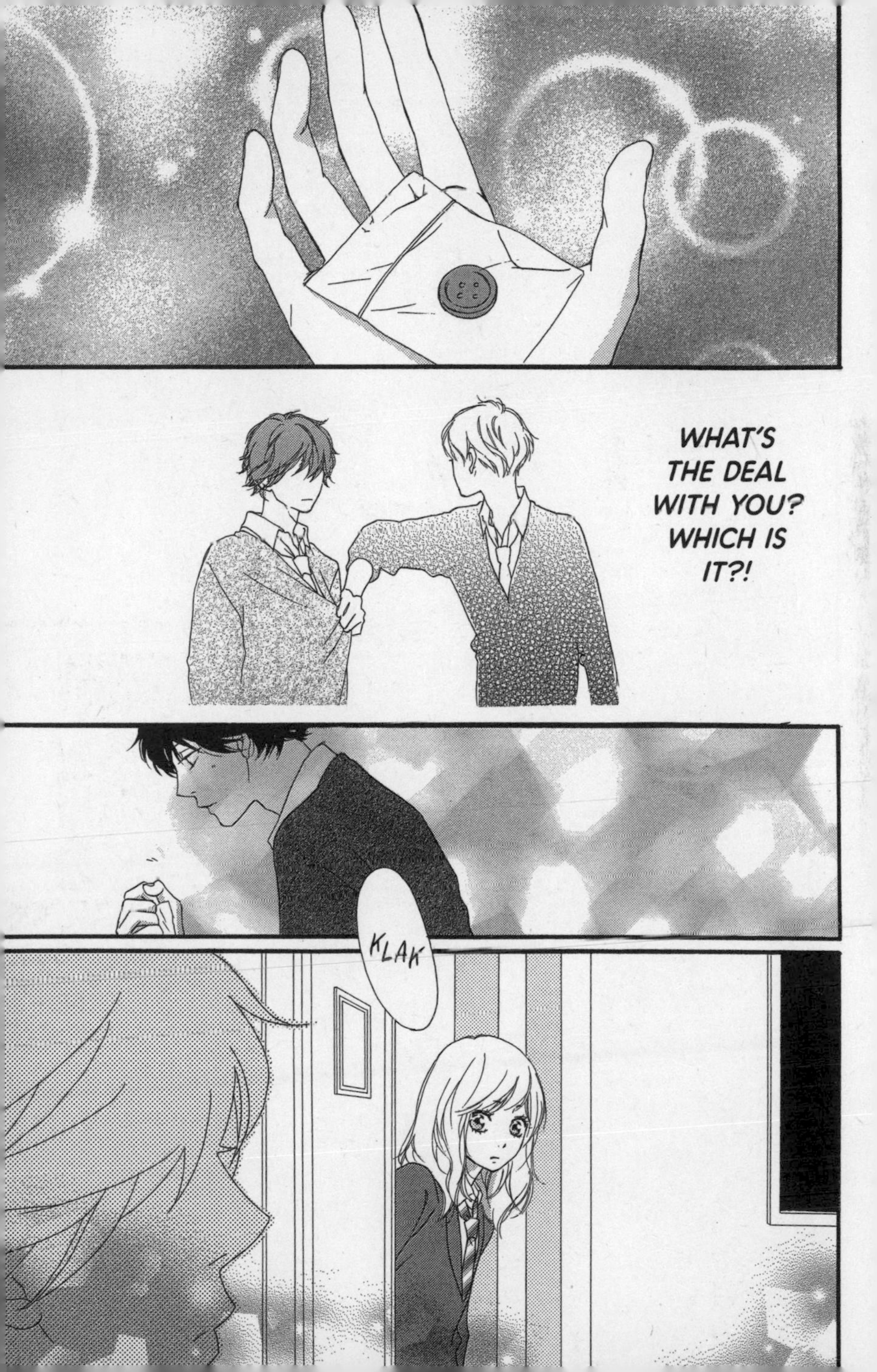
WHAT'S THE DEAL WITH YOU? WHICH IS IT?!
KLAK

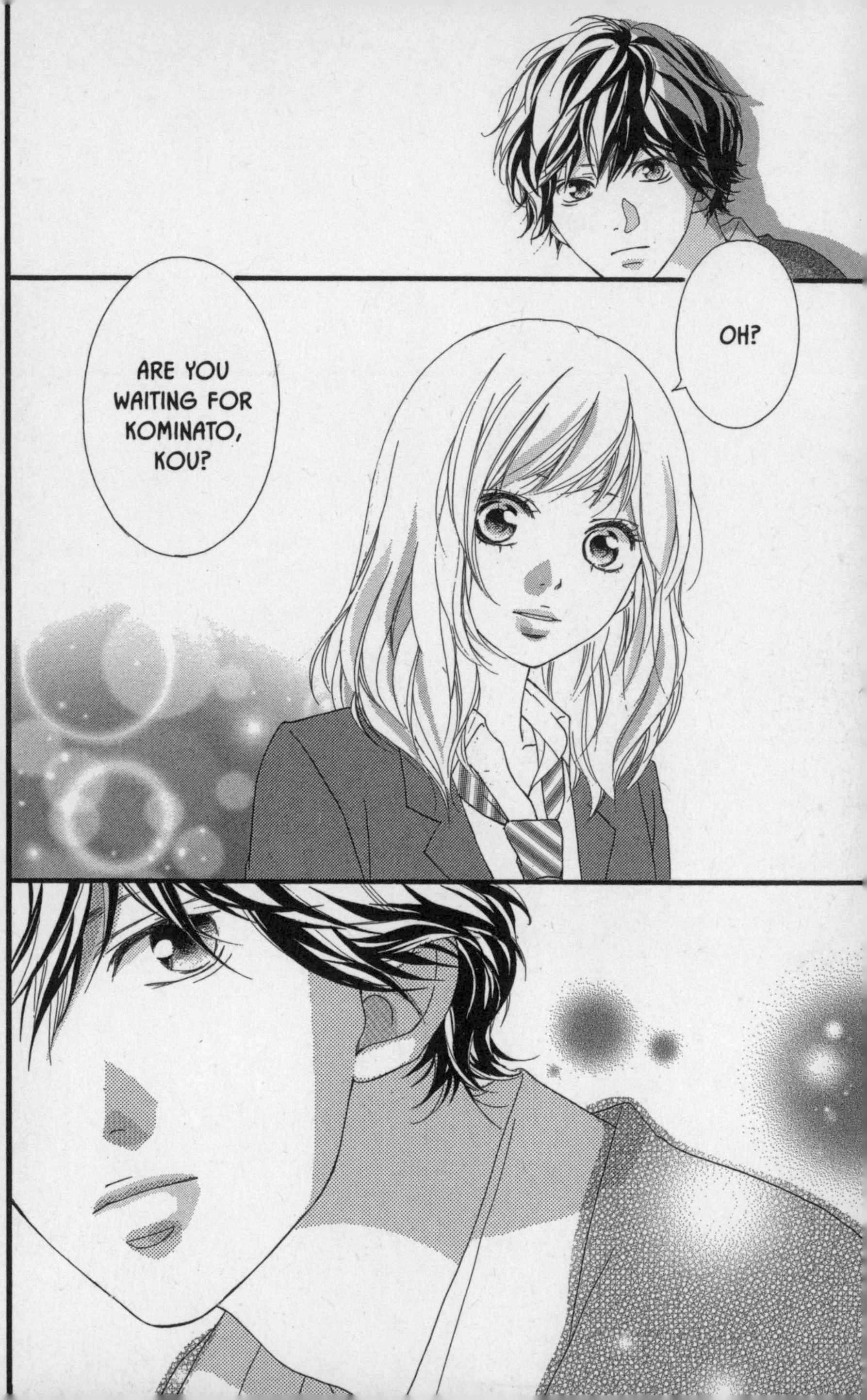
OH?
ARE YOU WAITING FOR KOMINATO, KOU?

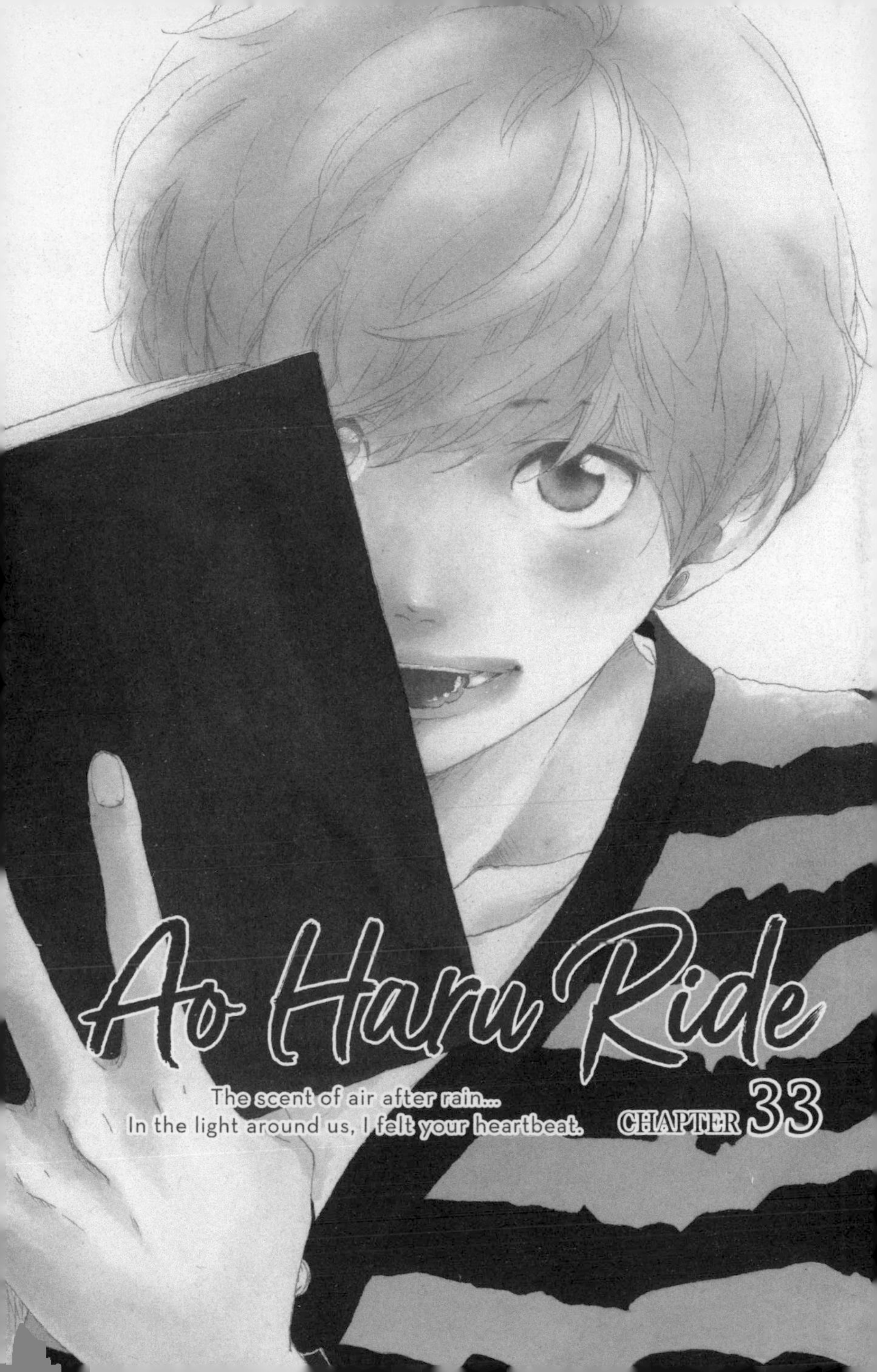
Ao Haru Ride
The scent of air after rain...
In the light around us, I felt your heartbeat.
CHAPTER 33

ANNOUNCEMENT

I have some exciting news to share with you.

Ao Haru Ride will be made into an animated series!!!!! Woo-hoo!!! Yaay!!! BOM BOM BOM! POOM POOM POOM!

I am absolutely thrilled. When I became a mangaka, I dreamed my work would one day become an anime, but I never expected it to actually happen. To think my dream is coming to fruition... It truly is a dream, and I'm so grateful to my readers, whether you're a loyal follower or just reading this for fun. Thank you, thank you, thank you from the bottom of my heart.

It's exciting to wonder about what these kids will look like in color and what their voices will sound like... I'm looking forward to the anime, and I hope you are too! Aah! I can't wait...!

In anticipation of the anime, volume 10 will be sold with a drama CD included!!! Woo-hoo!! Yay!!! BOM BOM BOM! POOM POOM POOM! The CD is only available with advance purchase in Japan, so if you want to be the first to hear Futaba's and Kou's voices, don't forget to reserve your copy! The deadline is 4/1/2014. I hope you'll enjoy it. ○

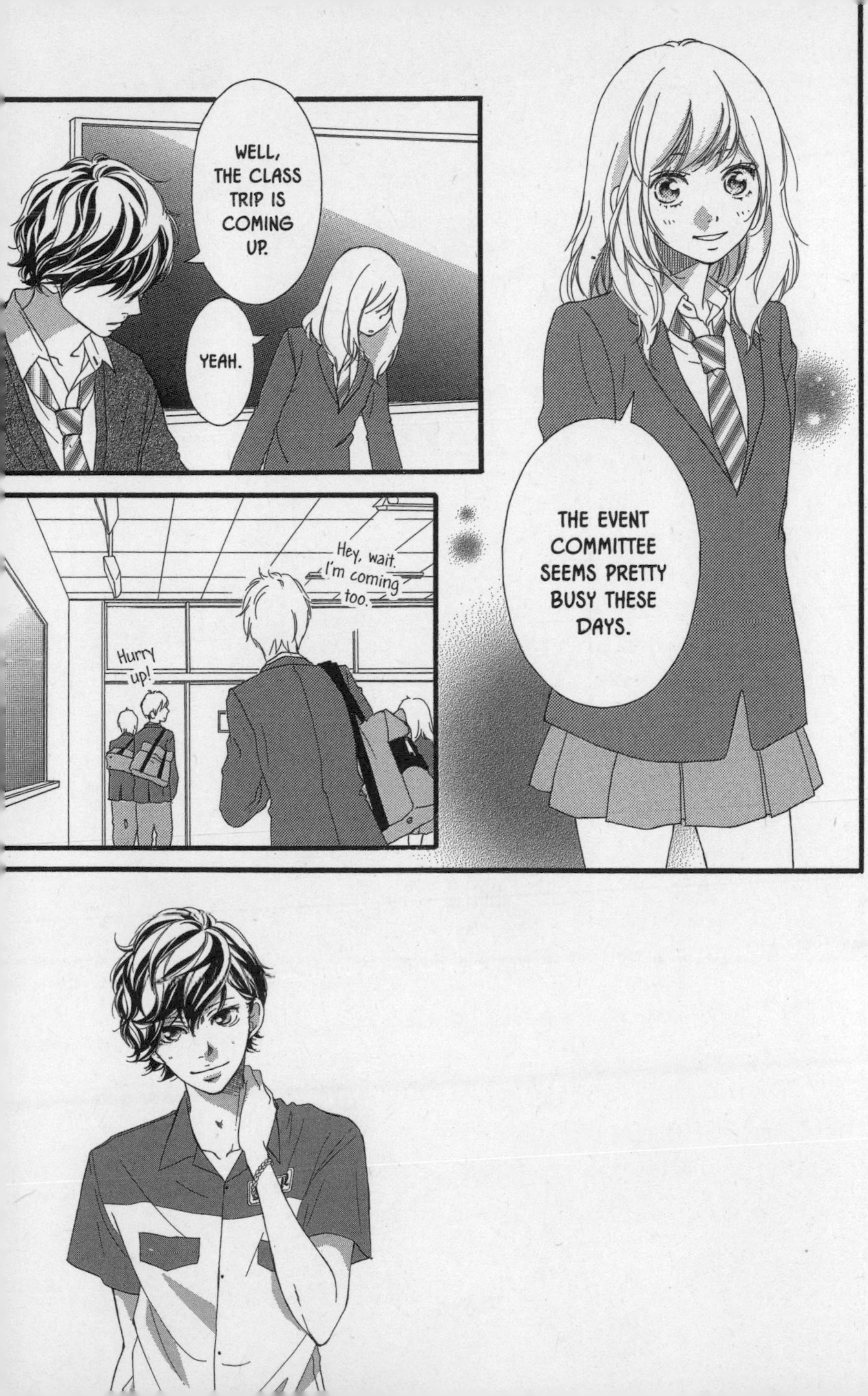
THE EVENT COMMITTEE SEEMS PRETTY BUSY THESE DAYS.
WELL, THE CLASS TRIP IS COMING UP.
YEAH.
Hey, wait. I'm coming too.
Hurry up!

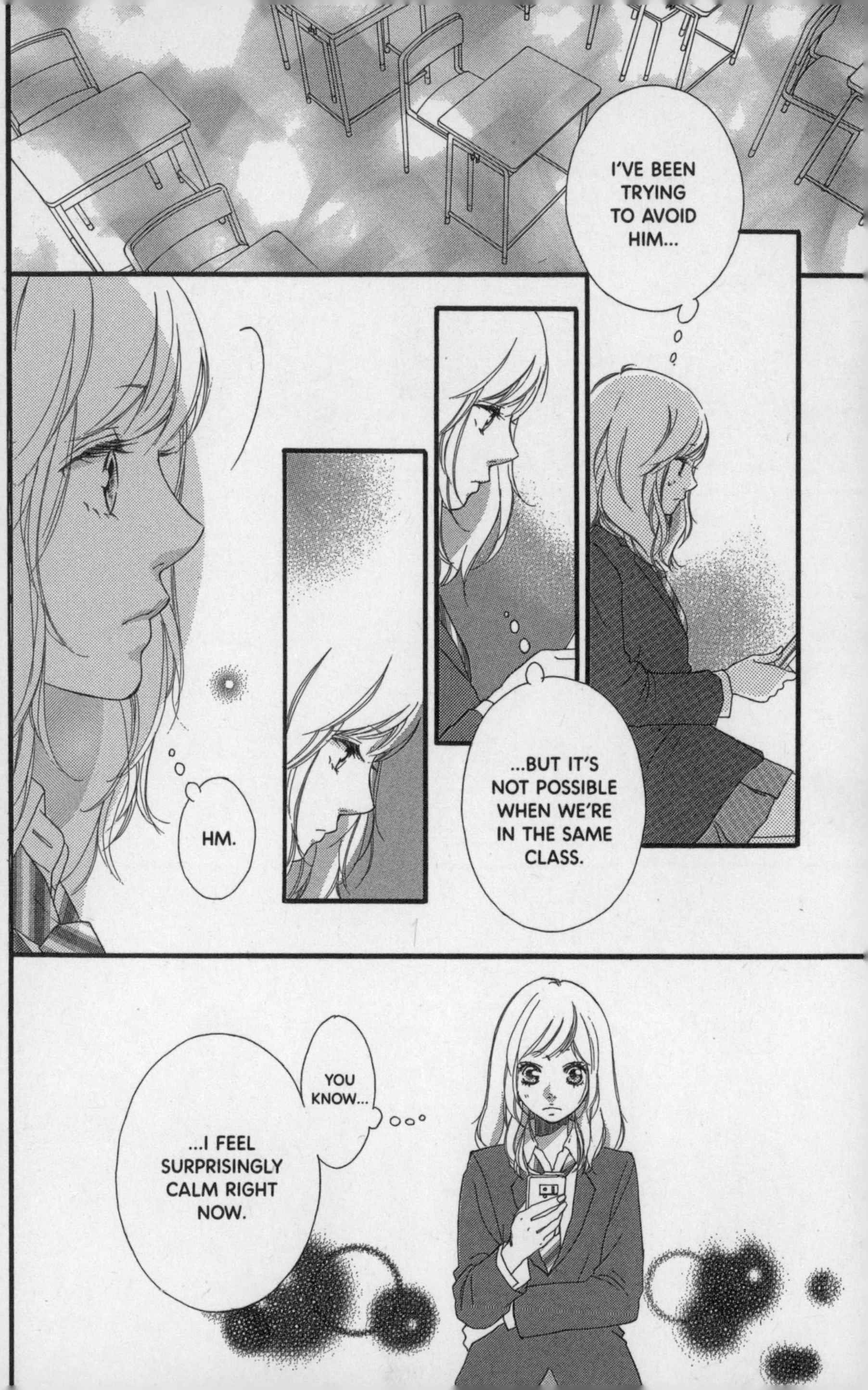
I'VE BEEN TRYING TO AVOID HIM...
...BUT IT'S NOT POSSIBLE WHEN WE'RE IN THE SAME CLASS.
HM.
YOU KNOW...
...I FEEL SURPRISINGLY CALM RIGHT NOW.

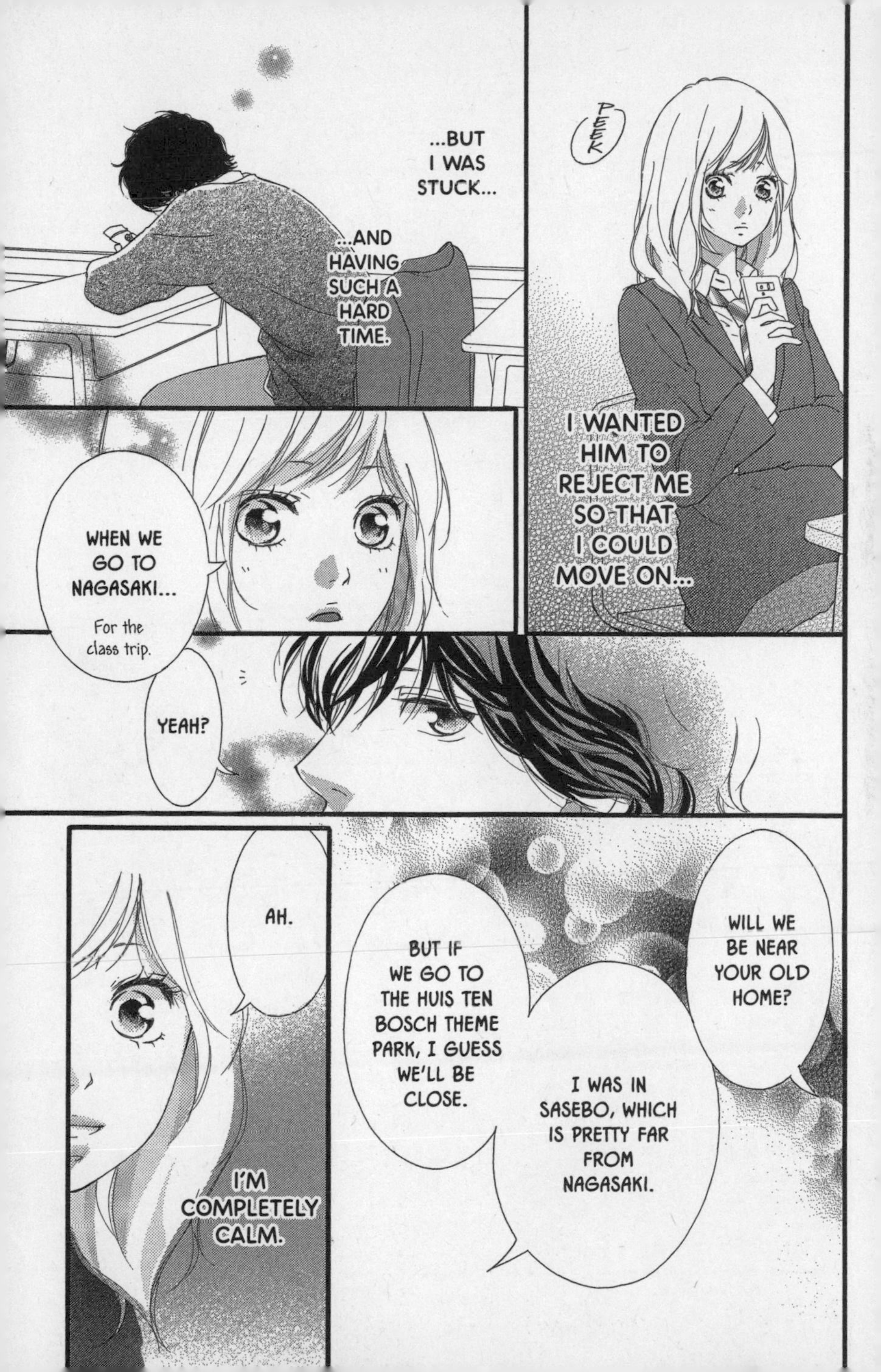
PEEK
I WANTED HIM TO REJECT ME SO THAT I COULD MOVE ON...
...BUT I WAS STUCK...
...AND HAVING SUCH A HARD TIME.
WHEN WE GO TO NAGASAKI...
For the class trip.
YEAH?
WILL WE BE NEAR YOUR OLD HOME?
I WAS IN SASEBO, WHICH IS PRETTY FAR FROM NAGASAKI.
BUT IF WE GO TO THE HUIS TEN BOSCH THEME PARK, I GUESS WE'LL BE CLOSE.
AH.
I'M COMPLETELY CALM.

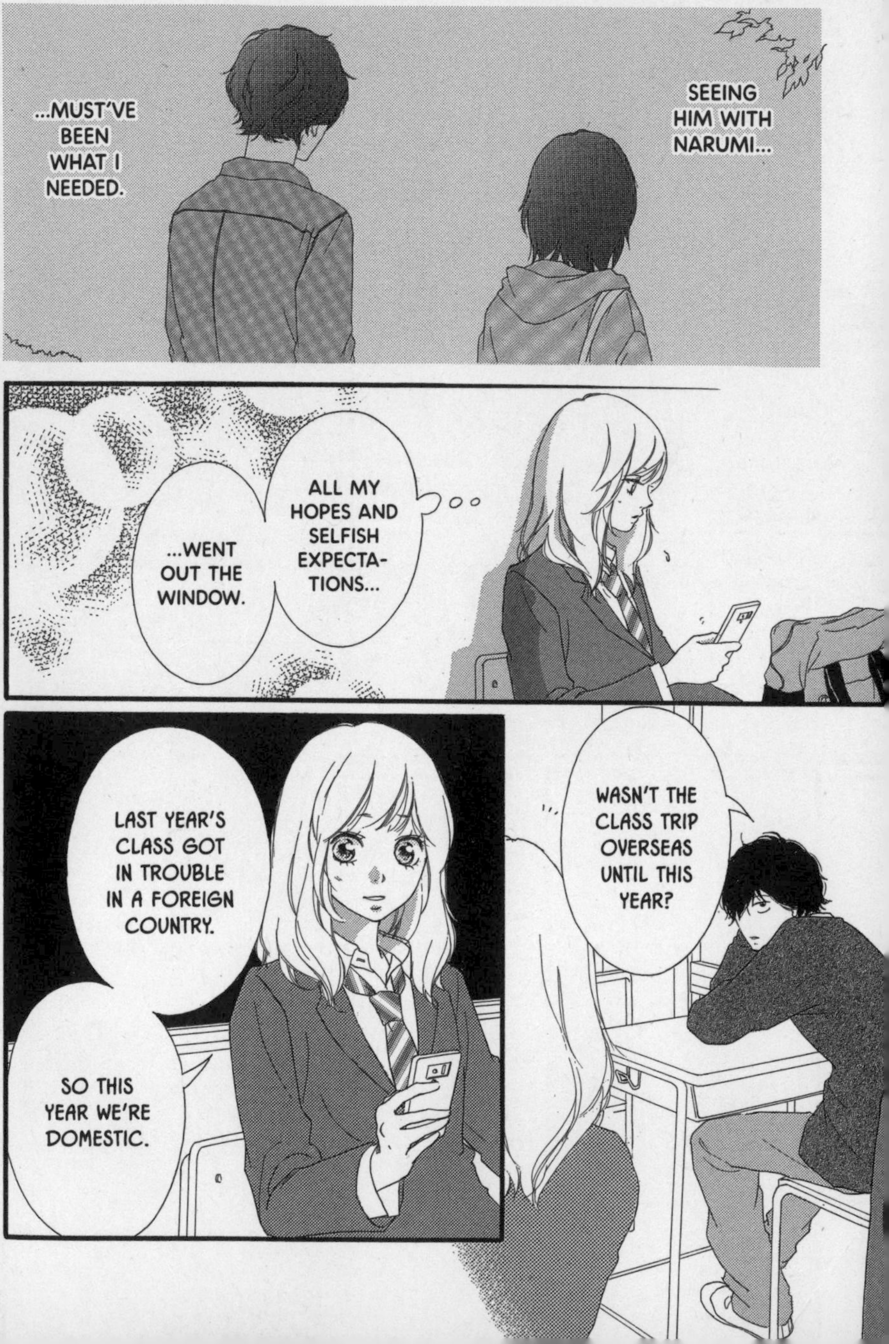
SEEING HIM WITH NARUMI...
...MUST'VE BEEN WHAT I NEEDED.
ALL MY HOPES AND SELFISH EXPECTATIONS...
...WENT OUT THE WINDOW.
WASN'T THE CLASS TRIP OVERSEAS UNTIL THIS YEAR?
LAST YEAR'S CLASS GOT IN TROUBLE IN A FOREIGN COUNTRY.
SO THIS YEAR WE'RE DOMESTIC.

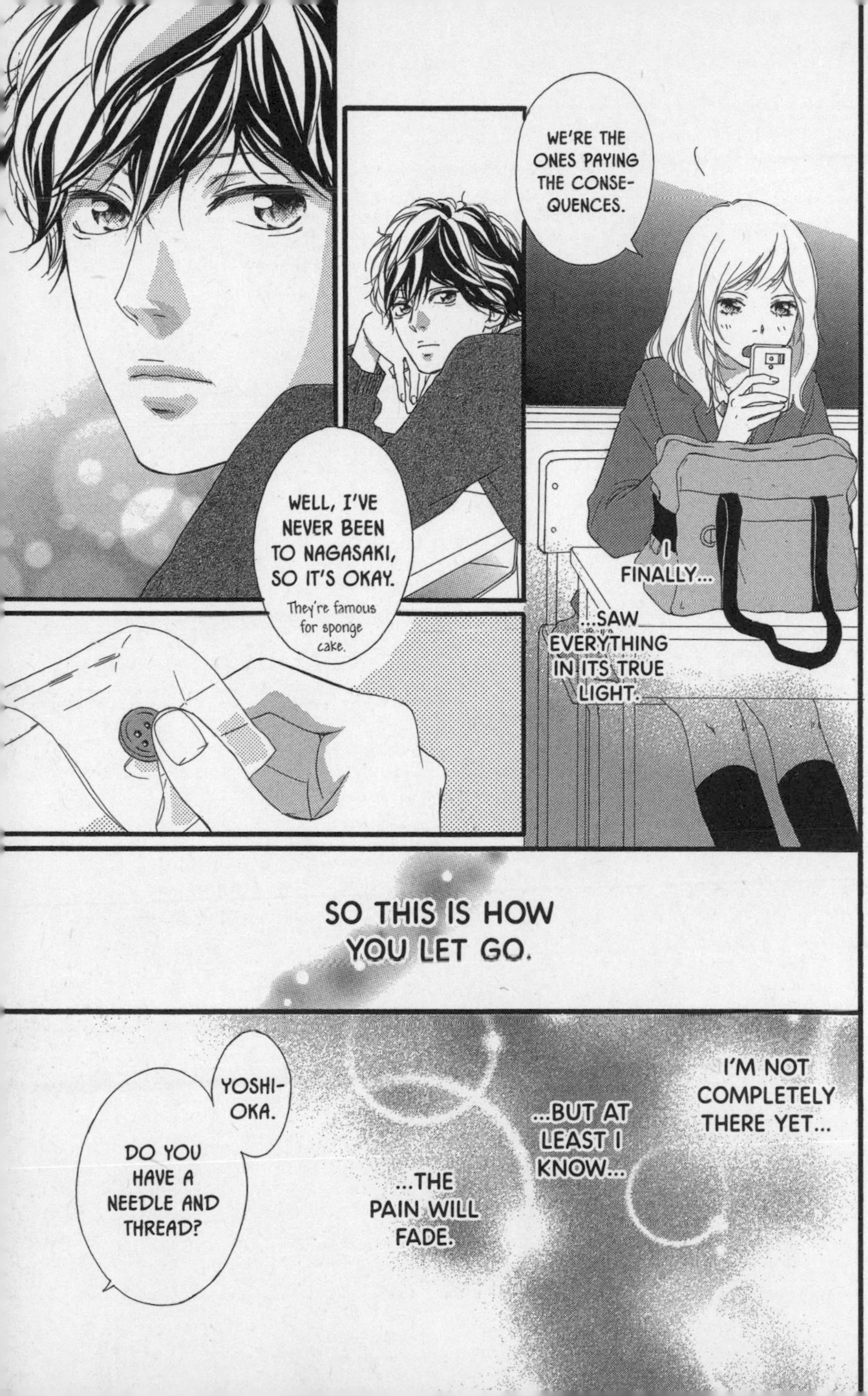
WE'RE THE ONES PAYING THE CONSE-QUENCES.
I FINALLY...
...SAW EVERYTHING IN ITS TRUE LIGHT.
WELL, I'VE NEVER BEEN TO NAGASAKI, SO IT'S OKAY.
They're famous for sponge cake.
SO THIS IS HOW YOU LET GO.
I'M NOT COMPLETELY THERE YET...
...BUT AT LEAST I KNOW...
...THE PAIN WILL FADE.
YOSHI-OKA.
DO YOU HAVE A NEEDLE AND THREAD?

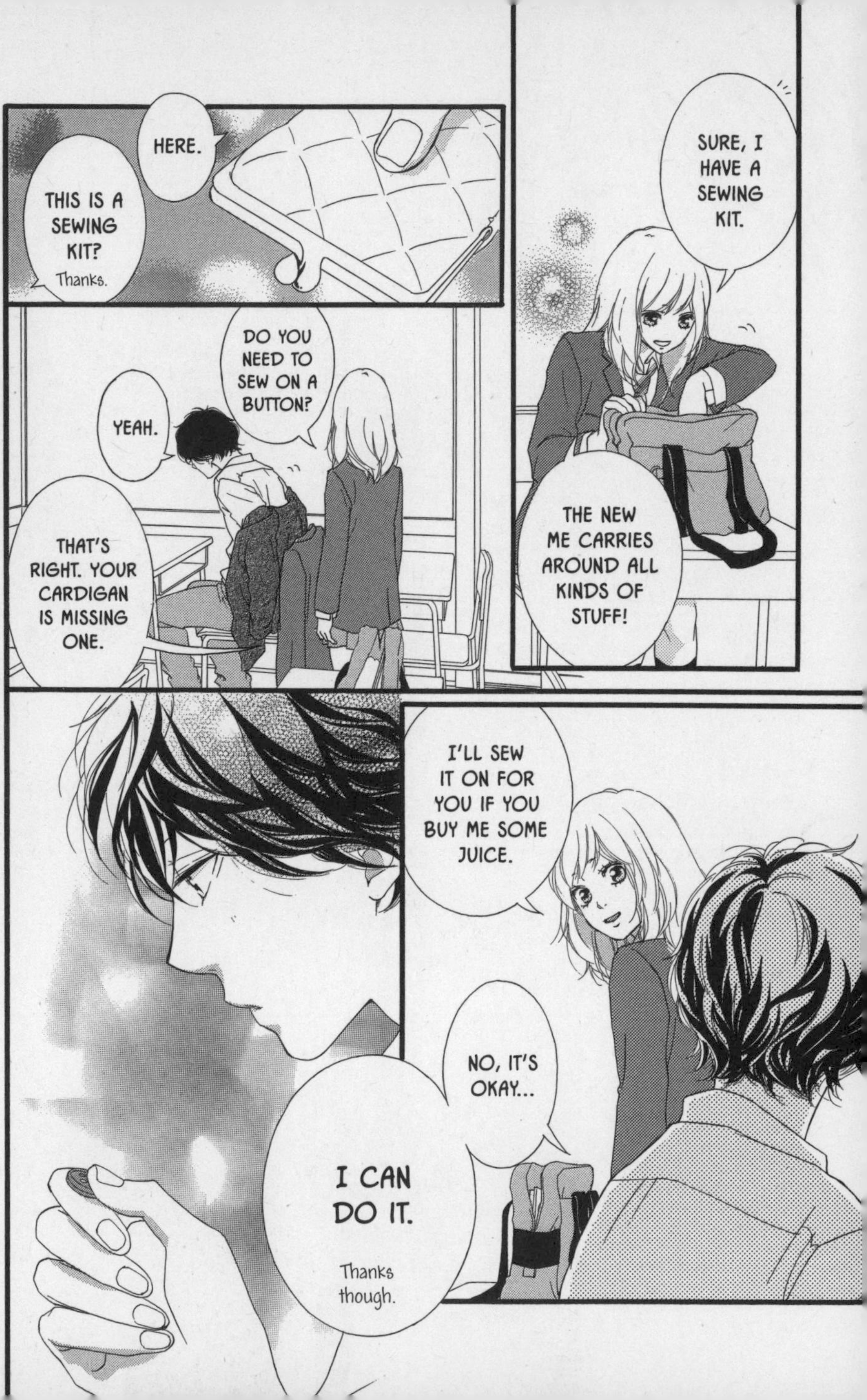
SURE, I HAVE A SEWING KIT.
THE NEW ME CARRIES AROUND ALL KINDS OF STUFF!
HERE.
THIS IS A SEWING KIT?
Thanks.
DO YOU NEED TO SEW ON A BUTTON?
YEAH.
THAT'S RIGHT. YOUR CARDIGAN IS MISSING ONE.
I'LL SEW IT ON FOR YOU IF YOU BUY ME SOME JUICE.
NO, IT'S OKAY...
I CAN DO IT.
Thanks though.

When I'm behind on a manuscript, I often don't have the time or energy to eat. I eat because I know I'll need the energy to keep going, but my eating habits are pretty awful. White rice with dried seasonings sprinkled on top is about as good as it gets when I'm up against a deadline. But sometimes I can't be bothered with the seasoning, so I just pour soy sauce on and eat that. As I was telling my assistants about my awful eating habits, S turned and said, "I do that too! It tastes like sushi!" I was shocked that she could think plain rice without fish was like sushi. I can only think she has unlimited imaginative potential. Meanwhile, my other assistant F looked at us completely bewildered and said, "Seriously?" Yes, F, yes. Your reaction was absolutely appropriate. A few days later, F, with her cute little voice and wide eyes, announced, "I tried soy sauce rice and it was good." I didn't expect her to try it. I'm sorry for bringing her into this.

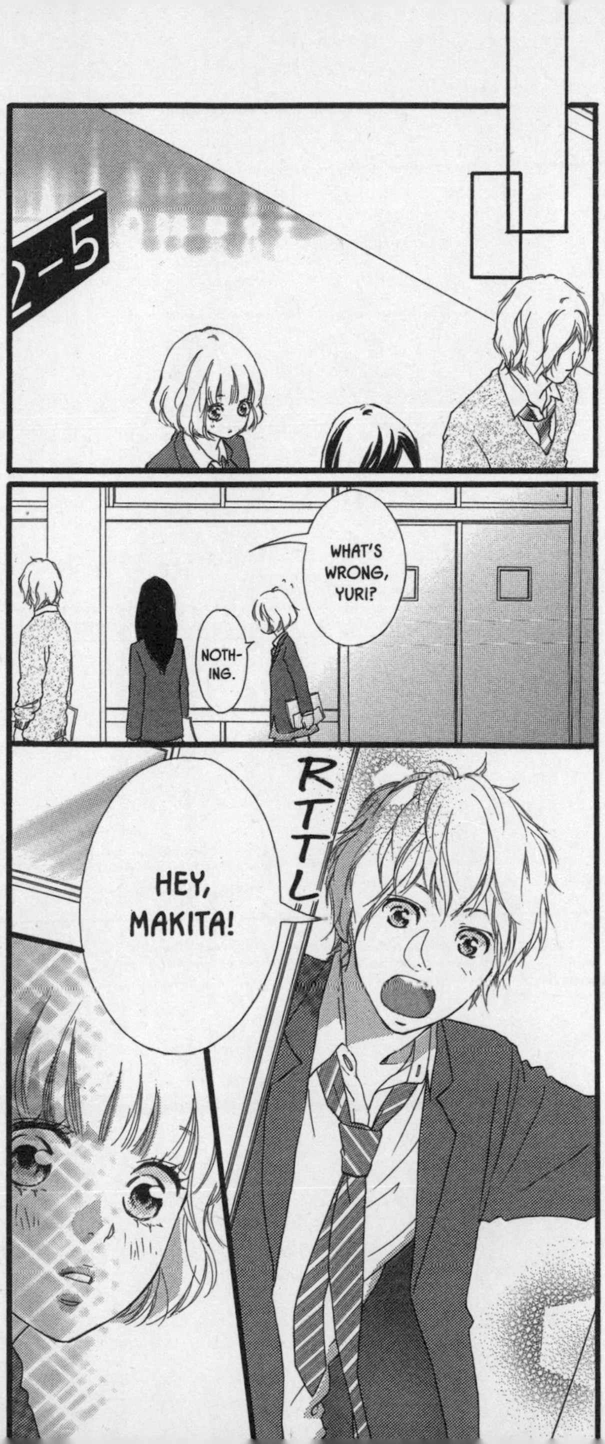
2-5
WHAT'S WRONG, YURI?
NOTHING.
RTTL
HEY, MAKITA!

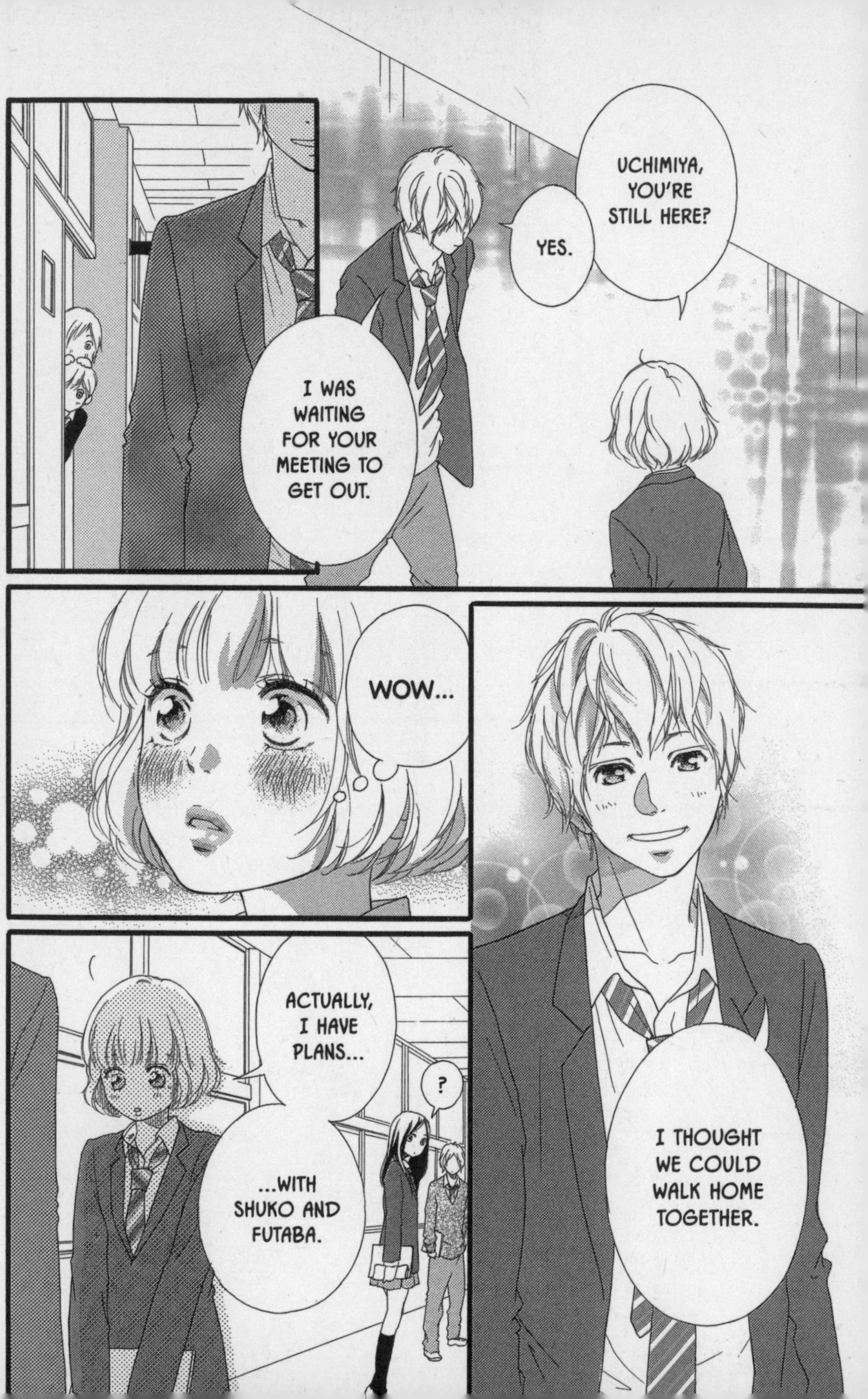
UCHIMIYA, YOU'RE STILL HERE?
YES.
I WAS WAITING FOR YOUR MEETING TO GET OUT.
I THOUGHT WE COULD WALK HOME TOGETHER.
WOW...
ACTUALLY, I HAVE PLANS...
?
...WITH SHUKO AND FUTABA.

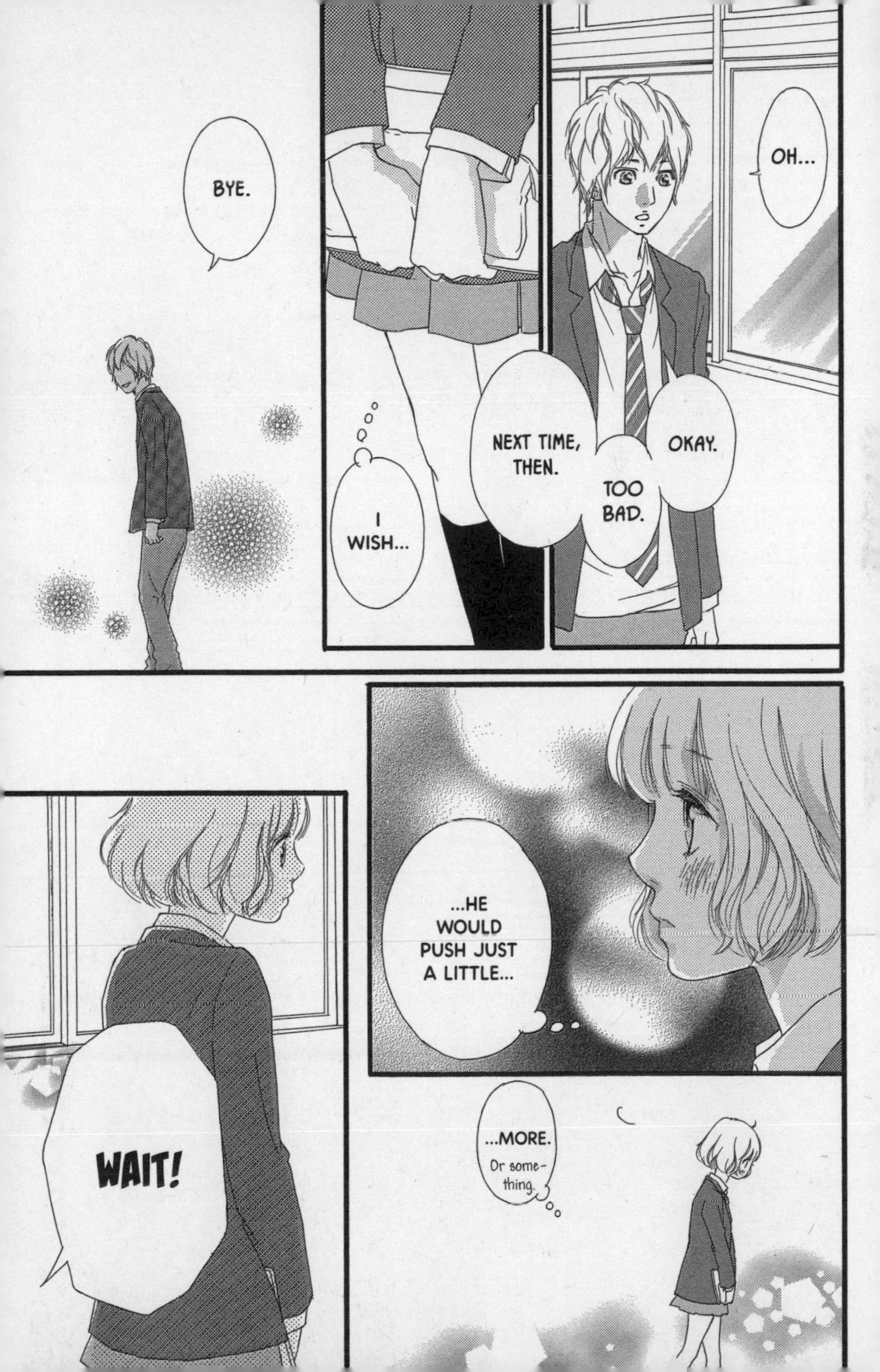
OH...
OKAY.
TOO BAD.
NEXT TIME, THEN.
I WISH...
BYE.
...HE WOULD PUSH JUST A LITTLE...
...MORE.
Or something.
WAIT!

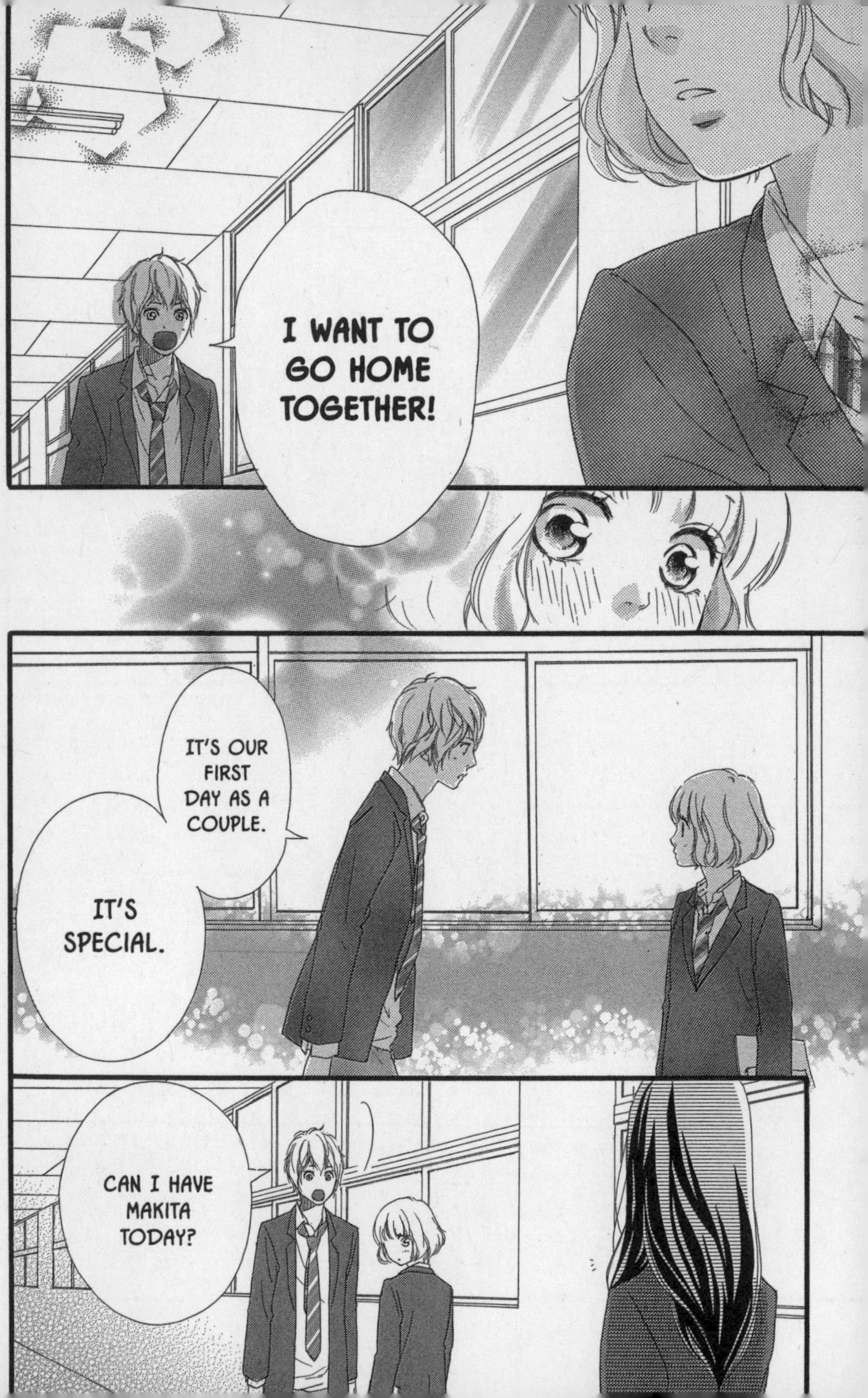
I WANT TO GO HOME TOGETHER!
IT'S OUR FIRST DAY AS A COUPLE.
IT'S SPECIAL.
CAN I HAVE MAKITA TODAY?

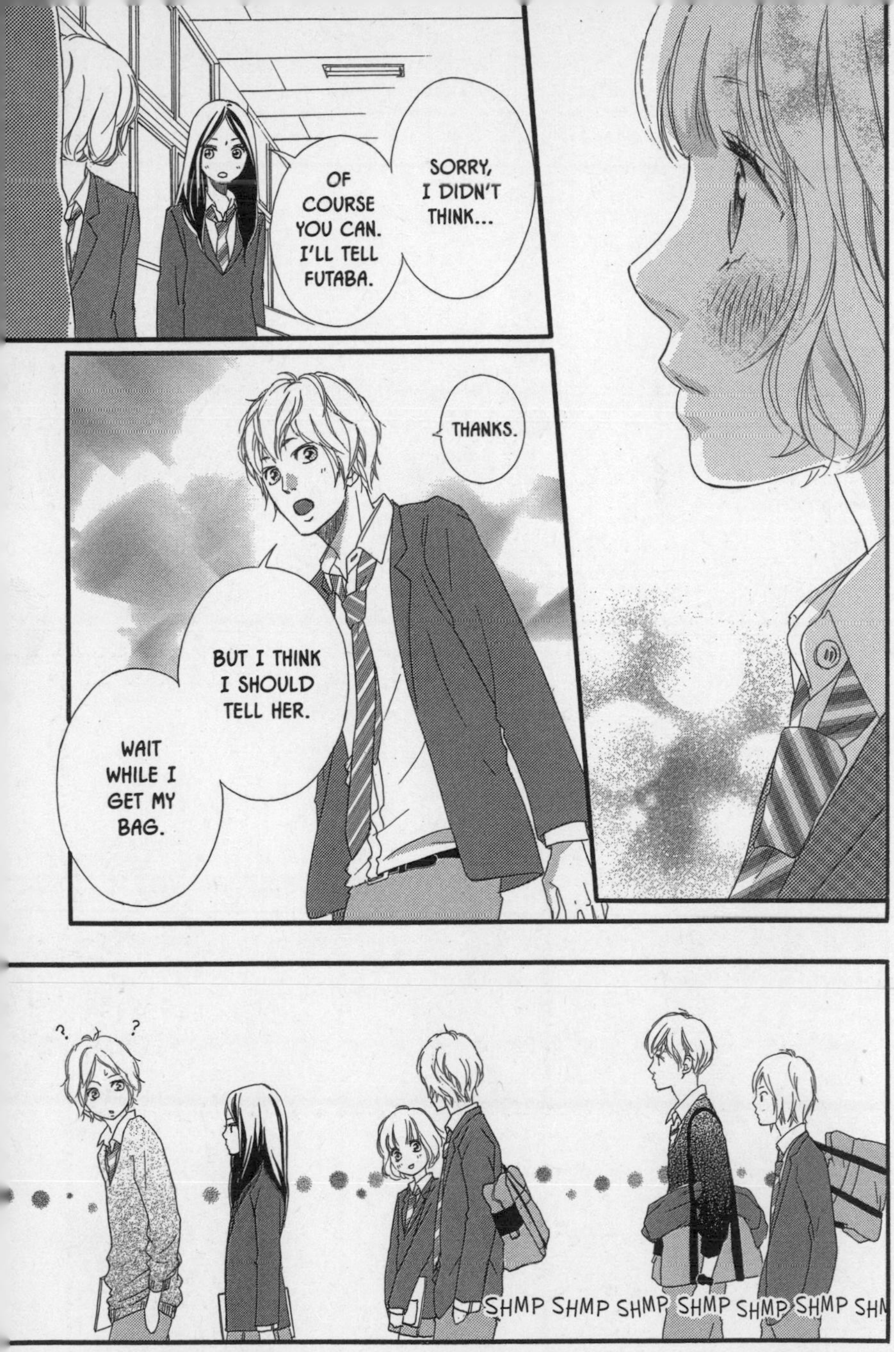
SORRY, I DIDN'T THINK...
OF COURSE YOU CAN. I'LL TELL FUTABA.
THANKS.
BUT I THINK I SHOULD TELL HER.
WAIT WHILE I GET MY BAG.
SHMP SHMP SHMP SHMP SHMP SHMP SHM

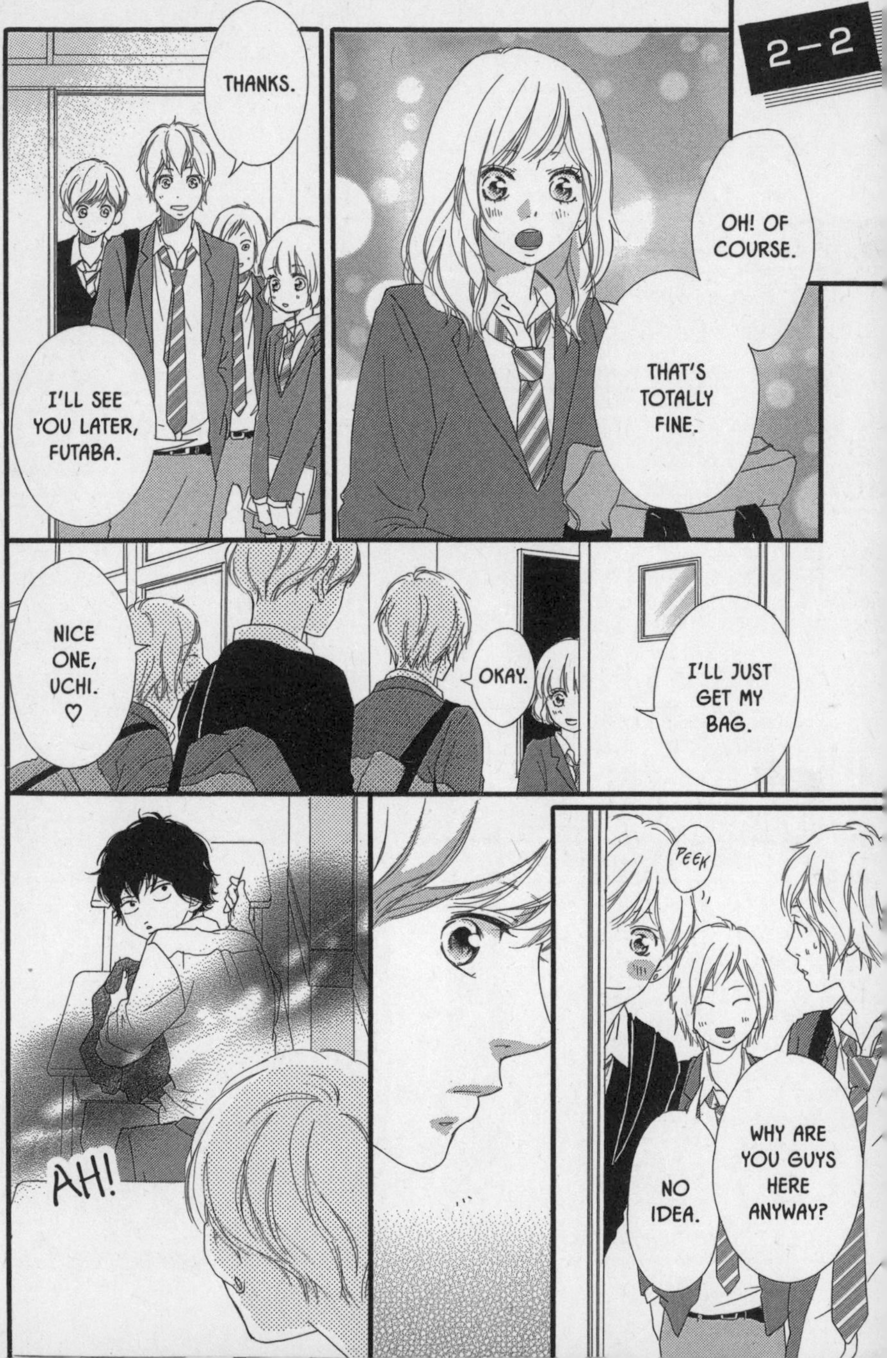
2-2
OH! OF COURSE.
THAT'S TOTALLY FINE.
THANKS.
I'LL SEE YOU LATER, FUTABA.
I'LL JUST GET MY BAG.
OKAY.
NICE ONE, UCHI. ♡
PEEK
WHY ARE YOU GUYS HERE ANYWAY?
NO IDEA.
AH!

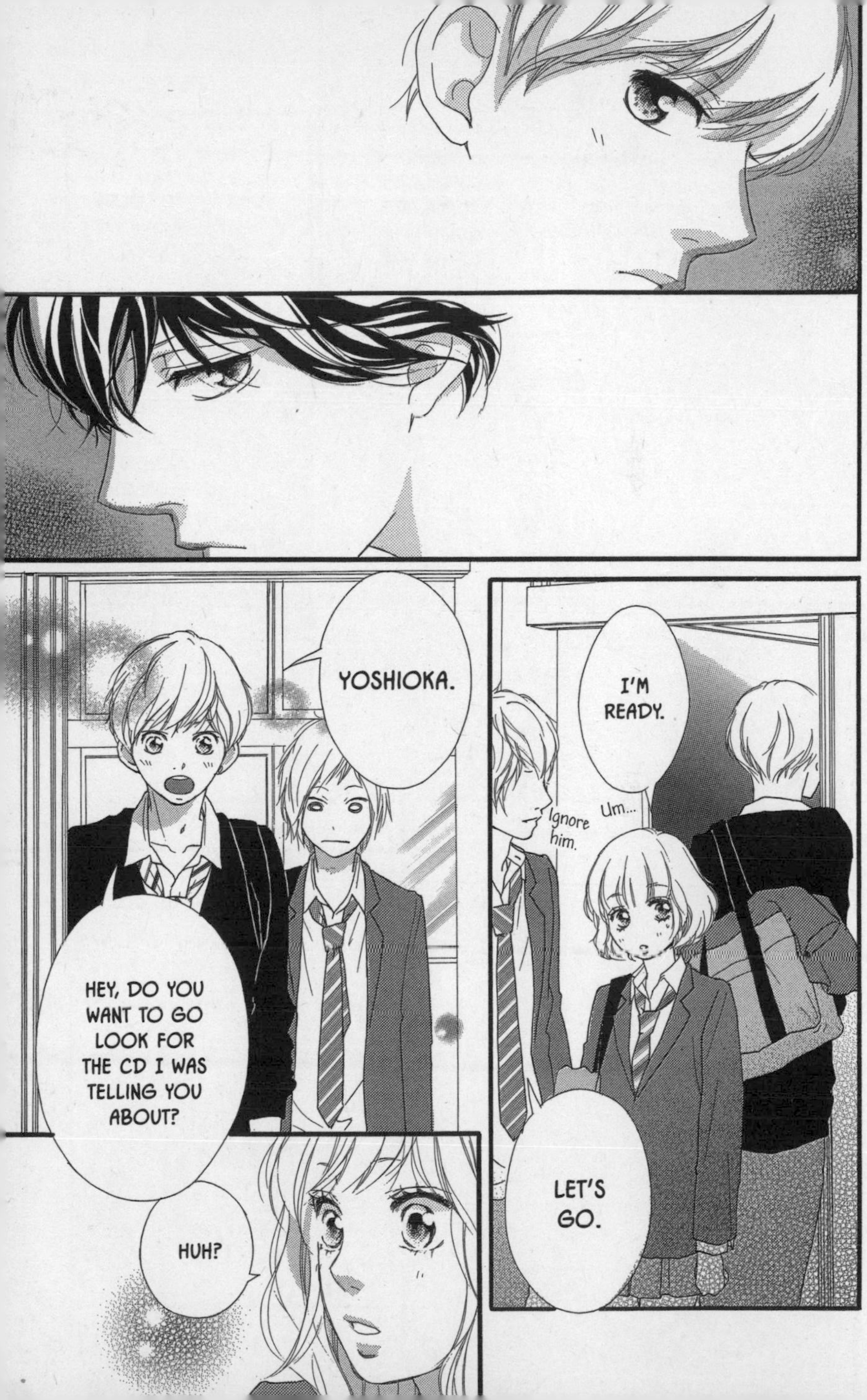
I'M READY.
Um...
Ignore him.
LET'S GO.
YOSHIOKA.
HEY, DO YOU WANT TO GO LOOK FOR THE CD I WAS TELLING YOU ABOUT?
HUH?

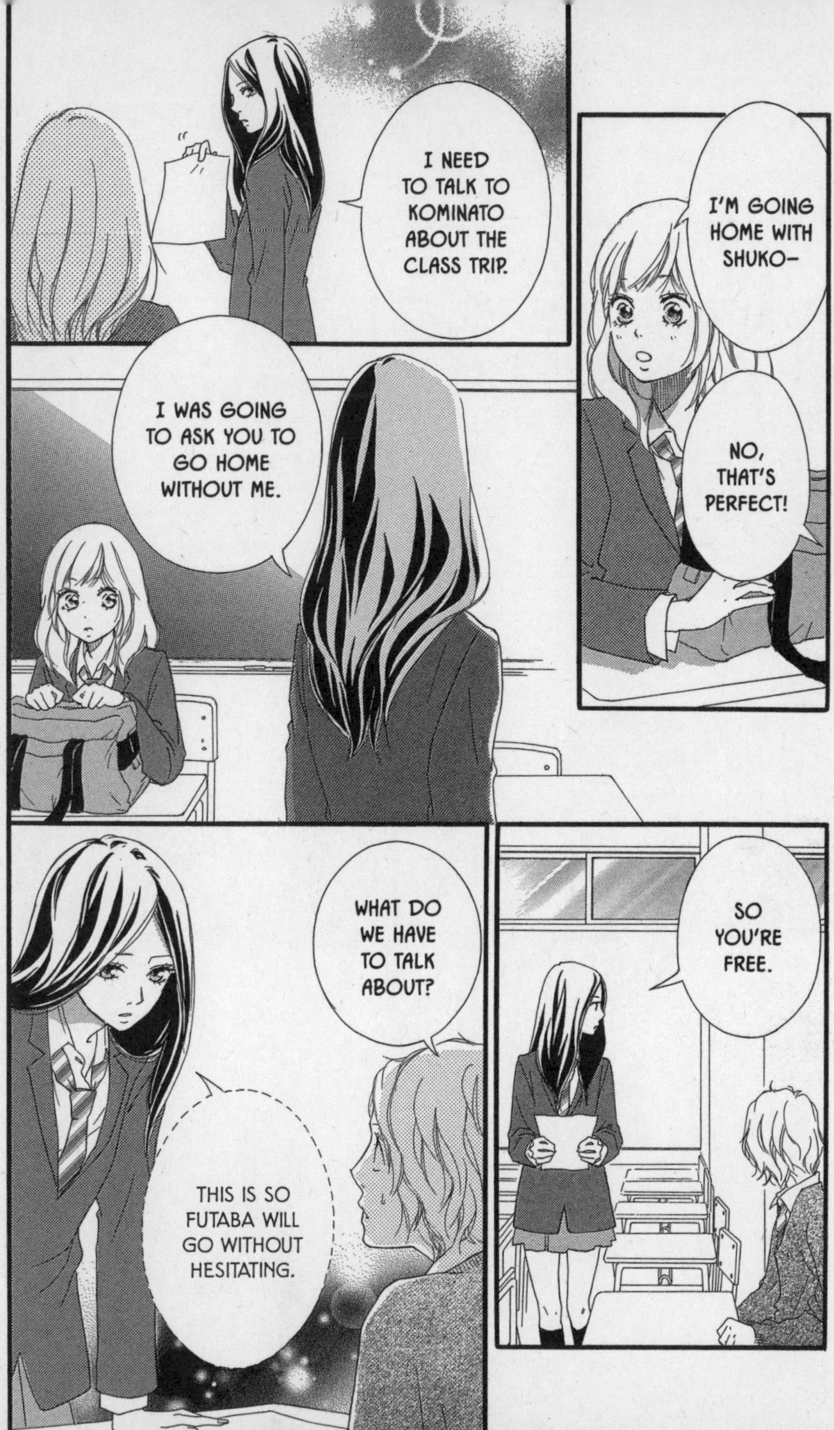
I'M GOING HOME WITH SHUKO-
NO, THAT'S PERFECT!
I NEED TO TALK TO KOMINATO ABOUT THE CLASS TRIP.
I WAS GOING TO ASK YOU TO GO HOME WITHOUT ME.
SO YOU'RE FREE.
WHAT DO WE HAVE TO TALK ABOUT?
THIS IS SO FUTABA WILL GO WITHOUT HESITATING.

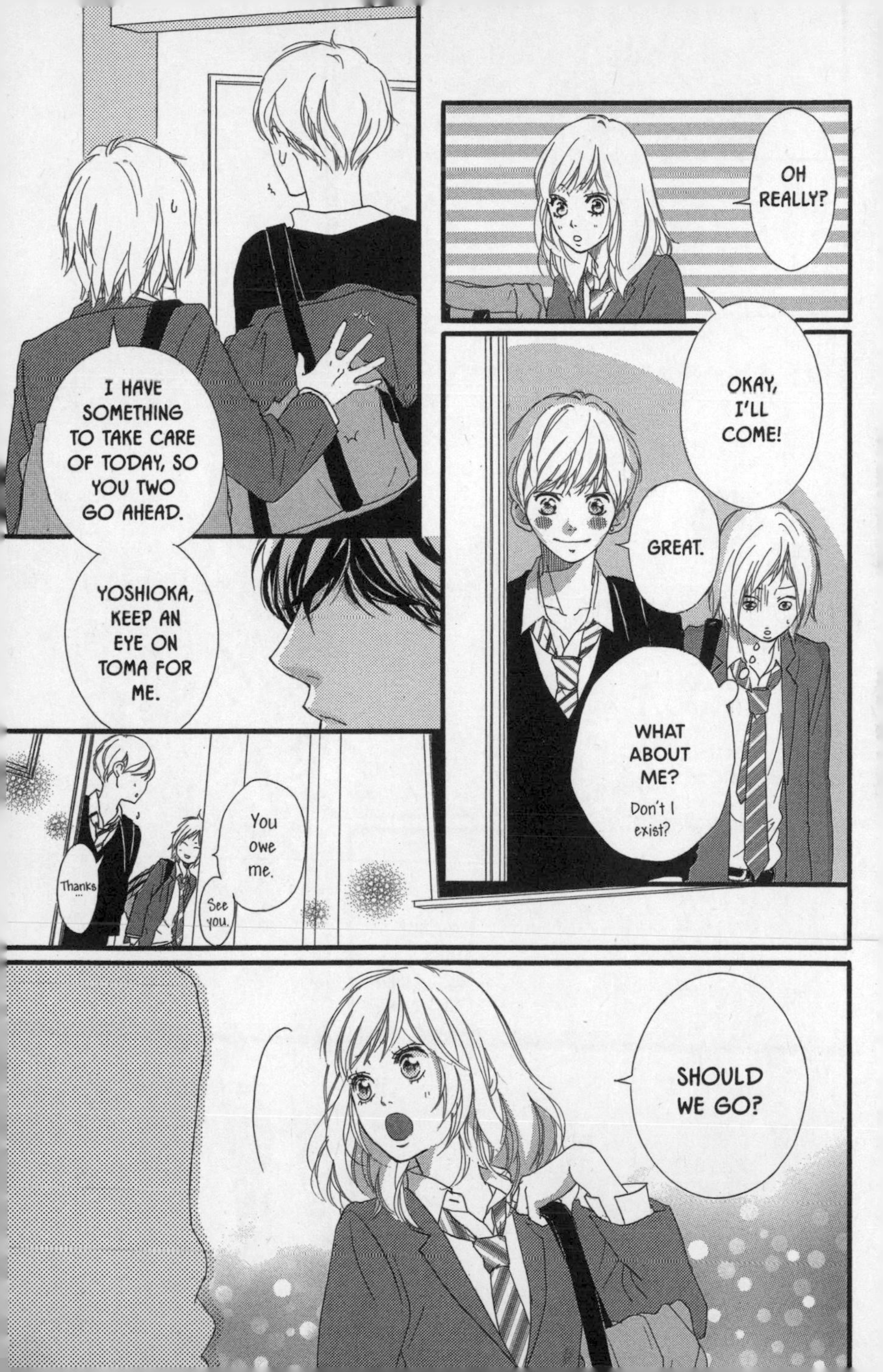
OH REALLY?
OKAY, I'LL COME!
GREAT.
WHAT ABOUT ME? Don't I exist?
I HAVE SOMETHING TO TAKE CARE OF TODAY, SO YOU TWO GO AHEAD.
YOSHIOKA, KEEP AN EYE ON TOMA FOR ME.
You owe me.
See you.
Thanks...
SHOULD WE GO?

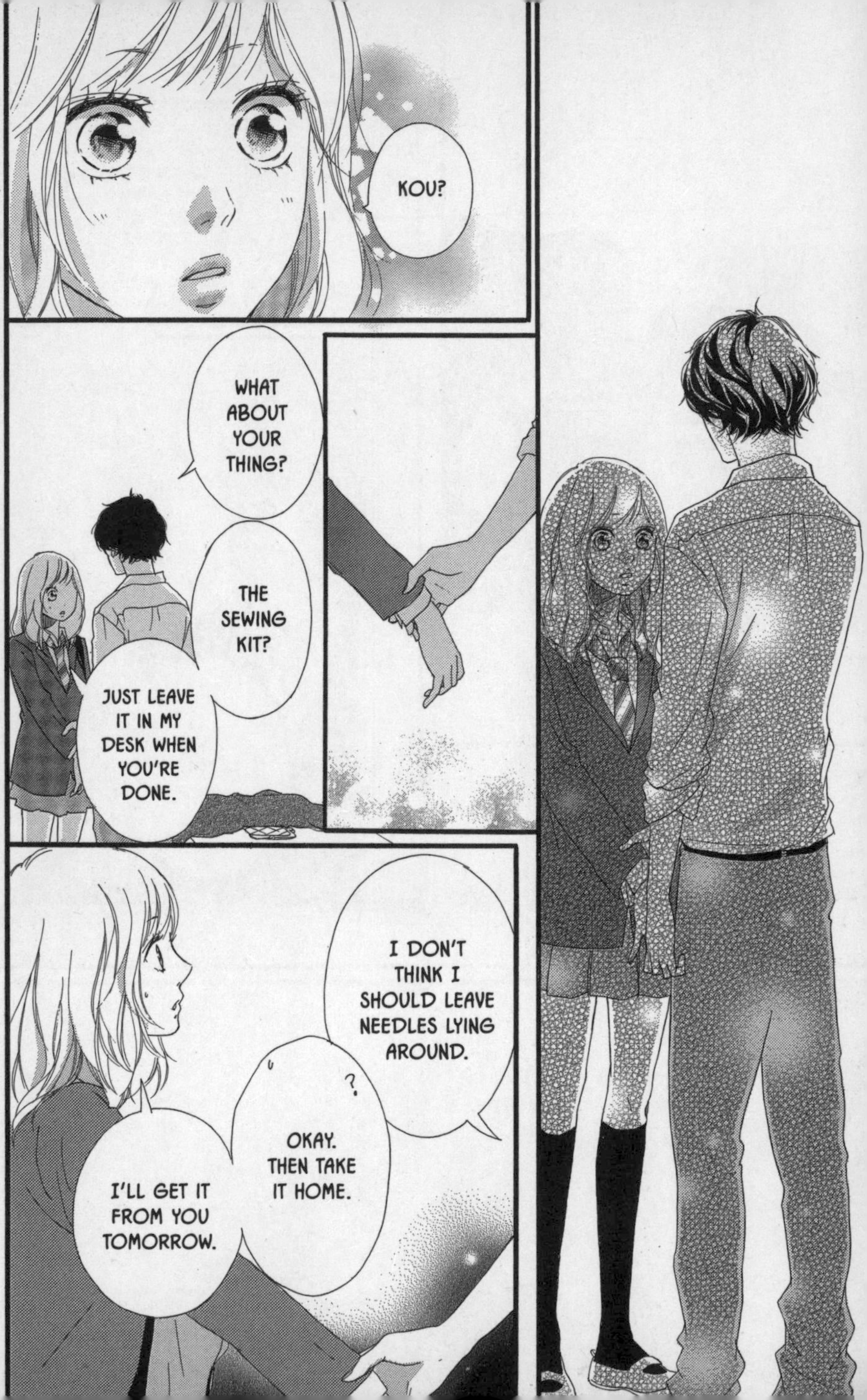
KOU?
WHAT ABOUT YOUR THING?
THE SEWING KIT?
JUST LEAVE IT IN MY DESK WHEN YOU'RE DONE.
I DON'T THINK I SHOULD LEAVE NEEDLES LYING AROUND.
OKAY. THEN TAKE IT HOME.
I'LL GET IT FROM YOU TOMORROW.

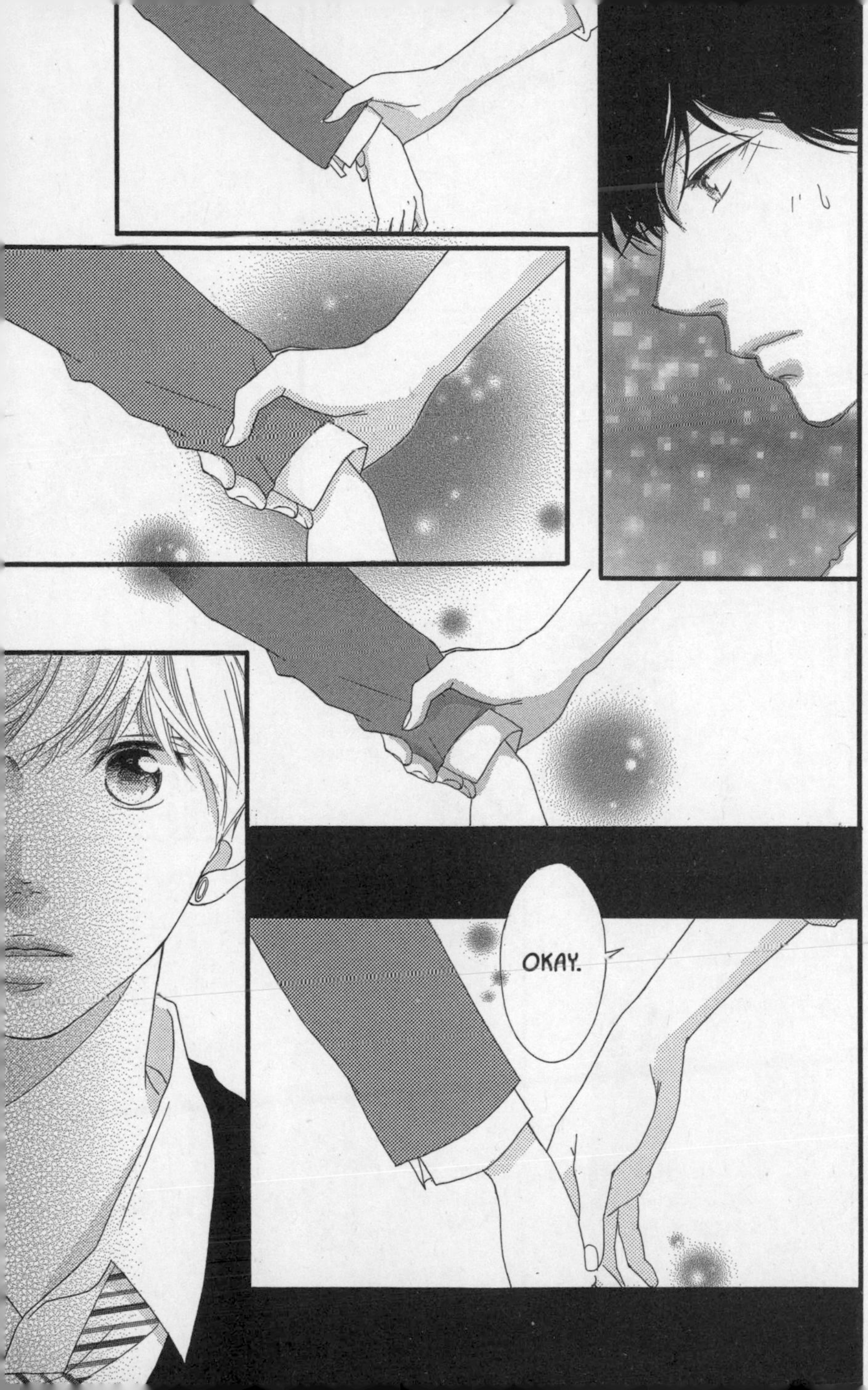
OKAY.

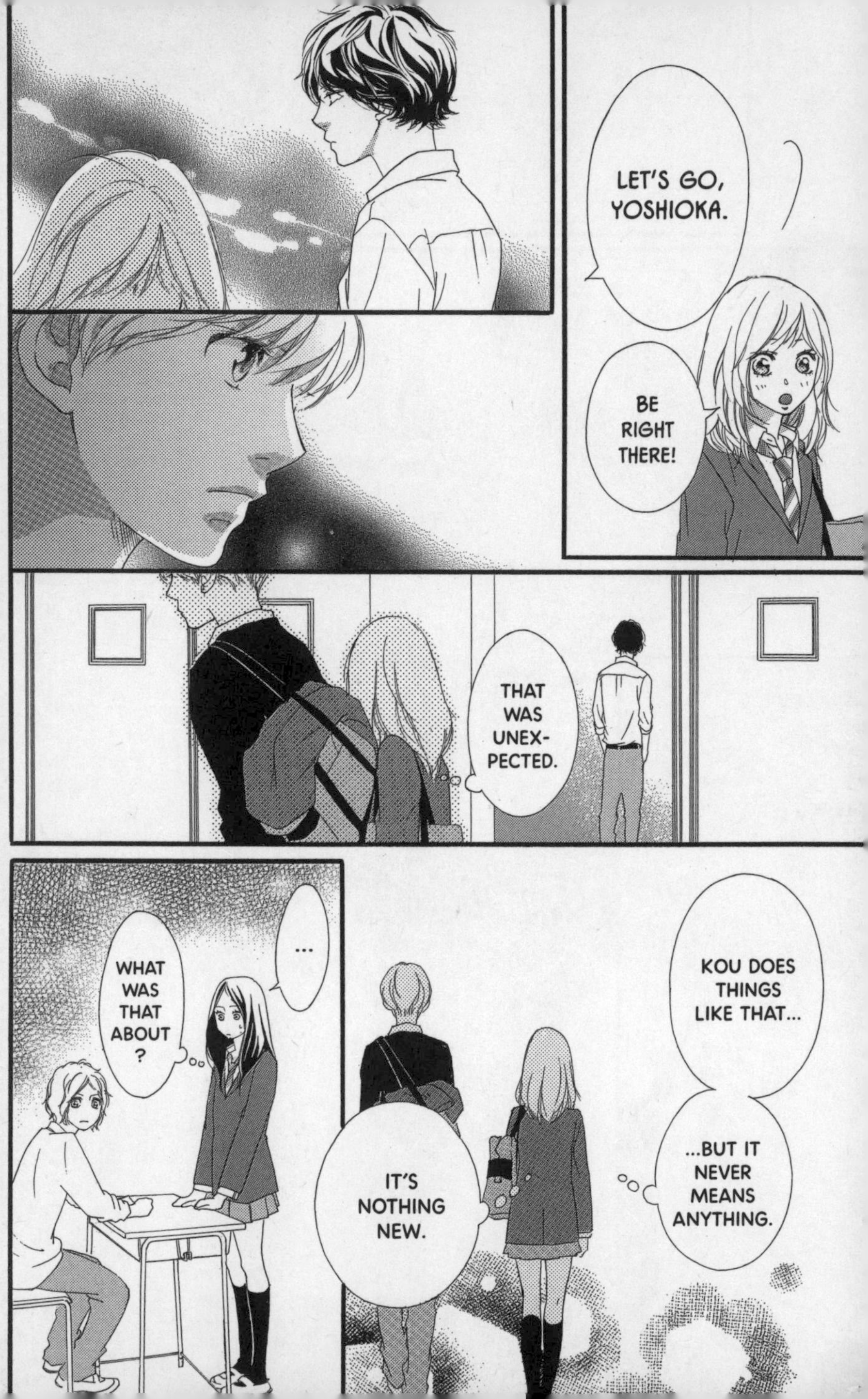
LET'S GO, YOSHIOKA.
BE RIGHT THERE!
THAT WAS UNEXPECTED.
KOU DOES THINGS LIKE THAT...
...BUT IT NEVER MEANS ANYTHING.
IT'S NOTHING NEW.
...
WHAT WAS THAT ABOUT?

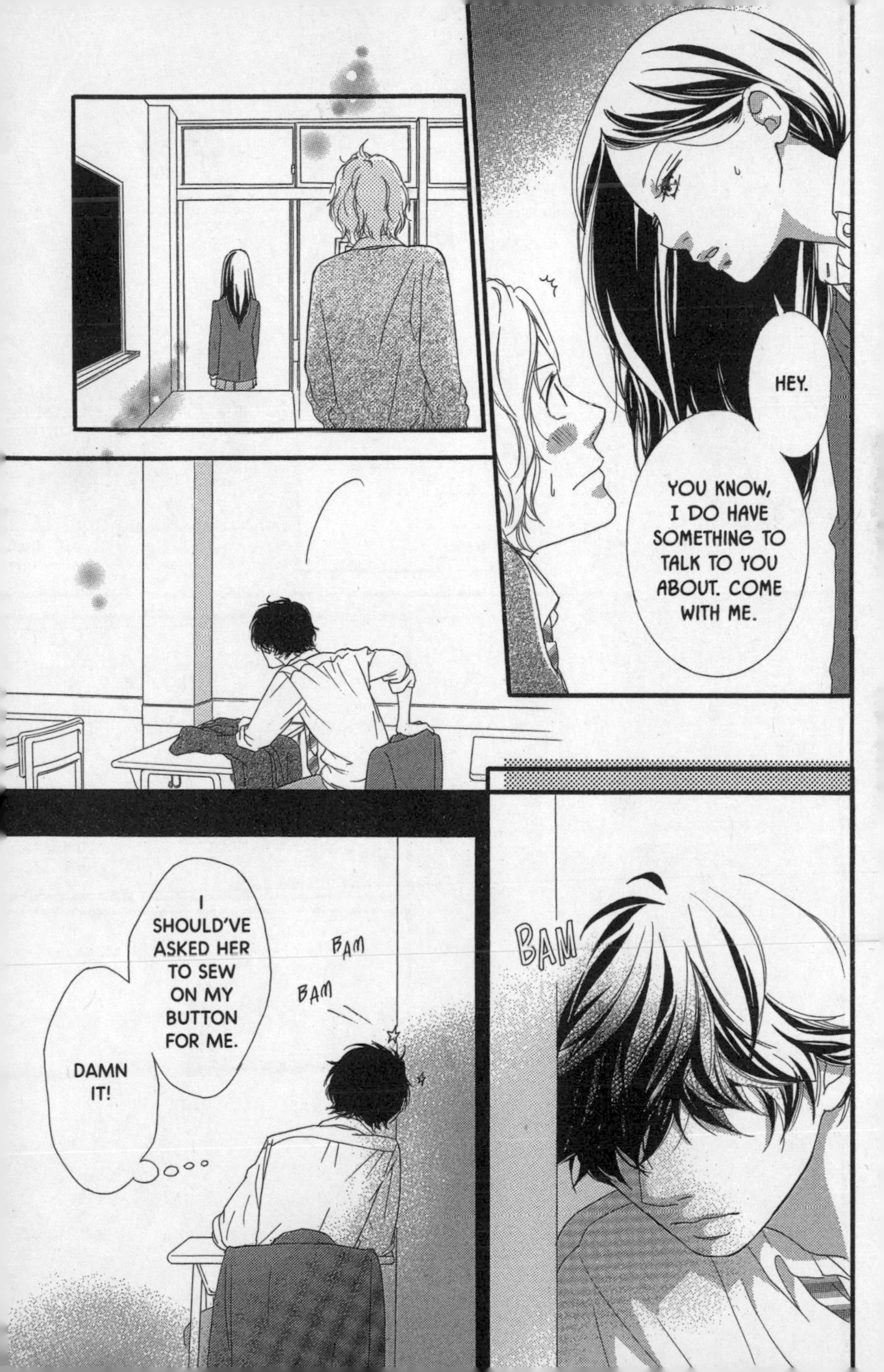
HEY.
YOU KNOW, I DO HAVE SOMETHING TO TALK TO YOU ABOUT. COME WITH ME.
BAM
I SHOULD'VE ASKED HER TO SEW ON MY BUTTON FOR ME.
BAM
BAM
DAMN IT!

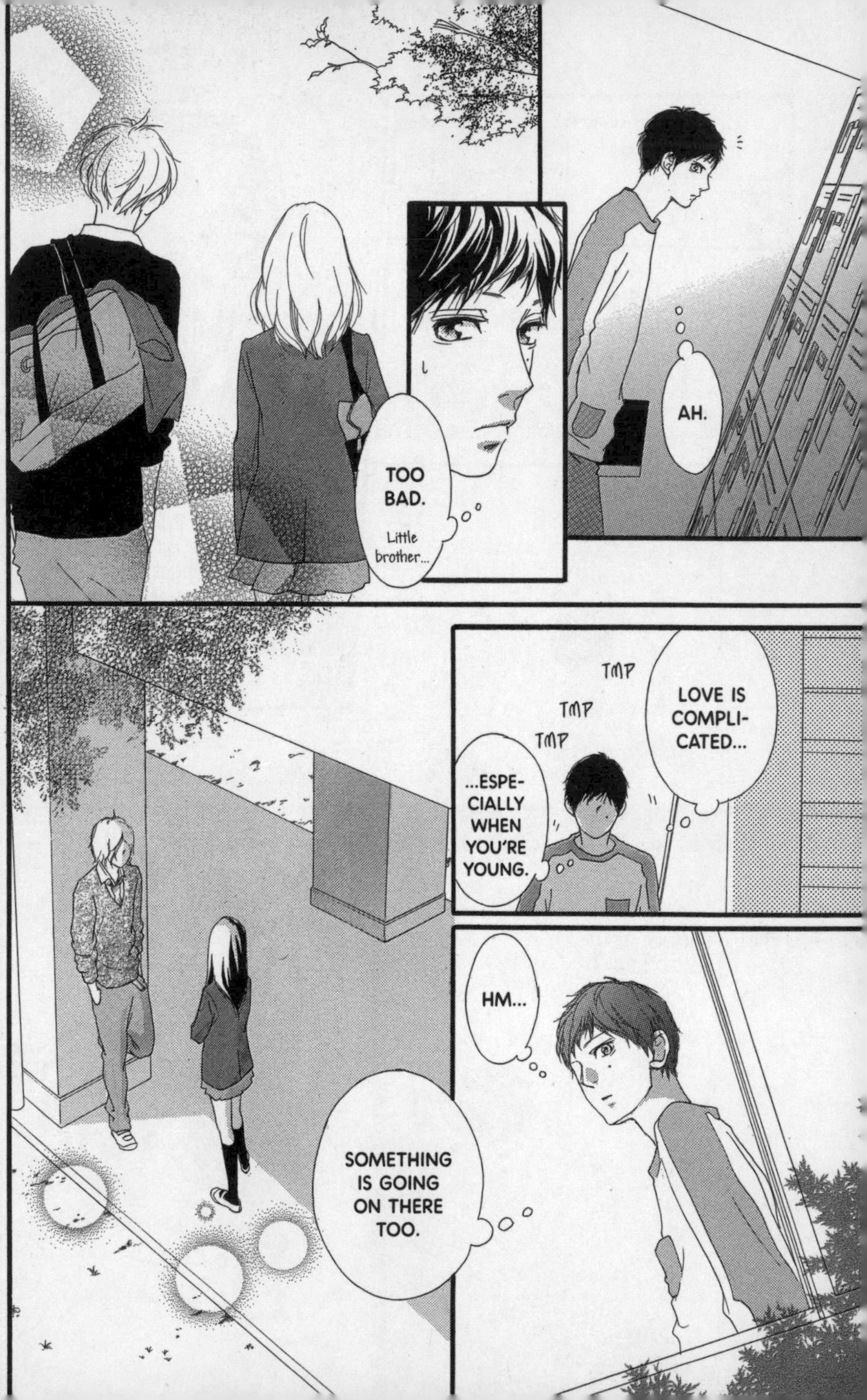
AH.
TOO BAD.
Little brother...
LOVE IS COMPLI-CATED...
TMP
TMP
TMP
...ESPE-CIALLY WHEN YOU'RE YOUNG.
HM...
SOMETHING IS GOING ON THERE TOO.

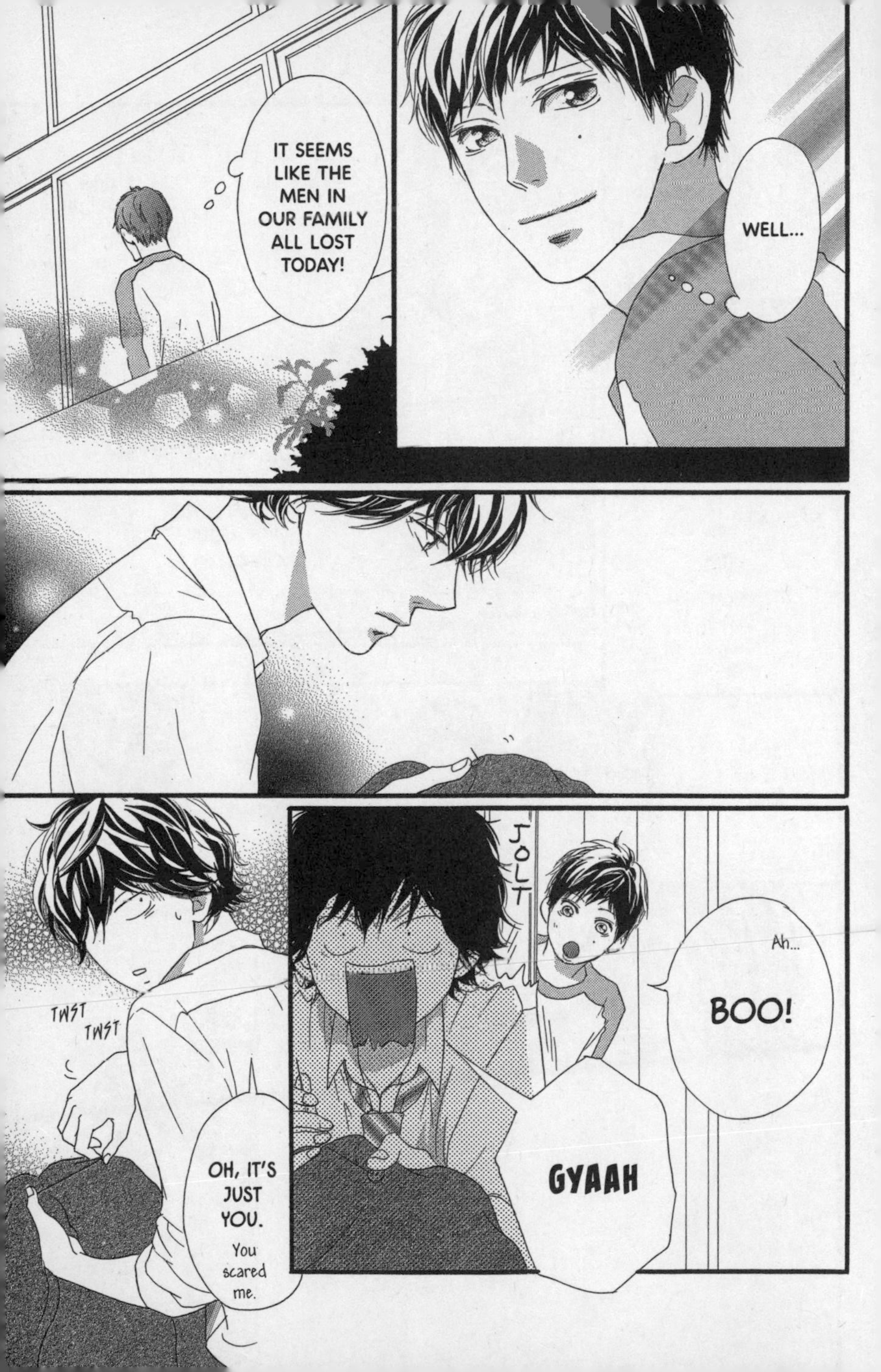
WELL...
IT SEEMS LIKE THE MEN IN OUR FAMILY ALL LOST TODAY!
Ah...
BOO!
JOLT
GYAAH
TWST TWST
OH, IT'S JUST YOU.
You scared me.

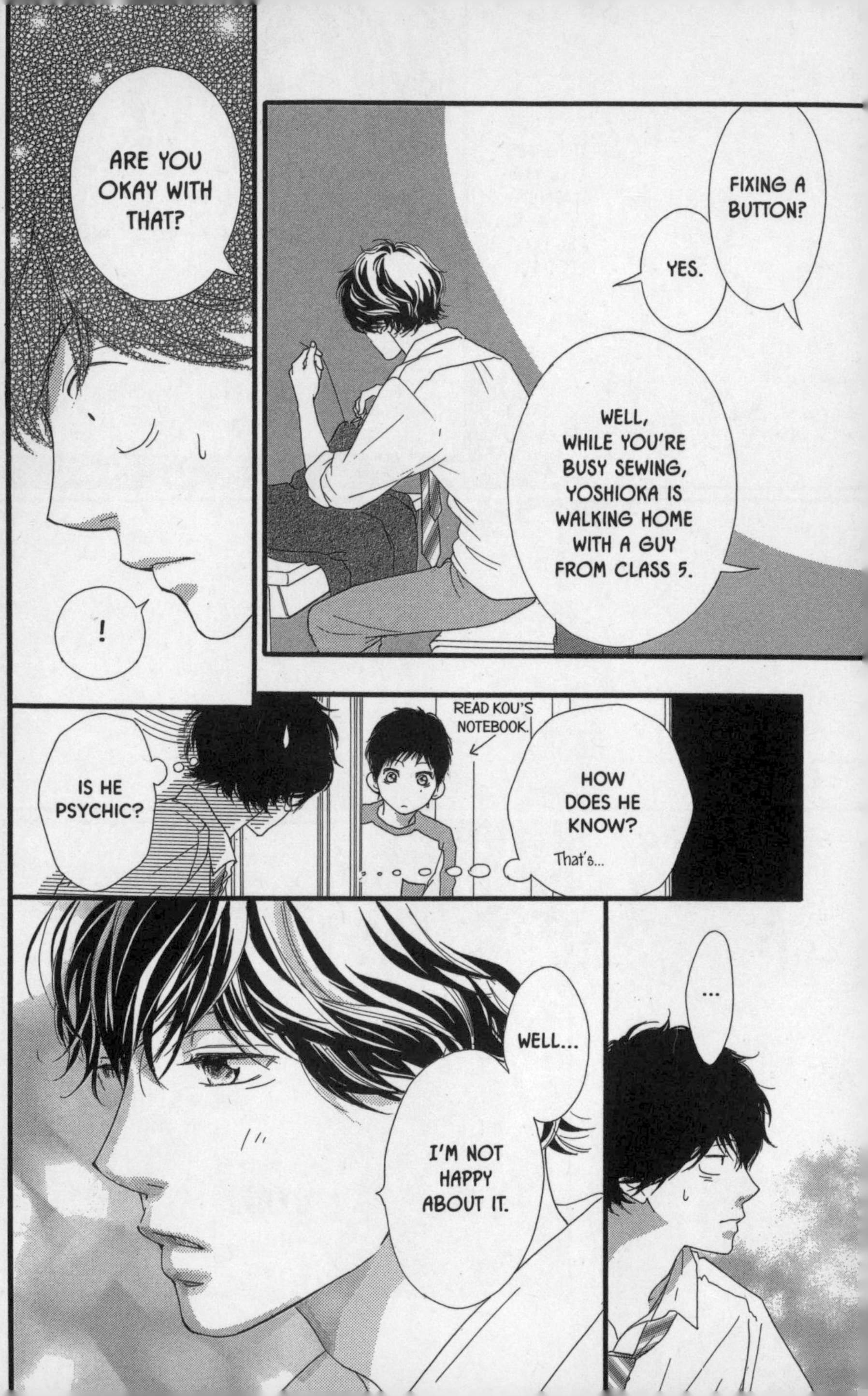
FIXING A BUTTON?
YES.
WELL, WHILE YOU'RE BUSY SEWING, YOSHIOKA IS WALKING HOME WITH A GUY FROM CLASS 5.
ARE YOU OKAY WITH THAT?
!
HOW DOES HE KNOW?
That's...
READ KOU'S NOTEBOOK.
IS HE PSYCHIC?
...
WELL...
I'M NOT HAPPY ABOUT IT.

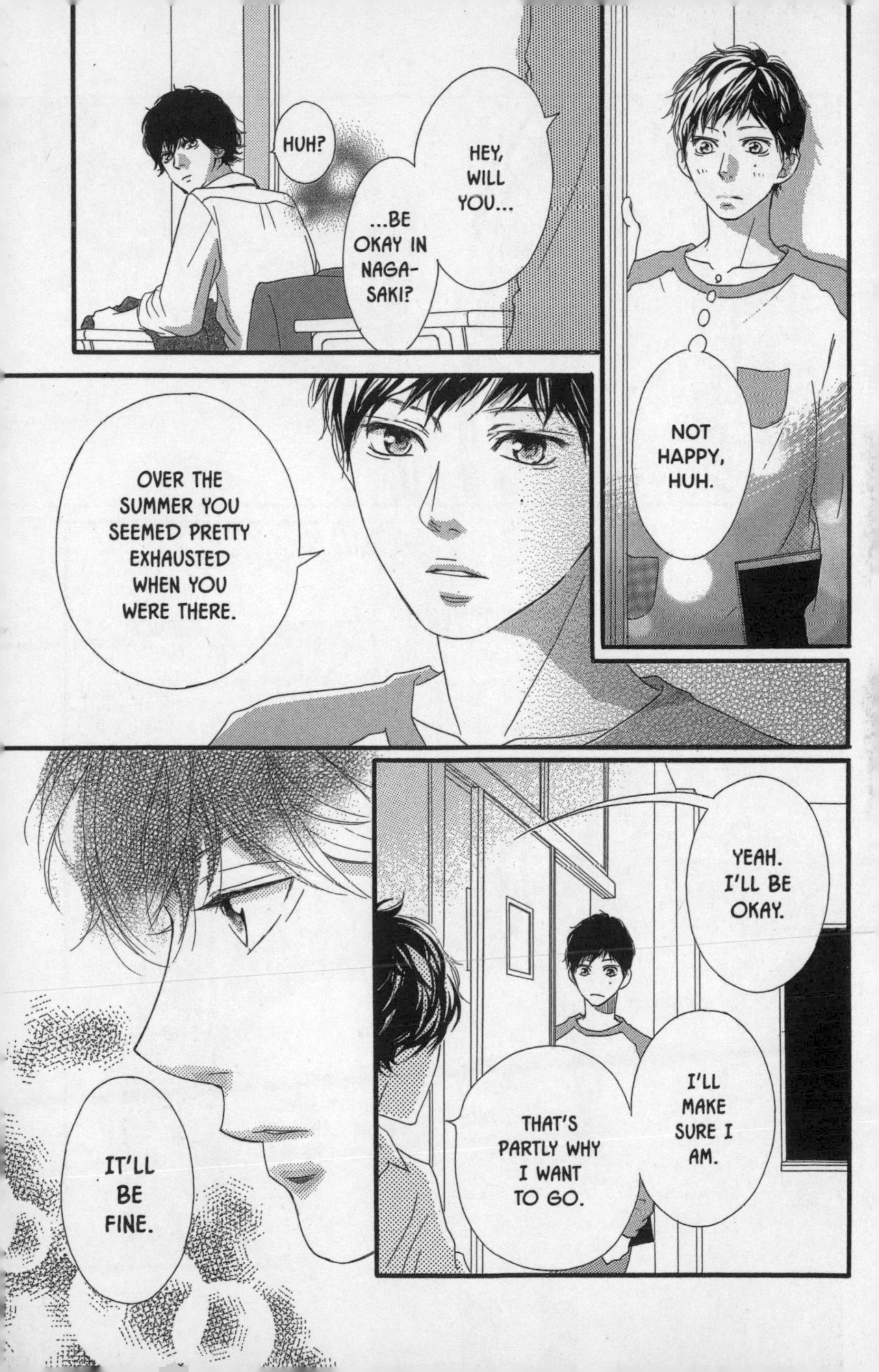
NOT HAPPY, HUH.
HEY, WILL YOU...
HUH?
...BE OKAY IN NAGA-SAKI?
OVER THE SUMMER YOU SEEMED PRETTY EXHAUSTED WHEN YOU WERE THERE.
YEAH. I'LL BE OKAY.
I'LL MAKE SURE I AM.
THAT'S PARTLY WHY I WANT TO GO.
IT'LL BE FINE.

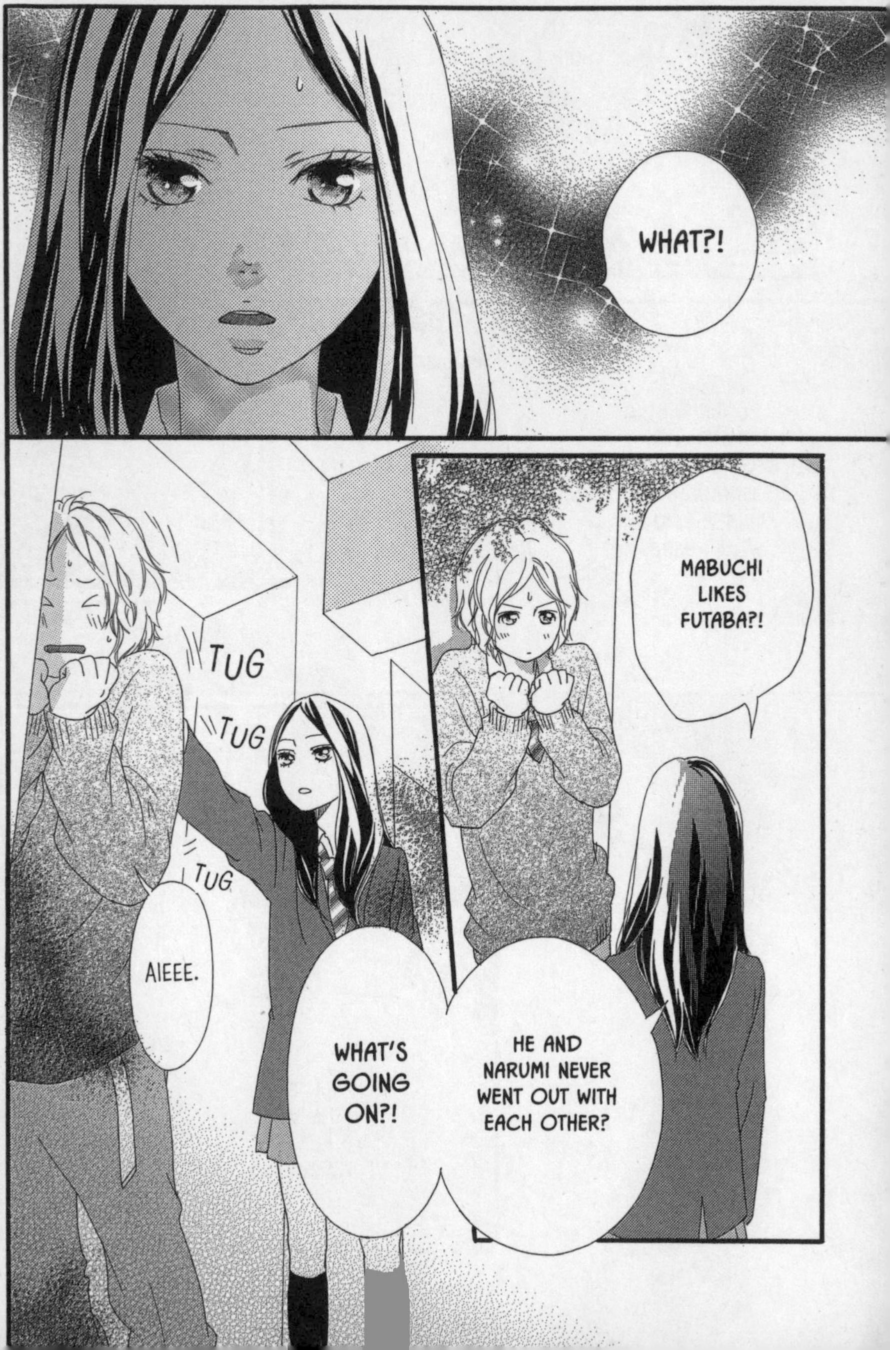
WHAT?!
MABUCHI LIKES FUTABA?!
HE AND NARUMI NEVER WENT OUT WITH EACH OTHER?
WHAT'S GOING ON?!
TUG
TUG
TUG
AIEEE.

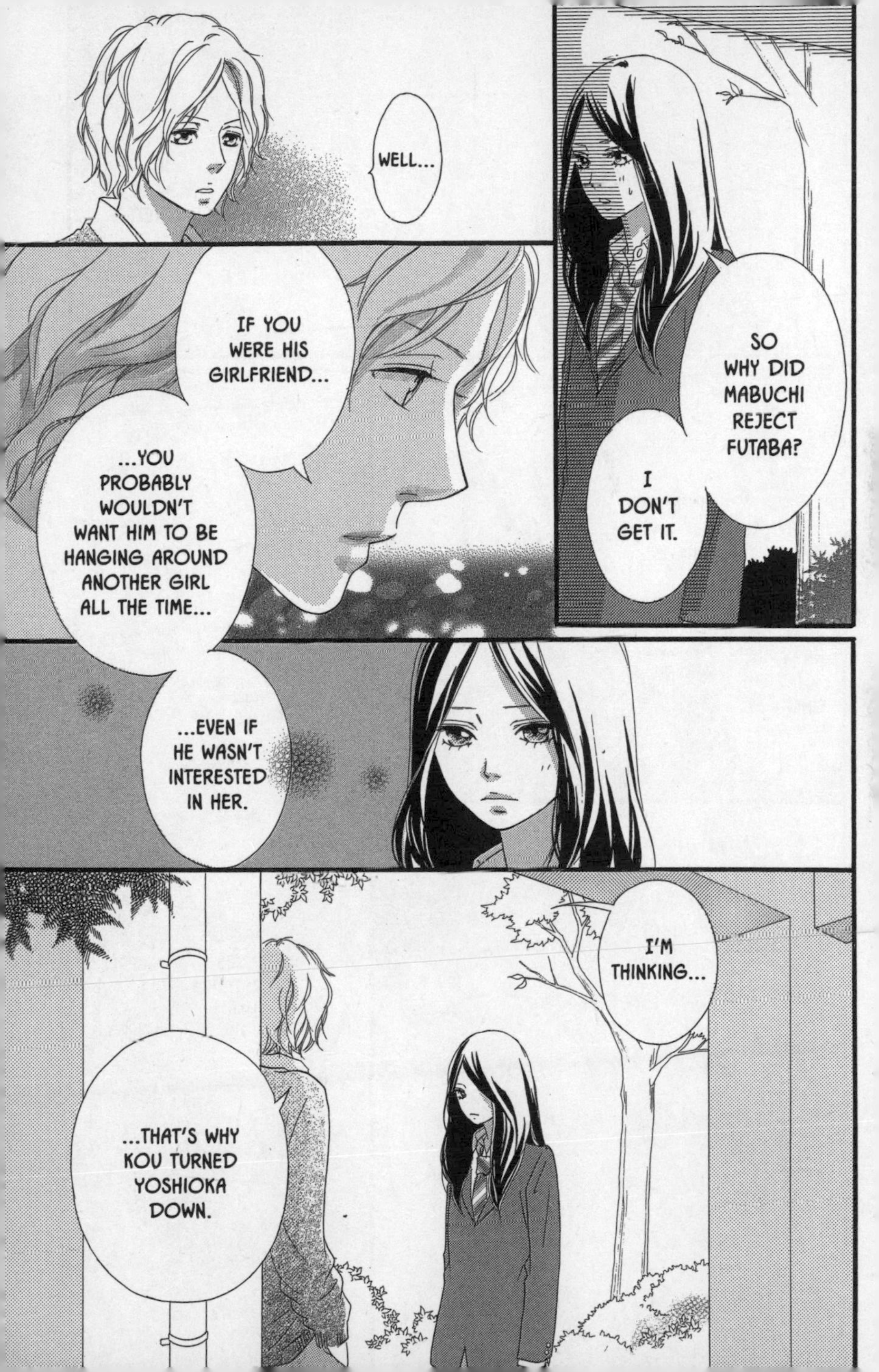
SO WHY DID MABUCHI REJECT FUTABA?
I DON'T GET IT.
WELL...
IF YOU WERE HIS GIRLFRIEND...
...YOU PROBABLY WOULDN'T WANT HIM TO BE HANGING AROUND ANOTHER GIRL ALL THE TIME...
...EVEN IF HE WASN'T INTERESTED IN HER.
I'M THINKING...
...THAT'S WHY KOU TURNED YOSHIOKA DOWN.

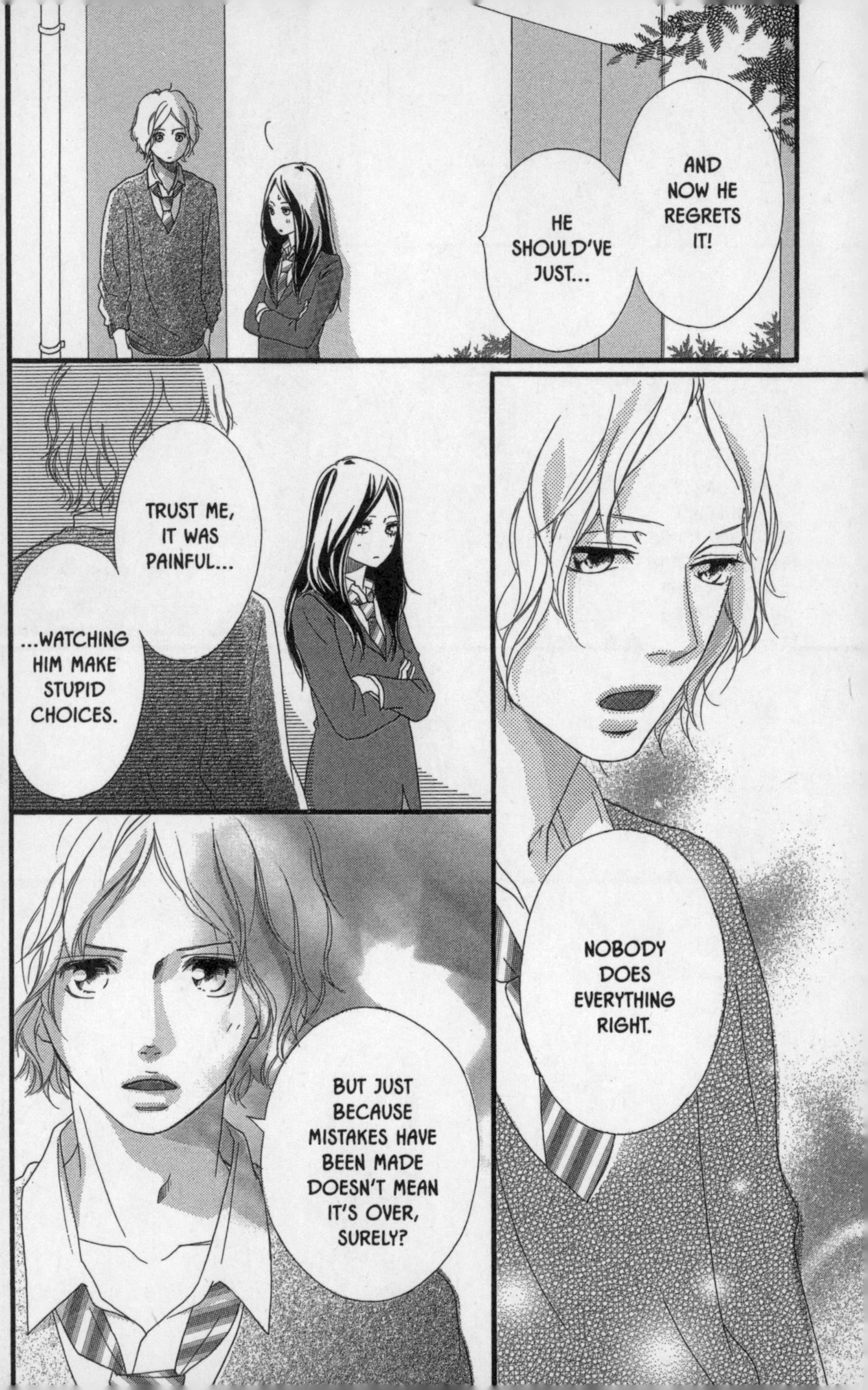
AND NOW HE REGRETS IT!
HE SHOULD'VE JUST...
NOBODY DOES EVERYTHING RIGHT.
TRUST ME, IT WAS PAINFUL...
...WATCHING HIM MAKE STUPID CHOICES.
BUT JUST BECAUSE MISTAKES HAVE BEEN MADE DOESN'T MEAN IT'S OVER, SURELY?

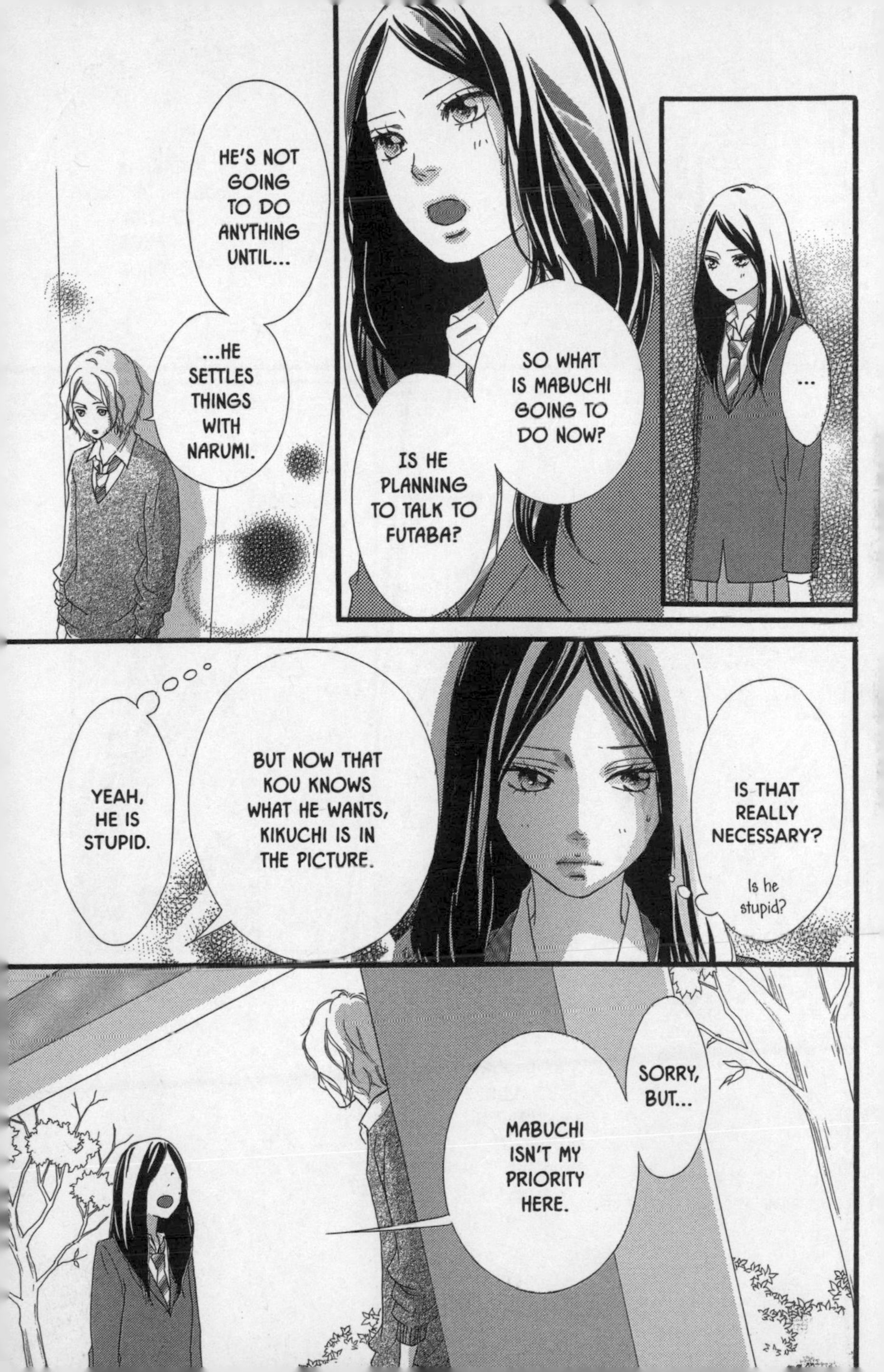
...
SO WHAT IS MABUCHI GOING TO DO NOW?
IS HE PLANNING TO TALK TO FUTABA?
HE'S NOT GOING TO DO ANYTHING UNTIL...
...HE SETTLES THINGS WITH NARUMI.
IS THAT REALLY NECESSARY?
Is he stupid?
BUT NOW THAT KOU KNOWS WHAT HE WANTS, KIKUCHI IS IN THE PICTURE.
YEAH, HE IS STUPID.
SORRY, BUT...
MABUCHI ISN'T MY PRIORITY HERE.

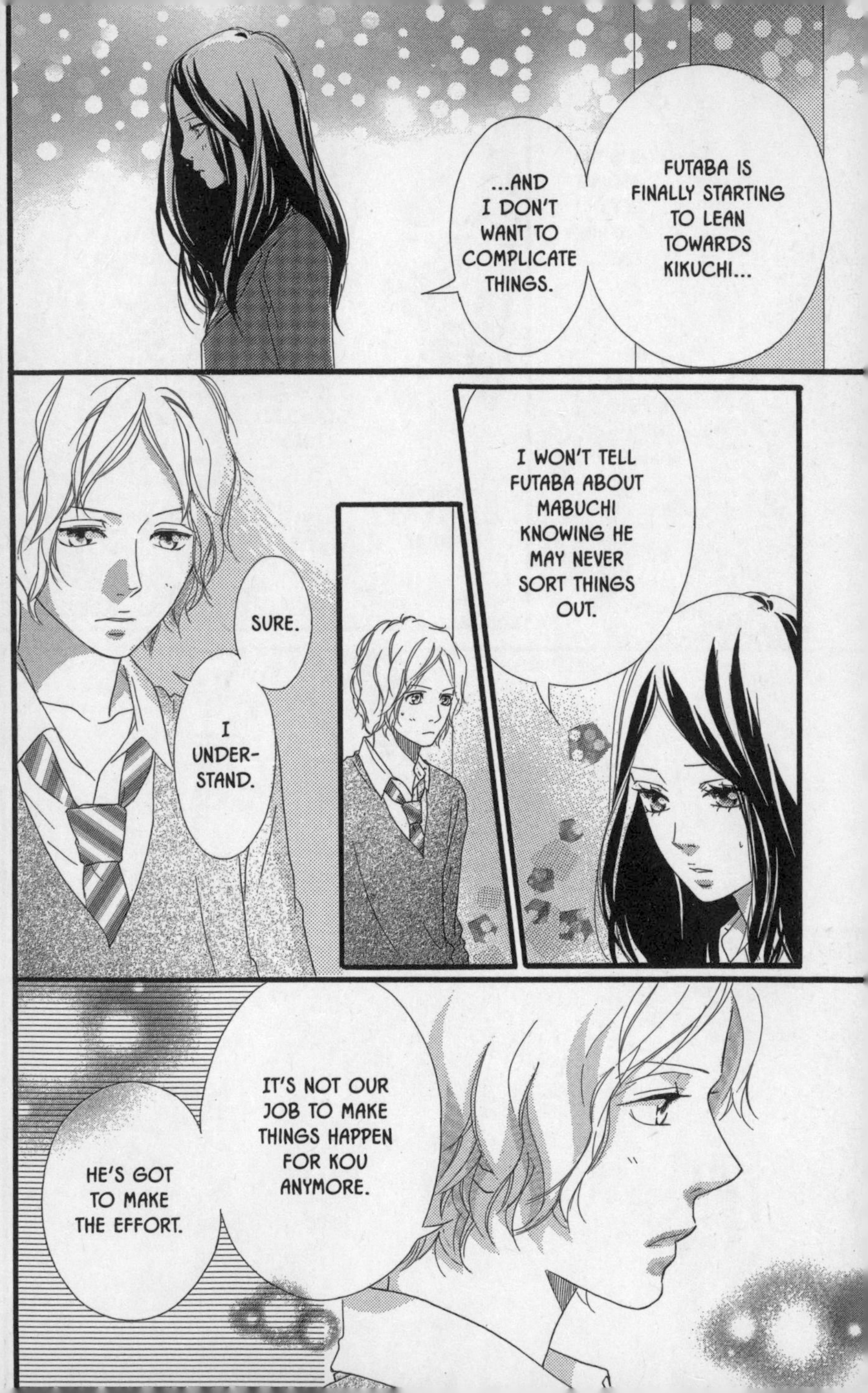
FUTABA IS FINALLY STARTING TO LEAN TOWARDS KIKUCHI...
...AND I DON'T WANT TO COMPLICATE THINGS.
I WON'T TELL FUTABA ABOUT MABUCHI KNOWING HE MAY NEVER SORT THINGS OUT.
SURE.
I UNDER-STAND.
IT'S NOT OUR JOB TO MAKE THINGS HAPPEN FOR KOU ANYMORE.
HE'S GOT TO MAKE THE EFFORT.

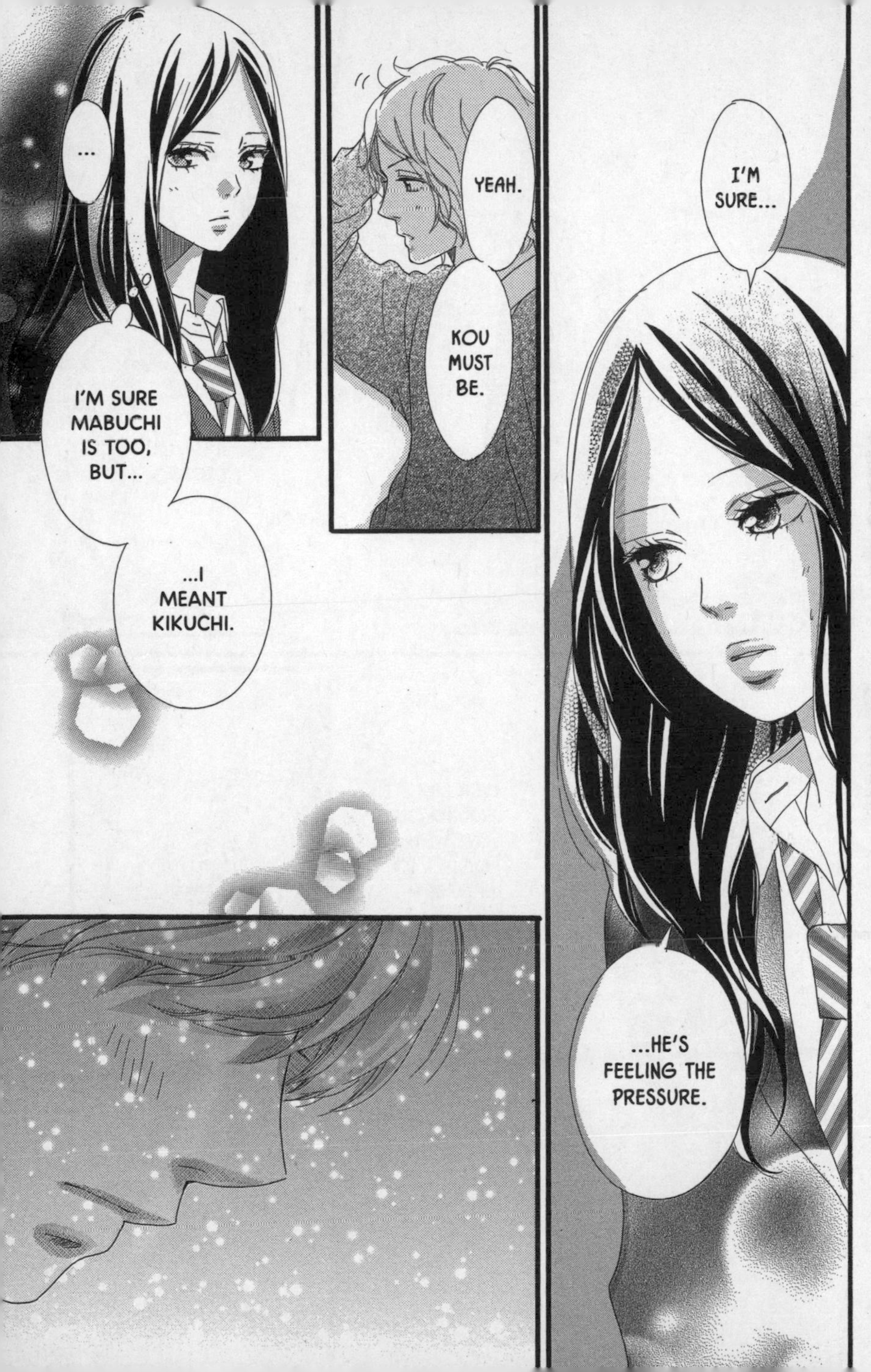
I'M SURE...
...HE'S FEELING THE PRESSURE.
YEAH.
KOU MUST BE.
...
I'M SURE MABUCHI IS TOO, BUT...
...I MEANT KIKUCHI.

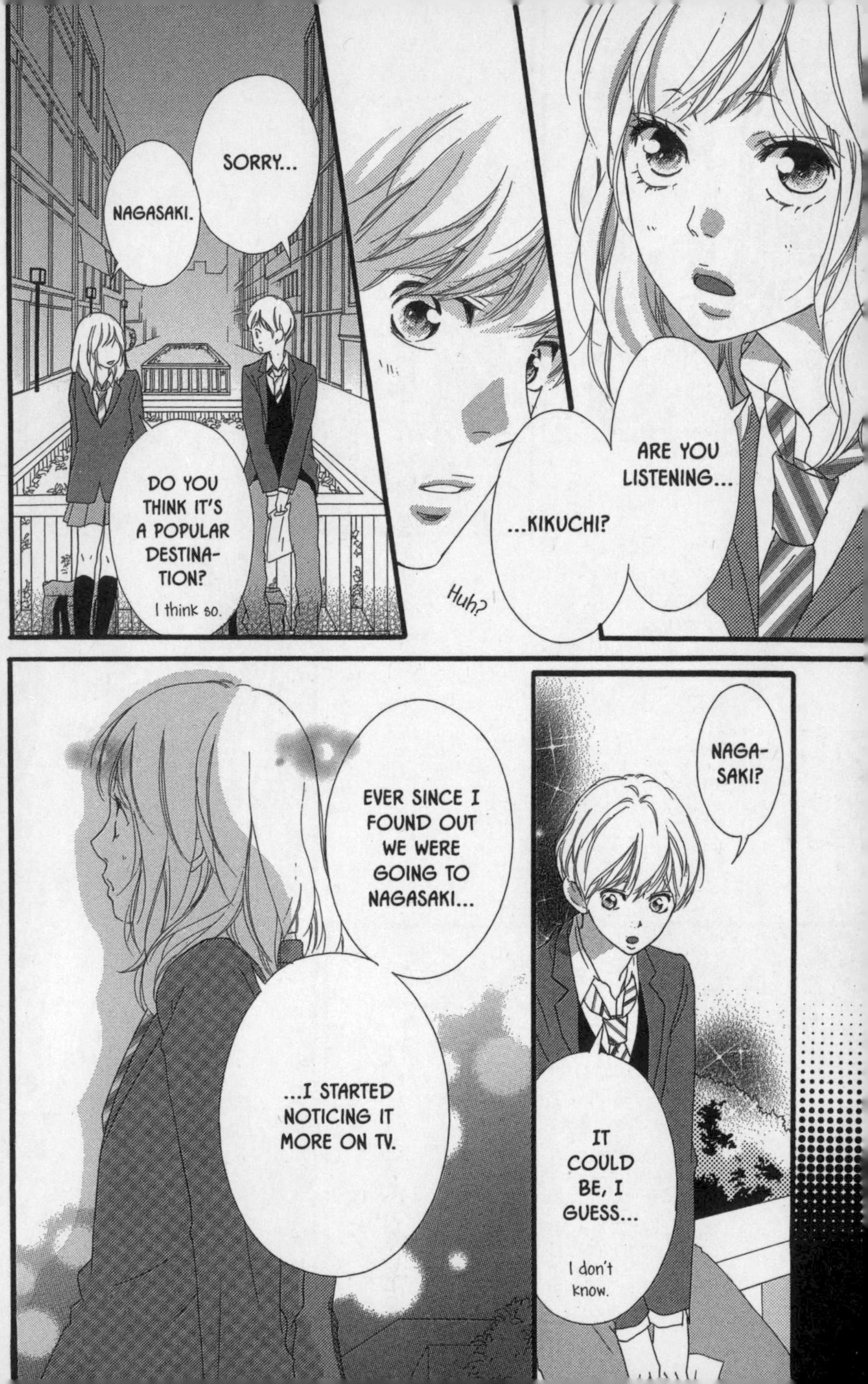
ARE YOU LISTENING...
...KIKUCHI?
Huh?
SORRY...
NAGASAKI.
DO YOU THINK IT'S A POPULAR DESTINA-TION?
I think so.
NAGA-SAKI?
IT COULD BE, I GUESS...
I don't know.
EVER SINCE I FOUND OUT WE WERE GOING TO NAGASAKI...
...I STARTED NOTICING IT MORE ON TV.

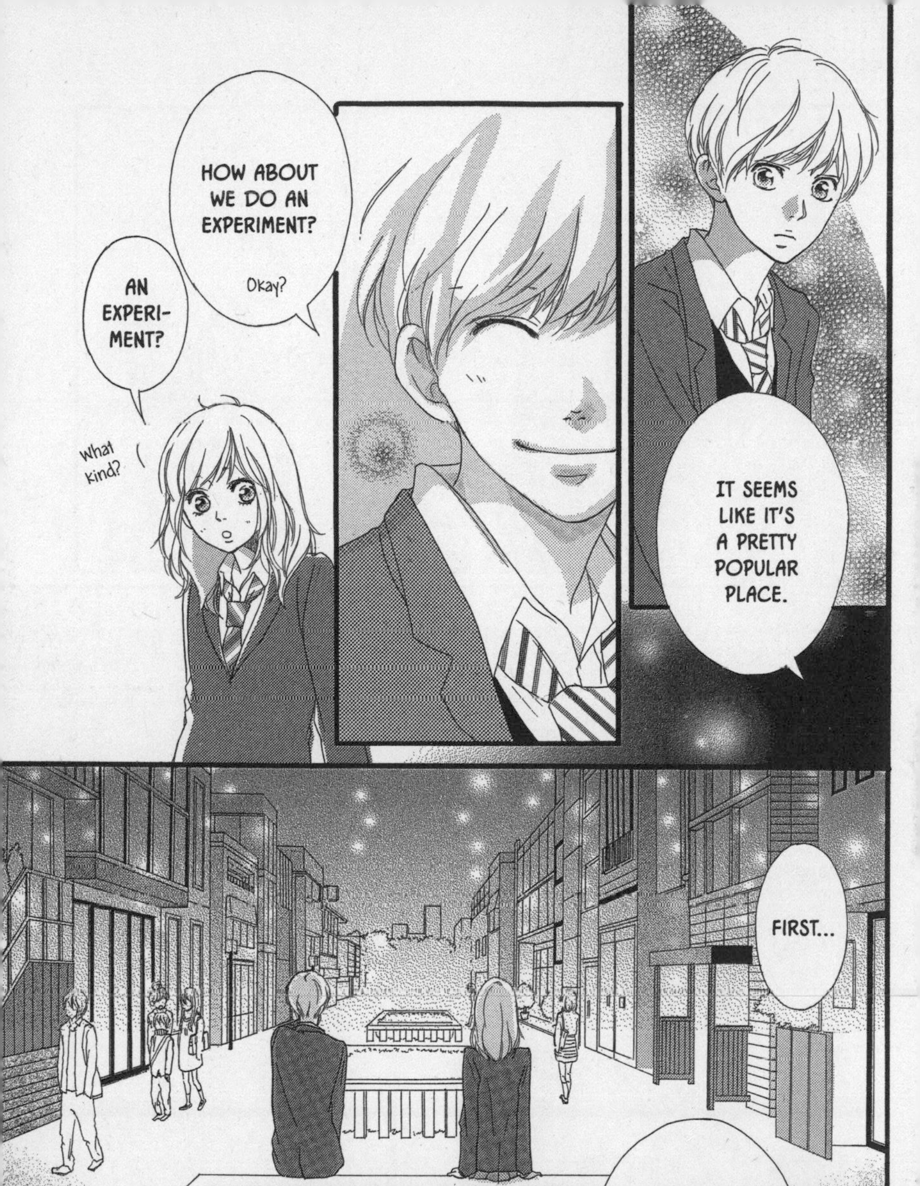
IT SEEMS LIKE IT'S A PRETTY POPULAR PLACE.
HOW ABOUT WE DO AN EXPERIMENT?
Okay?
AN EXPERI- MENT?
What kind?
FIRST...
LOOK ALL AROUND YOU- 180 DEGREES.

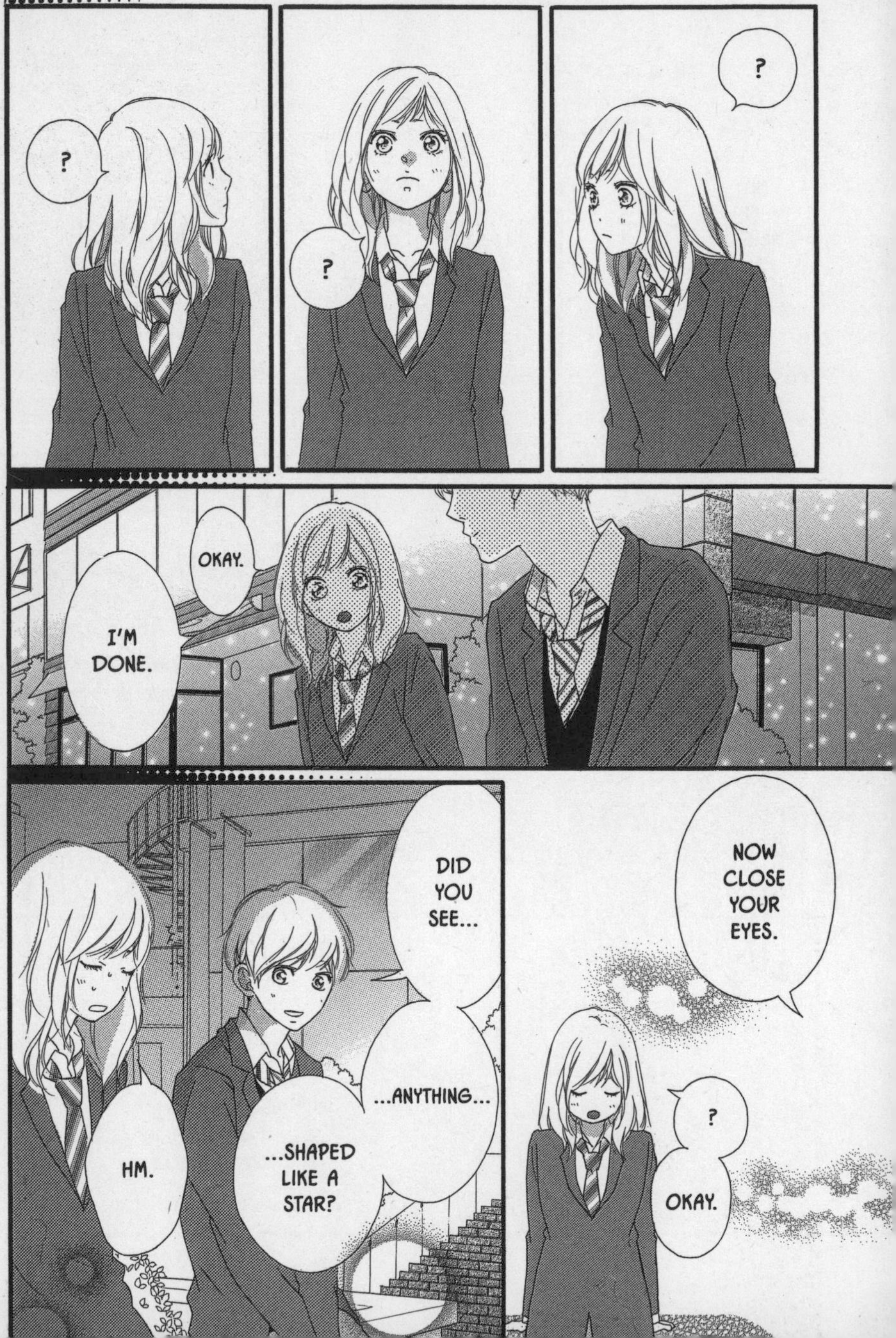
?
?
?
OKAY.
I'M DONE.
NOW CLOSE YOUR EYES.
?
OKAY.
DID YOU SEE...
...ANYTHING...
...SHAPED LIKE A STAR?
HM.

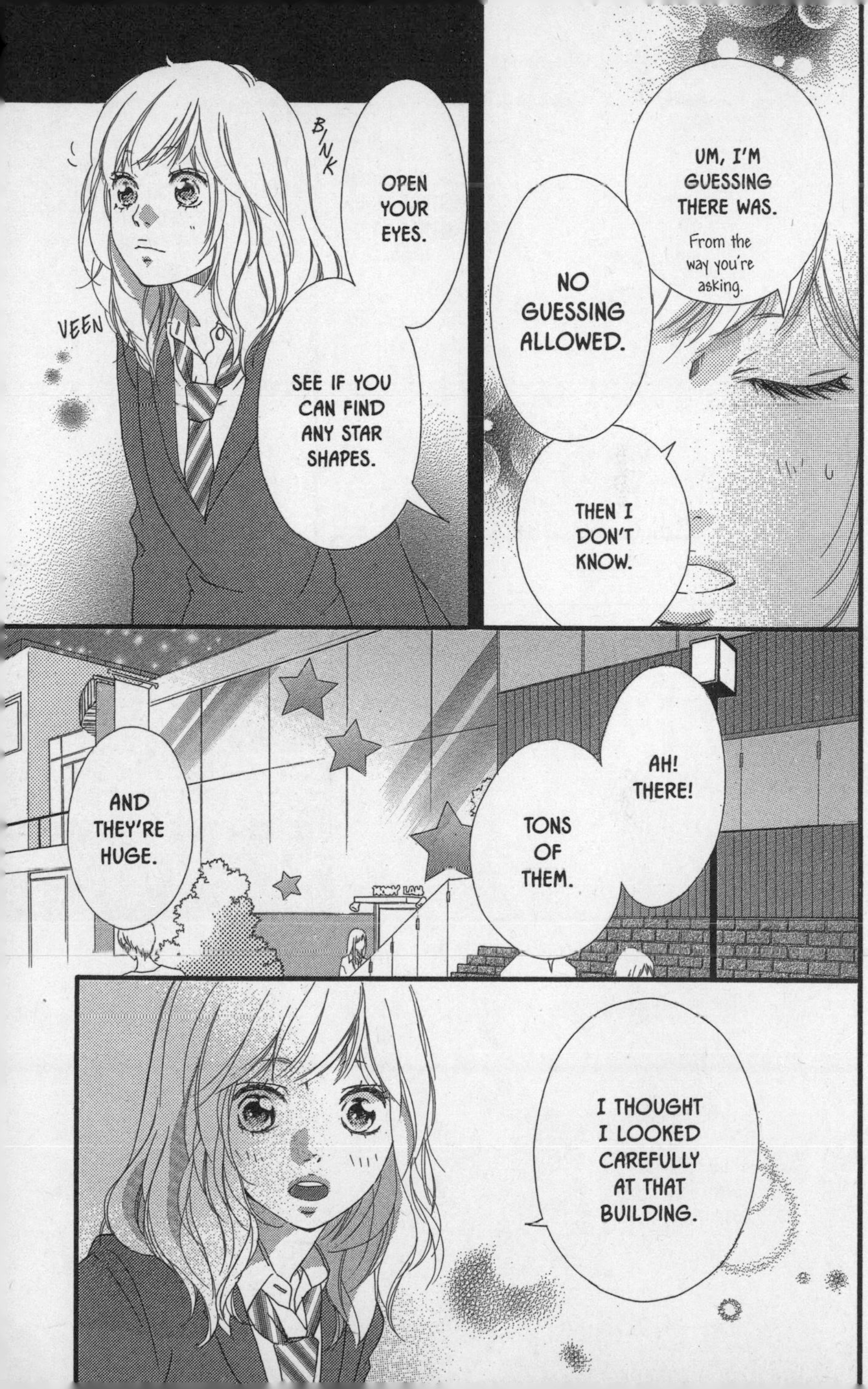
UM, I'M GUESSING THERE WAS.
From the way you're asking.
NO GUESSING ALLOWED.
THEN I DON'T KNOW.
BLINK
OPEN YOUR EYES.
SEE IF YOU CAN FIND ANY STAR SHAPES.
VEEN
AH! THERE!
TONS OF THEM.
AND THEY'RE HUGE.
I THOUGHT I LOOKED CAREFULLY AT THAT BUILDING.

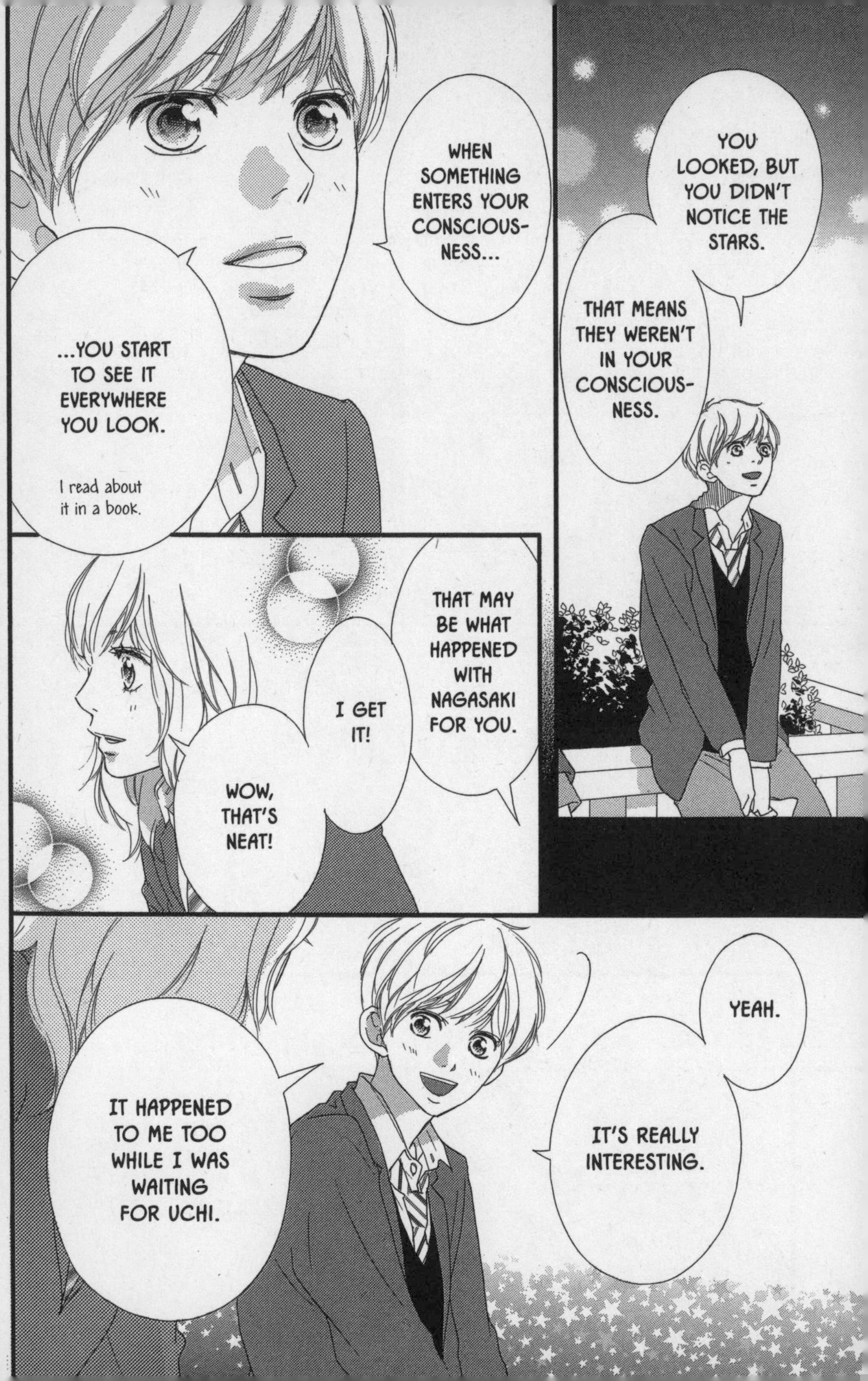
YOU LOOKED, BUT YOU DIDN'T NOTICE THE STARS.
THAT MEANS THEY WEREN'T IN YOUR CONSCIOUS-NESS.
WHEN SOMETHING ENTERS YOUR CONSCIOUS-NESS...
...YOU START TO SEE IT EVERYWHERE YOU LOOK.
I read about it in a book.
THAT MAY BE WHAT HAPPENED WITH NAGASAKI FOR YOU.
I GET IT!
WOW, THAT'S NEAT!
YEAH.
IT'S REALLY INTERESTING.
IT HAPPENED TO ME TOO WHILE I WAS WAITING FOR UCHI.

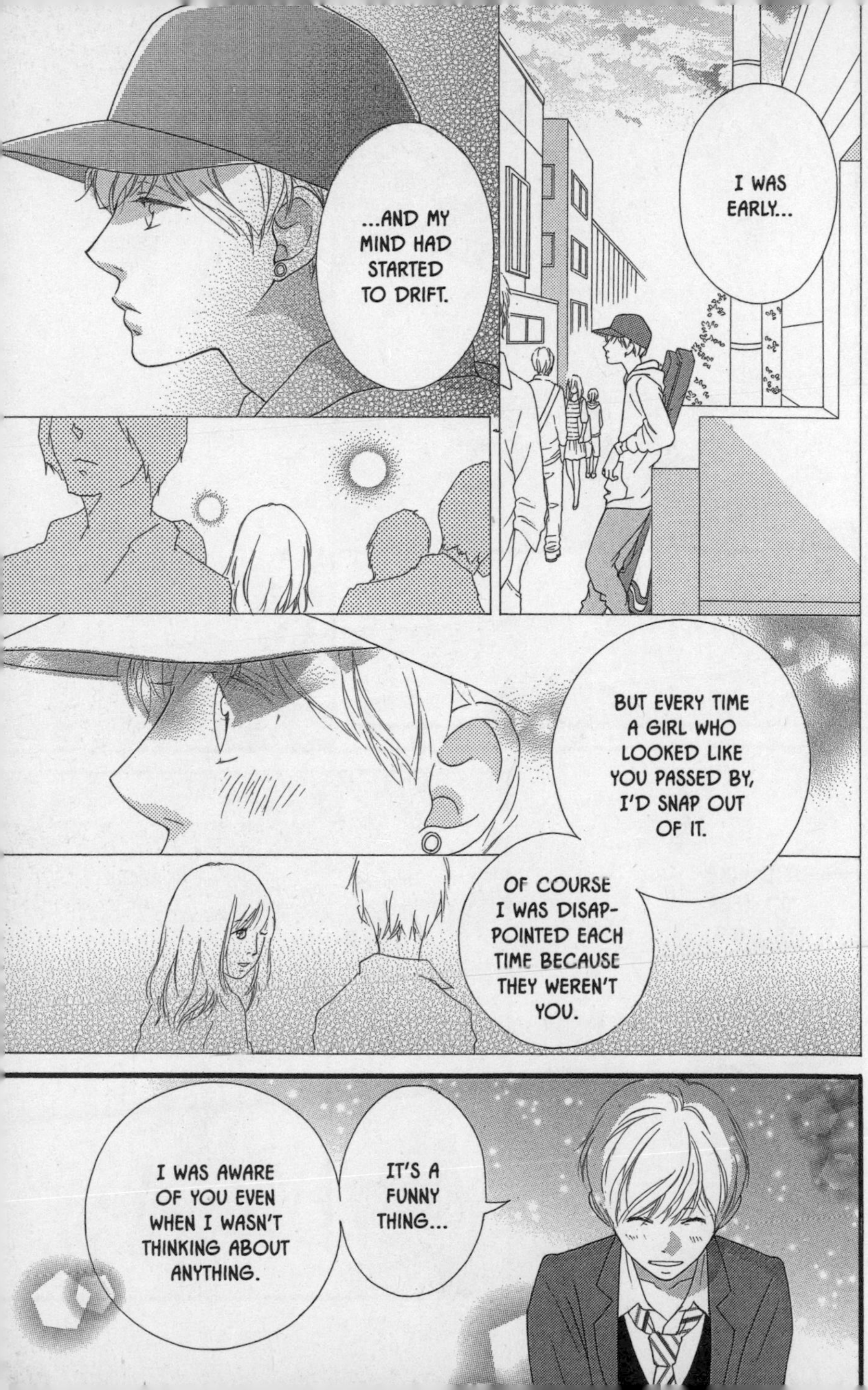
I WAS EARLY...
...AND MY MIND HAD STARTED TO DRIFT.
BUT EVERY TIME A GIRL WHO LOOKED LIKE YOU PASSED BY, I'D SNAP OUT OF IT.
OF COURSE I WAS DISAP-POINTED EACH TIME BECAUSE THEY WEREN'T YOU.
IT'S A FUNNY THING...
I WAS AWARE OF YOU EVEN WHEN I WASN'T THINKING ABOUT ANYTHING.

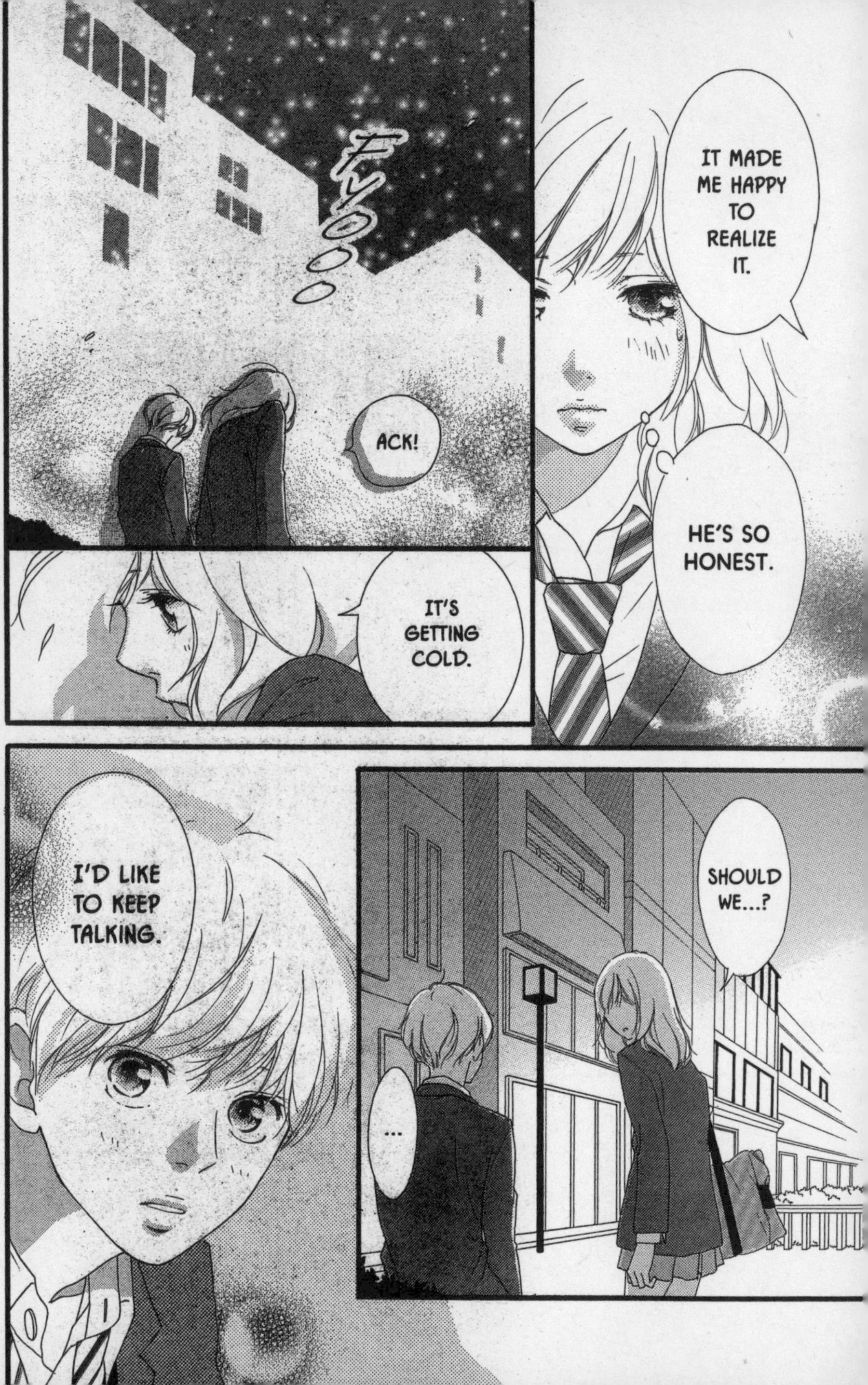
IT MADE ME HAPPY TO REALIZE IT.
HE'S SO HONEST.
FWOOO
ACK!
IT'S GETTING COLD.
SHOULD WE...?
...
I'D LIKE TO KEEP TALKING.

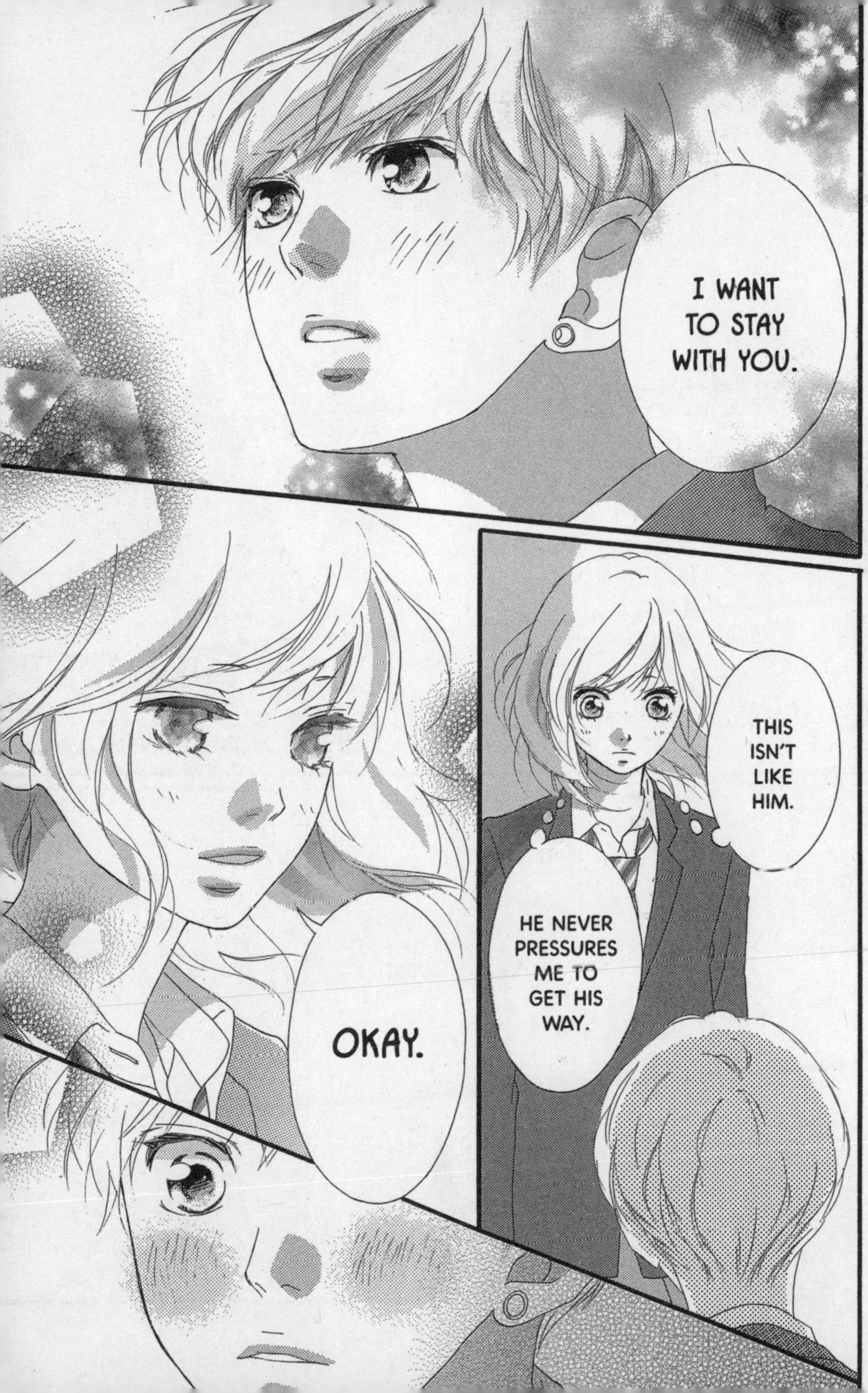
I WANT TO STAY WITH YOU.
THIS ISN'T LIKE HIM.
HE NEVER PRESSURES ME TO GET HIS WAY.
OKAY.

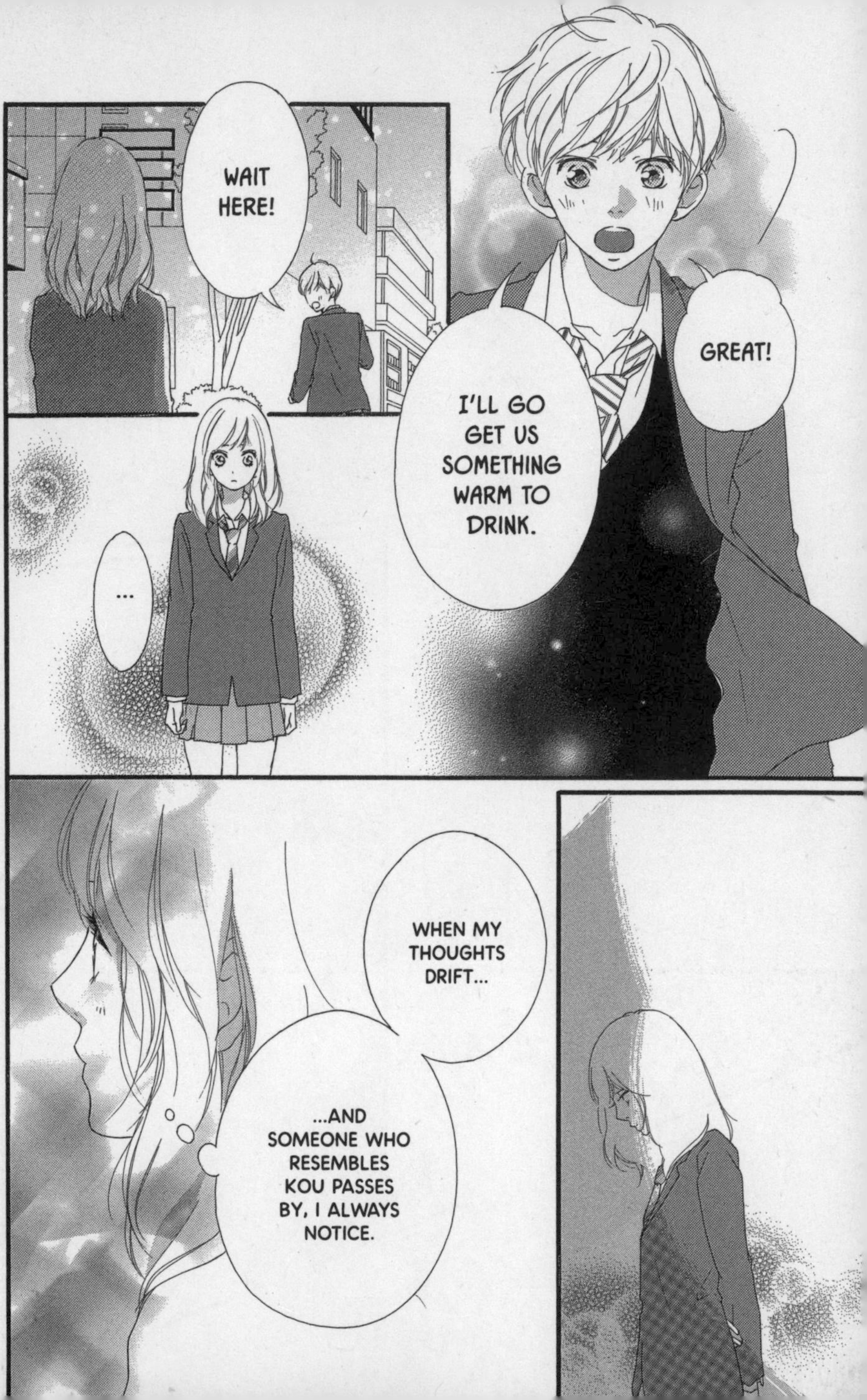
GREAT!
I'LL GO GET US SOMETHING WARM TO DRINK.
WAIT HERE!
...
WHEN MY THOUGHTS DRIFT...
...AND SOMEONE WHO RESEMBLES KOU PASSES BY, I ALWAYS NOTICE.

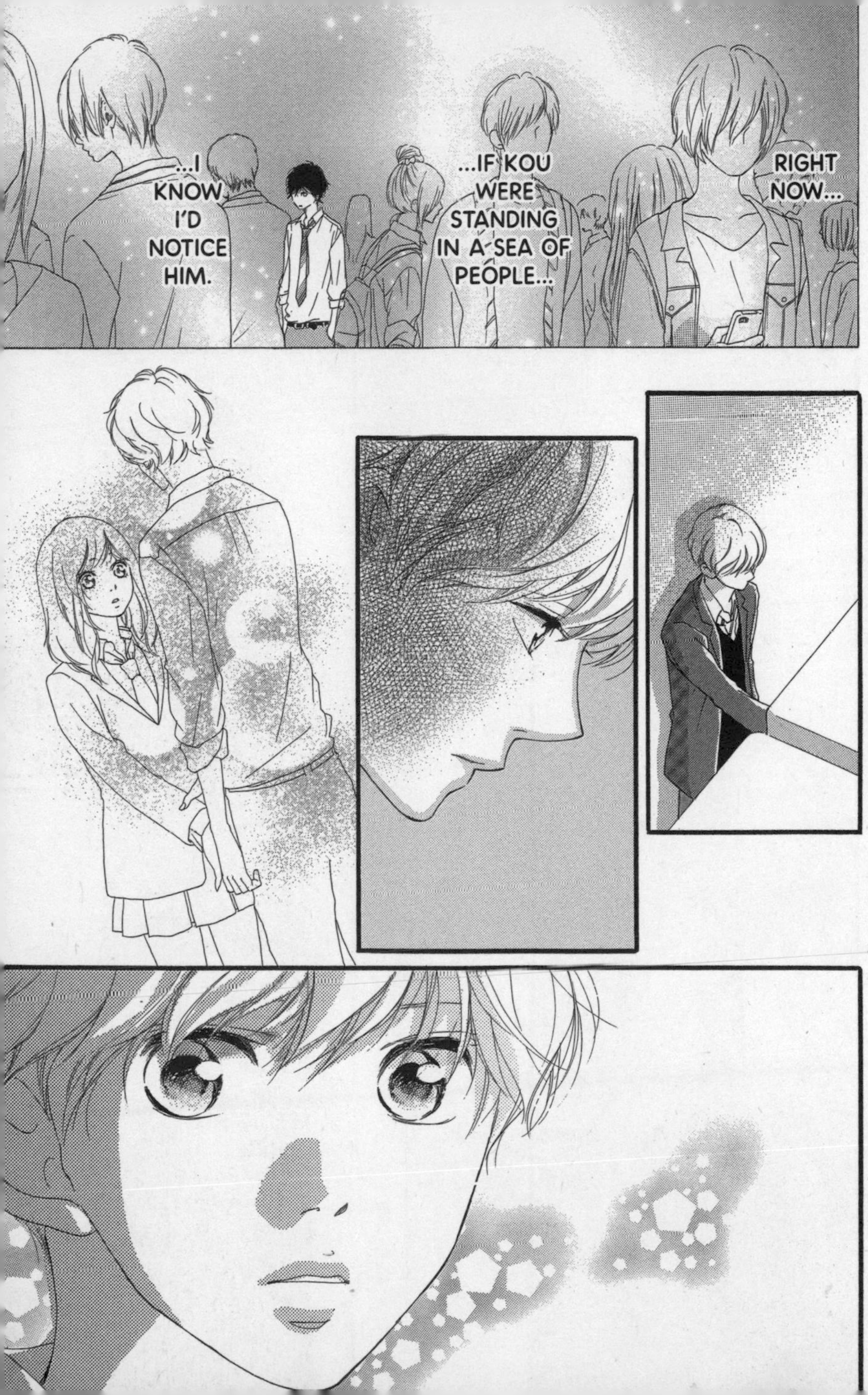
RIGHT NOW...
...IF KOU WERE STANDING IN A SEA OF PEOPLE...
...I KNOW I'D NOTICE HIM.

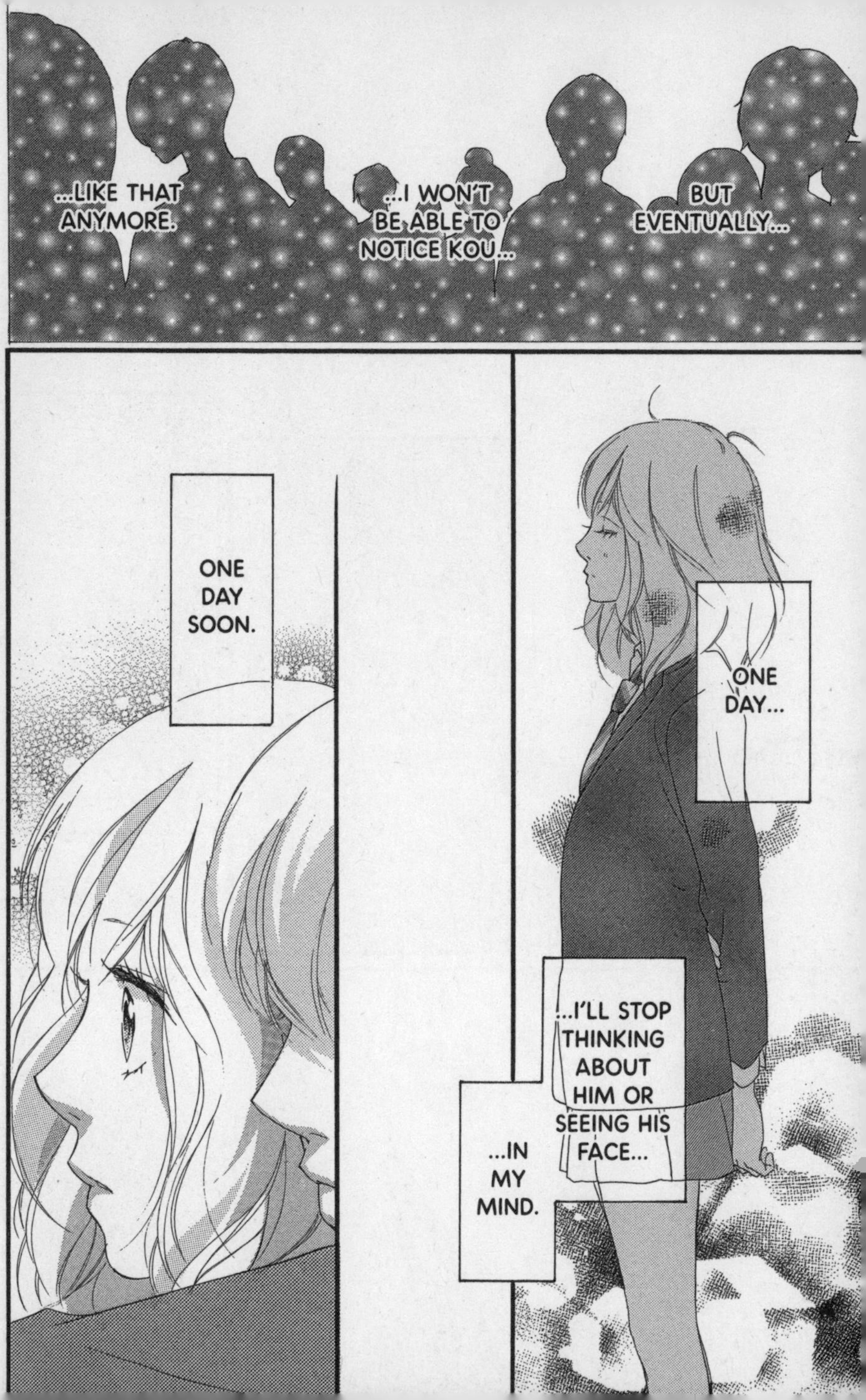
BUT EVENTUALLY...
...I WON'T BE ABLE TO NOTICE KOU...
...LIKE THAT ANYMORE.
ONE DAY...
...I'LL STOP THINKING ABOUT HIM OR SEEING HIS FACE...
...IN MY MIND.
ONE DAY SOON.

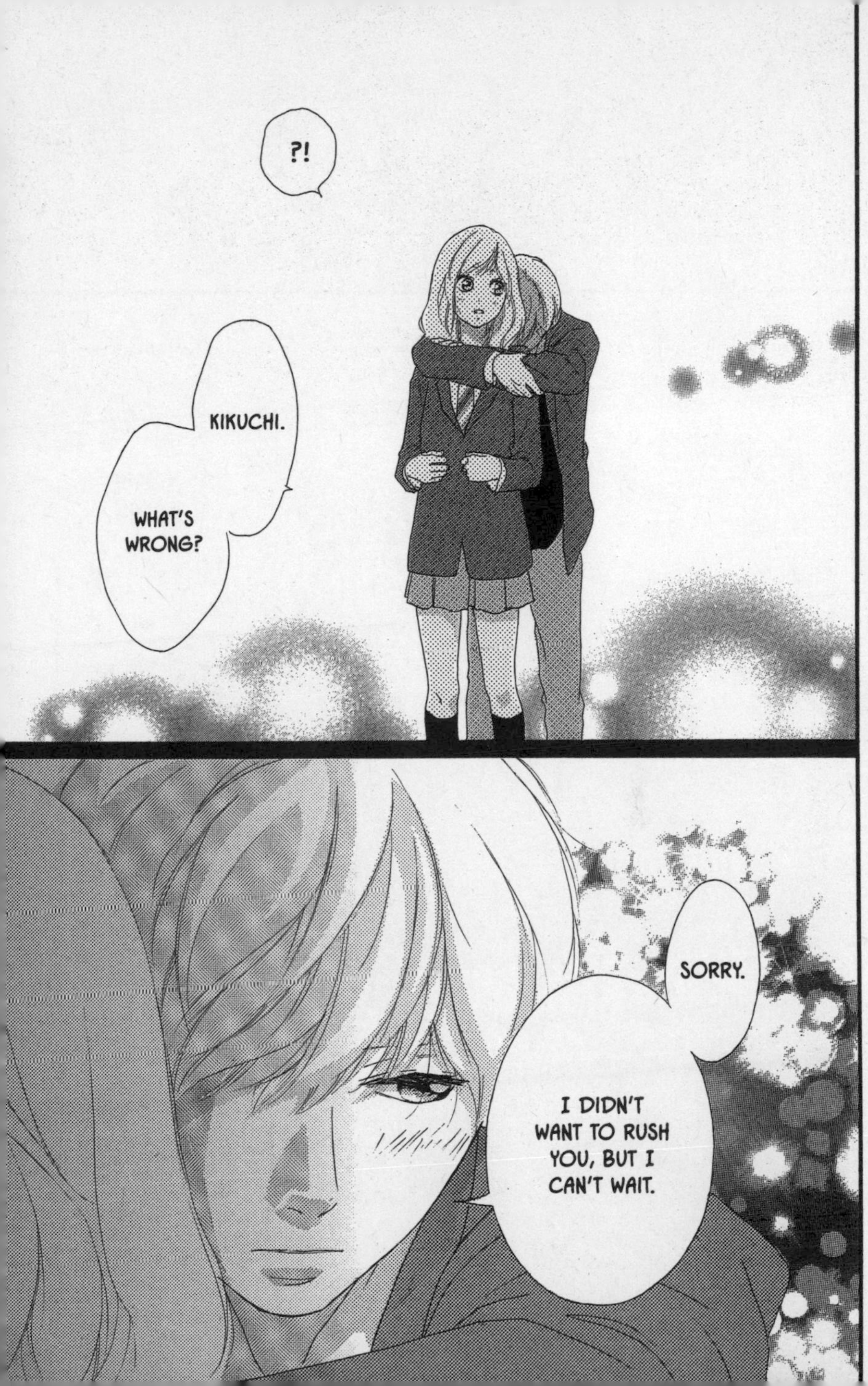
?!
KIKUCHI.
WHAT'S WRONG?
SORRY.
I DIDN'T WANT TO RUSH YOU, BUT I CAN'T WAIT.

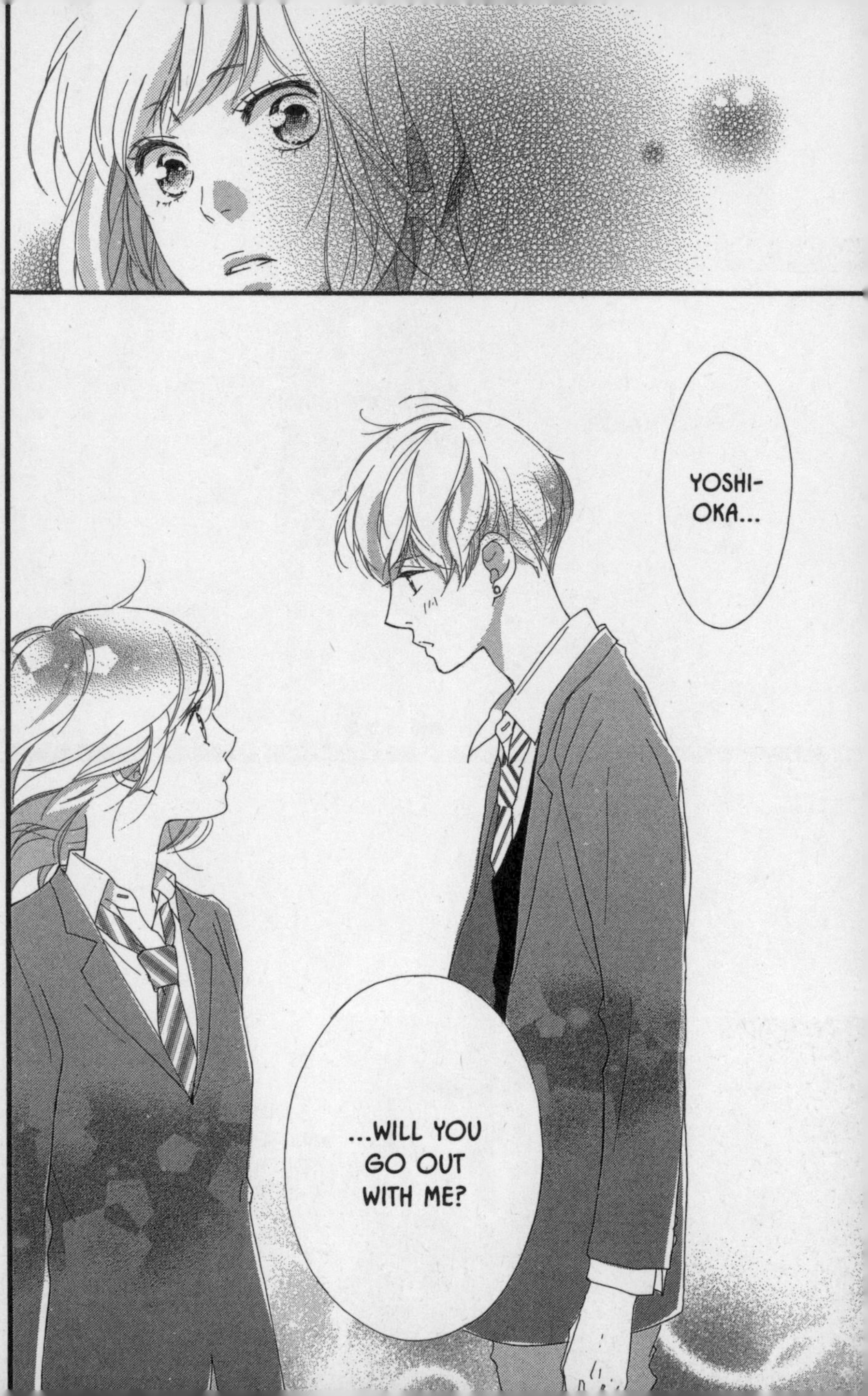
YOSHI-
OKA...
...WILL YOU GO OUT WITH ME?

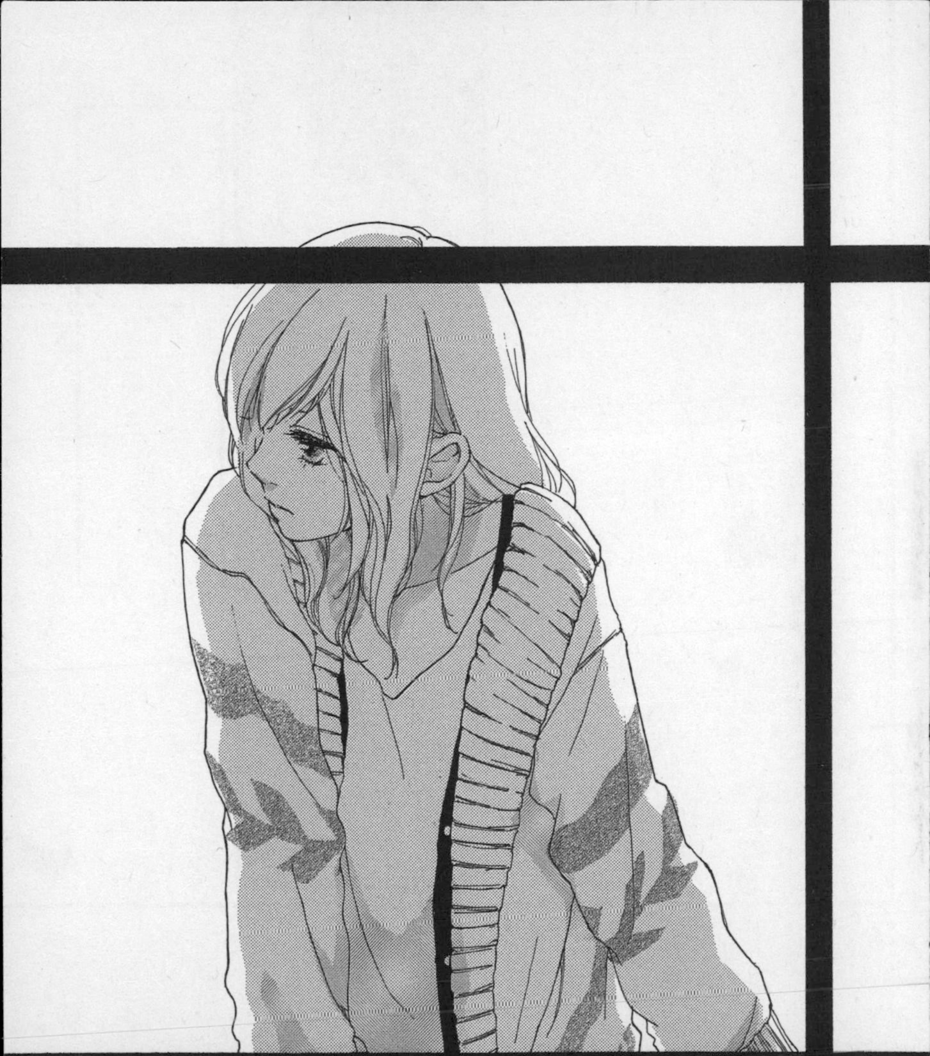

Ao Haru Ride

The scent of air after rain...
In the light around us, I felt your heartbeat.

CHAPTER 34

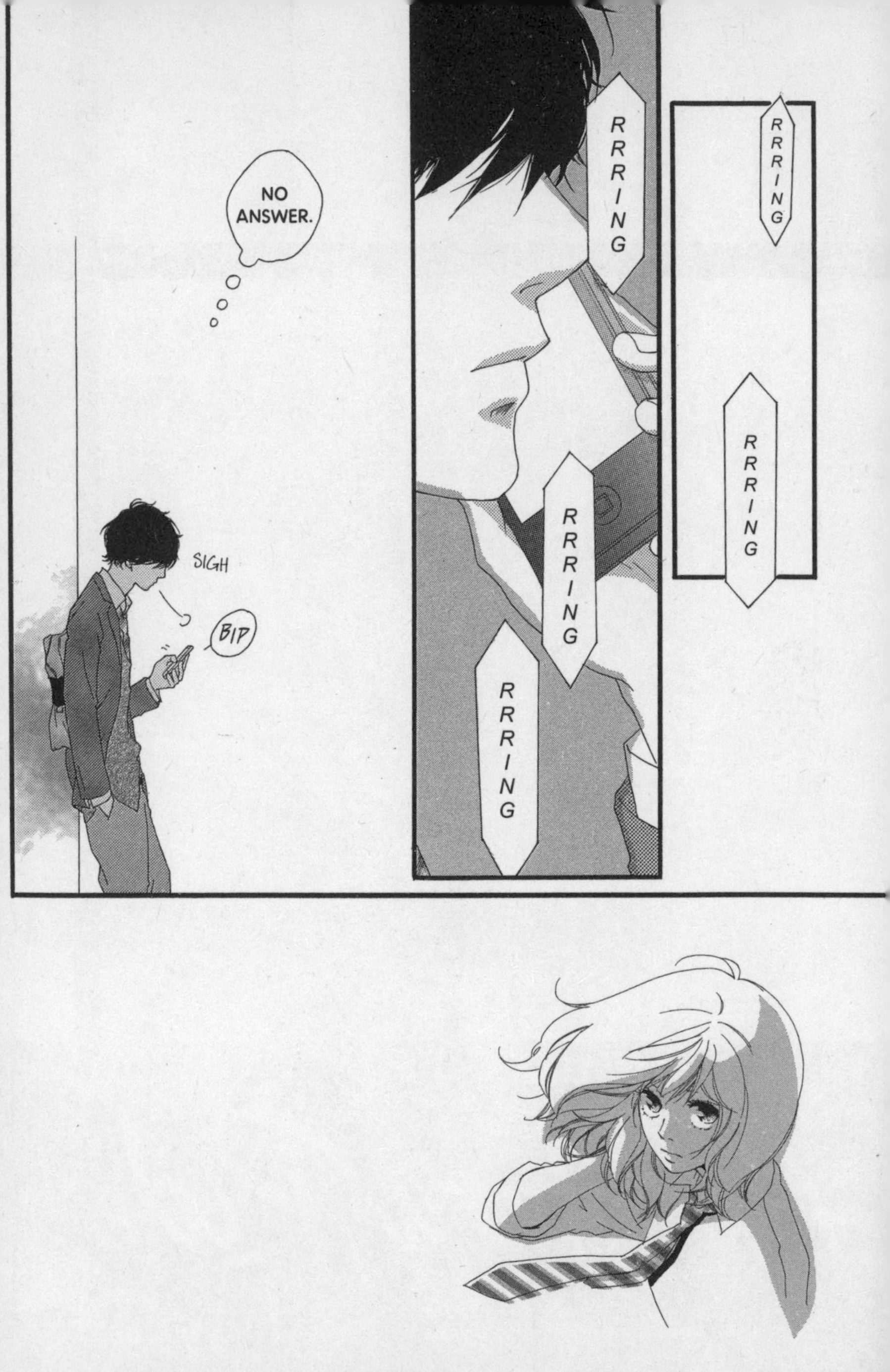
RRRING
RRRING
RRRING
RRRING
RRRING
NO ANSWER.
SIGH
BIP

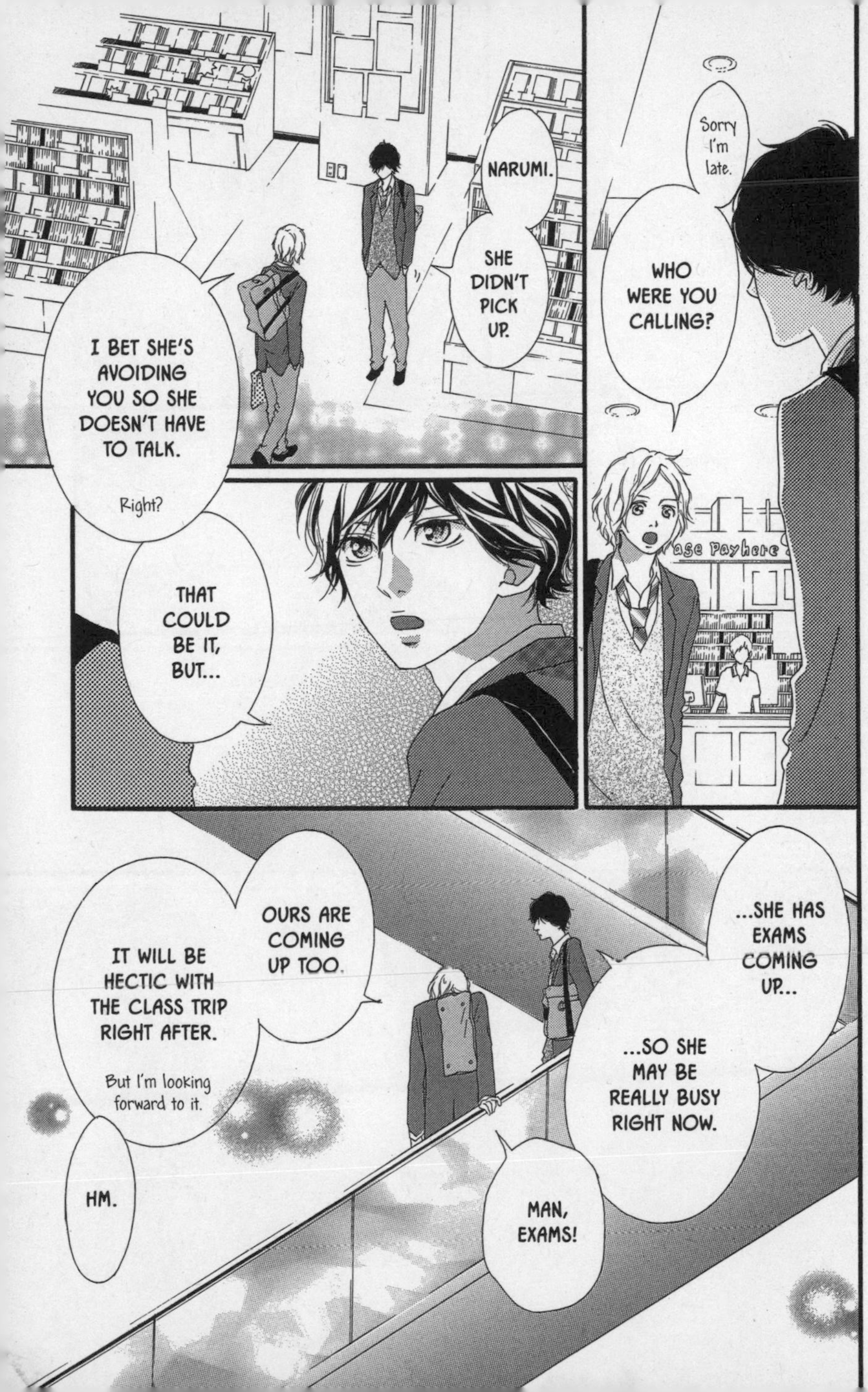
Sorry I'm late.
WHO WERE YOU CALLING?
NARUMI.
SHE DIDN'T PICK UP.
I BET SHE'S AVOIDING YOU SO SHE DOESN'T HAVE TO TALK.
Right?
THAT COULD BE IT, BUT...
...SHE HAS EXAMS COMING UP...
...SO SHE MAY BE REALLY BUSY RIGHT NOW.
OURS ARE COMING UP TOO.
IT WILL BE HECTIC WITH THE CLASS TRIP RIGHT AFTER.
But I'm looking forward to it.
MAN, EXAMS!
HM.

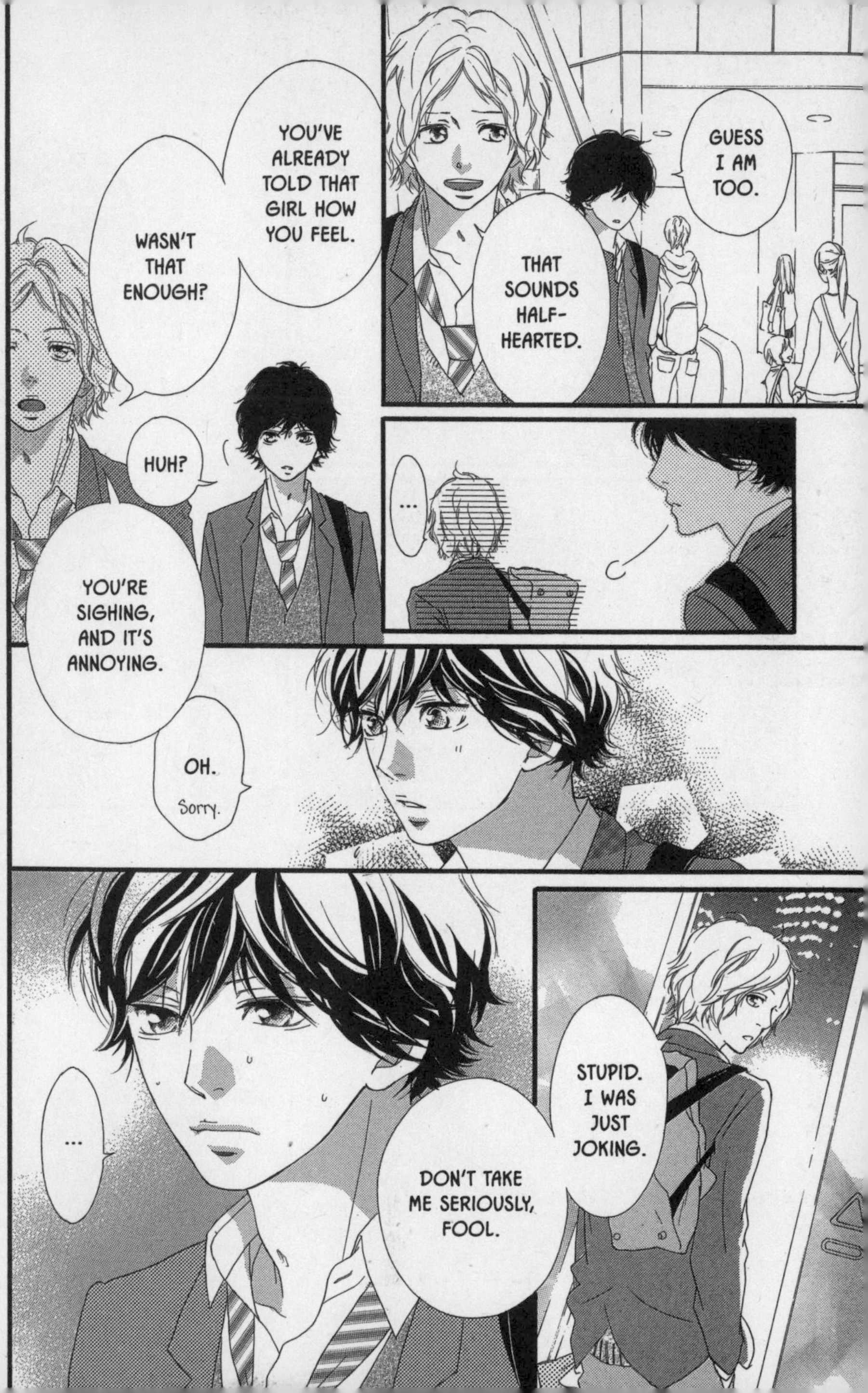
GUESS I AM TOO.
THAT SOUNDS HALF-HEARTED.
...
YOU'VE ALREADY TOLD THAT GIRL HOW YOU FEEL.
WASN'T THAT ENOUGH?
HUH?
YOU'RE SIGHING, AND IT'S ANNOYING.
OH.
Sorry.
STUPID. I WAS JUST JOKING.
DON'T TAKE ME SERIOUSLY, FOOL.
...

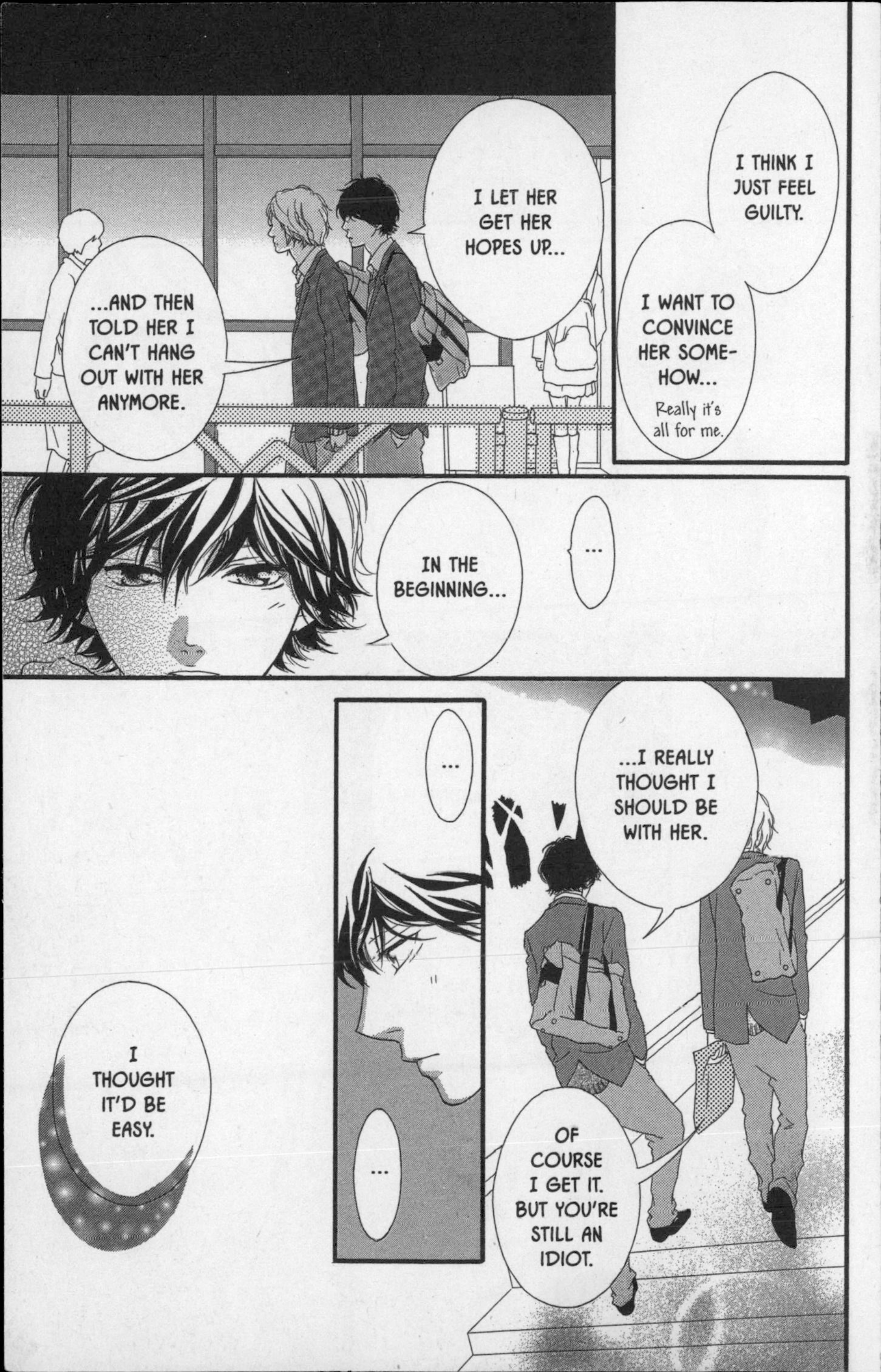
I THINK I JUST FEEL GUILTY.
I WANT TO CONVINCE HER SOME-HOW...
Really it's all for me.
I LET HER GET HER HOPES UP...
...AND THEN TOLD HER I CAN'T HANG OUT WITH HER ANYMORE.
...
IN THE BEGINNING...
...I REALLY THOUGHT I SHOULD BE WITH HER.
...
OF COURSE I GET IT. BUT YOU'RE STILL AN IDIOT.
...
I THOUGHT IT'D BE EASY.

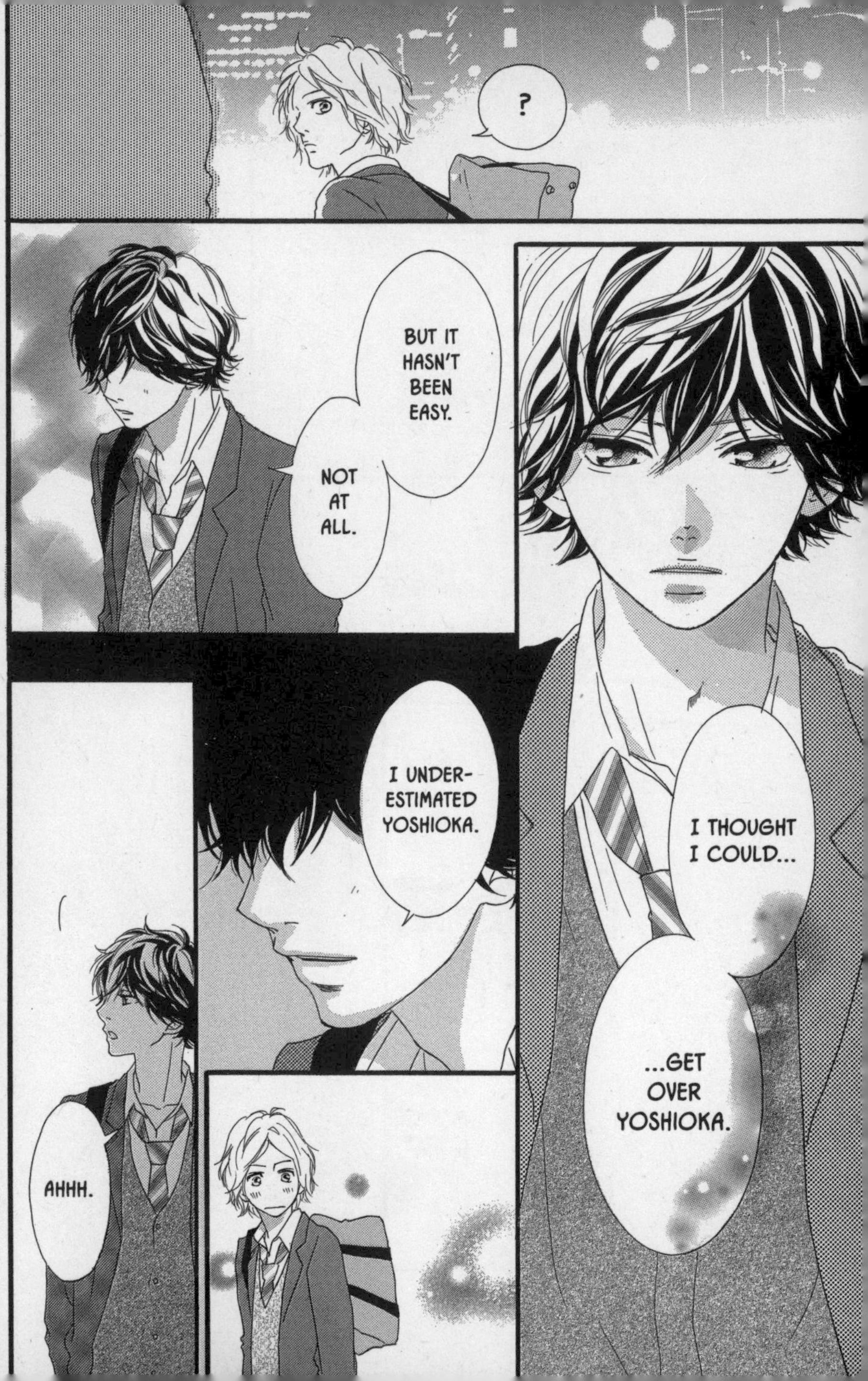
?
I THOUGHT I COULD...
...GET OVER YOSHIOKA.
BUT IT HASN'T BEEN EASY.
NOT AT ALL.
I UNDER-ESTIMATED YOSHIOKA.
AHHH.

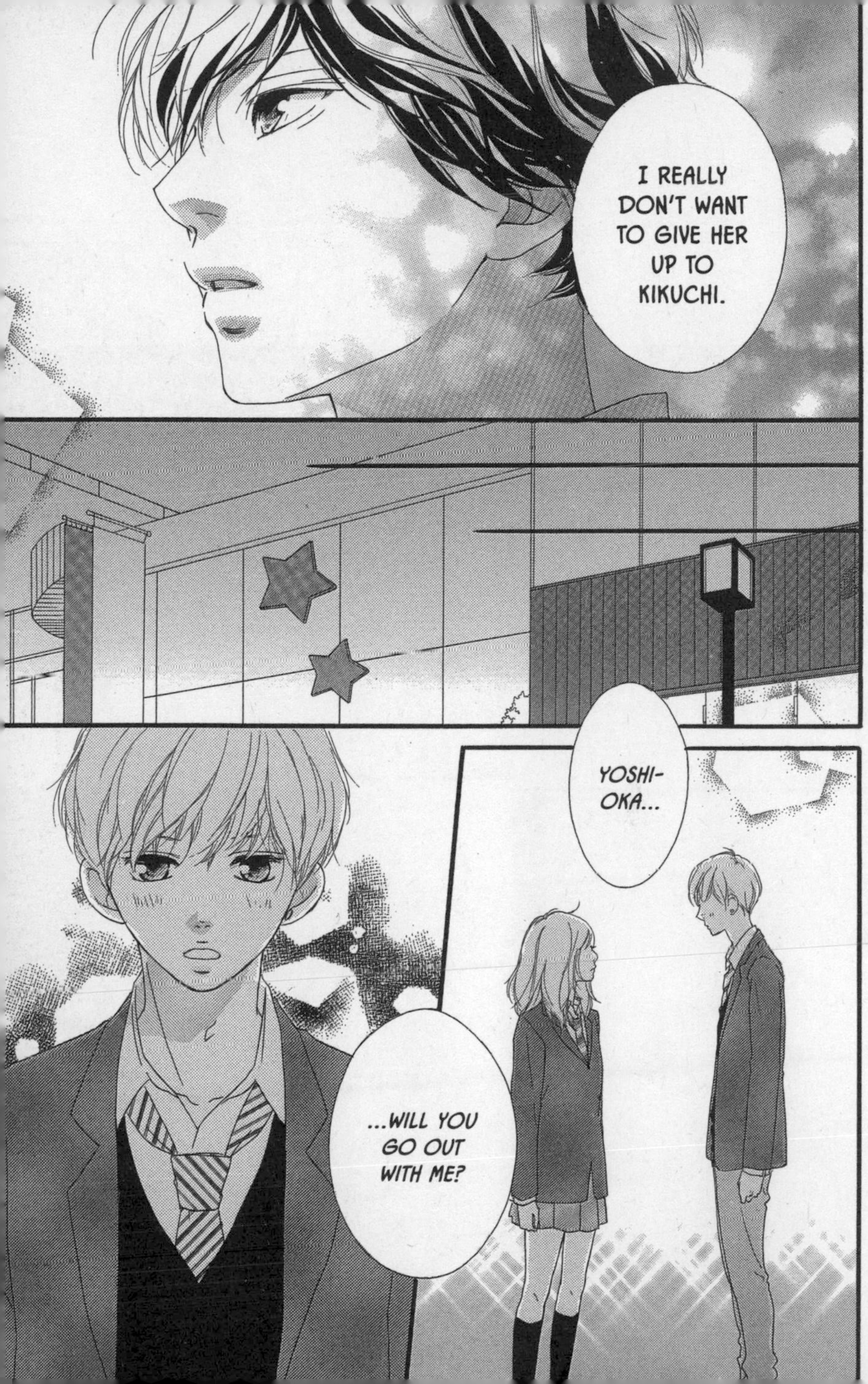
I REALLY DON'T WANT TO GIVE HER UP TO KIKUCHI.
YOSHI-OKA...
...WILL YOU GO OUT WITH ME?

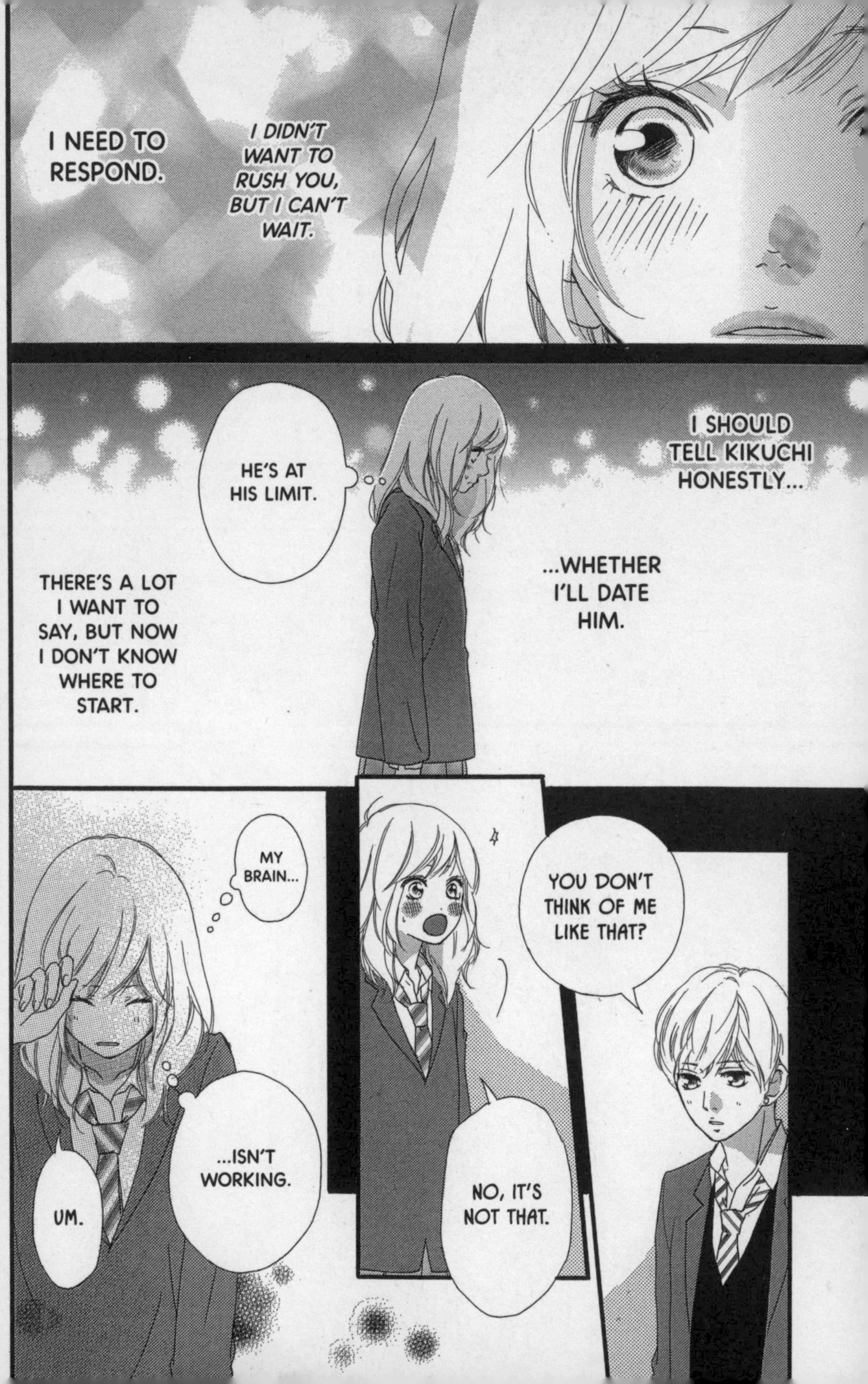
I DIDN'T WANT TO RUSH YOU, BUT I CAN'T WAIT.
I NEED TO RESPOND.
I SHOULD TELL KIKUCHI HONESTLY...
...WHETHER I'LL DATE HIM.
HE'S AT HIS LIMIT.
THERE'S A LOT I WANT TO SAY, BUT NOW I DON'T KNOW WHERE TO START.
YOU DON'T THINK OF ME LIKE THAT?
NO, IT'S NOT THAT.
MY BRAIN...
...ISN'T WORKING.
UM.

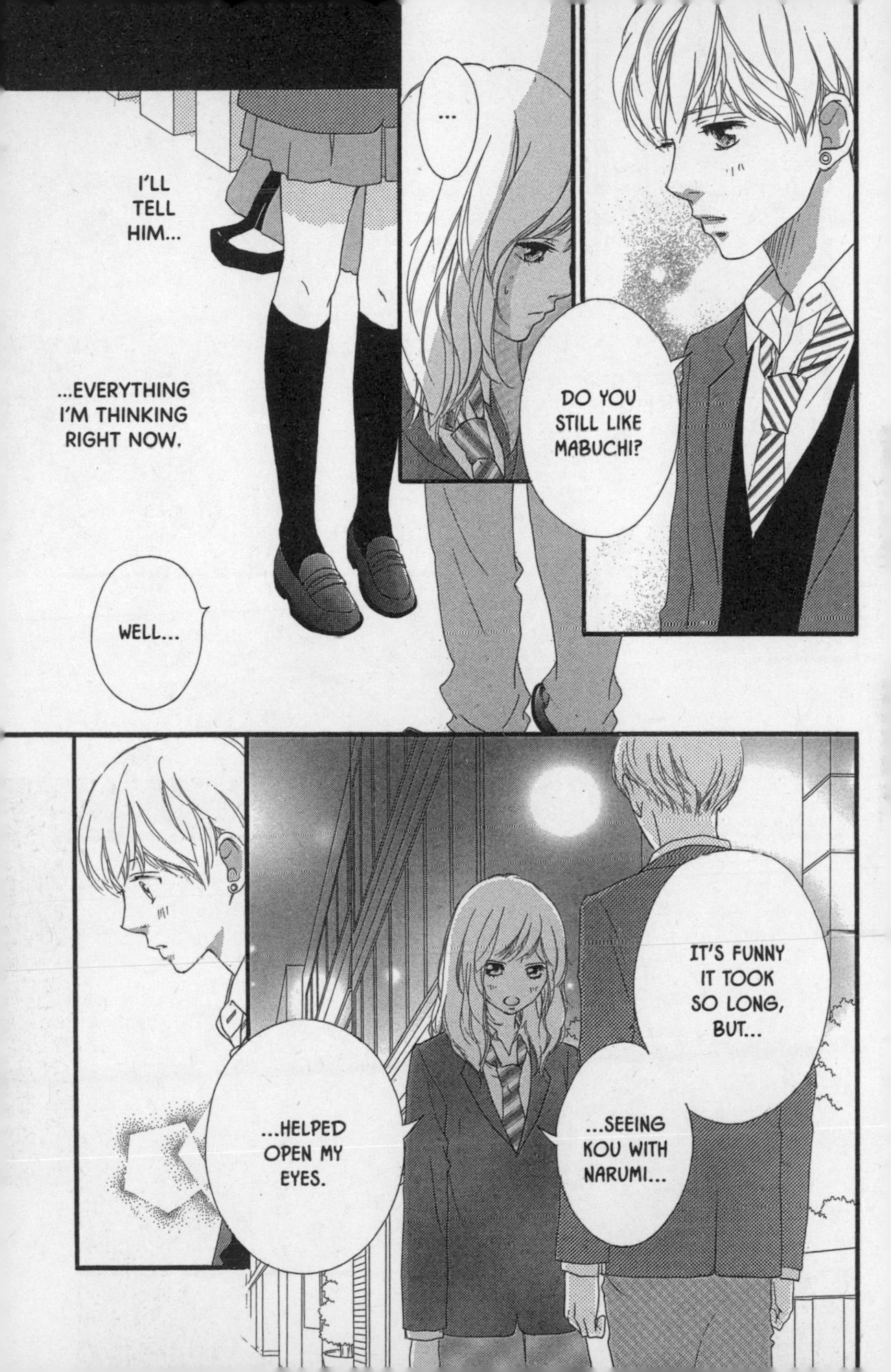
DO YOU STILL LIKE MABUCHI?
...
I'LL TELL HIM...
...EVERYTHING I'M THINKING RIGHT NOW.
WELL...
IT'S FUNNY IT TOOK SO LONG, BUT...
...SEEING KOU WITH NARUMI...
...HELPED OPEN MY EYES.

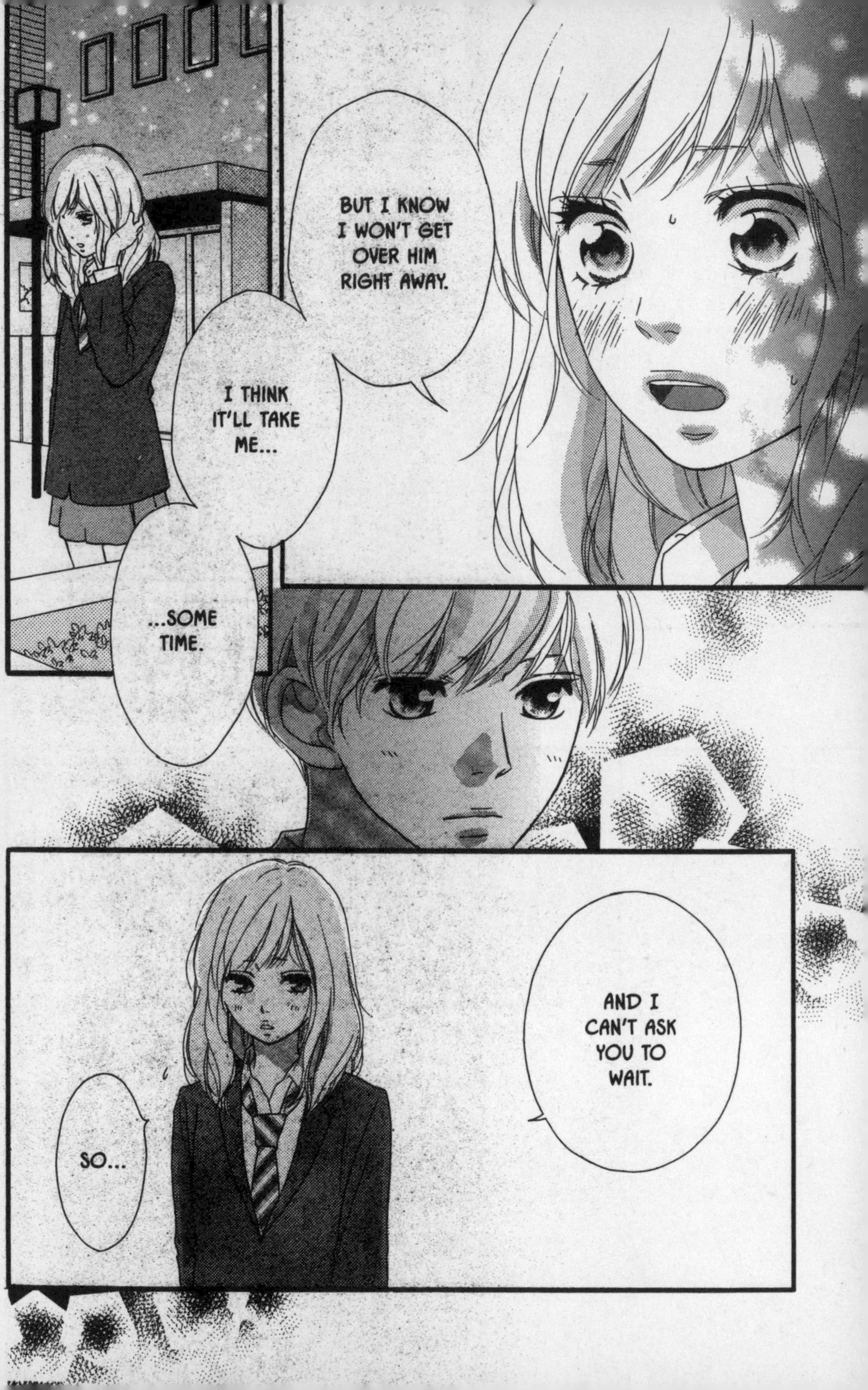
BUT I KNOW I WON'T GET OVER HIM RIGHT AWAY.
I THINK IT'LL TAKE ME...
...SOME TIME.
AND I CAN'T ASK YOU TO WAIT.
SO...

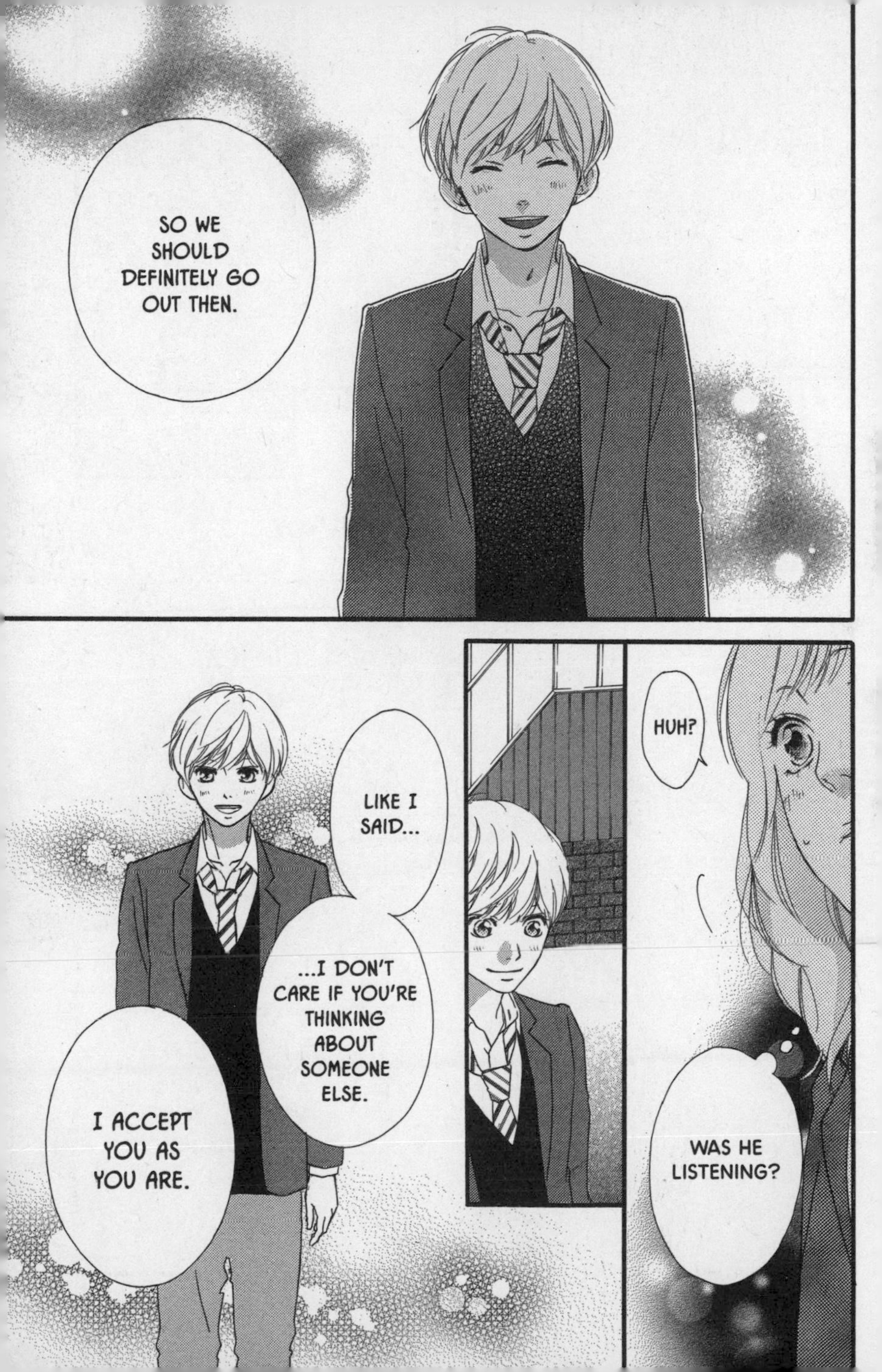
SO WE SHOULD DEFINITELY GO OUT THEN.
HUH?
WAS HE LISTENING?
LIKE I SAID...
...I DON'T CARE IF YOU'RE THINKING ABOUT SOMEONE ELSE.
I ACCEPT YOU AS YOU ARE.

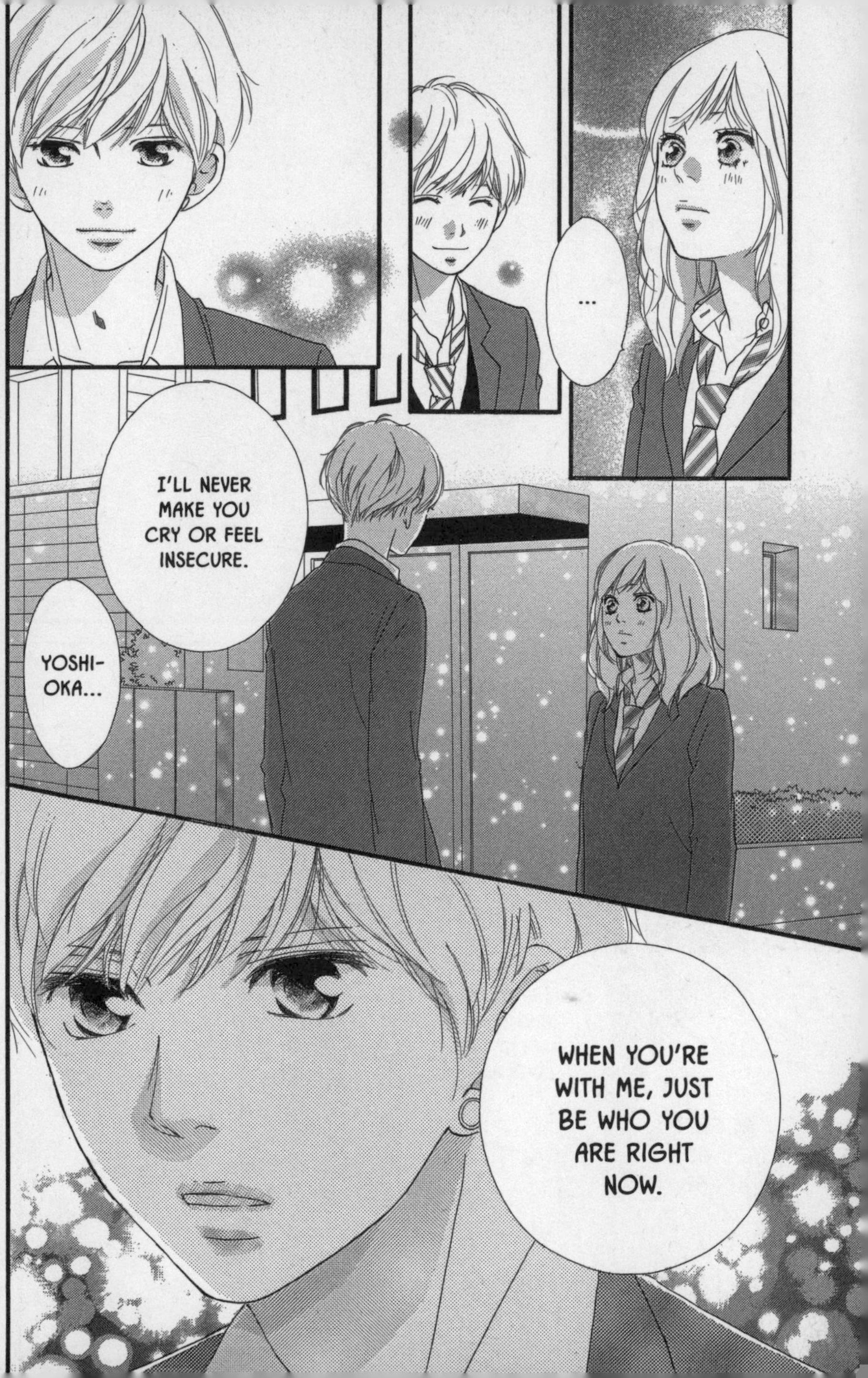
...
I'LL NEVER MAKE YOU CRY OR FEEL INSECURE.
YOSHI-OKA...
WHEN YOU'RE WITH ME, JUST BE WHO YOU ARE RIGHT NOW.

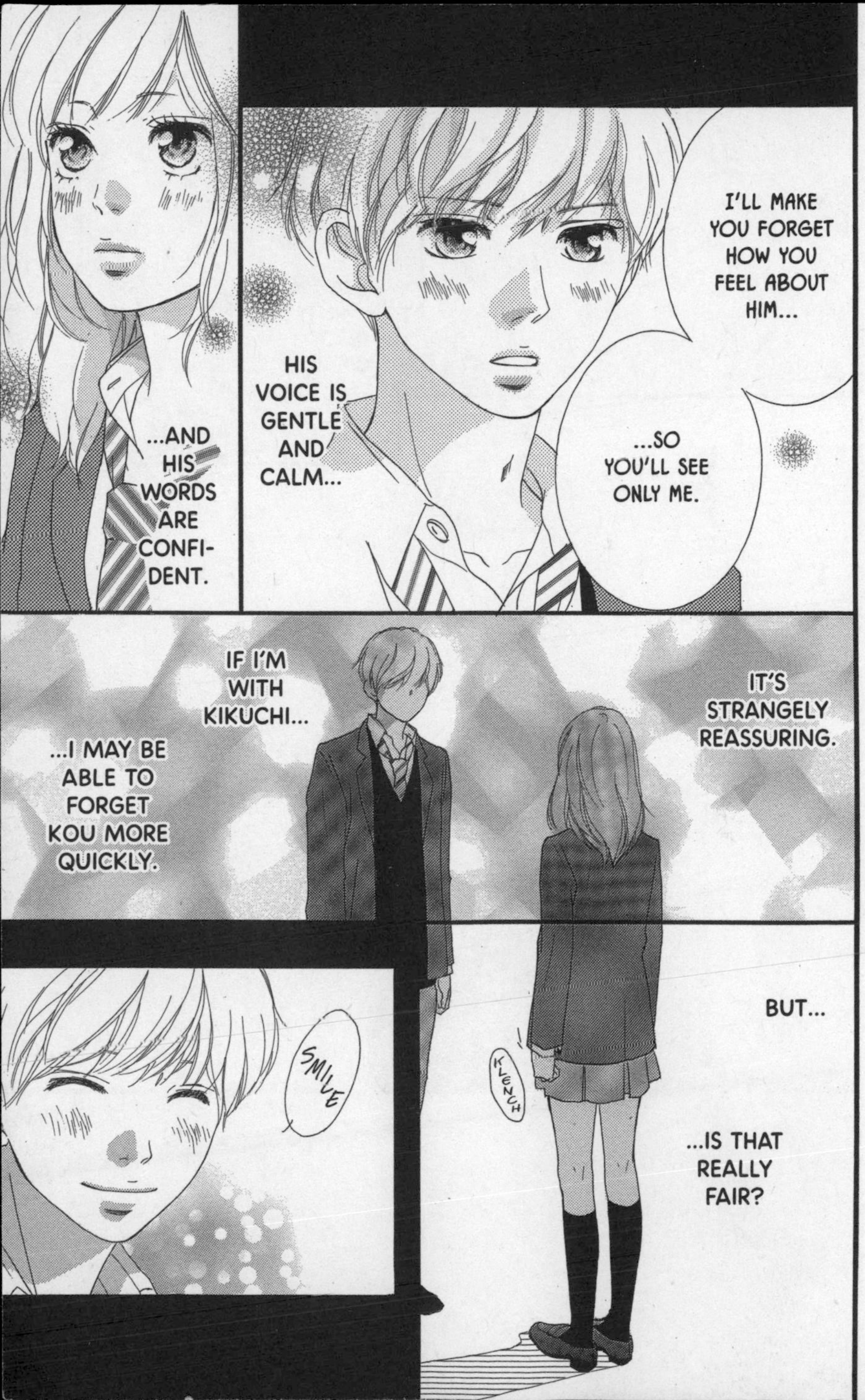
I'LL MAKE YOU FORGET HOW YOU FEEL ABOUT HIM...
...SO YOU'LL SEE ONLY ME.
HIS VOICE IS GENTLE AND CALM...
...AND HIS WORDS ARE CONFI-DENT.
IT'S STRANGELY REASSURING.
IF I'M WITH KIKUCHI...
...I MAY BE ABLE TO FORGET KOU MORE QUICKLY.
BUT...
KLENCH
...IS THAT REALLY FAIR?
SMILE

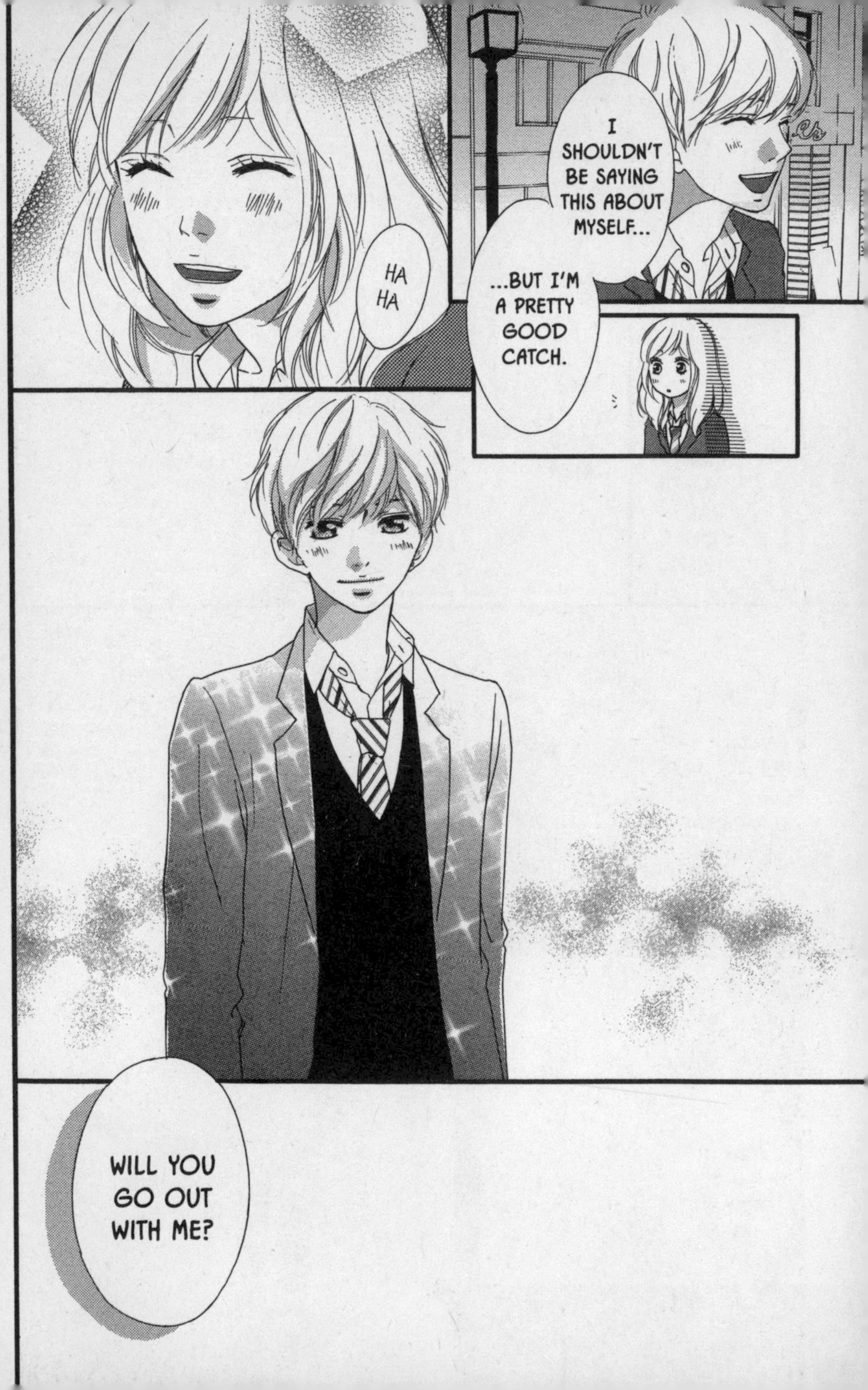
I SHOULDN'T BE SAYING THIS ABOUT MYSELF...
...BUT I'M A PRETTY GOOD CATCH.
HA HA
WILL YOU GO OUT WITH ME?

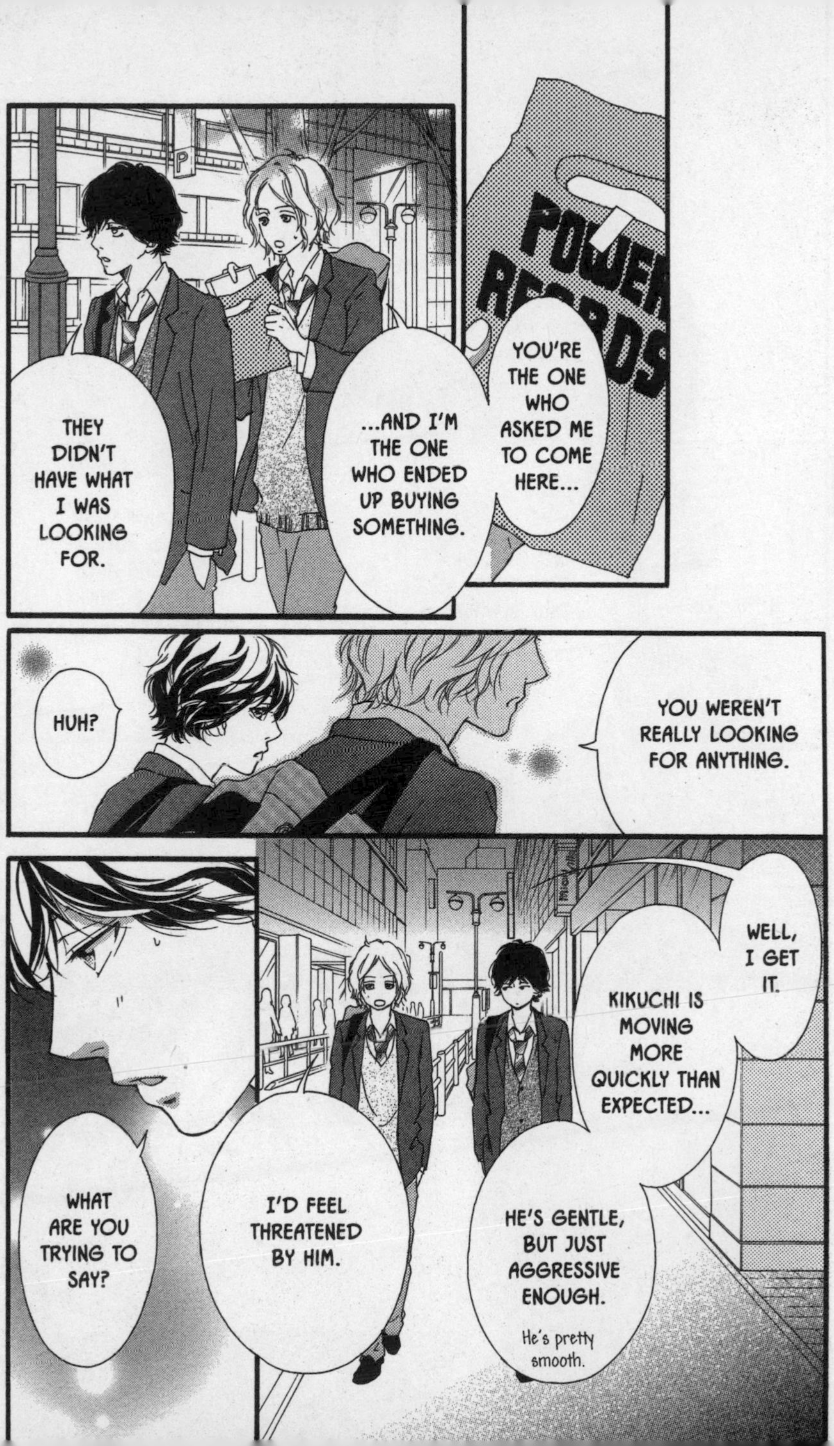
YOU'RE THE ONE WHO ASKED ME TO COME HERE...
...AND I'M THE ONE WHO ENDED UP BUYING SOMETHING.
THEY DIDN'T HAVE WHAT I WAS LOOKING FOR.
YOU WEREN'T REALLY LOOKING FOR ANYTHING.
HUH?
WELL, I GET IT.
KIKUCHI IS MOVING MORE QUICKLY THAN EXPECTED...
HE'S GENTLE, BUT JUST AGGRESSIVE ENOUGH.
He's pretty smooth.
I'D FEEL THREATENED BY HIM.
WHAT ARE YOU TRYING TO SAY?

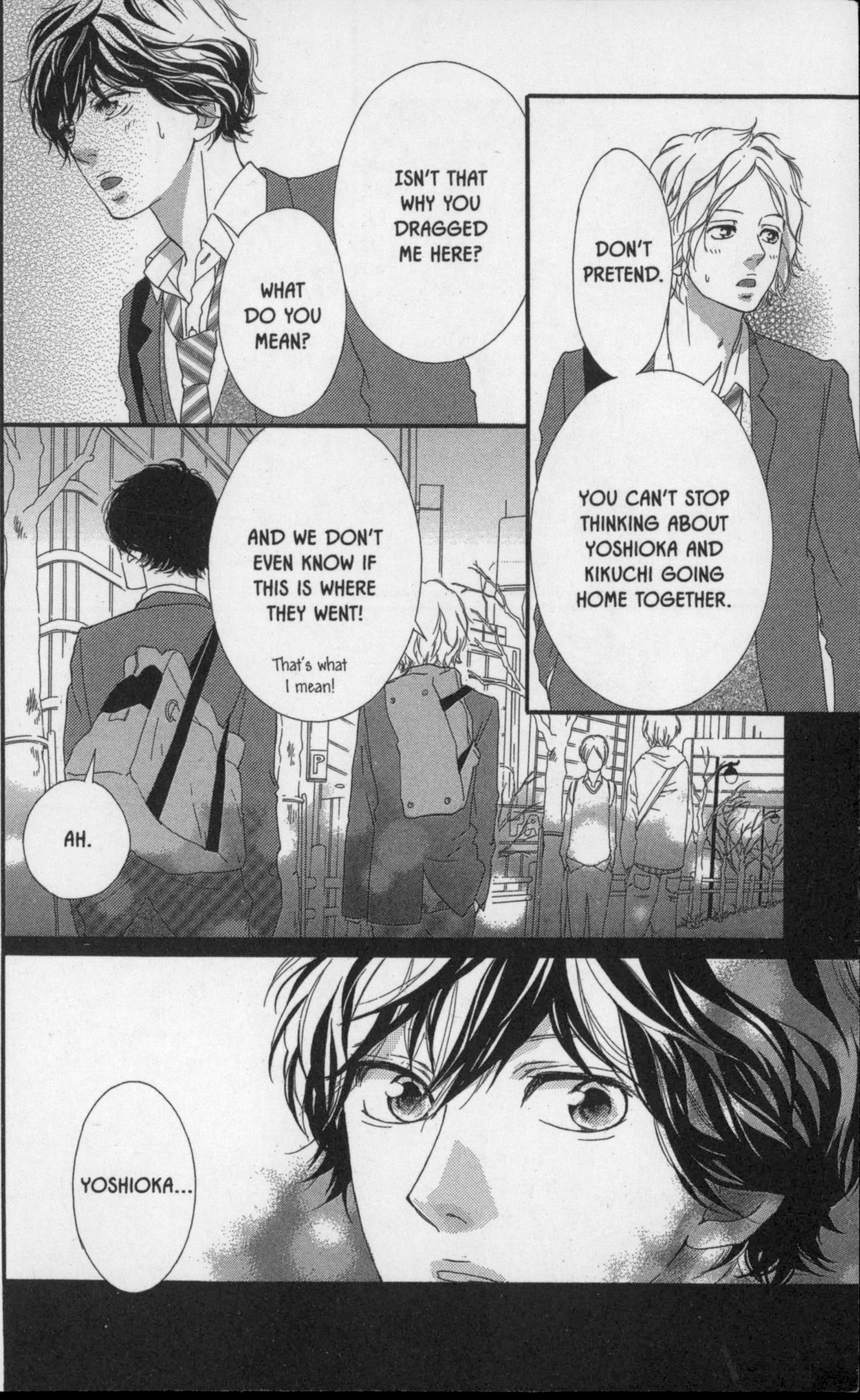
DON'T PRETEND.
YOU CAN'T STOP THINKING ABOUT YOSHIOKA AND KIKUCHI GOING HOME TOGETHER.
ISN'T THAT WHY YOU DRAGGED ME HERE?
WHAT DO YOU MEAN?
AND WE DON'T EVEN KNOW IF THIS IS WHERE THEY WENT!
That's what I mean!
AH.
YOSHIOKA...

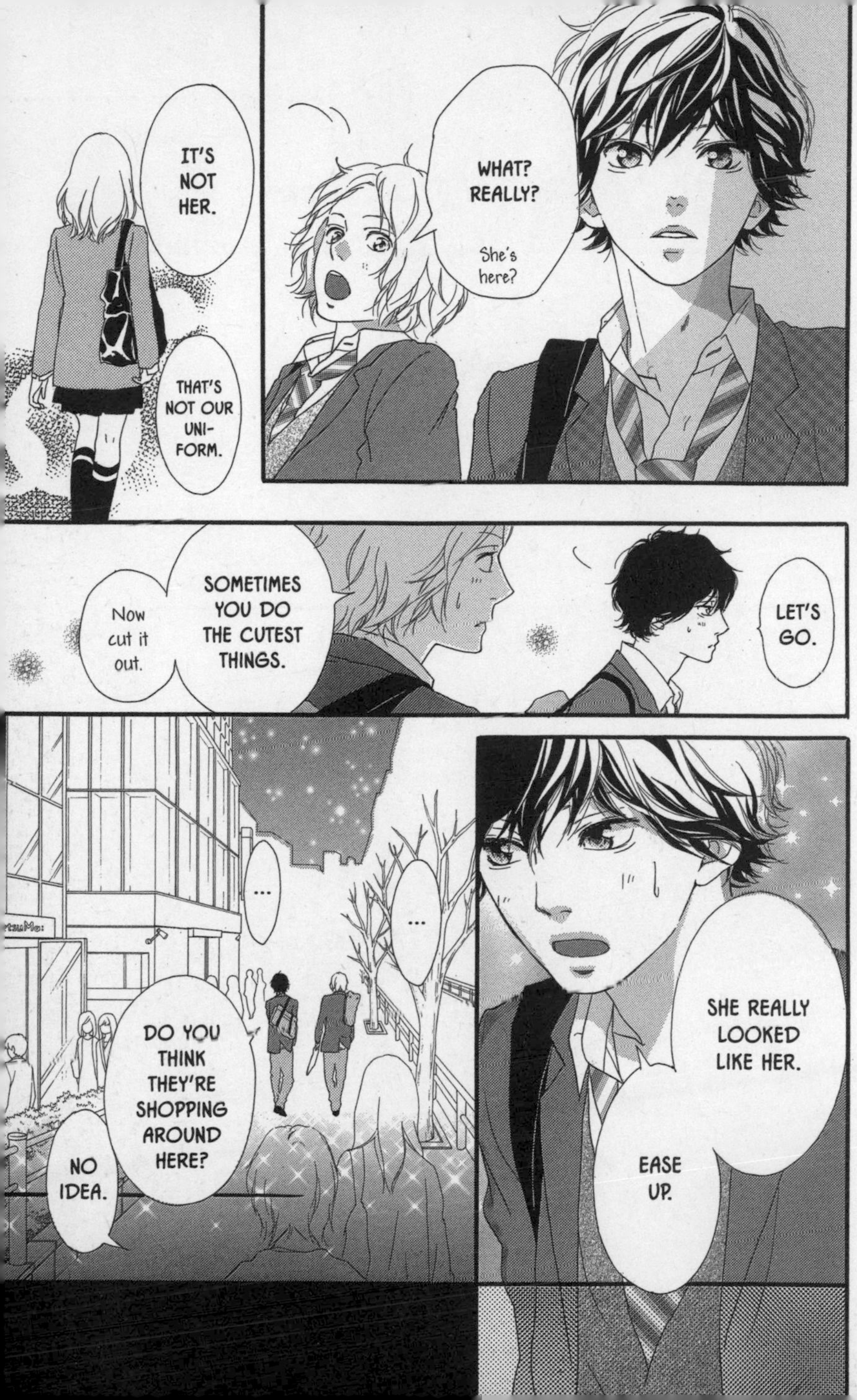
WHAT? REALLY?
She's here?
IT'S NOT HER.
THAT'S NOT OUR UNI-FORM.
LET'S GO.
SOMETIMES YOU DO THE CUTEST THINGS.
Now cut it out.
SHE REALLY LOOKED LIKE HER.
EASE UP.
...
...
DO YOU THINK THEY'RE SHOPPING AROUND HERE?
NO IDEA.

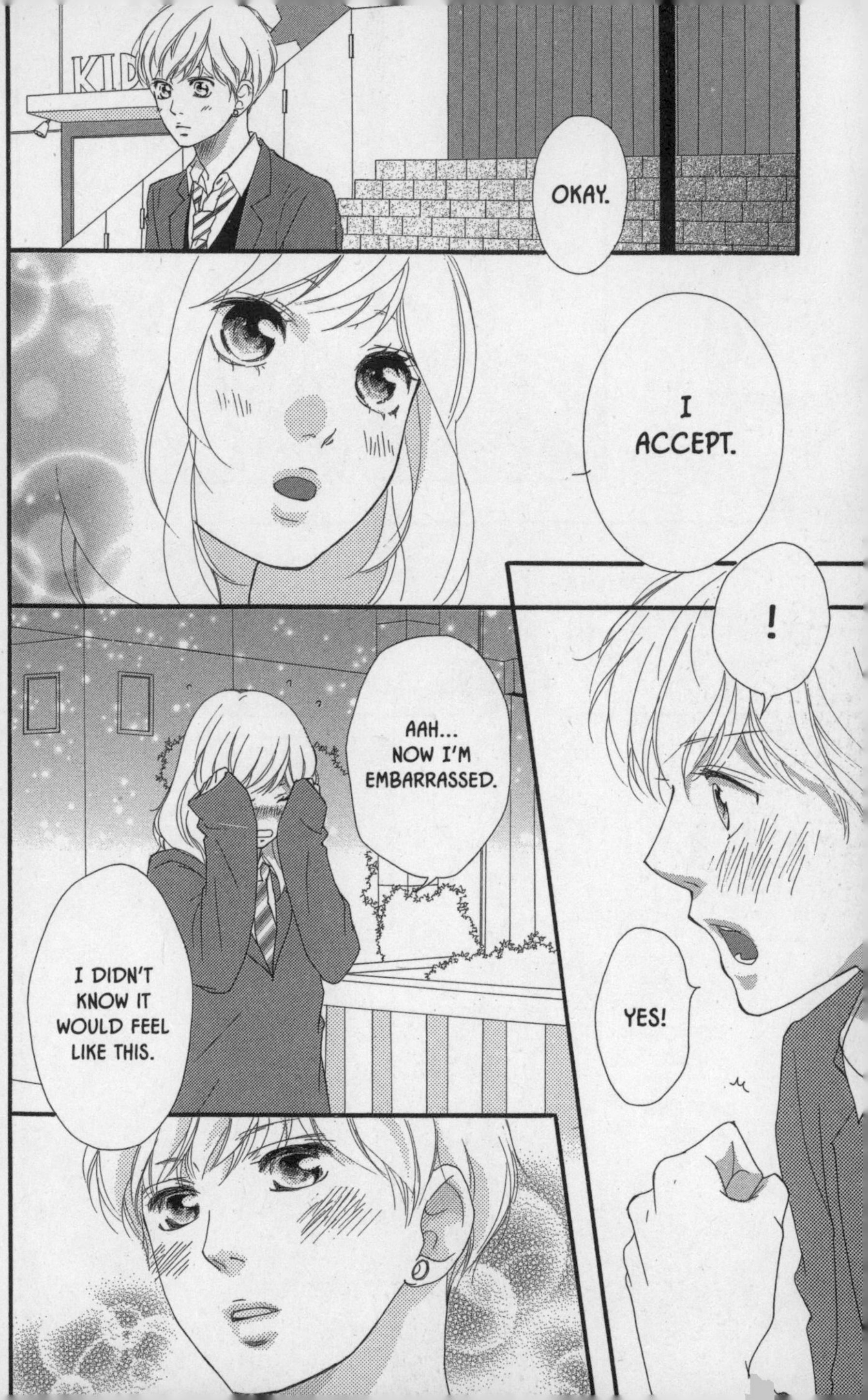
KID
OKAY.
I ACCEPT.
!
YES!
AAH... NOW I'M EMBARRASSED.
I DIDN'T KNOW IT WOULD FEEL LIKE THIS.

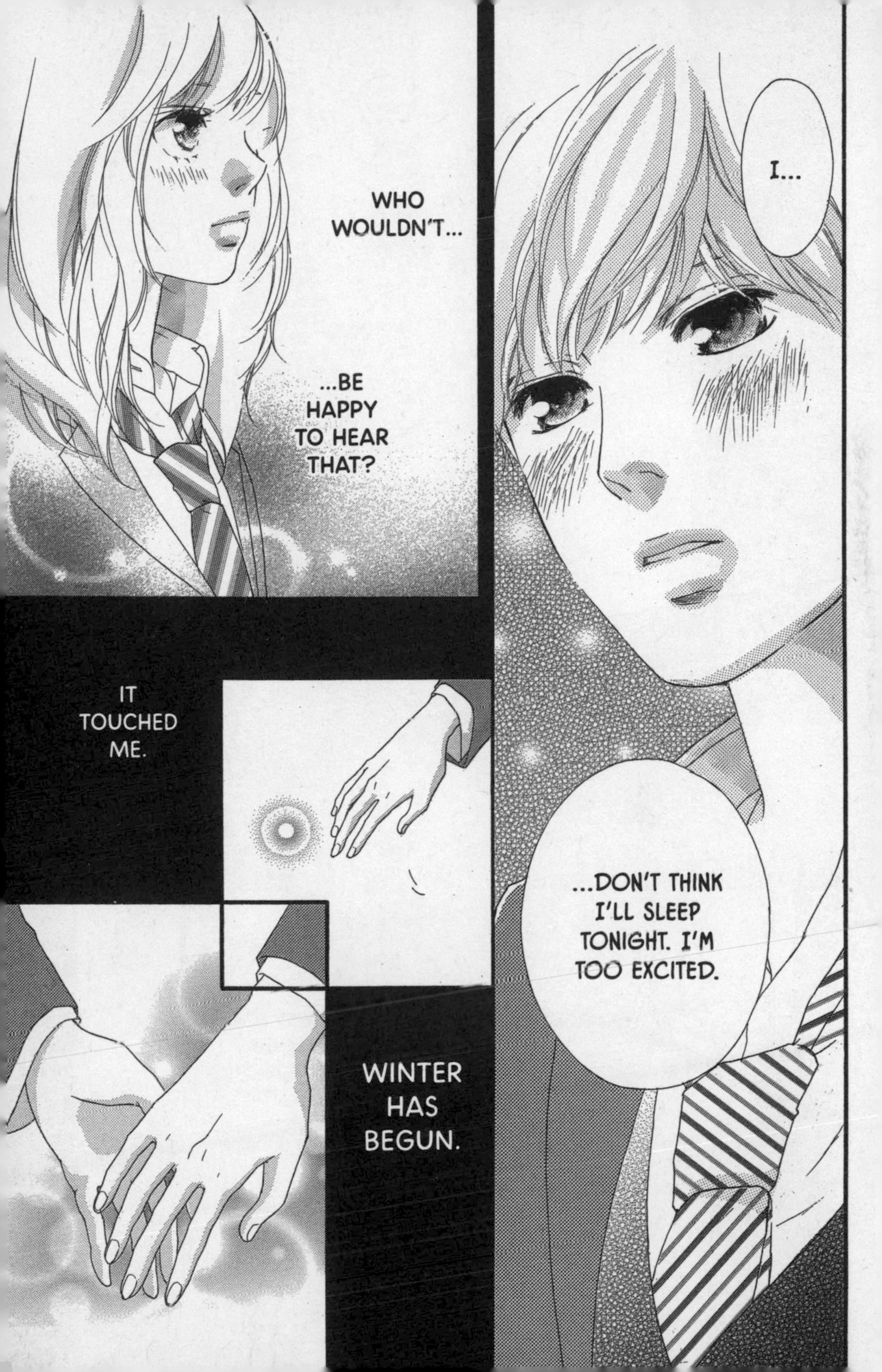
I...
...DON'T THINK I'LL SLEEP TONIGHT. I'M TOO EXCITED.
WHO WOULDN'T...
...BE HAPPY TO HEAR THAT?
IT TOUCHED ME.
WINTER HAS BEGUN.

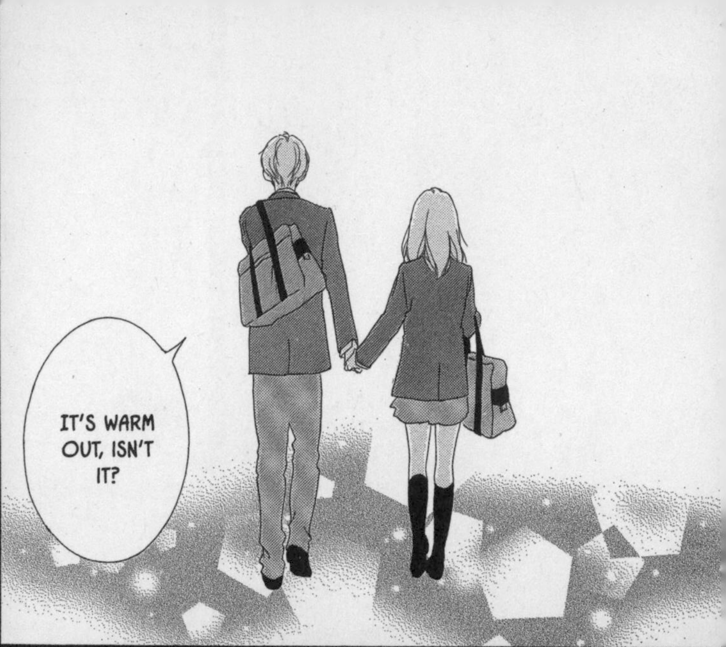
IT'S WARM OUT, ISN'T IT?

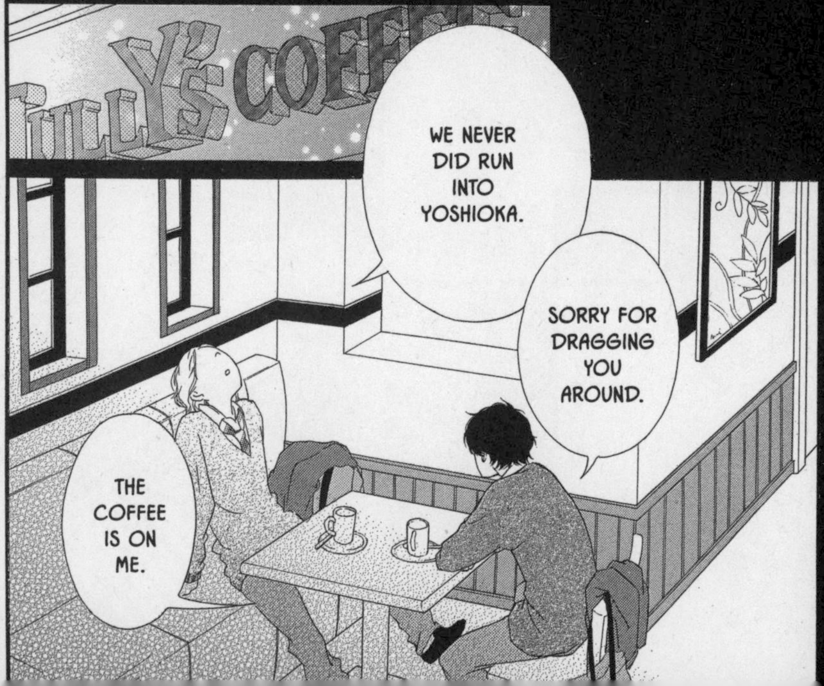
WE NEVER DID RUN INTO YOSHIOKA.
SORRY FOR DRAGGING YOU AROUND.
THE COFFEE IS ON ME.

One day someone gave me a branch of crape myrtle. They said it wasn't likely to take root, so I merely stabbed it into the soil by the entrance to my home. I didn't think much about its placement because I figured it would never grow, but it's grown quite a bit. It's still on the small side though it flowers. Not only that, but its branches grow as if they would grab anyone who walked by. I really wonder why they keep stretching out in that way. When I go to get my mail, I get poked if I'm not careful. Since I'm usually holed up inside working, it doesn't bother me that much, but I get a lot of deliveries, and I wonder what the delivery people must think. I do apologize. I truly didn't expect it to grow as much as it has. But gosh, I was really happy when I saw my little myrtle branch blossom!

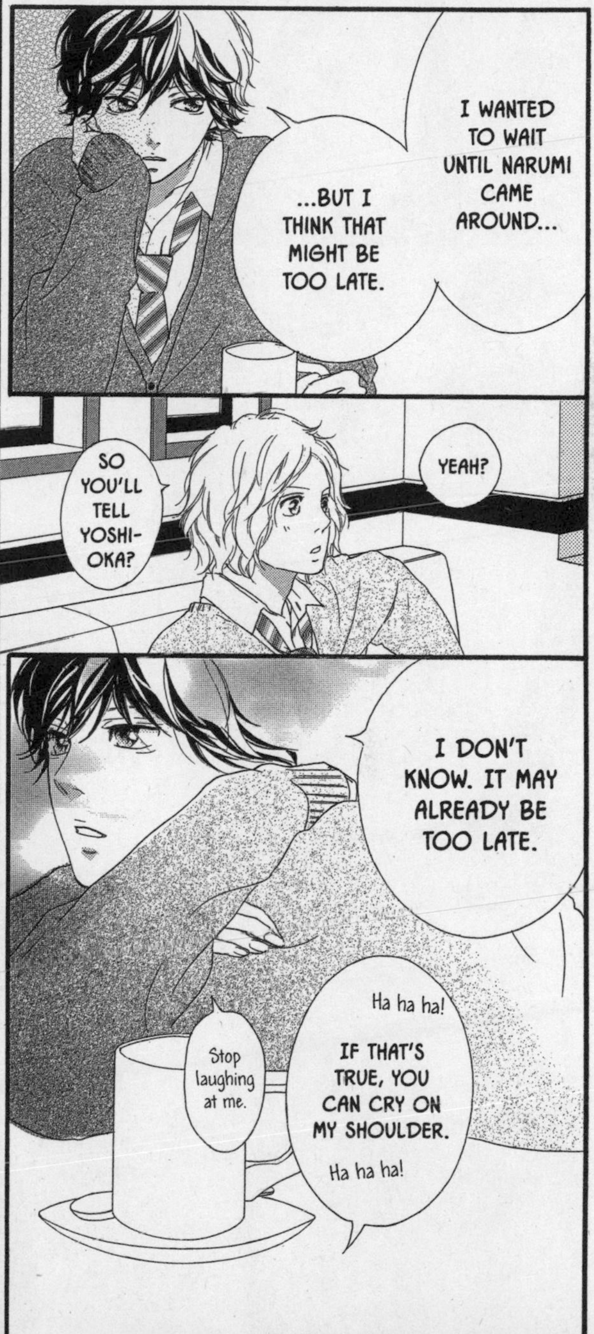
I WANTED TO WAIT UNTIL NARUMI CAME AROUND...
...BUT I THINK THAT MIGHT BE TOO LATE.
YEAH?
SO YOU'LL TELL YOSHI-OKA?
I DON'T KNOW. IT MAY ALREADY BE TOO LATE.
Ha ha ha!
IF THAT'S TRUE, YOU CAN CRY ON MY SHOULDER.
Ha ha ha!
Stop laughing at me.

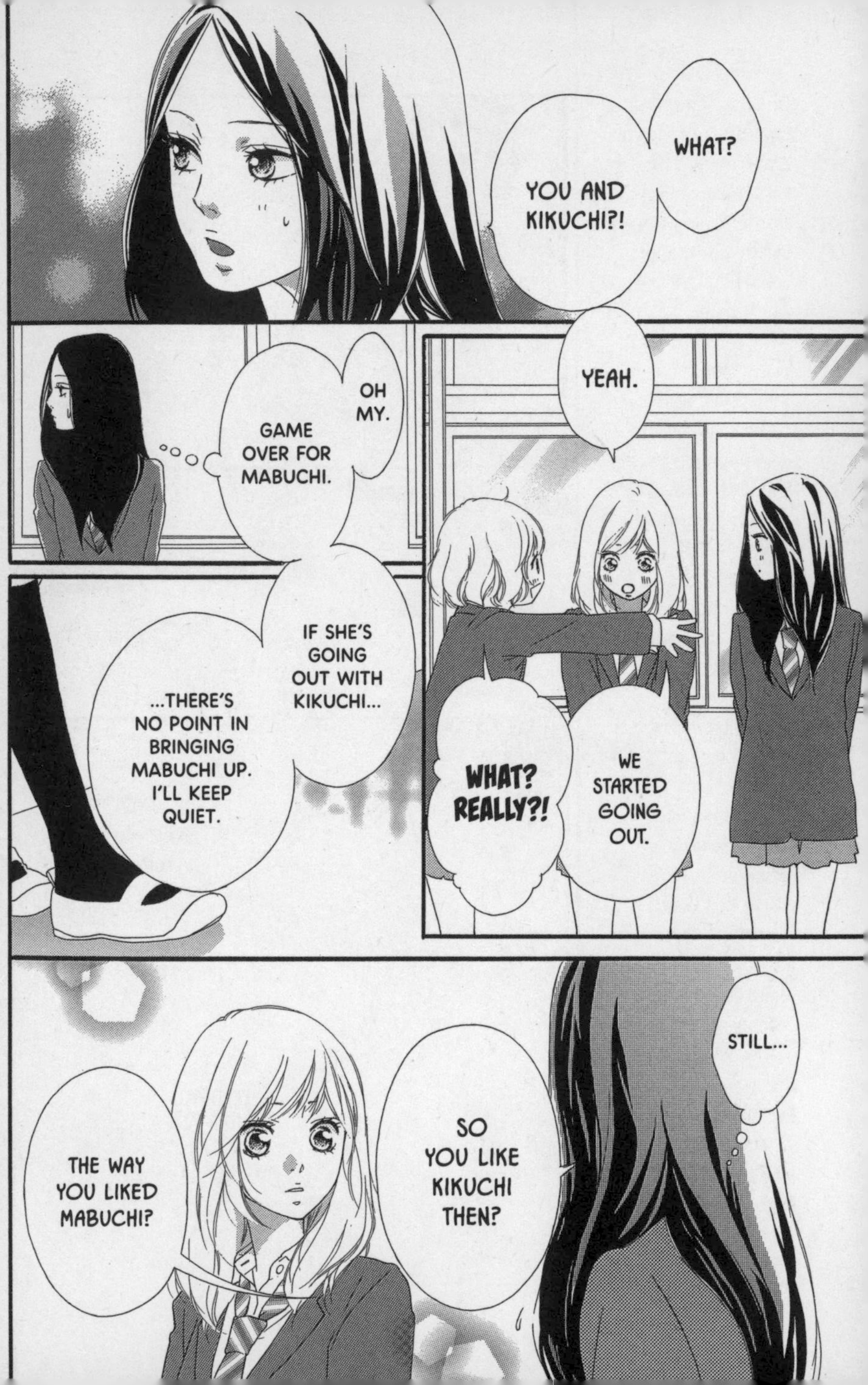
WHAT?
YOU AND KIKUCHI?!
YEAH.
WE STARTED GOING OUT.
WHAT? REALLY?!
OH MY.
GAME OVER FOR MABUCHI.
IF SHE'S GOING OUT WITH KIKUCHI...
...THERE'S NO POINT IN BRINGING MABUCHI UP. I'LL KEEP QUIET.
STILL...
SO YOU LIKE KIKUCHI THEN?
THE WAY YOU LIKED MABUCHI?

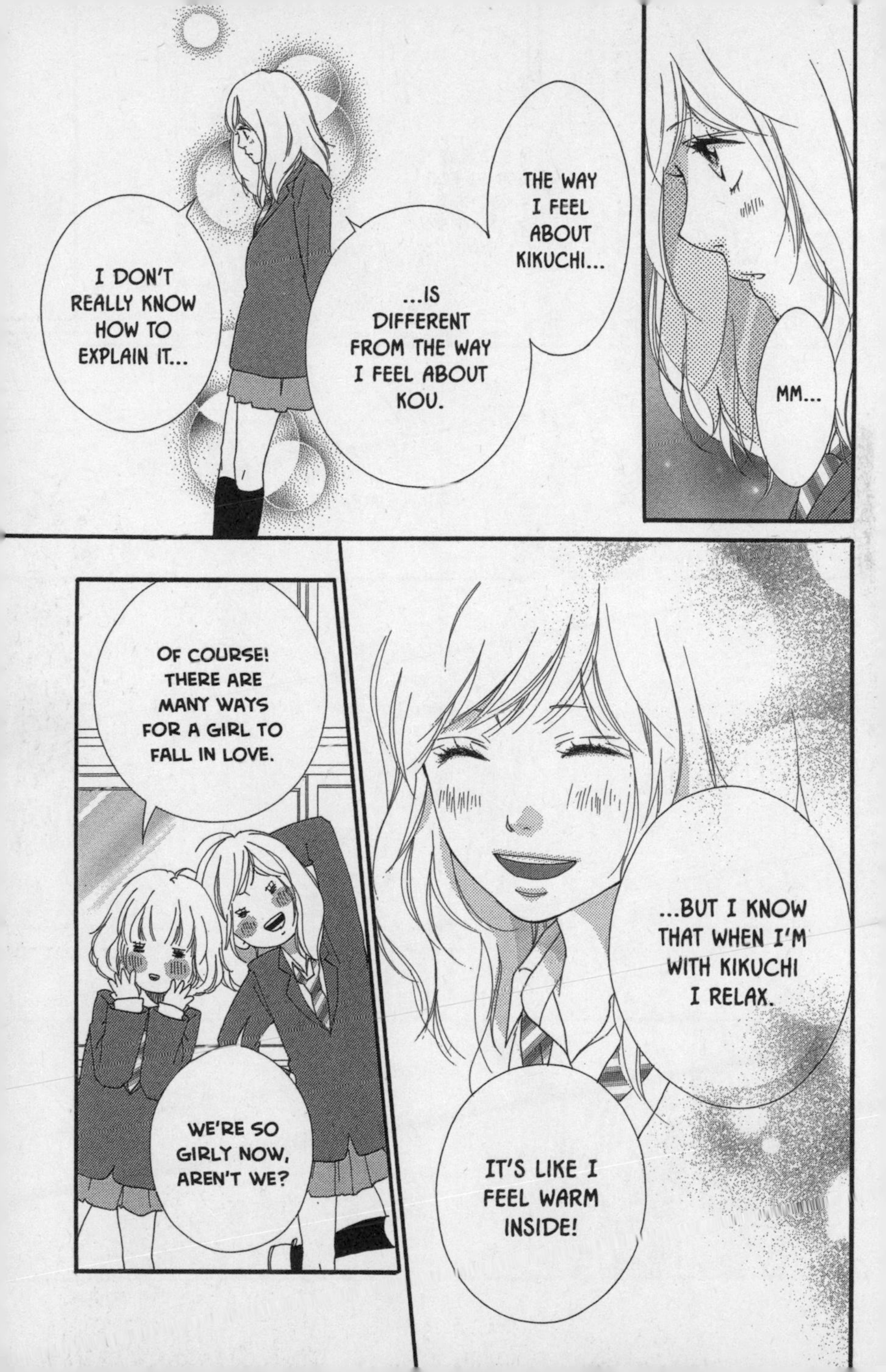
MM...
THE WAY I FEEL ABOUT KIKUCHI...
...IS DIFFERENT FROM THE WAY I FEEL ABOUT KOU.
I DON'T REALLY KNOW HOW TO EXPLAIN IT...
...BUT I KNOW THAT WHEN I'M WITH KIKUCHI I RELAX.
IT'S LIKE I FEEL WARM INSIDE!
OF COURSE! THERE ARE MANY WAYS FOR A GIRL TO FALL IN LOVE.
WE'RE SO GIRLY NOW, AREN'T WE?

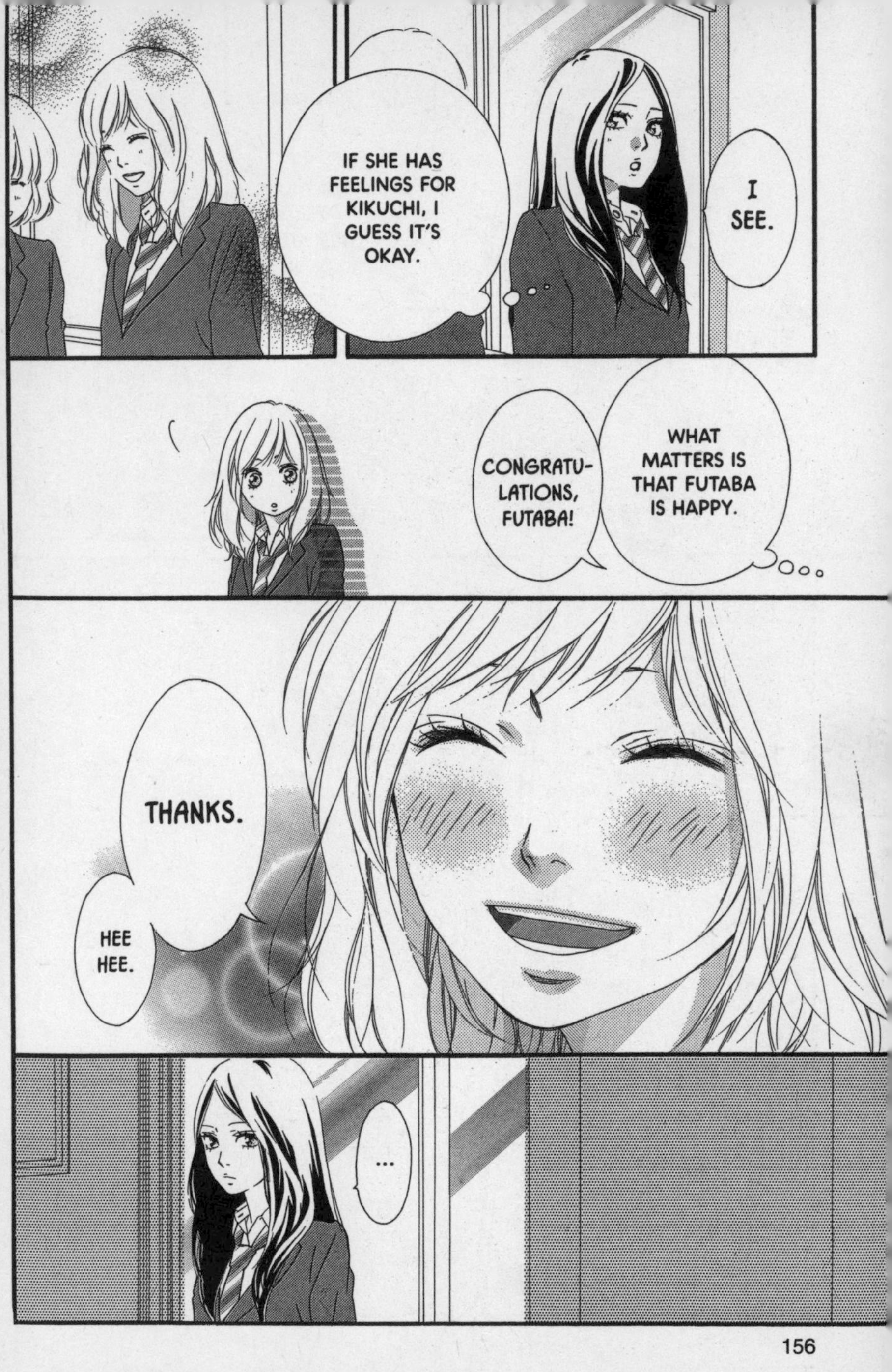
I SEE.
IF SHE HAS FEELINGS FOR KIKUCHI, I GUESS IT'S OKAY.
WHAT MATTERS IS THAT FUTABA IS HAPPY.
CONGRATU-LATIONS, FUTABA!
THANKS.
HEE HEE.
...

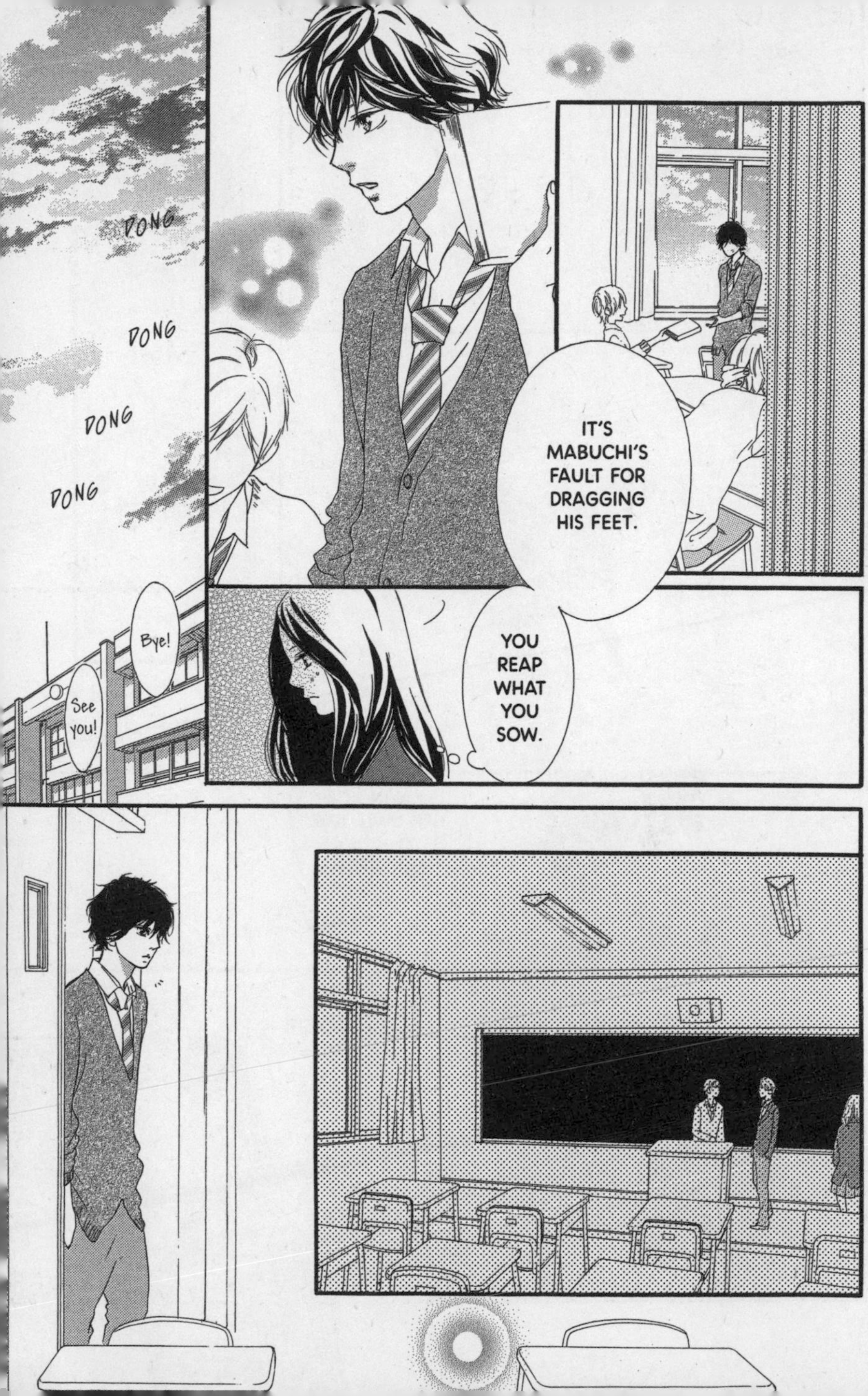

IT'S MABUCHI'S FAULT FOR DRAGGING HIS FEET.
YOU REAP WHAT YOU SOW.
DONG
DONG
DONG
DONG
Bye!
See you!

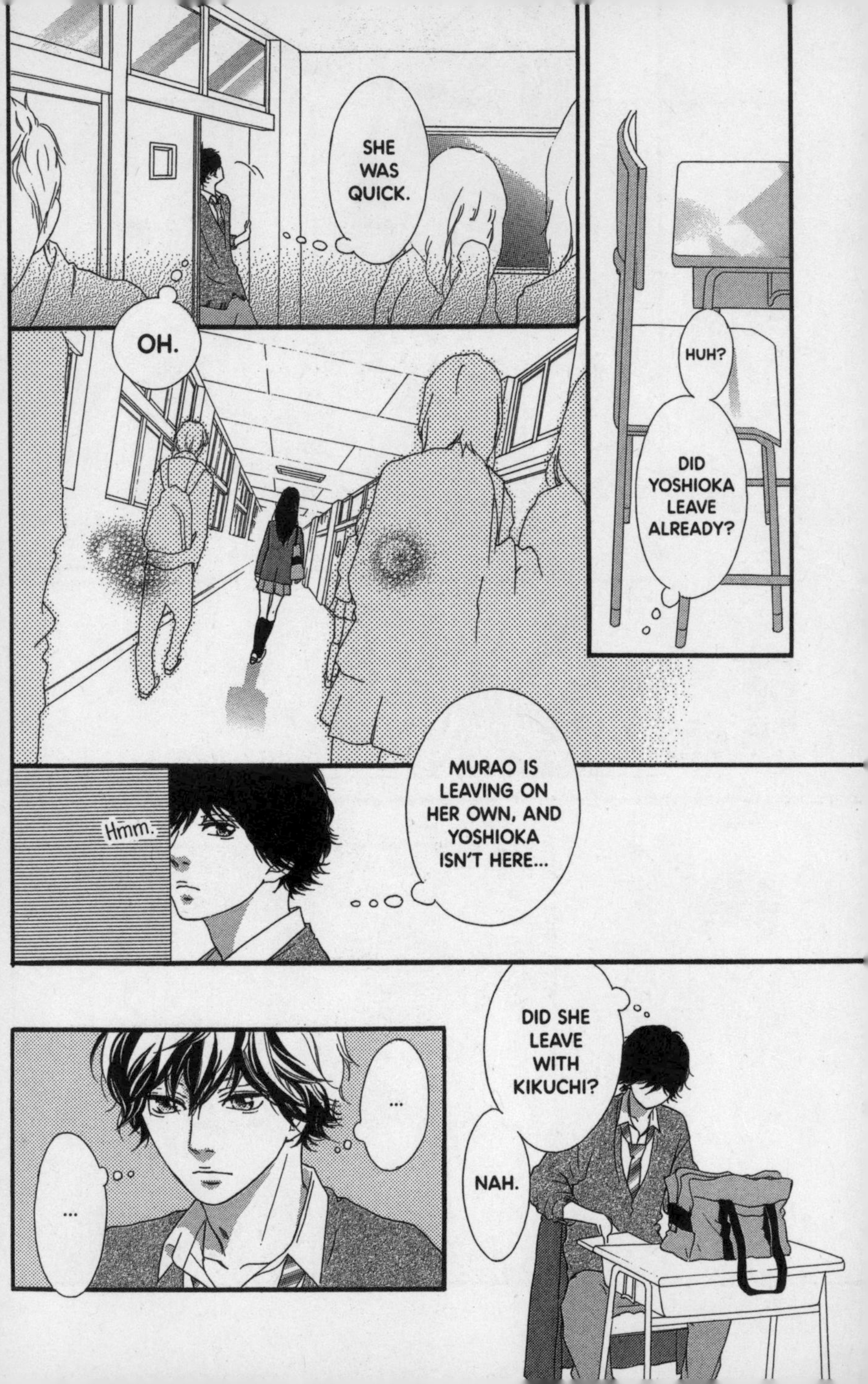
HUH?
DID YOSHIOKA LEAVE ALREADY?
SHE WAS QUICK.
OH.
MURAO IS LEAVING ON HER OWN, AND YOSHIOKA ISN'T HERE...
Hmm.
DID SHE LEAVE WITH KIKUCHI?
NAH.
...
...

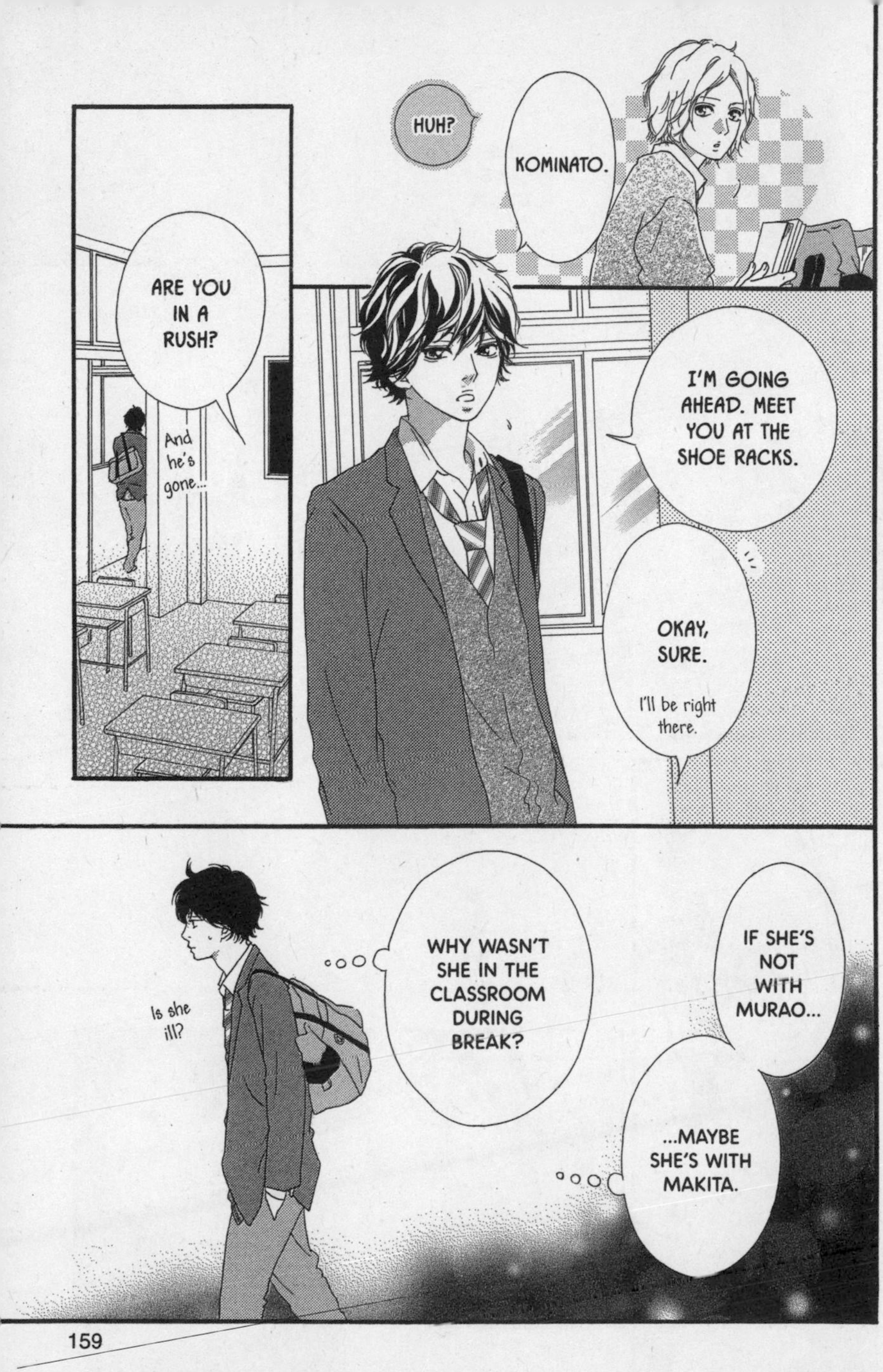
KOMINATO.
HUH?
I'M GOING AHEAD. MEET YOU AT THE SHOE RACKS.
OKAY, SURE.
I'll be right there.
ARE YOU IN A RUSH?
And he's gone...
IF SHE'S NOT WITH MURAO...
...MAYBE SHE'S WITH MAKITA.
WHY WASN'T SHE IN THE CLASSROOM DURING BREAK?
Is she ill?

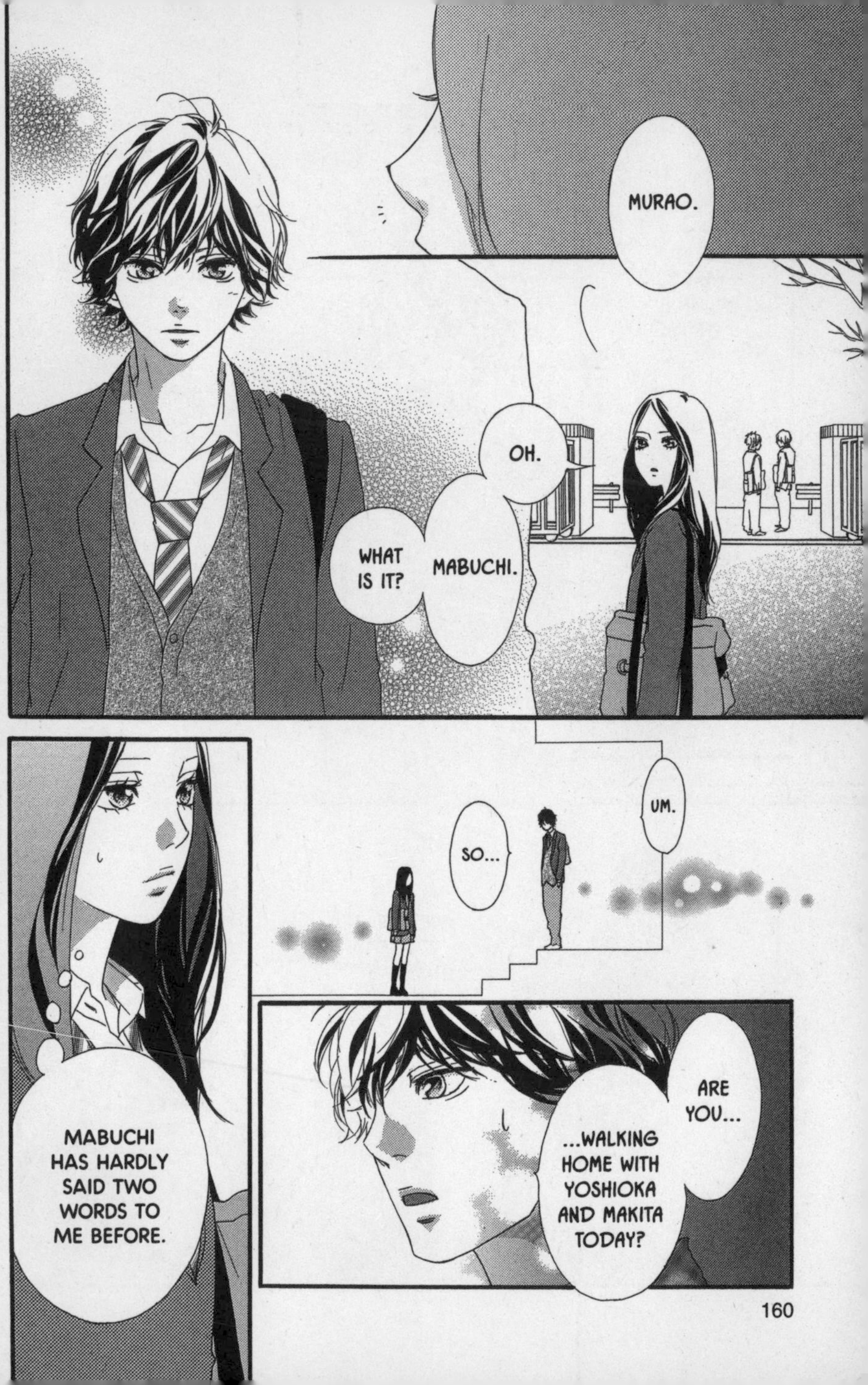
MURAO.
OH.
MABUCHI.
WHAT IS IT?
UM.
SO...
ARE YOU...
...WALKING HOME WITH YOSHIOKA AND MAKITA TODAY?
MABUCHI HAS HARDLY SAID TWO WORDS TO ME BEFORE.

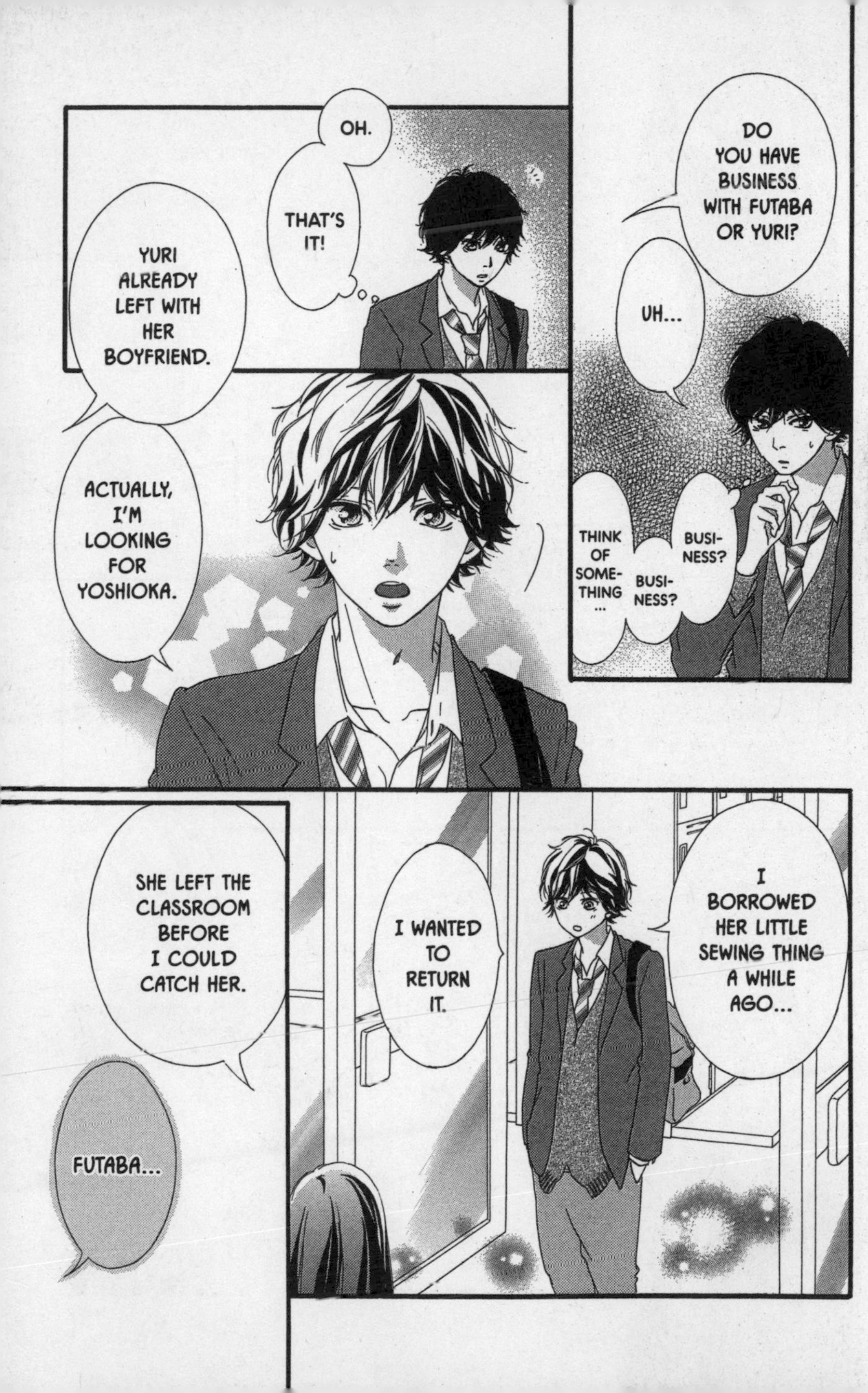
DO YOU HAVE BUSINESS WITH FUTABA OR YURI?
UH...
BUSI-NESS?
BUSI-NESS?
THINK OF SOME-THING...
OH.
THAT'S IT!
YURI ALREADY LEFT WITH HER BOYFRIEND.
ACTUALLY, I'M LOOKING FOR YOSHIOKA.
I BORROWED HER LITTLE SEWING THING A WHILE AGO...
I WANTED TO RETURN IT.
SHE LEFT THE CLASSROOM BEFORE I COULD CATCH HER.
FUTABA...

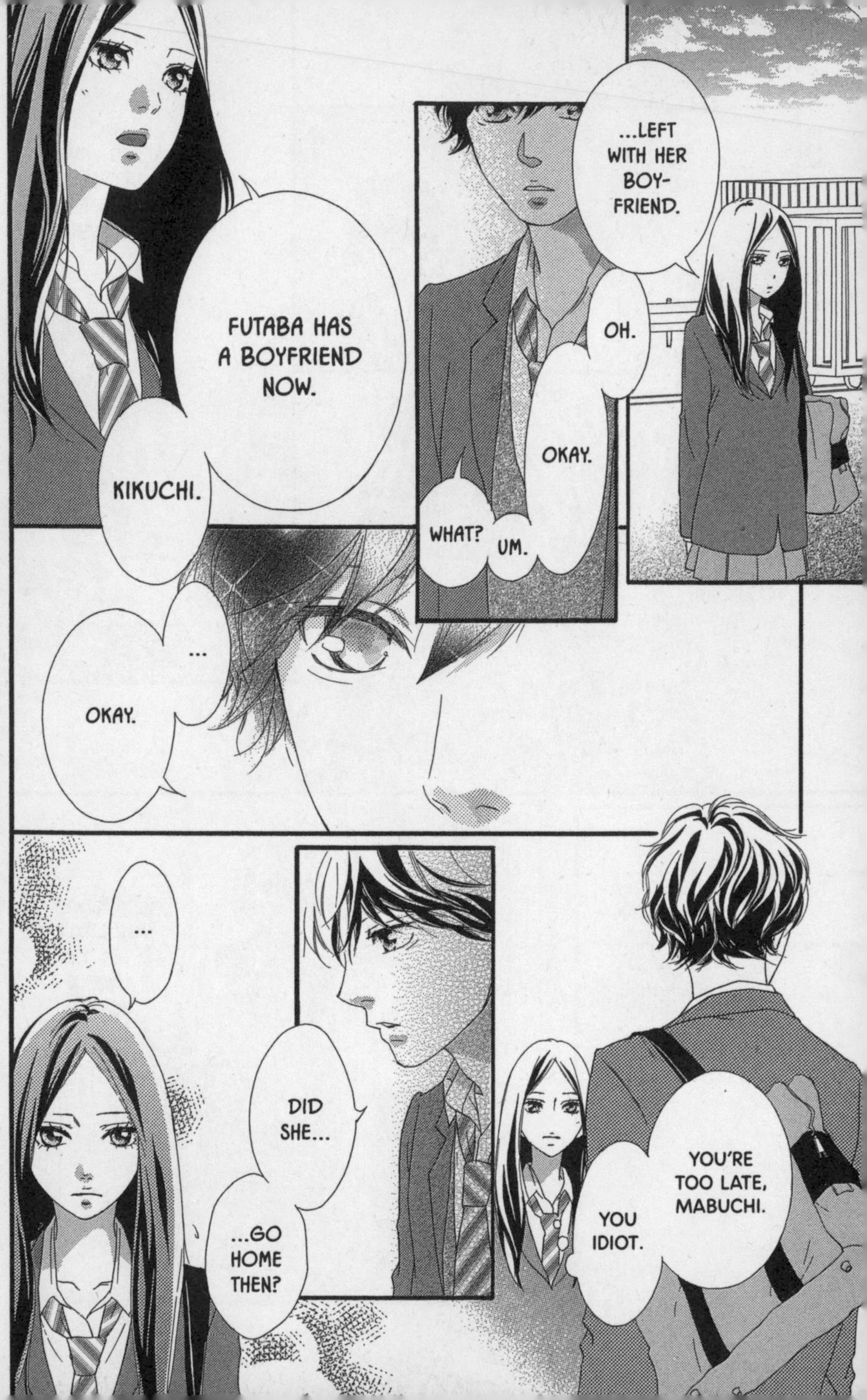
...LEFT WITH HER BOY-FRIEND.
OH.
OKAY.
UM.
WHAT?
FUTABA HAS A BOYFRIEND NOW.
KIKUCHI.
...
OKAY.
YOU'RE TOO LATE, MABUCHI.
YOU IDIOT.
DID SHE...
...GO HOME THEN?
...

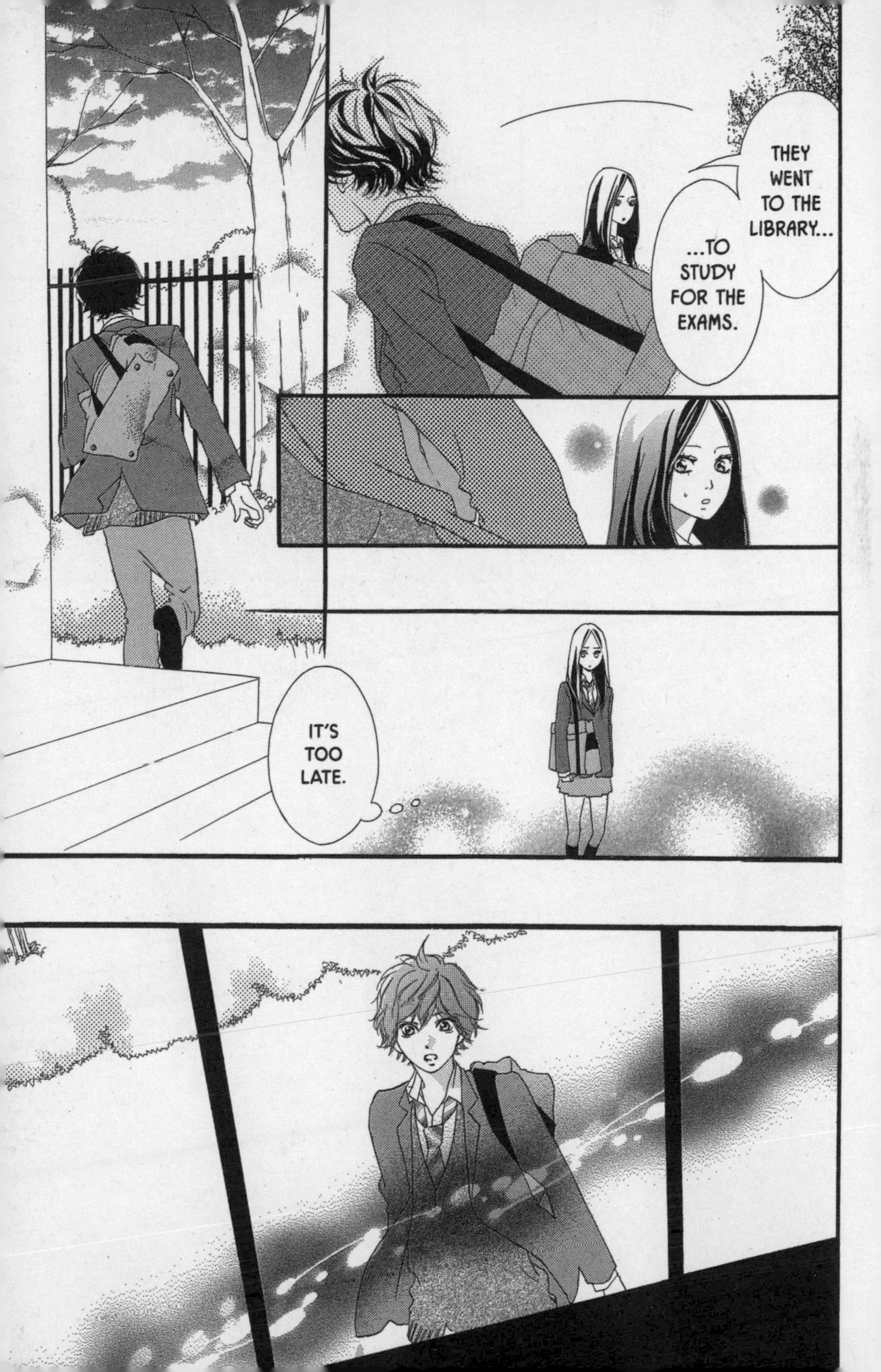
THEY WENT TO THE LIBRARY...
...TO STUDY FOR THE EXAMS.
IT'S TOO LATE.

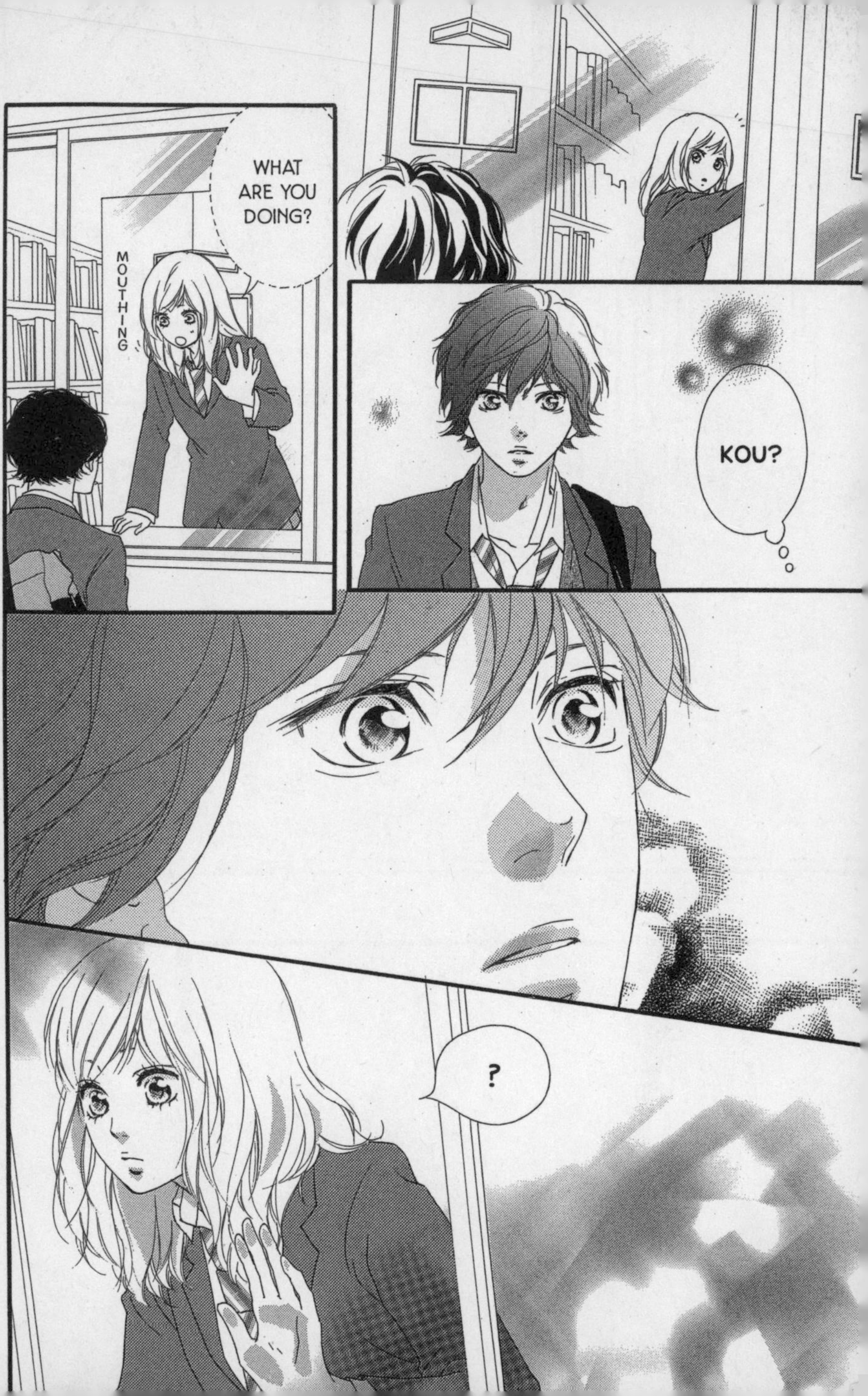
KOU?
MOUTHING
WHAT ARE YOU DOING?
?

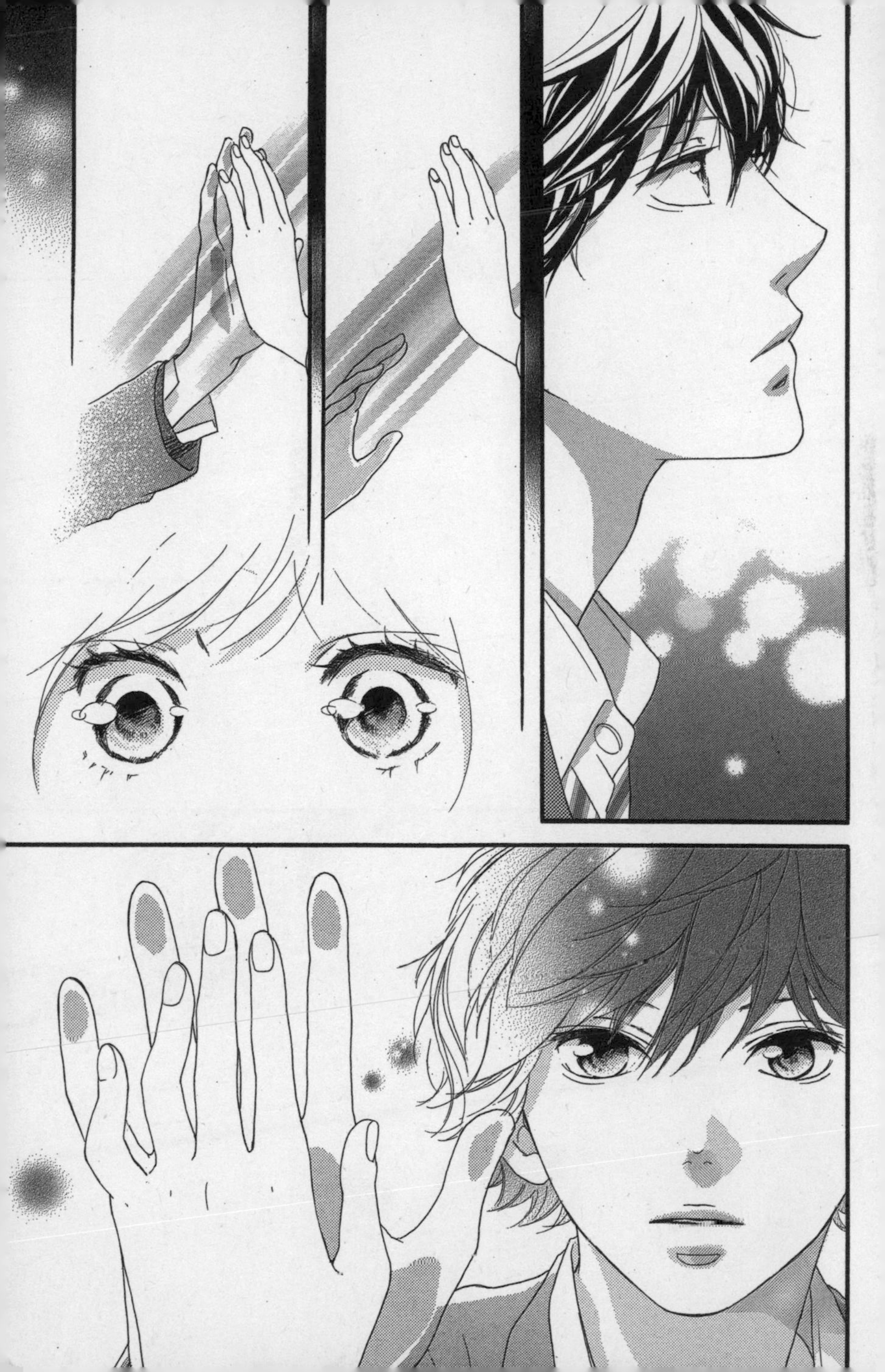

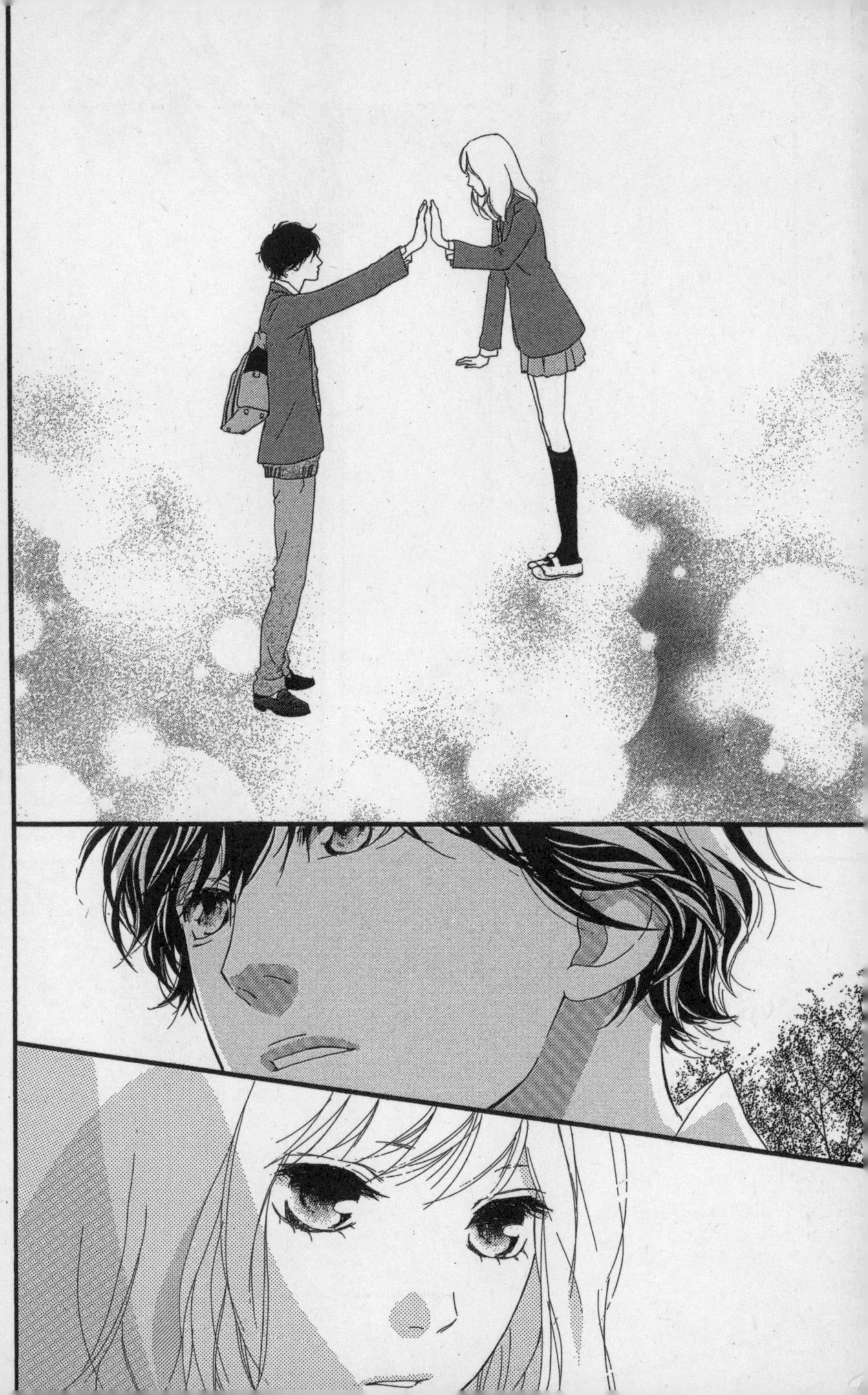

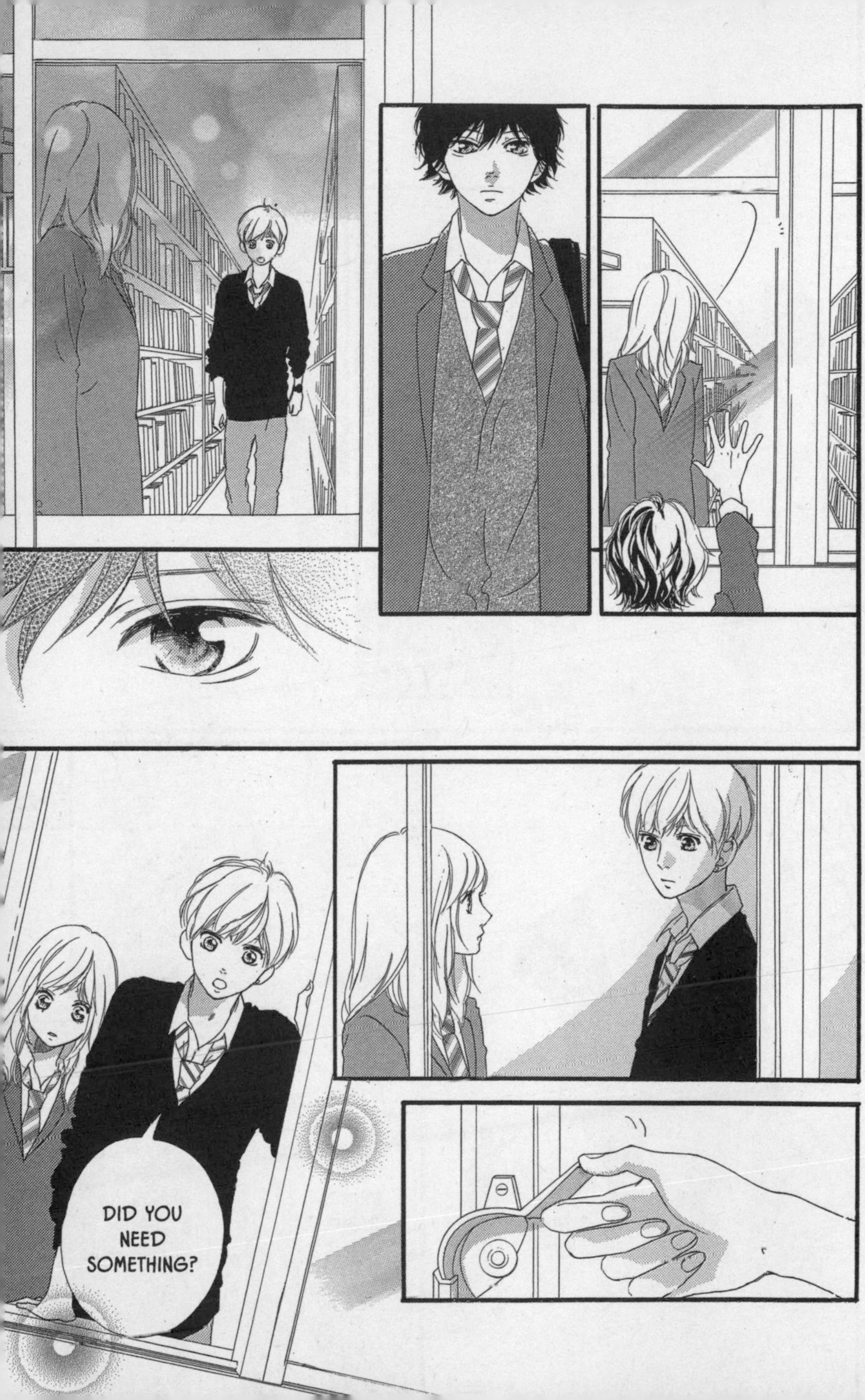
DID YOU NEED SOMETHING?

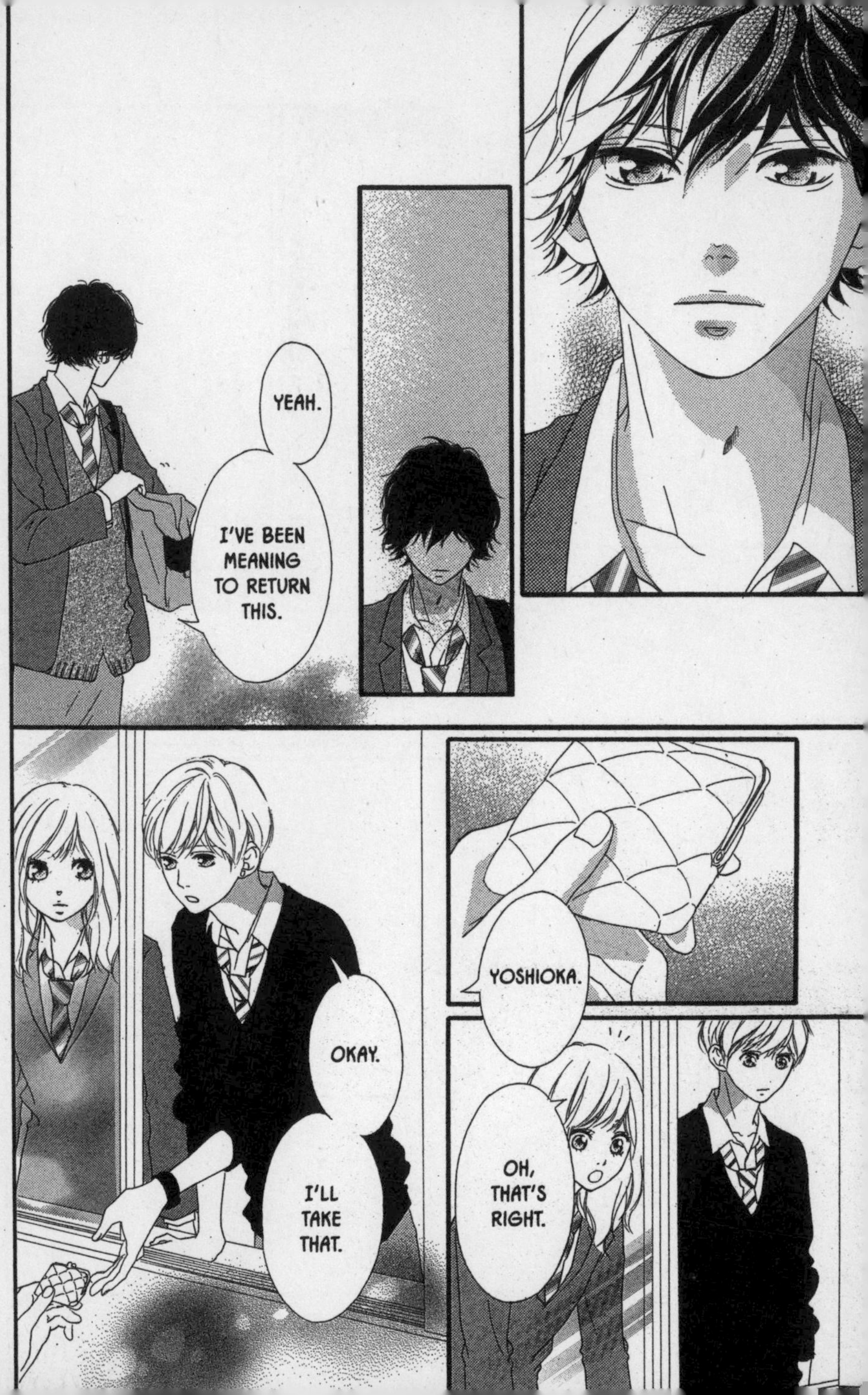
YEAH.
I'VE BEEN MEANING TO RETURN THIS.
YOSHIOKA.
OH, THAT'S RIGHT.
OKAY.
I'LL TAKE THAT.

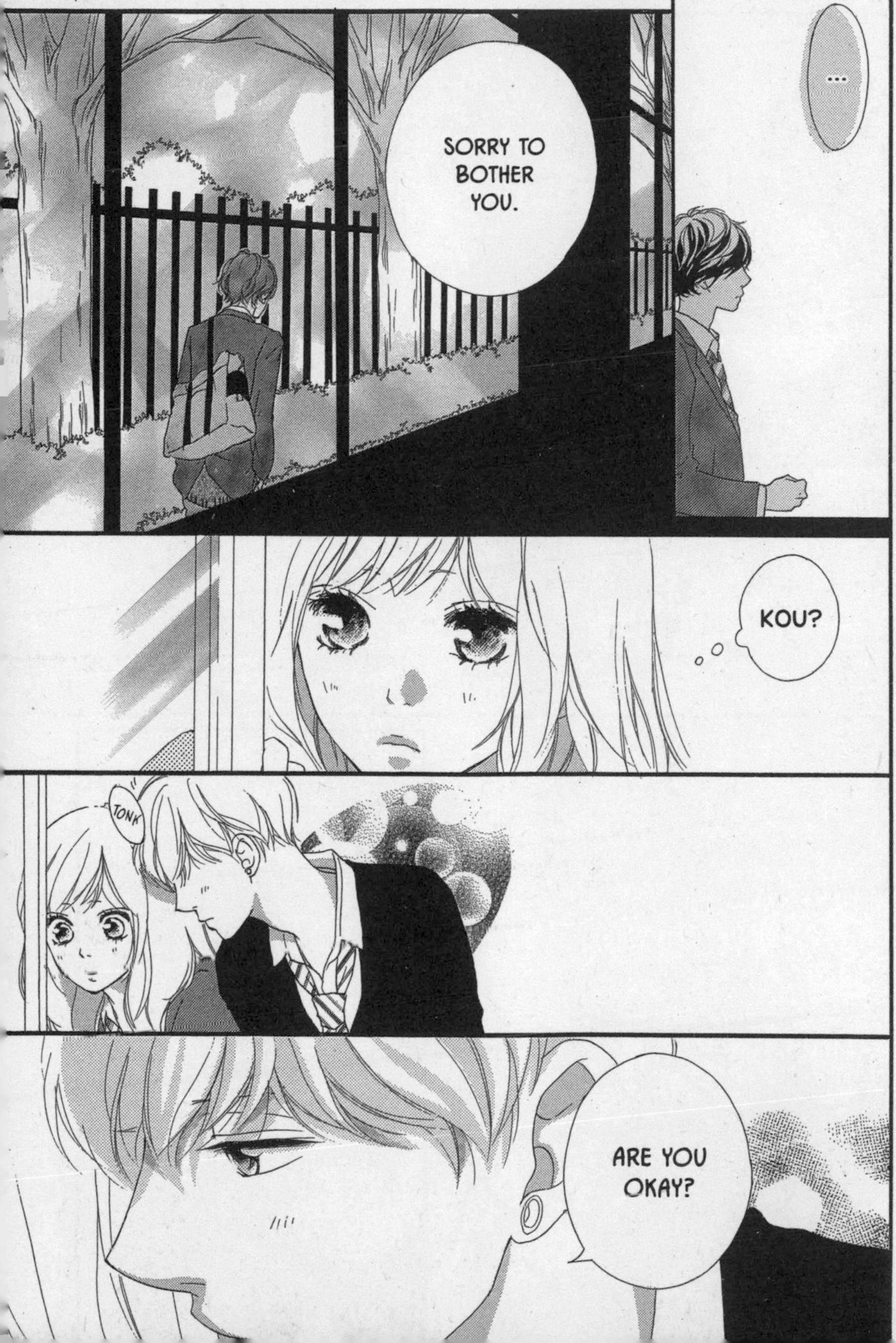
...
SORRY TO BOTHER YOU.
KOU?
TONK
ARE YOU OKAY?

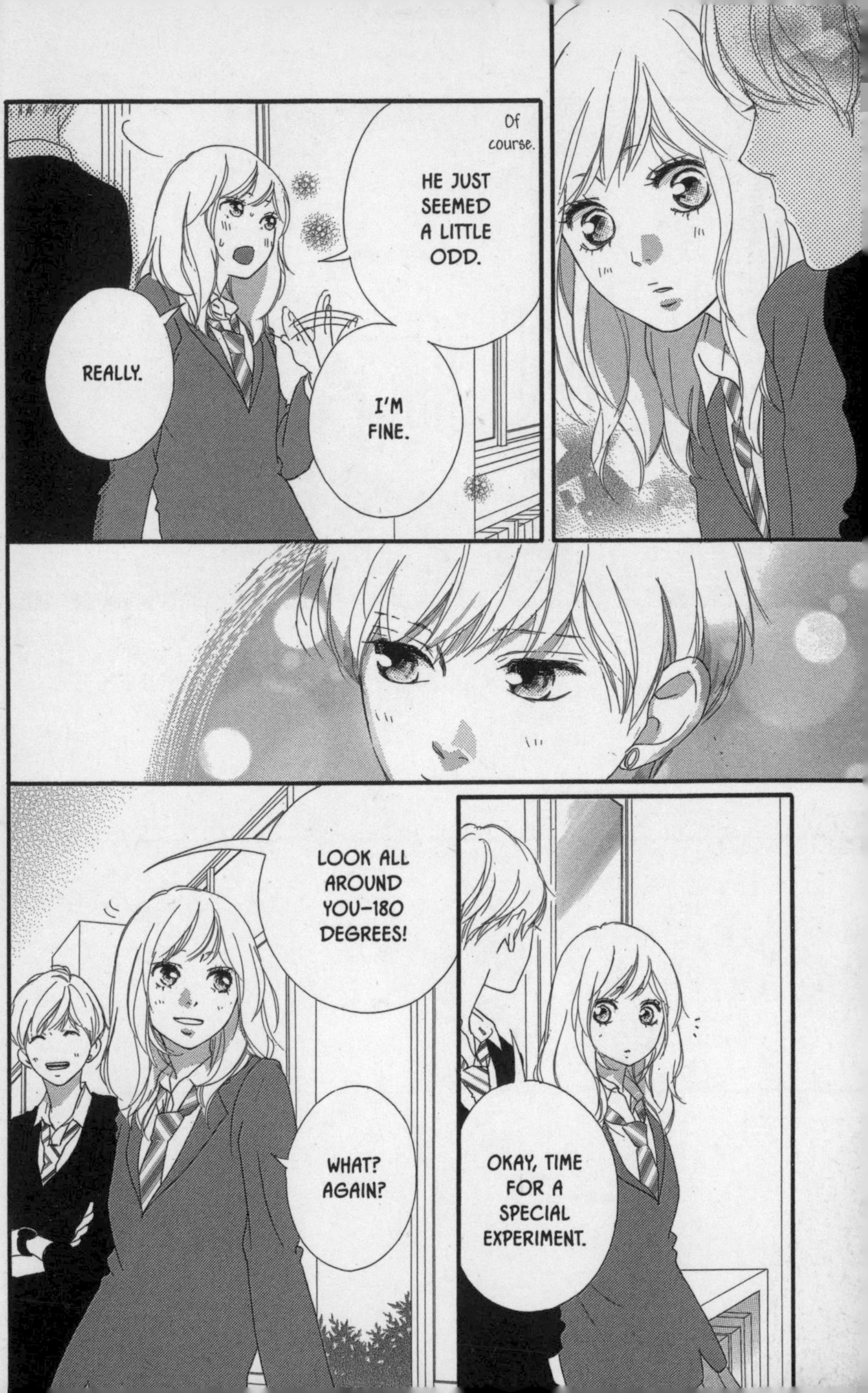
Of course.
HE JUST SEEMED A LITTLE ODD.
I'M FINE.
REALLY.
OKAY, TIME FOR A SPECIAL EXPERIMENT.
LOOK ALL AROUND YOU—180 DEGREES!
WHAT? AGAIN?

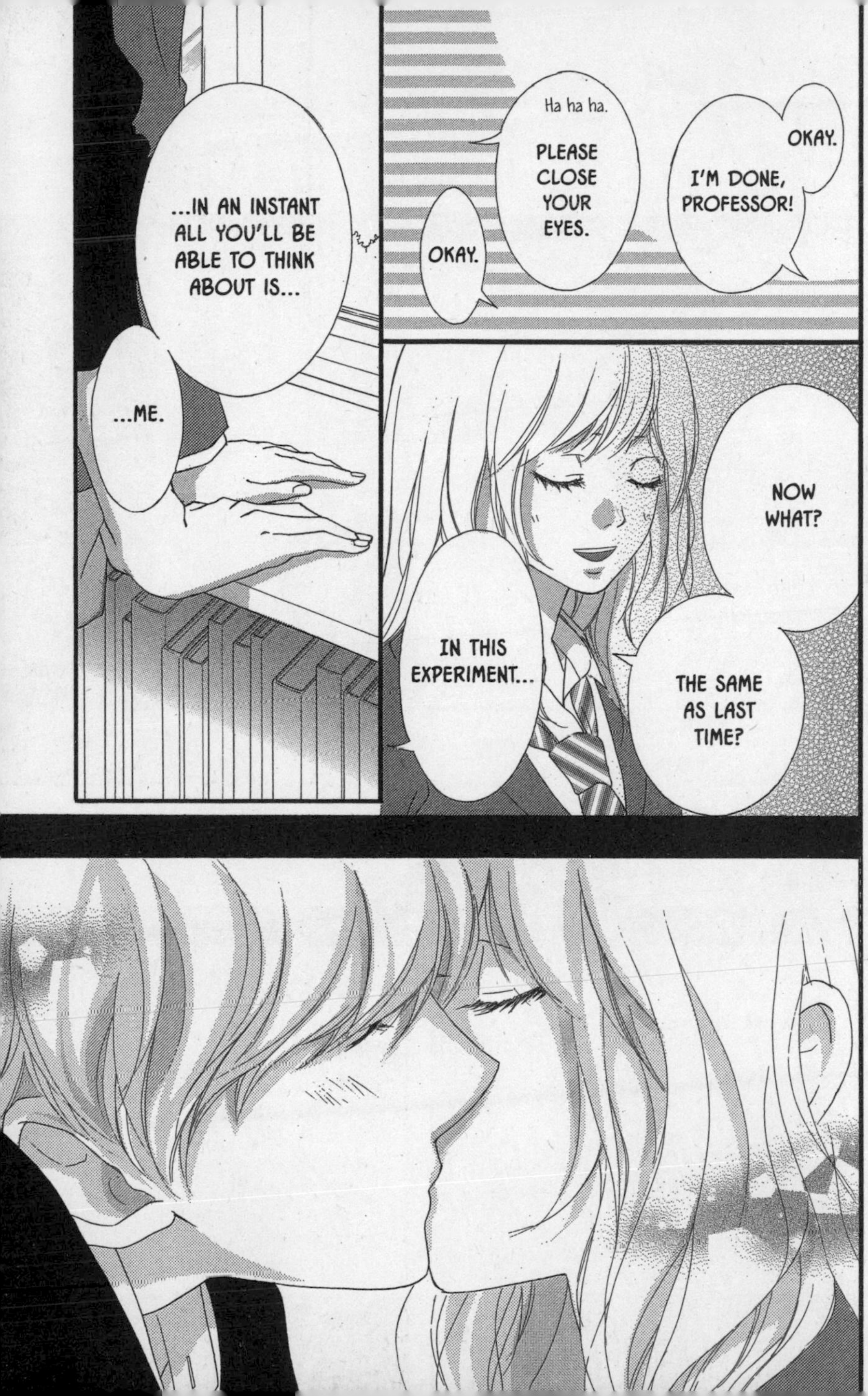
OKAY.
I'M DONE, PROFESSOR!
Ha ha ha.
PLEASE CLOSE YOUR EYES.
OKAY.
NOW WHAT?
THE SAME AS LAST TIME?
IN THIS EXPERIMENT...
...IN AN INSTANT ALL YOU'LL BE ABLE TO THINK ABOUT IS...
...ME.

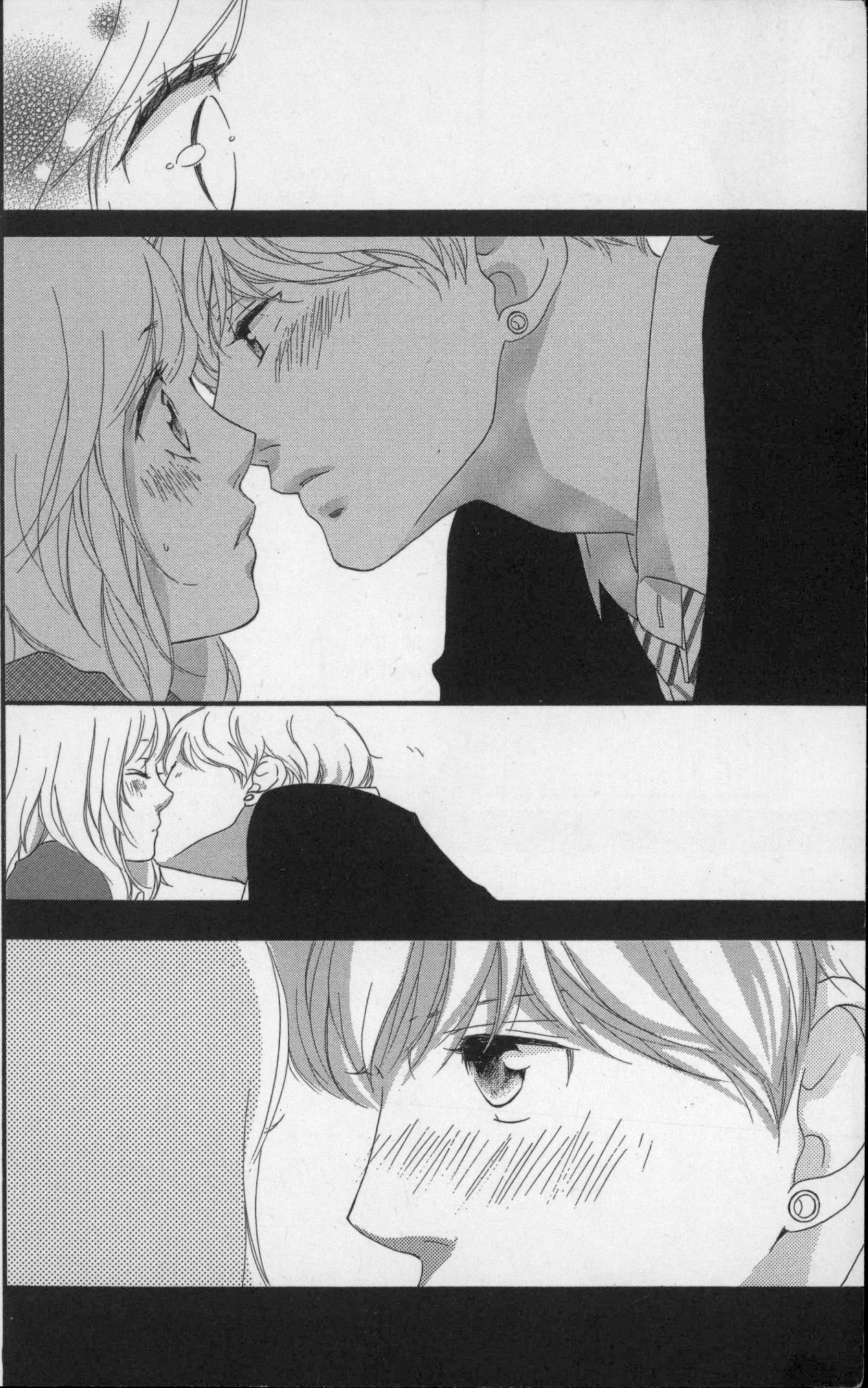

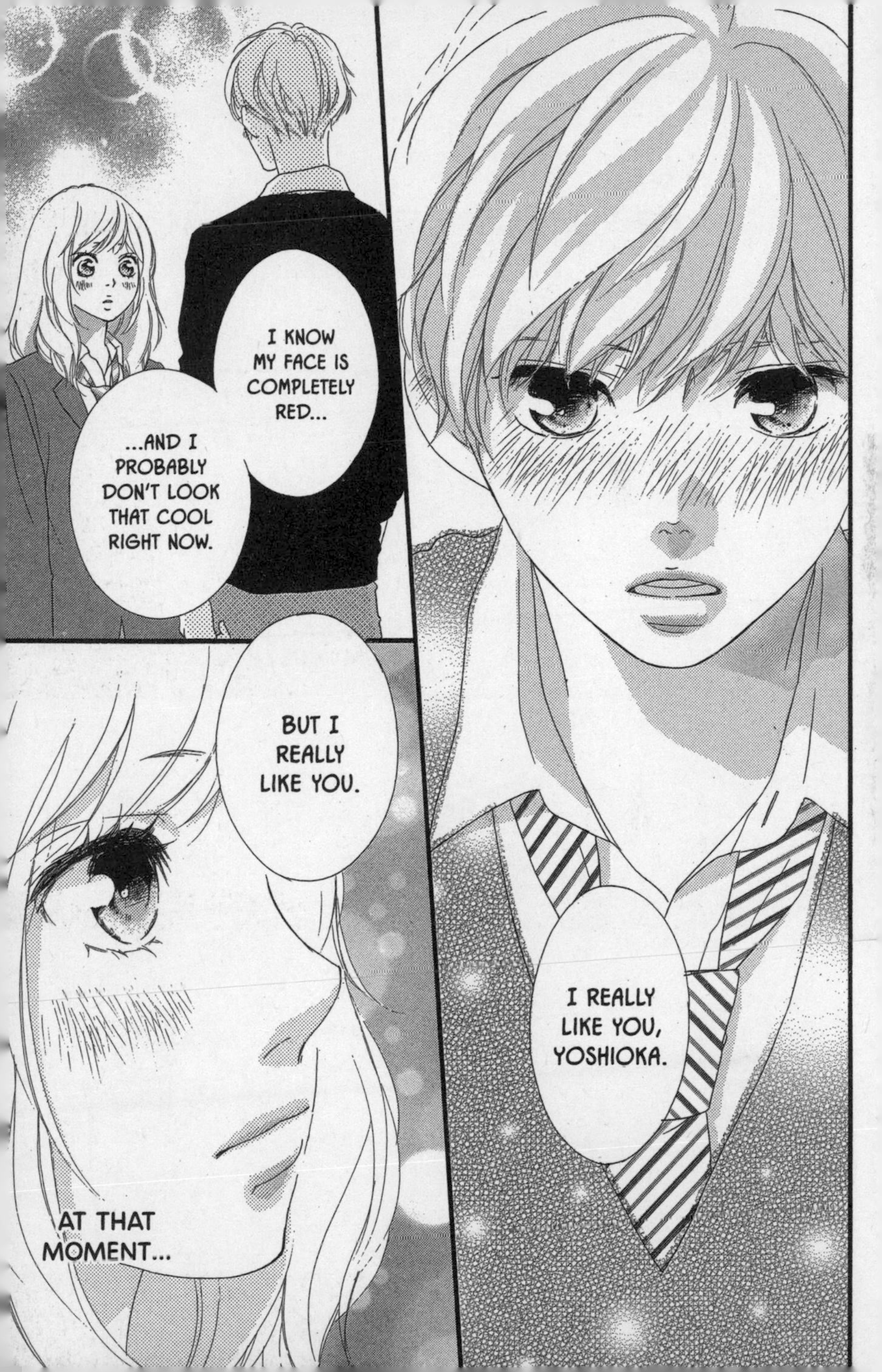
I REALLY LIKE YOU, YOSHIOKA.
I KNOW MY FACE IS COMPLETELY RED...
...AND I PROBABLY DON'T LOOK THAT COOL RIGHT NOW.
BUT I REALLY LIKE YOU.
AT THAT MOMENT...

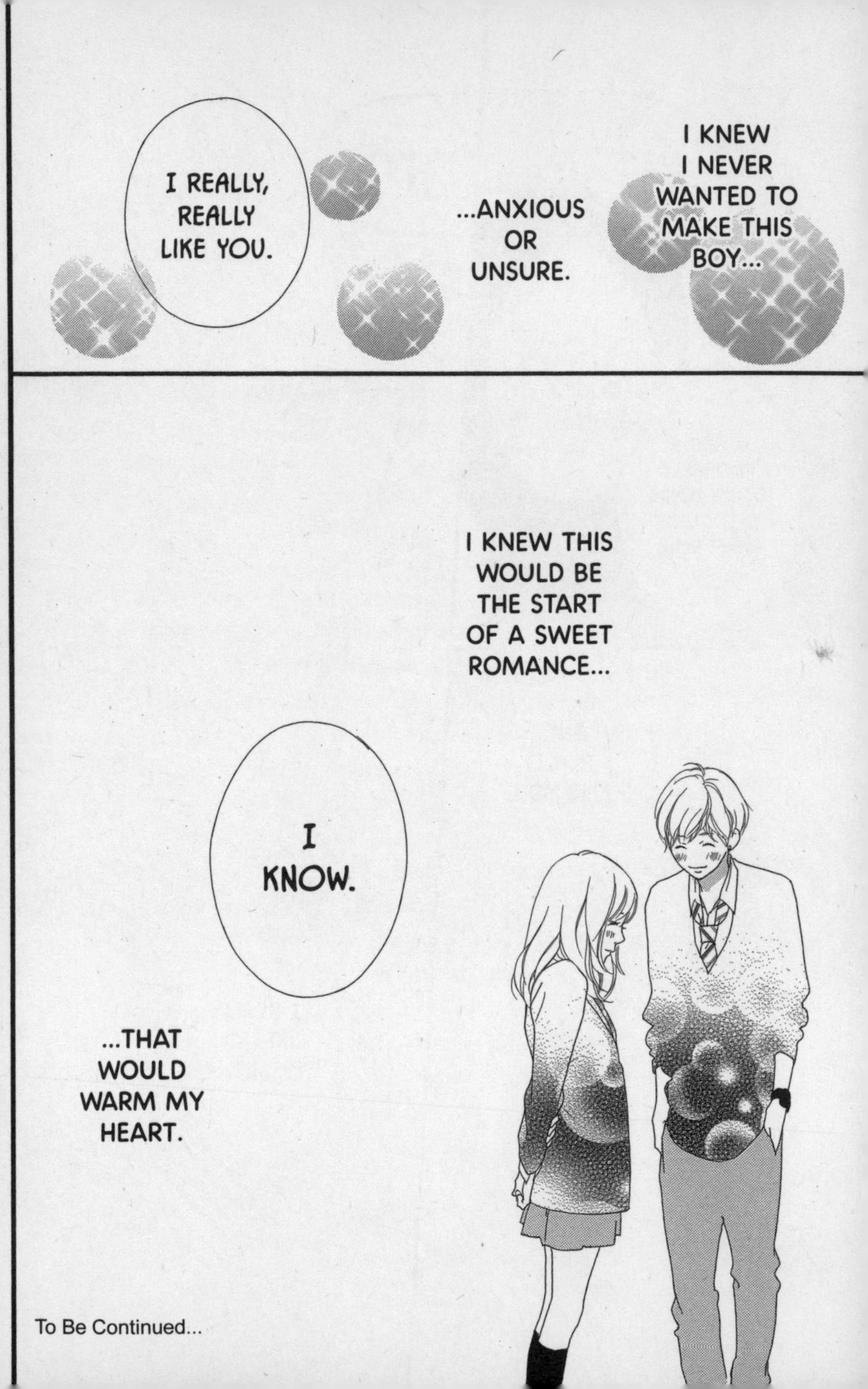
I KNEW I NEVER WANTED TO MAKE THIS BOY...
...ANXIOUS OR UNSURE.
I REALLY, REALLY LIKE YOU.
I KNEW THIS WOULD BE THE START OF A SWEET ROMANCE...
I KNOW.
...THAT WOULD WARM MY HEART.
To Be Continued...

Afterword

Thank you for reading through to the end!

When I was in preschool, there was one little girl that I absolutely adored. In my mind, she was the protagonist of our world. Since I had no idea how television shows were made back then, I assumed there were cameras hidden in the clouds and trees that were recording the story of her life. I did my best to play out my role as an extra in her show, which was super fun for me. I was a rather discerning child, but there were also times when I would act impulsively and go for a challenge. As an adult I find myself faced with challenges that I would normally write off as too difficult, but somehow a light switches on and I dive in absolutely determined to meet it. It's very strange impulsive behavior. Drawing manga was one such impulse. There was a time when I said that I could never be a mangaka. Looking back now, I am so glad that instead of discounting it, I followed my impulse and went out and bought myself some manga paper. One day I hope I'll be able to look back and feel that way about the many chances I've taken with my work.

See you in the next volume!

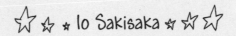

☆ ☆ ✳ Io Sakisaka ✳ ☆ ☆

I always go to the same hair salon,
and when I leave I make an appointment for
my next visit. (I get a discount that way.)

Last time I was there, I told my regular
stylist I was moving and wouldn't be back.
We bade each other a heartfelt farewell.

My plans ended up changing, and I still
haven't moved. But I can't bring myself
to go back to that salon...

IO SAKISAKA

Born on June 8, Io Sakisaka made her debut
as a manga creator with *Sakura, Chiru*. Her
works include *Call My Name*, *Gate of Planet*
and *Blue*. *Strobe Edge*, her previous work, is
also published by VIZ Media's Shojo Beat
imprint. *Ao Haru Ride* was adapted into an
anime series in 2014. In her spare time,
Sakisaka likes to paint things and sleep.

Ao Haru Ride

VOLUME 9
SHOJO BEAT EDITION

STORY AND ART BY **IO SAKISAKA**

TRANSLATION **Emi Louie-Nishikawa**
TOUCH-UP ART + LETTERING **Inori Fukuda Trant**
DESIGN **Shawn Carrico**
EDITOR **Nancy Thistlethwaite**

Printed in the U.S.A.

Published by VIZ Media, LLC
P.O. Box 77010
San Francisco, CA 94107

10 9 8 7 6 5 4 3 2 1
First printing, February 2020

ratings.viz.com RATED T TEEN

PARENTAL ADVISORY
AO HARU RIDE is rated T for Teen and is recommended for ages 13 and up. This volume contains the sweetness of youth.

VIZ MEDIA
viz.com

Shojo Beat
shojobeat.com

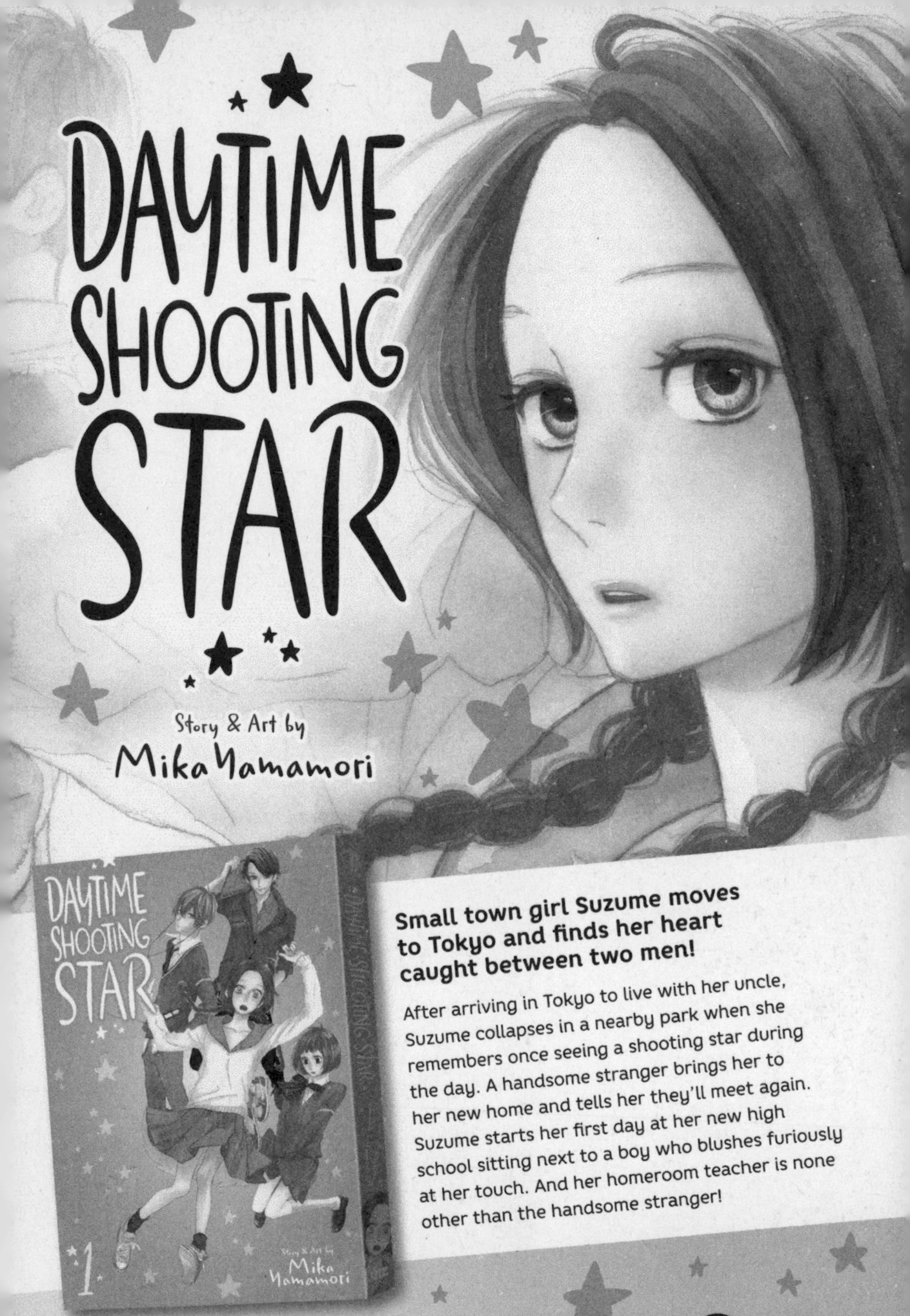
DAYTIME SHOOTING STAR
Story & Art by
Mika Yamamori
DAYTIME SHOOTING STAR
1
Story & Art by Mika Yamamori
Small town girl Suzume moves to Tokyo and finds her heart caught between two men!
After arriving in Tokyo to live with her uncle, Suzume collapses in a nearby park when she remembers once seeing a shooting star during the day. A handsome stranger brings her to her new home and tells her they'll meet again. Suzume starts her first day at her new high school sitting next to a boy who blushes furiously at her touch. And her homeroom teacher is none other than the handsome stranger!
RATED T TEEN
VIZ

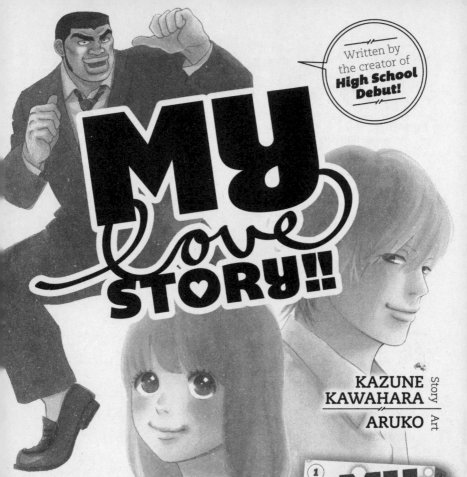

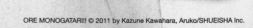

SHORTCAKE CAKE

STORY AND ART BY
suu Morishita

An unflappable girl and a cast of lovable roommates at a boardinghouse create bonds of friendship and romance!

When Ten moves out of her parents' home in the mountains to live in a boardinghouse, she finds herself becoming fast friends with her male roommates. But can love and romance be far behind?

RATED
T
TEEN

VIZ

Honey
So Sweet

Story and Art by Amu Meguro

Little did Nao Kogure realize back in middle school that when she left an umbrella and a box of bandages in the rain for injured delinquent Taiga Onise that she would meet him again in high school. Nao wants nothing to do with the gruff and frightening Taiga, but he suddenly presents her with a huge bouquet of flowers and asks her to date him—with marriage in mind! Is Taiga really so scary, or is he a sweetheart in disguise?

HONEY © 2012 by Amu Meguro/SHUEISHA Inc.

Lydia can see fairies—
but can she tell who the real villain is?

The Earl & the Fairy

Story & Art by **Ayuko**
Original Concept by **Mizue Tani**

Lydia Carlton is a fairy doctor, one of the few people with the ability to see the magical creatures who share our world. During one of her rare trips to London to visit her father, Lydia's quiet life is suddenly transformed when she is rescued from kidnappers by a mysterious young man!

Check your local manga retailer for availability!

Vol. 1 ~ ISBN: 978-1-4215-4168-6
Vol. 2 ~ ISBN: 978-1-4215-4169-3
Vol. 3 ~ ISBN: 978-1-4215-4170-9
Vol. 4 ~ ISBN: 978-1-4215-4171-6

STOP!

YOU MAY BE READING THE WRONG WAY.

In keeping with the original Japanese comic format, this book reads from right to left—so action, sound effects and word balloons are completely reversed to preserve the orientation of the original artwork.